An Illustrated History of the
LEWES
&
EAST GRINSTEAD
RAILWAY

Seal of the Lewes & East Grinstead Railway. *Bluebell Archives*

| TIME TABLE No. 65. | **LONDON BRIGHTON & SOUTH COAST RAILWAY.** |

LEWES & EAST GRINSTEAD LINE.

Lewes, New Barcombe, Newick and Chailey, Fletching and Sheffield Park, Horsted Keynes, West Hoathly, Kingscote, and East Grinstead.

SEPTEMBER, 1882,] LOCAL TRAIN SERVICE. **[and until further notice.**

TO EAST GRINSTEAD.		WEEK DAYS.							SUNDAYS.				
		a.m.	a.m.	p.m.	p.m.	p.m.			a.m.	p.m.	p.m.		
BRIGHTON	dep.	7 45	10 25	2 15	5 3	8 30	..	..	8 25	2 20	6 10	..	..
LONDON ROAD	,,	7 48	10 28	2 18	5 6	8 33	..	..	8 28	2 23	6 13	..	..
FALMER	,,	7 56	..	2 26	5 14	8 41	..	..	8 36	2 31	6 21	..	..
LEWES	,,	8 15	10 47	2 42	5 30	9 0	..	..	8 52	2 47	6 37	..	..
NEW BARCOMBE	,,	8 34	11 2	2 57	5 44	9 15	..	..	9 7	3 1	6 52	..	..
NEWICK and CHAILEY	,,	8 44	11 12	3 7	5 54	9 25	..	..	9 17	3 11	7 2	..	..
FLETCHING and SHEFFIELD PARK	,,	8 49	11 17	3 12	5 59	9 30	..	..	9 22	3 16	7 7	..	..
HORSTED KEYNES	,,	9 1	11 29	3 24	6 11	9 42	..	..	9 34	3 28	7 19	..	..
WEST HOATHLY	,,	9 12	11 40	3 35	6 22	9 53	..	..	9 45	3 39	7 30	..	..
KINGSCOTE	,,	9 17	11 45	3 40	6 27	9 58	..	..	9 50	3 44	7 35	..	..
EAST GRINSTEAD (New Station Low Level Platform)	arr.	9 25	11 53	3 48	6 35	10 6	..	..	9 58	3 52	7 48	..	..

FROM EAST GRINSTEAD.		WEEK DAYS.							SUNDAYS.				
		a.m.	a.m.	p.m.	p.m.	p.m.			a.m.	p.m.	p.m.		
EAST GRINSTEAD (New Station Low Level Platform)	dep.	6 45	9 55	1 20	5 45	9 10	..	..	10 35	4 20	8 15	..	..
KINGSCOTE	,,	6 51	10 1	1 26	5 51	9 16	..	..	10 41	4 26	8 21	..	..
WEST HOATHLY	,,	6 57	10 7	1 32	5 57	9 22	..	..	10 47	4 32	8 27	..	..
HORSTED KEYNES	,,	7 5	10 15	1 40	6 10	9 35	..	..	10 55	4 40	8 35	..	..
FLETCHING and SHEFFIELD PARK	,,	7 18	10 28	1 53	6 23	9 54	..	..	11 8	4 53	8 48	..	..
NEWICK and CHAILEY	,,	7 25	10 35	2 0	6 30	10 1	..	..	11 15	5 0	8 55	..	..
NEW BARCOMBE	,,	7 34	10 44	2 9	6 39	10 10	..	..	11 24	5 9	9 4	..	..
LEWES	,,	7 46	10 56	2 21	6 51	10 22	..	..	11 36	5 21	9 16	..	..
FALMER	,,	..	11 8	2 39	..	..	..	..	11 48	5 33	9 28	..	..
LONDON ROAD	,,	8 3	11 17	2 48	7 8	10 39	..	..	11 57	5 42	9 37	..	..
BRIGHTON	arr.	8 9	11 23	2 54	7 14	10 45	..	..	12 3	5 48	9 43	..	..

All Trains 1st, 2nd and Parly. between Brighton, Lewes and East Grinstead.

LONDON TRAIN SERVICE TO AND FROM EAST GRINSTEAD (via Three Bridges).

FROM LONDON.		WEEK DAYS.					B	C				
		a.m.	a.m.	a.m.	p.m.	p.m.	p.m.	p.m.	p.m.	p.m.	p.m.	
VICTORIA	dep.	7 35	10 15	11 40	12 55	1 20	2 0	4 0	..	7 8		
LONDON BRIDGE	,,	7 40	10 15	11 50	1 8	1 30	2 5	4 5	5 5	7 20		
EAST GRINSTEAD	arr.	9 29	11 43	1 5	2 20	2 59	3 59	5 27	6 11	8 49		

B Thursdays only.　　C Saturdays only.

TO LONDON.		D							
		a.m.	a.m.	a.m.	p.m.	p.m.	p.m.	p.m.	
EAST GRINSTEAD	dep.	6 45	8 10	9 35	12 2	3 11	4 3	6 52	..
LONDON BRIDGE	arr.	8 20	9 45	10 47	2 2	4 43	5 49	8 30	..
VICTORIA	,,	8 30	..	11 7	1 55	4 51	5 58	9 8	..

D Mondays only.

LONDON TRAIN SERVICE TO AND FROM LEWES.

FROM LONDON.		WEEK DAYS.																	
		a.m.	a.m.	a.m.	a.m.	a.m.	a.m.	a.m.	p.m.	p.m.	p.m.	p.m.	p.m.	p.m.	p.m.	p.m.	p.m.	p.m.	p.m.
VICTORIA	dep.	..	7 35	9 55	..	10 15	11 40	11 55	1 20	1 20	3 25	..	4 30	..	5 43	6 50	7 50	8 20	..
LONDON BRIDGE	,,	6 40	7 40	..	10 10	10 15	11 50	12 5	1 30	2 5	..	4 5	..	5 5	..	7 0	8 0	8 30	9 10
LEWES	arr.	7 55	10 1	11 11	11 34	12 8	1 11	1 57	3 1	3 59	4 45	5 25	5 52	6 17	7 15	8 42	9 28	9 50	11 10

TO LONDON.		WEEK DAYS.															
		a.m.	E a.m.	a.m.	a.m.	a.m.	p.m.	p.m.	p.m.	p.m.	p.m.	p.m.	p.m.	p.m.	p.m.	p.m.	
LEWES	dep.	7 27	7 55	9 30	11 20	11 25	12 29	12 55	2 39	3 10	5 4	6 5	6 18	8 20	8 28	10 4	..
LONDON BRIDGE	,,	9 15	9 24	10 50	12 45	..	2 2	2 20	4 16	4 43	6 35	7 25	7 45	9 52	9 57	12 8	..
VICTORIA	arr.	..	9 30	11 7	12 49	1 55	2 10	2 25	4 30	4 51	6 42	7 37	7 55	9 59	10 11	..	..

E Mondays only.

☞ **POSTAL TELEGRAPH.** All the Stations on this New Line are Postal Telegraph Stations by appointment of the Postmaster General.

London Bridge Terminus, August, 1882.

(By Order)　J. P. KNIGHT, General Manager.

500—23-8-82.

Waterlow and Sons Limited, Printers, London Wall, London.

The first timetable, which operated with slight seasonal amendments for the period while East Grinstead Low Level remained the northern terminus of the line until the extension to South Croydon was opened on 10 March 1884. *Bluebell archives*

An Illustrated History of the
LEWES
&
EAST GRINSTEAD
RAILWAY

Klaus Marx

Oxford Publishing Co

First published 2000

ISBN 0 86093 547 7

© Klaus Marx 2000

Published by Ian Allan Publishing

an imprint of Ian Allan Publishing Ltd, Terminal House, Shepperton, Surrey TW17 8AS.
Printed by Ian Allan Printing Ltd, Riverdene Business Park, Hersham, Surrey KT12 4RG.

Code: 0101/A3

Dedication

This book is dedicated to all members of the Bluebell Railway, and especially to those actively involved on the line itself, in the hope they will come to appreciate even more the goodly heritage into which they have entered.

SHEFFIELD PARK CRICKET GROUND.

LORD SHEFFIELD'S XI v. AUSTRALIANS, MAY 8TH. 9TH. & 10TH. 1890.

Front cover: 'C2X' class 0-6-0 No 32442, having arrived on a goods train from Norwood Yard, moves forward under the supervision of the signalling staff at East Grinstead South on 13 March 1958, three days prior to the line's final closure. A train for Three Bridges stands at the High Level platform.

Rear cover, above: In one of the earliest colour photographs to be taken on the line – on 30 April 1955 – the signalman at Sheffield Park hands the staff to the crew of Fairburn 2-6-4T No 42101 in charge of a Brighton to London Bridge working, the Maunsell 3 set in the contemporary carmine and cream livery.

Centre and below: View of West Hoathly and Kingscote take on the last day of BR services on 16 March 1958. *All R. C. Riley*

Above: A 'sectional' photograph of one of the most memorable cricket matches at Sheffield Park, showing the extensive ground and on the left several of the pavilions. The photographer, Hawkins of Brighton, has ingeniously built up a composite picture by joining at the correct points, four separate photographs. The framed picture hangs in one of the inns in the centre of Fletching. *Bluebell Archives*

Previous page: In 1966 a letter accompanying the above photograph delivered to Sheffield Park read, 'My grandfather's name was James Rawlins, and my mother, born in 1884, says she was 5-6 years of age at the time the picture was taken.' Stationmaster James Rawlins, seen holding his daughter's hand, was in charge of Sheffield Park from February 1898 to August the following year. Between these dates there was a considerable turnover of staff, so it is impossible to identify the rest of the posed team of two signal porters, a porter and a booking clerk. This fine view of the well-kept station in pristine condition shows on the left the rather grand glazed-roof lavatories, in the centre the North box, the station house with its pretty bargeboards, imitation-panelled upper floor and flower decoration, the humble station nameboard and ballast-covered permanent way. *Bluebell Archives*

Contents

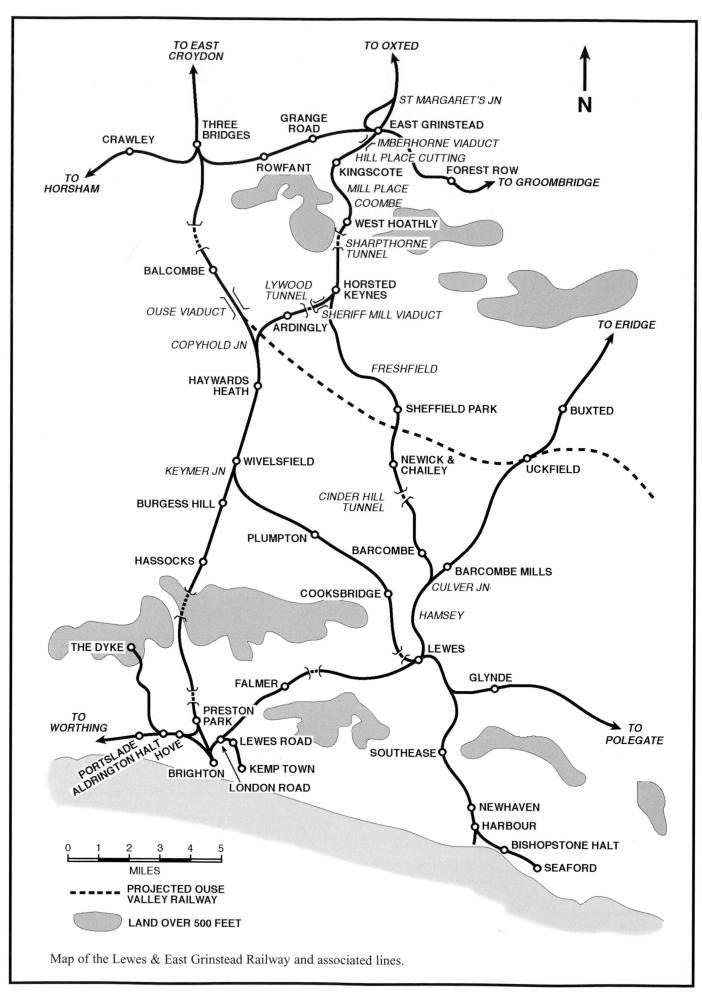

TO EAST
CROYDON

TO OXTED

N

CRAWLEY

THREE
BRIDGES

GRANGE
ROAD

ST MARGARET'S JN

EAST GRINSTEAD

TO
HORSHAM

ROWFANT

IMBERHORNE VIADUCT

HILL PLACE CUTTING

KINGSCOTE

FOREST ROW

TO GROOMBRIDGE

MILL PLACE
COOMBE

WEST HOATHLY

BALCOMBE

SHARPTHORNE
TUNNEL

LYWOOD
TUNNEL

HORSTED
KEYNES

OUSE VIADUCT

SHERIFF MILL VIADUCT

ARDINGLY

COPYHOLD JN

TO ERIDGE

FRESHFIELD

HAYWARDS
HEATH

SHEFFIELD PARK

BUXTED

WIVELSFIELD

KEYMER JN

NEWICK &
CHAILEY

UCKFIELD

BURGESS HILL

CINDER HILL
TUNNEL

PLUMPTON

BARCOMBE

HASSOCKS

BARCOMBE MILLS

CULVER JN

COOKSBRIDGE

HAMSEY

THE DYKE

LEWES

FALMER

GLYNDE

TO
WORTHING

PRESTON
PARK

LEWES ROAD

TO
POLEGATE

PORTSLADE
ALDRINGTON HALT
HOVE

BRIGHTON

KEMP TOWN

SOUTHEASE

LONDON ROAD

NEWHAVEN

HARBOUR

BISHOPSTONE HALT

SEAFORD

0 1 2 3 4 5

MILES

PROJECTED OUSE
VALLEY RAILWAY

LAND OVER 500 FEET

Map of the Lewes & East Grinstead Railway and associated lines.

Foreword

This history of a line of which the major part remains to this day, much loved by the many associated with its preservation, maintenance and operation, had its genesis in 1960 when I was asked to chair the infant Bluebell Railway's Museum and History Committee and become its archivist. One of the briefs was to produce a history of the Lewes-East Grinstead line and, full of youthful enthusiasm, I would mount my NSU 'Quickly' moped in school holiday time (for I was then teaching history at Great Walstead School, within earshot of the line at Freshfield) and visit all the possible railway contacts I could. Most were former staff, but among the gems were people who had built the line or witnessed it under construction, travelled on the first train, worked on the line and fought to save it. On one occasion I even met the redoubtable Miss Bessemer. It proved a matter of urgency for nearly all have since passed on. However, the long wait of 40 years until the calm of retirement has proved beneficial, so much additional information having come to light during the intervening period.

These personal accounts put the flesh on the bones, for railway history is not everybody's cup of tea, particularly the kind that wades in detail through obscure proposals, abortive schemes and Parliamentary bills, all ribbed in a solid framework of chronology. Every effort has been made to produce an interesting narrative without diluting the main points of emphasis. The story is exciting enough, a tale of individual enterprise, well in keeping with the pioneers of today's Bluebell Railway, who refused to be overawed by the big battalions and stuck to their guns to the very end. If one theme runs throughout, then it is the spirit of survival against all odds, opposition, financial stringency and ridicule. It is a challenge to those in charge today to carry on in the same spirit as their honest forebears.

If the account goes into considerable detail at times, it makes no excuse. It is, after all, the history of what the people to whom this book is dedicated would call 'Our own railway', one which many of us have come to know so intimately from the carriage window, platform edge or track level. Each bridge, each bend, each mile or signal post means something special to those who are frequently down on the line. The right way to regard history, some say, is to look upon it as a servant. Only the past can explain the present and answer many of the whys and wherefores of today's railway as we know it.

The account has also this to recommend itself. It is the detailed study of how a line was actually built, an aspect too frequently overlooked by railway historians in their desire to get to the train running stages as soon as is humanly possible. Though materials naturally play a prominent part, it is very much an affair of persons: promoters, committees, directors, engineers and contractors and their host of navvies, those rogues of Victorian railway construction with whom one cannot but often sympathise, through to the inspectors who let loose on the trains the public who had been so prominent behind the scenes all the while and who viewed the constructional phase as a mixed blessing. And the narrative runs through the 75 years or so of the line's operation, as seen through the eyes of station staff and local inhabitants, to the generation of those who fought a brilliant rearguard action against the closure of the line.

Every effort has been made to set the line against its correct backcloth, starting with its arrival in late Victorian society with its grim institution of the Dickensian workhouse, the full fervency of the Temperance movement, the respectful days of the master-servant relationship and the staggering extremes of wealth which graduated down to abysmal poverty. This was the restricted world of our great grandparents, for whom travel except for the well-to-do was indeed a rarity, the event of a lifetime if one was fortunate, and in the Sussex countryside there were many who had never been farther than their two feet could carry them. It was to such a rural neighbourhood that the railway came with as much novelty as it had come half a century before to the excited inhabitants of Merseyside. The railway continued to develop during a lifetime of unprecedented change, of which the arrival of the telegraph and the internal combustion engine, to name just two inventions, were decisive.

With such a large canvas it has been necessary to keep within the publisher's guidelines. It confines itself strictly to the lines of the Lewes & East Grinstead Railway including the link to the Brighton main line at Copyhold Junction, and does not seek to cover in any great detail the end stations at Lewes, Haywards Heath or East Grinstead (except for the Low Level station), majoring on the intermediate stations which came into being with the inaugural Act. A crucial decision arose as to whether to cover the line from north to south (logical?) or come up from Culver Junction, 'up' being the operative word, scaling the line's many rising stretches of grades of 1 in 75. The best argument for the latter is the fact that, against the general pattern, mileages were reckoned from Culver Junction. East Grinstead is a good enough place to finish up whether in 1882 or 2002!

Some explanation is required as to the arrangement of the text. Footnotes and appendices have been dispensed with to avoid the inconvenience of page hopping, all sources and contributors being mentioned in the main text. A selective index is provided at the rear of the book and numerous chapter sub-headings have been incorporated to assist ready reference.

Out of the countless photographs taken of the line, this evocative portrait of the 7.23pm Newick-Lewes captured on the descent to Barcombe on 25 May 1955 truly encapsulates the character of the line — an all-Brighton train hauled by 'E4' radial tank No 32482 chases the evening shadows, having just run down one of the line's formidable 1 in 75 grades. *S. C. Nash*

With regard to photographs, the great majority have been selected from those deposited in the Bluebell Archives and, where known, the photographer's name and the source has been acknowledged. My sincere thanks to each and every one of them. No apology is made for the condition of some of the very early ones. They provide vital evidence and it is a miracle that they survived at all.

Acknowledgements for helpful assistance in research are also due to the staff of the former British Railways Board Historical Records Department at 66 Porchester Road, for all the early research was carried out there (with an occasional glance out of the fire door across over the turntable at Ranelagh Bridge and the exit from Paddington), and their successors at the Public Record Office, Kew; also to the staff at the House of Lords Record Office and at the Civil Engineers' Plan Store 'under the arches' in the old Waterloo, to the willing assistance of the staff at the East Sussex Record Office at Pelham House and now at its new quarters at the Maltings behind Lewes Castle, and to those at the British Museum Newspaper Library at Colindale in the 1960s, when one could still handle with great care all the actual Victorian newspapers.

The fuller story could not have been completed without the help of so many others — my numerous friends involved in the Bluebell Railway and the Brighton Circle — who have assisted with material and contributed personally to this history. They are just too numerous to mention by name and there is always the danger of leaving someone out. Their names are pinpointed at the relevant place in the text. However, there have been those who have more than gone out of their way in their willingness to assist with this enterprise and simply must feature in these acknowledgements; in particular Mike Cruttenden, Chairman of the Brighton Circle, and fellow members Peter Hay, Bill Howe, Dick Kirkby and Sid Nash who made their records so readily available, and especially to my mentor over the years, Dick Riley, Ed Hart who has read the proofs and suggested improvements, and supremely to Alan Braithwaite who has painstakingly placed the text and captions onto disk. Finally my thanks to Ian Allan Publishing Ltd, the publisher, to the late Handel Kardas for editing the manuscript and to Peter Waller in particular for his enthusiasm and support in carrying this project through to completion.

It remains for me to remind the reader, should he have missed it or turned over the leaf, that this book is dedicated to all members of the Bluebell Railway, and especially to those actively involved on the line itself, in the hope they will come to appreciate even more the goodly heritage into which they have entered.

Klaus Marx
Autumn 2000

List of Sources and Selected Bibliography

Books

1885/6	*East Grinstead and its Environs — A Guide to the New Railway* (Farncombe)
1887	*Life of Joseph Firbank*; F. McDermott
1956	*A Centenary of Signalling*; Westinghouse Brake & Signal Co
1963	*Contractors' Locomotives Part 1; Brassey — Firbank — Walker* (Union Publications)
1963	*A History of the Southern Railway*; C. F. Dendy Marshall (Ian Allan)
1969-74	*Locomotives of the LB&SCR Vols 1-3*; D. L. Bradley (RCTS)
1977	*A Pictorial Record of Southern Signals*; G. A. Pryer (OPC)
1978	*Bluebell Line Historical Album*; Klaus Marx (Bluebell Railway)
1979	*Sussex Railway Architecture*; John Hoare (Harvester)
1979	*The London Brighton & South Coast Railway Vol 3*; J. Howard Turner (Batsford)
1984	*Branch Lines to East Grinstead*; Vic Mitchell and Keith Smith (Middleton)
1986	*The Signal Box*; Signalling Study Group (OPC)
1988	*Rails to Sheffield Park*; Michael S. Welch (Kingfisher)
1988	*The Bluebell Railway*; Klaus Marx, Peter Thomas, John Potter (Ian Allan)
1992	*The Bluebell Railway*; Terry Gough (Past and Present)
1995	*Branch Lines to Horsted Keynes — Then and Now*; Michael S. Welch (Runpast)

Documents

Minute Book; Lewes, East Grinstead & London Railway
Minute Book; Lewes & East Grinstead Railway
Minute Book of General Meetings; Lewes & East Grinstead Railway Company (All, PRO RAIL 364 1-3)
Minutes of LBSCR Board of Directors (PRO RAIL 414 75-85)
Minutes of LBSCR Engineering Committee (PRO RAIL 414 153-62)
1877: Bill and Evidence — House of Lords Record Office
1878: Contract for Construction with Joseph Firbank (PRO RAIL 414 455)
1879: Arrangements between LBSCR and J. Wolfe Barry (PRO RAIL 414 319)
LBSCR Staff Registers (PRO RAIL 414 750-796)
Architectural Drawings. Civil Engineers' Plan Store, Railtrack (Southern)
Land Documents — East Sussex Record Office

Journals

The Railway News
Railway Gazette
The Railway Magazine
Southern Railway Magazine
The Brighton Circular
Bluebell News
Railway World
Steam Days
Sussex County Magazine
The Railway Observer

Newspapers

(County)	(National)
Brighton and Sussex Daily Post	*Daily Express*
Brighton Daily News	*Daily Mail*
Brighton Gazette	*Daily Telegraph*
Brighton Observer	*Evening News*
Brighton Times	*Evening Standard*
East Grinstead Courier	*Manchester Guardian*
East Grinstead Observer	*News Chronicle*
East Sussex News	*Sunday Express*
Evening Argus (Brighton)	*The Observer*
Mid-Sussex Times	*The Times*
North Sussex Gazette	
Sussex Advertiser	
Sussex Daily News	
Sussex Express and County Herald	
West Sussex County Times	

BECKENHAM, LEWES AND BRIGHTON

RAILWAY.

(Capital £2,250,000.)

NEW LINE BETWEEN LONDON AND BRIGHTON.

BOARD OF DIRECTORS.

SIR JOHN VILLIERS SHELLEY, Bart., M.P.

FRANCIS BARCHARD, Esq., Horsted Place, Sussex.

CHARLES BEARD, Esq., Rottingdean, Sussex.

J. G. BLENCOWE, Esq., M.P., Bineham, Sussex.

Lieut.-Gen. F. DAVIES, Danehurst, Sussex.

Lieut.-Col. ELSEY, Director of the Bank of London, West Lodge, Ealing.

JAMES INGRAM, Esq., Chailey, Sussex.

With power to add to their Number.

SOLICITORS.

Messrs. FRESHFIELDS & NEWMAN, 5, New Bank Buildings.

ENGINEER.

F. T. TURNER, Esq., 15, Parliament Street.

SURVEYOR.

F. VIGERS, Esq., 3, Frederick's Place, Old Jewry.

BROKERS.

Messrs. KNIGHT, COLEMAN & CO., 1, Royal Exchange Buildings.

BANKERS.

THE BANK OF LONDON.

SECRETARY.

CHARLES LENNOX PEEL, Esq.

OFFICES—15, PARLIAMENT STREET.

The object of the undertaking, independently of the accommodation of a large suburban and agricultural district not yet served by railways, is to afford a second and independent means of communication between London and Brighton, with access to new Termini in London, now so much required, owing to the enormous increase in the population of London and Brighton, and in the traffic of the existing line, which has more than quadrupled during the last 14 years.

Brighton, although the nearest watering-place to London, and therefore almost the sole convenient place of resort for a vast proportion of those requiring a marine residence whose business necessitates their constant attendance in London, is the only town of corresponding population in the kingdom which has not already the advantage of two independent communications with the Metropolis.

The population of Brighton in April, 1861, amounted to 87,317, showing an increase of upwards of 38,000 in the resident population since the opening of the railway in 1841, as against an increase of 7,100 only in the 10 preceding years; and the resident population of Brighton for a large portion of the year is more than doubled by the influx of visitors.

The number of passengers by the railway is daily increasing, whilst the means of conveyance over the existing rails are incapable of increase, and the line has already proved to be inadequate for the exigencies of the present traffic.

It would be invidious here to criticize the conduct of the Brighton Company in the management of their traffic. Assuming that management to be, as they state, most excellent, it affords no reason for withholding from the inhabitants of Brighton, and the district through which the proposed line will pass, the advantages of an increased and independent accommodation, and a connection with the several Railway Termini in the Metropolis, more particularly as there can be no doubt that the scale

1.
Promotion

Early Schemes

In the middle years of the 19th century the railways were the only practicable way of travelling in any speed or comfort. The roads were slow and bad, and in many rural areas like Sussex wear and tear without proper repair were the constant butt of complaint in the local papers. The canals, the pride of the 18th century, were slipping into a slow and irreversible decline due to the devastating competition of the 'iron roads'. Railway companies vied to have their own exclusive territory yet had no scruples to invade that of their neighbours. Large tracts of land regarded as 'grey areas' in times of recession left uneasy truces, while prosperous years would see rival companies putting schemes before a fickle Parliament in an attempt to corner the market. The centre of East Sussex was one such border zone and a transport wasteland. The River Ouse had been made navigable up to Balcombe by 1812, but by the middle of the century was in decline.

It was against this background and late in the annals of railway history that the Bluebell line we know today came into being. The Lewes-East Grinstead line was only the tail-end of a large number of schemes mooted during the frantic rivalry-ridden days of the mid-19th century railway mania. The railway history of the immediate neighbourhood opens way back in 1835, when Palmer's route to Brighton, one of six proposed, was planned to run through East Grinstead and West Hoathly to Lindfield and on south through Wivelsfield. The scheme stood an excellent chance owing to the directness of the route, but was eventually turned down in view of the high expense of construction through the hilly Sussex Weald.

Only a year later another scheme was afoot, from East Preston and Seaford to London, the main line of which passed through Chailey North Common, Lindfield and Hoathly Hill, to link up at either Godstone or Oxted to the proposed South Eastern line. Had this 'South Eastern, Brighton, Lewes & Newhaven Railway' succeeded, the LBSCR might never have come into existence. In 1837, however, Rennie's route to Brighton via Balcombe was given approval by Parliament, though alternative South Eastern-Newhaven schemes were planned as late as 1840.

With the Brighton and South Eastern companies firmly established by the middle of the 19th century, the territory between the Brighton and Hastings lines of the respective

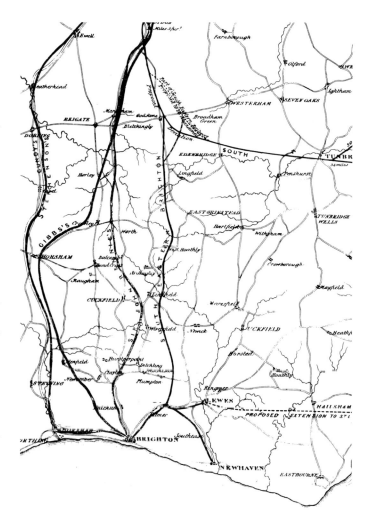

companies became a veritable battleground, riddled with intrigues and legal bickerings. By 1855 the LBSCR had reached East Grinstead from Three Bridges, but it was in the 1860s that battle was joined in earnest between the two hostile companies. The plum was still, of course, the passenger traffic to Brighton, whose population had trebled between 1841 and 1876. First in 1862 the prospectus of the Beckenham, Lewes & Brighton Railway, sponsored by the South Eastern and Chatham companies, was circulated. It was to pass through

Left: Title page of the prospectus of the proposed Beckenham, Lewes & Brighton Railway of 1863. *Bluebell Archives*

Above right: Map from the prospectus of the South Eastern, Brighton, Lewes & Newhaven Railway of 1836. *Bluebell Archives*

difficult country via East Grinstead, Newick and Lewes to a terminus at Kemp Town. The following year the Bill was revised to incorporate branches to Westerham and Eastbourne and a terminus in the heart of Brighton at Old Steine. In 1864 the same combination through an independent company had promoted the Surrey & Sussex Junction Railway from Croydon to Groombridge through the vicinity of East Grinstead. The following year a London, Lewes & Brighton Railway, this time via Orpington, was proposed.

In order to preserve the territory intact, the LBSCR resorted to defensive tactics which attempted to clinch the issue once and for all. The immediate repercussions were the East Grinstead & Tunbridge Wells, the Uckfield line and the Kemp Town branch, all undertaken by the 'Brighton'. But the threat to Eastbourne remained, the SER and LCDR companies obtaining Royal Assent in 1866 for a direct route there. Foreseeing this, the LBSCR had sanctioned the Ouse Valley Railway in 1863, from the well-known Ouse Viaduct via Lindfield and Sheffield Bridge to Uckfield and Hailsham, with a further extension the following year from Hellingly to St Leonards. Contractors were already at work — witness surviving embankments and bridges today near Lindfield and Uckfield — when the boom of the railway mania of the 1860s collapsed in spectacular fashion with the failure of the important banking house of Overend & Gurney in 1866, causing the weaker brethren to amalgamate, and even the strongest to retrench their expenditure. Both rival schemes went by the board, but a mere matter of months might have produced an Ouse Valley line which would have rendered the future Lewes-East Grinstead line pointless. Yet for another 10 years the East Grinstead-Haywards Heath-Uckfield triangle was to remain empty on the railway map.

The early 1870s saw a continuation of the bitter rivalry in central and East Sussex between the LBSCR and its closest competitors. On its eastern flank the SER and LCDR renewed their promotion of 'penetrating' lines aimed at tapping into the traffic to Brighton, while the LBSCR patronised 'blocking' lines to fend off these threats. The next bout of schemes started in 1872 with a Brighton, Eastbourne & London Railway which, coming south through East Grinstead, Saint Hill and Danehill, was to branch at Fletching, go south via Sheffield Bridge, Barcombe, Lewes and Bevendean to Brighton, and east to Uckfield, Chiddingly, Hailsham and the east end of Eastbourne. This ambitious scheme foundered, being fiercely contested by the LBSCR.

By 1875 things were once again at fever pitch. In the last week of that year the *North Sussex Gazette,* based in East Grinstead, saw fit to take stock of the town. It was a mixed review, typical of the mid-Victorian period, of changes for better or for worse — excitement over church reseating as private pews gave way to public benches; commiseration over the closing of the schools in the summer for lack of funds ('The poorer children have for the most part run wild ever since') — the long-talked-of Town Hall had been built, together with a hall for the JPs at the Police Station — the Sanitary Authority of the Board of Guardians had promised a drainage system, the regular cleaning and watering of the streets and the erection of water works.

But in one sector prospects seemed bleak indeed: 'We regret that we cannot speak well of railway matters.' Notwithstanding a large increase in traffic of all kinds at the station, which lay near the mid-point of the single line connecting Three Bridges with Tunbridge Wells, the Brighton company was accused of continuing its habitual neglect of the requirements of the town. Passenger trains had been more than ever unpunctual, goods traffic had been grossly neglected, the darkness of the railway bridge outside the railway station had continued and ladies had been forced to grope about for their carriages in the dark, no shelter having yet been provided outside the station against the wet and stormy wintry weather. Communications with Lewes via the main line appeared worse than ever and all trains continued to arrive at Tunbridge Wells just in time to miss the up trains of the SER to Tonbridge and Sevenoaks. 'In fact,' commented the newspaper sarcastically, 'it would be difficult to arrange a more awkward series of trains than we now have. It is no wonder that the new Metropolitan and Brighton scheme is hailed with delight for, happens what will, railway matters cannot be worse than they are now.'

Ever since the financial collapse of 1866 which had damped down the rivalry of the railway companies over East Sussex, an uneasy peace had remained between the Brighton and South Eastern companies. The latter, casting envious eyes westwards, would still dearly have liked to move into the central South Coast routes. Similar ambitions were entertained by the London, Chatham & Dover concern which inspired a direct ingression by a proposed 'Metropolitan & Brighton Railway' in 1875. It was to begin by a double junction with the SER and LCDR at Beckenham, running via Oxted, Godstone (with spurs connecting with the former South Eastern main line, pointing at the very least to indirect SER influence and backing), following a route similar to Palmer's of 1835 via East Grinstead, Newick, Lewes and Rottingdean, and ending in an underground terminus opposite the Royal Pavilion in Brighton, a distance of 46½ miles. The railway historian Dendy Marshall states that it failed to appeal to the public and was therefore dropped, but the more likely reason for its demise was simply that the local gentry could wait no longer and had other plans afoot of a kindred nature. Brighton Corporation for its own reasons certainly put in its oar against it.

The Promoters

1876 opened at East Grinstead with an accident to a horse and trap, collecting passengers off the 5.20pm, as it turned by the unlit railway bridge, stumbling and breaking the shaft of the carriage. What was wanted by the whole locality, rated for its independent spirit, was not 'A light in our darkness' nor a wider station road, but a new railway. Local landowners and businessmen decided they had had enough. If no one else would finance a railway to give their area the modern communications it so desperately needed, they would do it themselves. The will to achieve this lay with a pressure group that had been on the boil for over 10 years, namely the independent-minded local sponsors who had met in January 1866 at the Sheffield Arms hotel near Sheffield Park to oppose the Brighton-imposed Ouse Valley line by backing the SER and LCDR's London, Lewes & Brighton scheme, notwithstanding that the backing companies, sensing the grip of financial recession, had cold feet over their counter-scheme. In the chair was Viscount Pevensey, the future Earl of Sheffield, who now with much the same group of local gentry gathered to promote a completely independent railway, the

Right: Map of the proposed Beckenham, Lewes & Brighton Railway of 1863. *Bluebell Archives*

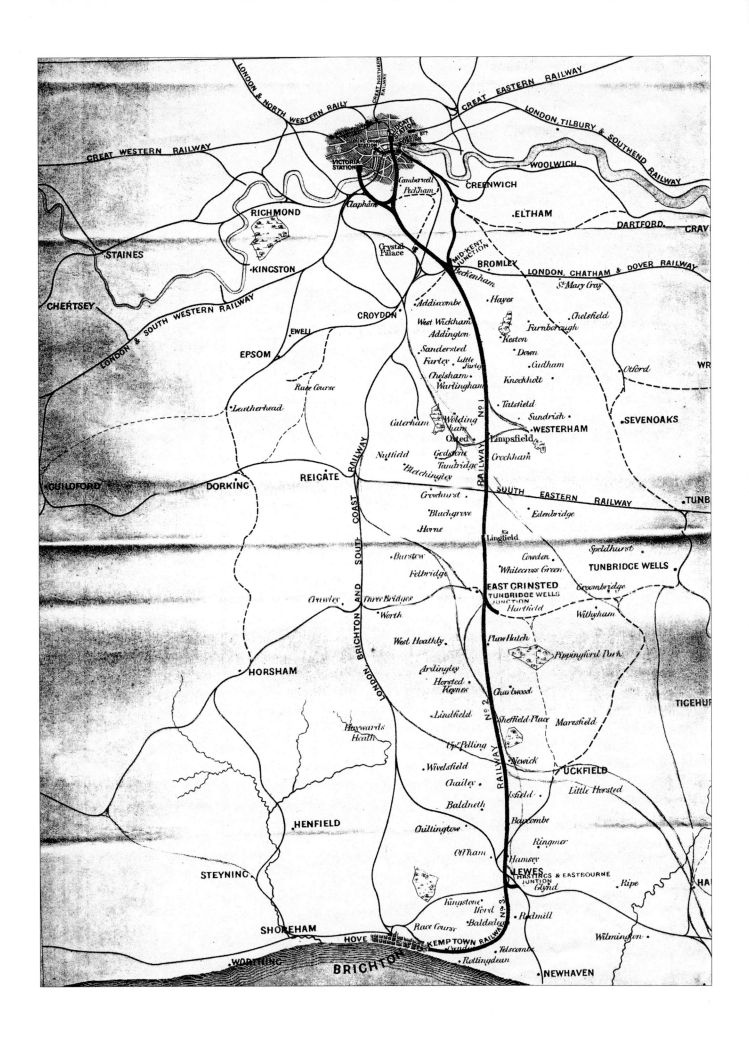

METROPOLITAN AND BRIGHTON RAILWAY,

VIÂ BECKENHAM.

From Cannon Street, Charing Cross, London Bridge, of the South Eastern Railway.

From Ludgate Hill, Holborn Viaduct, Victoria, of the London Chatham and Dover Railway.

From Moorgate Street and the other Stations of the Metropolitan Railway system to the proposed Pavilion Station at **Brighton.**

TO BE INCORPORATED BY ACT OF PARLIAMENT,
CAPITAL £2,100,000
IN 105,000 SHARES OF £20 EACH.

Deposit £1 on application, and the balance in instalments of not more than £3 each, payable after the passing of the Act, at intervals of not less than four months.

On the passing of the Act and payment of the first instalment, the Banker's receipt for the deposit and the letter of acceptance will be exchanged for Share Certificates.

If the Act be not obtained the expenses incurred will be paid by the Provisional Committee, and the deposit of £1 per Share returned in full.

PROVISIONAL COMMITTEE (*with power to add to their number*).

BENJAMIN WHITWORTH, Esq., M.P., 11, Holland Park, Director of the Metropolitan Railway.

DONALD LARNACH, Esq., Brambletye, East Grinstead, Sussex.

JAMES WYLLIE, Esq., 13, Leadenhall Street, Director of the Consolidated Bank.

OSWALD AUGUSTUS SMITH, Esq., Hammerwood, East Grinstead, Sussex.

ELI LEES, Esq., 102, Lancaster Gate.

J. H. PULESTON, Esq., M.P., Marden Park, Godstone, Surrey.

JAMES SHEPHERD, Esq., 10, Old Broad Street.

P. G. CARVILL, Esq. (Francis Carvill and Son), 13, Leadenhall Street.

J. R. LINGARD, Esq., Beckenham, Kent.

JOHN H. GARTSIDE, Esq., Staley, Cheshire.

JAMES HOLDEN, Esq., Fulshaw Park, Wilmslow, Cheshire, Director of the Staveley Coal and Iron Company.

J. G. HOLDEN, Esq., Royton, Oldham, Director of the Sheepbridge Coal and Iron Company.

EDMUND A. PONTIFEX, Esq. (Pontifex and Wood), Shoe Lane.

W. R. ARBUTHNOT, Esq., Plawhatch, West Hoathly, Sussex.

J. BROOMHALL, Esq., J.P., The Manor House, Penge, Director of the National Temperance and Genl. Prov. Inst.

WILLIAM WALKER, Esq., 64, Old Broad Street, Director of the Bank of South Australia.

JAMES S. WALKER, Esq., J.P., Hunsdon Bury, Herts.

EDWARD WIMBLE, Esq., Milbourne Lodge, Putney.

F. A. DU CROZ, Esq., Courtlands, East Grinstead, and 52, Lombard Street.

MAJOR-GENERAL HITCHINS, R.E., East Lodge, Brighton.

BANKERS.

The LONDON JOINT STOCK BANK, Princes Street, London.

The CONSOLIDATED BANK, Threadneedle Street, London, and Manchester.

Messrs. SMITH, PAYNE, and SMITHS, 1, Lombard Street.

SOLICITORS.

Messrs. BURCHELL, 5, Broad Sanctuary, Westminster.

ENGINEERS.

EDWARD WILSON.

Messrs. NIMMO and MACNAY.

SECRETARY (*pro tem*).

CHARLES ELEY.

OFFICES.

110, CANNON STREET, CITY.

H.R.

14

Left: Title page of the prospectus of the Metropolitan & Brighton Railway of 1876. Note the name of F. A. Du Croz, whose objections to the LEGR caused alteration of the route through the Sharpthorne ridge. *Bluebell Archives*

Above: The Star Hotel in the High Street, Lewes, where the promoters of the London, Lewes & East Grinstead Railway met on Saturday, 30 September 1876. The hotel stood on the site of the ancient Star Inn, in the cellar of which 17 Protestant martyrs were imprisoned during Mary Tudor's reign, and went up the steps to their deaths at the stake. Some of the store rooms survive under today's Town Hall. *Copyright Sussex Archaeological Society/Reeves Collection*

Lewes, East Grinstead & London Railway Co, comprising three sections: north and south of East Grinstead and a short branch from Horsted Keynes to the Brighton main line near Copyhold Farm.

Though there was undoubtedly a degree of support from the local townsmen of Lewes and East Grinstead, who wished for a more direct link between their respective towns, both already served by rail, a contemporary correspondent was well justified in regarding the venture as 'a landowner's line with somebody possibly behind them,' for certainly it ran through one of the most rural areas of Sussex, the home of large estates of gentry great and small. As far as that 'somebody' was concerned, all the financial evidence pointed towards Henry North Holroyd, third Earl of Sheffield.

Saturday, 30 September 1876, the year of succession to his earldom, found him in the chair of a meeting at Lewes of the Provisional Committee of the London, Lewes & East Grinstead Railway. This influential gathering of local landowners, having property between Lewes and East Grinstead, was held at the old Star Hotel. The purpose of the meeting was to consider the question of applying to Parliament for the power to construct a railway between these towns and northwards on to London. Many of those present had at various times expressed considerable dissatisfaction that the numerous previous schemes had come to nothing, due to circumstances outside their control, namely the roughshod political decisions and arrangements between the large rival railway companies, with the result that 'railway accommodation' looked as if it would never be forthcoming for the several large villages situated some distance from the Brighton main line.

The neighbourhood of the line was well represented, both in profession and estate. Beside the Earl of Sheffield there were present (in *Minute Book* order): J. C. Blencowe of Chailey,

Lewes and East Grinstead Railway.

(Incorporation of Company—Construction of Railways from London, Brighton, and South Coast Railway Company's Railway near Barcombe Station to their Railway near East Grinstead Station, with a Branch to their Main Line between Hayward's Heath and Balcombe Stations—Compulsory Purchase of Lands—Tolls—Special Power to limited Owners, &c., of Land—Running Powers over certain Railways of, Facilities against, Agreements with and other Provisions affecting London, Brighton, and South Coast Railway Company and other Companies—Amendment of Acts.)

NOTICE is hereby given, that Application is intended to be made to Parliament in the ensuing Session for leave to bring in a Bill for effecting the purposes or some of the purposes following, that is to say:—

1. To incorporate a Company, and to authorise the Company so to be incorporated (in this notice called "the Company") to make and maintain in the county of Sussex, the railways hereinafter mentioned, or some or one of them, or some part or parts thereof respectively, together with all proper and sufficient bridges, viaducts, rails, sidings, turntables, stations, approaches, roads, buildings, yards, and other works and conveniences connected therewith, that is to say:—

(1.) A Railway (No. 1) commencing in the parish of Barcombe, by a junction with the Brighton, Uckfield, and Tunbridge Wells Branch of the London, Brighton, and South Coast Railway Company (in this notice called "the Brighton Company"), at a point about 770 yards (measured along the said Railway) south-westward from the south end of the passenger platform at Barcombe Station, and terminating in the parish of East Grinstead, at a point about 240 yards south-westward from the bridge by which the Three Bridges and Tunbridge Wells Branch of the Brighton Company's Railway is carried over a road leading southward from Killick's Farm, the said bridge being distant about 260 yards westward from the passenger platform at East Grinstead Station, which intended Railway No. 1 will be made or pass from, in, through, or into the parishes, townships, and places following, or some of them, that is to say: Barcombe, Chailey, Newick, Fletching, Lindfield, Horsted-Keynes, West-Hoathly, and East Grinstead.

(2.) A Railway (No. 2) wholly in the parish of East Grinstead, commencing by a junction with the intended Railway No. 1 at its termination, and terminating by a junction with the Three Bridges and Tunbridge Wells Branch Railway above-mentioned, at a point about 200 yards westward from the Booking Office at the East Grinstead Station thereon.

(3.) A Railway (No. 3) commencing in the parishes of Ardingly and Cuckfield, or one of those parishes, by a junction with the Main Line of Railway of the Brighton Company at a point about 25 yards northward from the Bridge carrying the Road known as Copyhold Lane, over the said Main Line, and terminating in the parish of Horsted-Keynes, by a junction with the intended Railway No. 1 in Leamland Wood, at a point about 570 yards north-west from Great Odynes Farm House, and about 600 yards westward from the House known as Leamland, which intended Railway No. 3 will be made, or pass from, in, through, or into the parishes, townships, and places of Ardingly, Cuckfield,

Balcombe, West-Hoathly, Lindfield, and Horsted-Keynes.

2. To authorise the Company to deviate laterally from the lines of the intended works to the extent shown on the plans hereinafter mentioned, or as may be provided by the Bill, and also to deviate vertically from the levels shown on the Sections hereinafter mentioned.

3. To empower the Company to cross, divert, alter, or stop up, whether temporarily or permanently, all such turnpike and other roads, highways, streets, pipes, sewers, canals, navigations, rivers, streams, bridges, railways, and tramways within the parishes, townships, extra-parochial and other places aforesaid, or any of them, as it may be necessary or convenient to cross, divert, alter, or stop up, for the purposes of the intended works, or any of them, or of the Bill.

4. To authorise the Company to purchase and take by compulsion, and also by agreement, lands, houses, tenements, and hereditaments, for the purposes of the intended railways and works, and of the Bill; and to vary or extinguish all rights and privileges in any manner connected with the lands, houses, tenements, and hereditaments so purchased or taken.

5. To enable and authorise any tenant for life of, or other person having a limited estate or interest in, any lands which would or might be benefited or improved in value by, or would derive facilities or accommodation from the construction or working of the intended railways, or any or either of them, or any part or parts thereof respectively, to subscribe to and hold shares in the undertaking of the Company, and to raise the moneys necessary for that purpose by mortgage of, and to charge the same upon such lands and the fee simple and inheritance thereof, and to grant and convey to the Company any lands required for the construction of the intended railways, or any or either of them, or any part or parts thereof respectively, or any stations, sidings, roads, approaches, works, or conveniences connected therewith, either without payment or other consideration, or for such considerations, pecuniary or otherwise, and upon such terms and conditions as may have been, or may be, agreed upon between any such person and the Company, and to sanction and confirm any agreements which may have been, or may be, made between any such person and the Company, or any person or persons on their behalf respectively, with respect to any of the matters aforesaid.

6. To enable the Company to levy tolls, rates, and duties upon, or in respect of, the intended railways and works, and upon the railways and portions of railways, stations, and works hereinafter mentioned belonging to the Brighton Company, and to alter the tolls, rates, and duties which the Brighton Company are now authorised to take, and to confer exemptions from the payment of such tolls, rates, and duties respectively.

7. To empower the Company and any Company or persons for the time being working or using the railways of the Company, or any part thereof, either by agreement or otherwise, and on such terms and conditions, and on payment of such tolls and rates as may be agreed on, or as may be settled by arbitration or provided by the Bill, to run over, work, and use with their engines, carriages, and wagons, officers, and servants, whether in charge of engines and trains, or for any other purpose whatsoever, and for the purposes of their traffic of every description, the railways or portions of railways hereinafter mentioned, that is to say:—(a.) So much of the railways of the Brighton Company as lies, or will lie, between the junctions therewith of the intended

16

William Langham Christie, MP for Lewes 1874-85, who lived at Glyndebourne, Robert Crosskey, County Magistrate of Lewes, Edward Easton of West Hoathly, later to become Chairman of the LEGR, W. H. Sainsbury Gilbert, Burwood Godlee of Lewes, James Ingram, the Reverend William Powell, Rector of Newick 1868-85, and Henry James Sclater JP of Newick. An equal number, though unable to attend, had expressed interest and willingness to stand for the new Committee.

Also in attendance was the man the assembled company had really come to hear in order to be informed as to the practicability of the scheme: Mr John Wolfe Barry, who was to be the line's engineer. The Provisional Committee received his report favourably to a man, and instructed him to proceed at once with a survey. It was agreed that steps should be taken immediately to prepare a Bill and plans and sections for deposit in the coming session of Parliament, and that a fund limited to the amount of each gentleman's subscription be raised to defray the Parliamentary and other expenses. As the press report put it, 'The preliminary expenses were guaranteed.' The promoters at this stage appointed as solicitors Messrs Hunt, Curry & Nicholson of Lewes, and Peerless, Head & Sons of East Grinstead for the long haul of legal and clerical labours ahead.

The other most important business was the appointment of an Executive Committee which was to place the carrying through of the scheme in the hands of a smaller, more manageable group of men, with the natural expectation that matters would be more easily expedited. The Earl of Sheffield, who had dug deeply into his purse for the initial expenses, was appointed Chairman of the new Committee which consisted of Edward Easton (Vice Chairman) and Messrs Blencowe, Christie, Crosskey, Godlee, Hallett (of Lindfield), Ingram, Rev Powell, Sclater, and Smith (of Paddockhurst). The Committee had powers to add to its numbers and did so immediately at the first meeting by co opting F. A. Du Croz, who lived at Courtlands and owned land around Sharpthorne astride the course of the proposed line. Other new faces soon to be involved were the Hon D. E. Holroyd, the Earl's cousin, Charles Fox, General Hepburn and W. V. K. Stenning, who was later to own the timber yards at East Grinstead and Kingscote.

The Plans and Bill

For the next few months, until the Company was formed with a Board of Directors, the progress of the scheme was pushed forward by the Committee. Its places of meeting varied from the Terminus Hotel, London Bridge, to the Royal Crescent Hotel, Brighton. During this time it approved a railway gradient for the line of 1 in 70, adopted Wolfe Barry's report and opened a bank account. Wolfe Barry must have worked fast, for his report was before the Committee on 8 November. It resolved 'that the whole line as described be proceeded with and that this meeting hereby pledges itself to use its best endeavours to obtain the necessary Act of Parliament,' and even made bold to solicit subscriptions from the owners of property north of East Grinstead for, after all, they were bent on going through to London.

The Bill for the railway south from East Grinstead, as eventually deposited, embraced the plans for the line to be

constructed in three separate sections. The 'main line' comprised Railway No 1 and was to run from a point '770 yards along the railway south westwards from the south end of the passenger platform at Barcombe station and terminate in the parish of East Grinstead about 240 yards south westwards from the bridge by which the Three Bridges-Tunbridge Wells branch of the Brighton Railway is carried over a road leading southwards from Killick's Farm, the said bridge being distant about 260 yards westward from the passenger platform at East Grinstead station.'

Railway No 2 was wholly in the parish of East Grinstead, commencing by a junction with intended Railway No 1 at its termination, and terminating 'by a junction with the Three Bridges & Tunbridge Wells branch railway at a point about 200 yards westward from the Booking Office at the East Grinstead [2nd] station thereon.'

Railway No 3 left the Brighton main line at a junction '25 yards north of Copyhold Lane, terminating with a junction to intended Railway No 1 in Leamland Wood at a point 570 yards northwest from Great Odynes Farm and 600 yards westward from the house known as Leamland.'

In the first week of December 1876, the public read in their papers that the plans for the LEG and London Railways had been duly deposited. Once the subscription list had been opened with adequate support, the law required that plans and sections and a book of reference with attendant documents, such as estimates and a list of lessees, occupiers and owners of land on which the railway was to be built, be deposited at the Private Bill office of the House of Lords, which examined the project in committee. Bills were first sent up to the Clerk of Parliaments, whose body of examiners, provided all standing orders had been complied with, issued a certificate upon which the Lord Chancellor was then informed that the Bill could proceed. This authority came through on 9 February 1877, and three days later a petition of suitors for the Bill comprising Messrs Christie (MP for Lewes), Gregory (Sussex East) and Fortescue Harrison (Renfrew) begged leave to bring in, read and present it to the Commons. It required a second reading on 21 February and was referred to a committee under a Mr Ruskes.

Meanwhile the Brighton Board of Directors had been keeping a wary eye on the scheme's progress. Though it had initially agreed to let the promotion take its independent course in the way of which it would not stand, it had on 14 February given the solicitors the go-ahead with the LEGR Bill (Nos 1 and 2) at an Extraordinary Special General Meeting of the Proprietors of the LBSC, before whom the LEGR Bills were presented.

On the first day of June 1877 Mr Ruskes' committee reported back that they had examined the allegations contained in the preamble of the Bill and amended the same by omitting certain recitals referring to powers to use the lines of the LBSCR for securing and facilitating the transmission of traffic. Several other clauses with respect to working and other arrangements were struck out. The Brighton company obviously had a powerful Parliamentary lobby to watch over its interests. The amendments made and report printed, it was considered by the House of Commons and recommended for a third reading on 6 June. A similar process was repeated in the Lords. On 3 July Mr Cope, the LEGR's solicitor, reported to his own directors that 'the Company's Bill would go unopposed before the Committee of the House of Lords this

Left: First page of LEGR Bill deposited in Parliament in 1877. *Bluebell Archives*

CHAPTER ccxviii.

An Act for incorporating the Lewes and East Grinstead A.D. 1877.
Railway Company ; and for other purposes.

[10th August 1877.]

WHEREAS the construction of the railways by this Act authorised from the Brighton, Uckfield, and Tunbridge Wells branch of the London, Brighton, and South Coast Railway Company (in this Act called " the Brighton Company "), near Barcombe Station, to their Three Bridges and Tunbridge Wells branch near East Grinstead Station, with a branch to their main line between Hayward's Heath and Balcombe Stations, would be of great public and local advantage :

And whereas the several persons herein-after named, with others, are willing at their own expense to carry the undertaking into execution on being incorporated into a company for the purpose :

And whereas it is expedient that the agreement between the promoters of the Company and the Brighton Company (a copy of which is set forth in the Schedule to this Act) should be sanctioned and made binding on the Company and the Brighton Company :

And whereas plans and sections showing the lines and levels of the railways authorised by this Act, and also books of reference containing the names of the owners and lessees, or reputed owners and lessees, and of the occupiers of the lands required or which may be taken for the purposes or under the powers of this Act, were duly deposited with the clerk of the peace for the county of Sussex, and are herein-after respectively referred to as the deposited plans, sections, and books of reference :

And whereas the purposes of this Act cannot be effected without the authority of Parliament :

May it therefore please Your Majesty that it may be enacted ; and be it enacted by the Queen's most Excellent Majesty, by and with the advice and consent of the Lords Spiritual and Temporal,

[*Local.–218.*]　　　　A　　　　1

Above left: Title page of the Act of 10 August 1877 incorporating the Lewes & East Grinstead Railway Co. *Bluebell Archives*

Above: Henry North Holroyd, who had just succeeded to the earldom as third Earl of Sheffield, chaired the first meeting of the Provisional Committee at Lewes. He was the principal backer of the LEGR scheme in terms of support

day at 3 o'clock'. After a quibble by the Board of Trade regarding the inclination for a road crossing was overruled, the Bill received its third reading in the Lords on 27 July, was agreed by the Commons on 6 August and the Royal Assent, '*Soit fait comme il est desiré*', was granted on 10 August 1877.

The passing of the Act was the authorisation for construction, enabling the company to purchase land and undertake the necessary works. This did not however imply that the deposited plans had to be carried out to the exact detail. In practice the engineer and contractor found problems on the ground, sometimes at a late stage, and certain lavishness had often to be curtailed because money was running short.

Finance

The LEGR Committee had realised that to take on two opposing established major railway companies at the same time, which were jointly determined that the northern extension should not succeed independently, was like knocking their heads against a brick wall. Virtually no small private lines had succeeded on their own in the South of England, and the days of light railways still lay in the future. History showed that many undertakings begun as independent schemes had been swallowed up at an early stage by the more financially viable major companies, which had both the capital and the experience, the equipment and the rolling stock to hand, often before a divot of the proposed trackbed had been turned.

Moreover, not only had the northern line insufficient financial backing — many doubtless withheld their support while the major companies refused to contemplate it — but even the funds for the LEGR proper were being spent faster than the money was coming in. The scheme had begun with a gentleman's fund to defray the preliminary expenses, and such was the initial enthusiasm for the line that land was given to the company by Lord Sheffield and the Rector of Barcombe. The second meeting decided to call up monies subscribed and open an account at the Old Bank, Lewes, in the name of the chairman and vice-chairman. The press noted in December 1876: 'The promoters have necessarily become responsible for considerable sums on account of preliminary expenses. We observe that subscription lists to help meet these expenses have been opened up with good results in Lewes and other localities, and we hope the inhabitants of East Grinstead will not be behind in doing their part. Subscriptions may be paid into either of the banks in this town.' But early in 1877 they were soliciting subscriptions from property owners north of East Grinstead, and the stepping up of subscriptions by half was the first sign of financial difficulties ahead.

By early summer the reserves had run out and the LEGR directors were at their wits' end for financing the completion of the Bill through Parliament, for without it they had little that would carry weight in the delicate negotiations with the LBSCR that lay ahead. They needed a sum of £3,000 for future preliminary expenses in connection with the passage of the Bill. If they were unable to find this amount, the scheme was finished. The decision lay with the chairman. He had already contributed more capital than all the others put together and he probably felt he had already invested too large a stake in the venture to throw in his hand at this well-advanced stage. He therefore made the vital decision recorded in the minutes: 'Lord Sheffield expressed his willingness to advance that amount of interest, and the repayment of such loan with interest at five per cent to be made to his Lordship out of the first capital to be raised upon the passing of the Act, and to be secured in the meantime by the personal guarantee of the following gentlemen [directors and others] each to pay Lord Sheffield £300 (with the proportion of interest thereon).' Six of the directors each took a share, two others were taken by Wolfe Barry, the engineer, and Cope, the solicitor, the remaining two being taken generously enough by Lord Sheffield himself. Edward Easton took the chair while the terms were accepted that the seal of the company be affixed and letters of guarantee be drawn up and despatched. But a key decision had been taken, providing funds that saw the Bill through to a successful conclusion and gave the company licence to raise capital to cover at the minimum the £311,296 estimate of expenses published by Wolfe Barry on 30 December 1876. But whether the vast capital could effectively be raised was open to question, and especially so in the minds of the LEGR directors.

The Deputations

It had been apparent for some time that funds for the scheme were not coming in as well as the promoters had been led to expect. As far as their independence was concerned, the writing was already on the wall. Someone more than the Earl of Sheffield was required if their fortunes were to be retrieved. Almost from the beginning, it had been realised that an approach would have to be made to the Brighton company, if only to see how the land lay, and probably no more than this was involved or expected when on 21 October 1876 the Committee deputed some of their number, the chairman, vice-chairman and Messrs Smith and Hallett, to seek an interview with the directors of the LBSCR. It is fortunate that the outcome, which was crucial to all future plans and progress, is recorded not only in the minute books of both railway companies but also in a full-length report in the *Sussex Advertiser*. Lined up against each other, the issues at stake, seen from different angles, are left in no doubt. The body of men who went to London Bridge on 8 November styled itself 'A Deputation of the Executive Committee of the proposed East Grinstead, Lewes and London Railway', and they had every intention of going through with their 'northern extension' to London. The group introduced by the Earl of Sheffield was a formidable one, far larger than the original delegation, and included several new and influential personages from north of East Grinstead. The deputation, according to the Press, 'was cordially received . . . and a discussion of extremely friendly and satisfactory character took place'.

The Earl of Sheffield and Edward Easton having explained the objects of the scheme and the views of the deputation, Samuel Laing, the Brighton Chairman, stood up to reply, saying that, although his company could not promise to give any pecuniary assistance, it would not oppose an application to Parliament for powers to carry out a scheme between Barcombe and East Grinstead. The LEGR interpretation of these points was that 'the Brighton Co would not only not oppose the project . . . but were willing to enter into any fair arrangement for working the line, etc, on terms to be mutually agreed upon or, failing agreement, to be settled by arbitration of the Board of Trade.'

However, with regard to the proposed line north of East Grinstead, the LBSCR was not in a position to pledge itself as to its course of action, on account of its relationship with the SER, the Brighton company's minutes specifically referring to 'the proposed line north of the SE Co's line' [ie Godstone]. The LEGR minutes add the further information that 'if the line was postponed to another year the Brighton Co might make an arrangement for dividing profit with the SE Co as they did in other instances, and thus the Act would be obtained without opposition.' The independents had read the minds of 'Big Brother' aright, sensing the advantages they now saw would accrue from the LEGR scheme if it was linked by a direct route to London.

The press report for this initial meeting provides the first detailed mention of the route contemplated, being from Lewes via Hamsey, Barcombe, Isfield, Newick, Fletching and West Hoathly, across to East Grinstead, a course which in parts swung a mile or two to the east of the one that was finally adopted. The project was stated to be warmly supported by the landowners and residents along the route designated, being primarily concerned with direct communication between the two terminal points, 'instead of the indirect, not to say roundabout, way at present existing by means of Uckfield and Tunbridge Wells [no Birchden spur] or by way of Three Bridges.'

The northern project contemplated using part of the Surrey and Sussex line 'arrested in its progress', a very material consideration, and the report summed up the outcome: 'So far as the matter has already gone, the prospects of success of the undertaking may be considered as highly favourable. The landowners along the line evince the strongest interest.' It makes the assumption, correctly but long before any official mention appears in either company's minutes, that 'The line would be worked by the Brighton Co so as to be included in their system.' It concludes: 'The residents of the district must not forget that "Heaven helps those who help themselves" and no effort ought therefore to be grudged to strengthen the hands of the promoters who have so zealously laid the foundation of the good work.'

At the conclusion of the meeting in the Brighton company's boardroom, the deputation moved round the corner at London Bridge to the Terminus Hotel and, joined by others, met in full committee. They resolved that, after the expressions of opinion of the Brighton Railway Board directors, the line between Lewes and East Grinstead be proceeded with immediately and that the necessary Parliamentary powers be obtained. Naturally, in view of Mr Laing's veiled threat, they could not move ahead in similar manner over the northern extension. This now meant that the extension to London fell out of step with the LEGR proper, eventually by as much as two years. However, they further ordered that the *whole* line as described in Mr Barry's report be proceeded with, and stated that 'This meeting pledges itself to use its best endeavours to obtain the necessary Act of Parliament.' That

Samuel Laing, Chairman of the LBSCR, took control of that company following the financial collapse of 1866 and was responsible for guiding it on a sound and successful basis. He was one of the pair of Brighton directors appointed as a result of the 'takeover' deal whereby the LBSCR became responsible for the completion of the line.
John Minnis collection

In a flood of verbiage, Chairman Samuel Laing requested that 'the No 2 Bill deposited by the promoters for a railway from East Grinstead to London be withdrawn at once.' On its part the Brighton board would undertake to recommend its proprietors to apply to Parliament next session for powers, jointly with the South Eastern company, 'to construct a railway over the Surrey and Sussex line at or near the Godstone station from which point the Brighton Co would continue to East Grinstead so as to join the line projected by the promoters under their No 1 Bill from East Grinstead to Barcombe.' A short discussion ensued, following which the deputation promised to consider the proposal.

But, polite as the promise may have been, once round the corner in the Terminus Hotel, their independent spirit revived and they published a special minute resolving that 'After hearing the communication just made by Mr Laing (without prejudice), it is still the opinion of the meeting that the northern line should be proceeded with.' The consideration that weighed so heavily with the promoters was the importance to them of having through trains to London, a factor that was strangely to repeat itself a century later when the Bluebell Railway first contemplated its northern extension. Back in the mid-19th century the major companies had betrayed the hopes of the locals so often, and they had no wish to see their truncated scheme become a minor branch line from Lewes.

However, when the Committee next met on 22 January, after hearing the vice-chairman's progress report, they decided to have a third confrontation with the Brighton board. They resolved unanimously 'that the Directors of the Lewes & East Grinstead, and the East Grinstead and London Railway Cos (acting jointly) do communicate with the directors of the LBSCR Co, requesting them to state in writing the terms which they wish the promoters of the new lines to agree, so that they may be carefully considered and an agreement if possible arrived at.' Lord Sheffield was now suggesting that a letter be written to Mr Laing, offering 'to have a conference with him should he think it desirable, and, should that be the case, that he together with the Earl de la Warr and Buckhurst and Edward Easton be deputed to attend.' What had suddenly changed their thinking? The moment of crisis lay ahead, from which they were to emerge with their wings clipped and their independence considerably reduced.

The Takeover

In simple terms, the surrender of independence stemmed from the financial weakness of the LEGR promoters and their supporters, and from the paramount strength of the main-line company to call the tune as required. Lewes to East Grinstead presented no problems to the LBSCR, provided the promoters did not flirt with the South Eastern or Chatham companies, but farther north, beyond Godstone, the enterprise entered hotly disputed territory where an independent concern could, if under considerable pressure, much more easily fall to the opposition's camp. Hence the Brighton company's peremptory demand that the No 2 Bill be withdrawn and the offer, as an inducement, of active support for the No 1 Bill if this were done.

It was in the light of this that the deputation met the Brighton directors and returned to their own board's meeting on 26 January 1877 to consider the heads of the proposed agreement with the LBSCR. Discussions ensued and the following alterations were suggested, which Mr Cope was to take to his opposite number on the Brighton company, Mr

they had in no way relinquished their hopes for the London section was underlined by the minute: 'Further subscription be solicited from the owners of property north of East Grinstead.'

Meanwhile on 15 November 1876 the deputation's proposals had been discussed at a meeting of the Brighton & South Eastern Joint Committee, and comments on the report sent to Sir Edward Watkin, the South Eastern Chairman, who was not present, were awaited. This was quickly rendered irrelevant, when it was learned in January 1877 that plans for the Lewes, East Grinstead & London Railway had been deposited and the LEGR Committee had resolved unanimously to go ahead with the line north of East Grinstead as well as the southern section to Lewes. Thoroughly alarmed by the news, the LBSCR acted like lightning, inviting, almost summoning, a second deputation of the Lewes, East Grinstead & London Railway promoters to attend their board. Added to their numbers were Lord de la Warr, Lord Arthur Hill and Mr Charles Hill, representatives indicative of the support and concern of the gentry along the northern extension.

Brewer, namely:

'That when the Lewes & East Grinstead Railway and the railways described in Articles 2 & 3 are completed, they shall be worked as a through line between London and Lewes and vice versa.

'That a standing Arbitrator, to be agreed upon, shall decide in the case of difference between the Brighton Co and the promoters.

'That Bill No 2 be withdrawn at once if the whole thing is accepted.

'That there be four passenger trains daily with through connections to and from London. [This was the clause that gave Miss M. Bessemer leverage to reopen the line in 1956.]

'That two directors to be elected to the LEGR Committee are to be directors of the Brighton Co.'

But there was still one sticking point. If an agreement were to be arrived at, it would have to stipulate that 'the Brighton Co help with capital'. By February the LEGR was saying that 'If the proposed arrangement was carried out and the line when continued did not earn enough to pay interest on the capital, the Brighton Co would make up the deficiency.' This proved quite the trickiest part of the negotiations, which culminated in an interview on 18 July at 3 Whitehall Place between Edward Easton and Samuel Laing, 'on the subject of capital'.

Laing must have known, if only from previous experience with such independent ventures, how precariously things stood, for, speaking from a position of strength, he straightly proposed that his company should take up and carry out the undertaking itself, 'to which Mr Easton demurred'. It was an empty gesture of defiant independence, but it was the money that spoke, and the inevitable outcome was a suggestion that, to enable the LBSCR to arrange for the advance of the requisite funds for constructing the line through a contractor of its own nomination, purchasing the land and providing other necessary expenditure, an agreement should be entered into between the two companies, by which the LBSCR would exercise its option of acquiring the undertaking when completed on the terms of the existing agreements. At the least this would enable the LEGR to proceed at once with the work without losing further time, and when Easton reported to his colleagues, there could be (and in fact was) no dissent. Nor was there any negative reaction among members of the Brighton board, who instructed the solicitors of both companies to get together and draft an agreement, 'on the basis of this Company *taking over the line*'.

It was also resolved 'that the chairman and Sir Philip Rose be and are hereby appointed the directors of the company to sit upon the board of the LEGR.' This minute sealed the 'taking over of the line' and just over a year later the General Manager, Mr Knight, was reminding the LEGR board to send him a copy of the minutes of *each* meeting. A few weeks before the line opened, Mr Knight confidently told his directors that 'the undertaking of the LEGR and all the real and personal property thereof etc, etc will become vested in the company in pursuance of its Act of 1878.' But, as will be seen, he was counting chickens before they were hatched.

After this enforced surrender, money matters moved from major to minor keys. The new Act empowered the LBSCR to raise capital and debentures to the extent of £533,000. The LBSCR was to find the money necessary to build the railway, which on completion was to revert to that company, and one of the final acts of the LEGR was for the director and secretary to sign a return to this effect. Much time was now taken up ironing out the forced marriage, for it was not exactly a shotgun wedding, the Brighton board being far too cautious, and time was on their side. Certainly the LEGR board had by mid-1878 incurred some large financial liabilities and, though they had in no way been reckless, they had proceeded on the understanding that the engagement between the two companies would eventually result in union.

On 17 July 1878 the LEGR board made out a requisition of £50,000 to provide funding for disbursements and liabilities, which included £10,000 for the costs of engineers, solicitors and parliamentary agents, interest, directors' fees and petty disbursements, £30,000 for land purchases in the quarter ahead and £10,000 for a start on the works. The Brighton board's reply proposed that a meeting be held for the purpose of determining the mode of procedure for financing the company, which two of the newly elected Brighton directors would attend. As a result of this it was agreed to establish credit of £50,000 in the books of the Lewes company, and that cheques would be drawn in favour of the latter company by Samuel Laing and Sir Philip Rose, to enable them to pay all necessary expenses certified by the LBSCR's solicitors and engineers. Also agreed was the payment of the directors' fees in connection with the Royal Assent for the Bill (£300 to date), £50pa for each director — £25 as a fixed sum, the remaining £25 to be divided between them according to attendance during the year at the henceforth monthly board meetings — and also secretarial expenses. The LBSCR opened this special account for LEGR transactions on 1 August, was already paying fresh instalments in by the end of November and continued to do so until 23 November 1883. The process of drawing cheques became a routine practice and, in October, Wolfe Barry was noted as giving the contractor a cheque for £10,000.

The Directors

The last meeting of the Committee and its reconstitution as a meeting of directors had taken place on 22 January 1877, and marked the transition from a subscribed list of promoters to a railway company with its allocation of shares and a seal of its own. This was confirmed on 5 June when letters of guarantee were sent out, while a minute of 3 July states that, 'Subject to altering the relative positions of the town arms of Lewes and East Grinstead, the design for the company's seal was approved and the secretary instructed to order it.' On 25 August the officials for the ensuing year were appointed. 'It was resolved unanimously that the Right Hon Henry North, Earl of Sheffield, be and is hereby elected Chairman of the directors.' Edward Easton was to be Deputy Chairman, Mr Robert Gilbert Howard Secretary, Mr John Wolfe Barry Engineer and Cope & Co solicitors. It was resolved that the first ordinary meeting of the company be held at the Royal Crescent Hotel, Brighton, on 12 September at 3pm.

The first general meeting of the shareholders duly took place and provided the sole entry in the Lewes & East Grinstead Railway Co minute book of general meetings. The directors were to be Lord Sheffield, Lord Arthur Hill, William Langham Christie MP, Edward Easton, William Henry Hallett and John Henry Sclater, and the remuneration was fixed at £250pa, to be apportioned by the directors among themselves as they saw fit. The secretary's salary was to be £150pa, including the use of his offices and petty disbursements. However, for reasons not disclosed on 16 June 1878, a letter was received from R. Gilbert Howard tendering his resignation. It was accepted and £150 voted for his services in the past year. Mr Frederick Sanders was appointed at the same salary, and one of his first tasks was to write to a Mr Firbank 'that the directors wish him to attend the next board meeting of which he will receive due notice'. Mr Sanders was already secretary to the Beltim Land & Irrigation Co Ltd, and his offices at 11 Delahay Street, Westminster, conveniently became the headquarters of the LEGR Co.

Fortunately a report of the second ordinary general meeting of the company, held on 28 February, 1878, at Abingdon Street, Westminster, with the Earl of Sheffield in the chair, appeared in the *North Sussex Gazette*. The following progress report of the directors was adopted.

'Your directors have the satisfaction of reporting that after making the necessary survey and trial borings, the engineer has so far completed the plans for the railway that a contract can now be entered into for its construction. The notice plans for the purchase of land for about eight miles of the line have now been completed, and the notices are in the process of being served on the respective owners and occupiers. The Brighton Co have in accordance with the agreement entered into with this company, deposited in Parliament the Bill for the northern half of the line from East Grinstead to Croydon, and your directors have presented a petition for the purpose of seeing that clauses for the due fulfilment of the agreement are inserted therein, and have every reason to believe that the Bill will become law this session. Your directors can therefore now congratulate you and the County of Sussex on the approaching carrying out of this very desirable and important undertaking.'

A brief survey of board attendances is worthy of comment, indicating the degree of interest in the scheme. Lord Sheffield was Chairman and a regular attender for the first two years, when matters of the greatest moment and decision were thrashed out. He was absent from meetings in late June and July, when he was away on his annual holiday on his cruise yacht, but attendances then became intermittent, with the last one on 27 May 1879. By then the important details had been settled and the meeting dealt with minor routine matters, and the Earl had many interests of greater importance on his plate. Edward Easton as selected Vice-Chairman stood in on these absences, and himself missed only once, on 9 August 1882 (a

few days after the opening!), in 43 attendances over nine years. He was the mainstay behind the independent spirit of the LEGR. Also absent on that same day was William Hallett, who only missed four times in all. James Sclater JP attended roughly half the meetings till about the time Lord Sheffield left and then entered upon a final run of 13 attendances to the end without missing a meeting. William Christie MP, who held Lewes throughout this period, attended all but two meetings up to the end of 1878, and half of the remainder. Lord Arthur Hill first put in an appearance at the meeting prior to the inaugural director's meeting and put in less than a third of possible attendances between February 1879 and August 1882.

The two Brighton directors, Mr Samuel Laing MP and Sir Philip Rose Bt, appointed 19 June 1878, made their first attendance on 30 July that year, when a letter was read from the LBSCR's secretary instructing that, under powers conferred by Section 27 of the LEGR Act, its two nominees be received as directors of the LEGR Co. The two Brighton-implanted directors were present through to their final appearances on 1 February 1882, Rose missing out twice and Laing five times. The former, incidentally, was a solicitor and senior partner in the firm of Norton, Rose & Brewer, which acted as solicitors on behalf of the LBSCR.

The last board meeting labelled in the minute book as 'directors' was that of Lord Sheffield's final attendance on 27 May 1879, and thereafter the chair was usually taken by Edward Easton as deputy. On the occasion of his rare absence Mr Sclater took over, but 26 October 1881 was a meeting with minimal business and, with both of the above-mentioned present, Samuel Laing for some reason took the chair. During the period July 1879 to February 1882 the 10 meetings convened — a far negation from the monthly meetings ordered — took place at the LBSCR offices at London Bridge, doubtless to convenience the Brighton directors, but, once they relinquished attending, the meetings returned to the offices of the LEGR at 11 Delahay Street, apart from one on 28 February 1883 back at London Bridge. For this final period, attendances averaged four LEGR directors, the Secretary, Mr Waites of Messrs Cope & Co, and the odd attendance from Wolfe Barry.

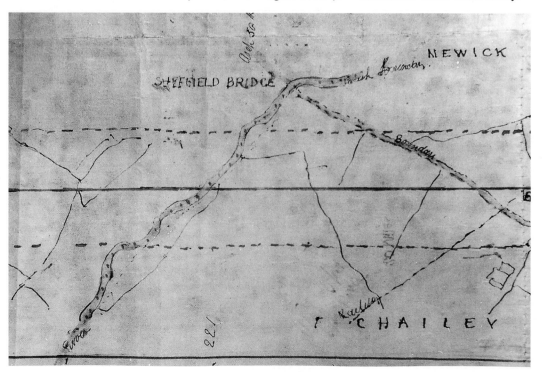

Rough plan on vellum of the single line section from Ketches Farm through to Barcombe, formerly in the possession of Sir William Grantham JP. The section illustrated shows the future site of Sheffield Park station, the River Ouse and, most interestingly, in the lower right-hand corner, the course of the incomplete Ouse Valley Railway, which would have had a station at Sheffield Bridge. The line of track would have been purchased and pegged out, but had lain derelict following cessation of work in 1867.
Bluebell Archives

2.
Preparation

The Engineers

'Mr John Wolfe Barry CE, attended the meeting and received instructions to proceed at once with the survey.' So read the minutes of the Provisional Committee which met at Lewes on 30 September 1876. Which of the promoters had the personal contact with Wolfe Barry to bring him into the scheme may never be known, but certainly the latter had been involved for some time earlier in the year, doing sufficient of the spadework to have his report favourably and unanimously received at the above meeting, for the promoters to resolve that 'it is desirable that steps be taken at once to prepare a Bill and plans and sections for deposit in the coming session of Parliament.'

Certainly John Wolfe Barry was a most reputable fish for such a minor independent venture to hook. Born in Scotland in 1836, the son of Sir Charles Wolfe Barry who built the Houses of Parliament, he was educated at Glenalmond School and went on to King's College, London. He trained as an engineer in the shops of Lucas Bros and was a pupil of John Hawkshaw, who built Charing Cross and Cannon Street stations, together with the bridges over the Thames. In 1867 he started on his own as a consulting engineer with the Metropolitan District Railway with regard to its Ealing and Fulham branches. He had already begun to make his mark in the engineering world when the Lewes & East Grinstead project came into view, having presented papers to the Institution of Civil Engineers in 1868, and published his first book in 1876, entitled *Railway Affairs*, in which he pointed out that 'baulk road' laying showed an economy in timber as well as iron. Barry proved that with a gauge as wide as 7ft the use of cross sleepers would have consumed more timbers than the longitudinals. It was advice that came rather too late in the day for the GWR, which had by that date virtually completed the laying of broad gauge track. Certainly Barry took some inspiration from his friendship with the Brunel family, and about this time took Isambard's second son, Henry Marc, into partnership. McDermott in his Firbank biography cites the Chief Engineers of the LEGR contract as Wolfe Barry and M. Brunel, and the Resident Engineers as J. Robinson and Brereton. The former, John Robinson MICE of Newick, held the title of Executive Engineer.

An outline draft of the plans had been circulating earlier in the summer among the more prominent of the landowners through whose territory the proposed line would pass, giving them an idea of the extent to which they would be affected. One such outline plan, inked on vellum, which survived in the hands of the Grantham family of Barcombe, is among the treasures of the Bluebell Archives. Meanwhile, before the section plans could be ready to go forward before Parliament, quite a bit of tidying up and delineation had to be done. Following the settling of the ruling gradient at 1 in 70 in October 1876, a further report was accepted in the November meeting that Barry should proceed with 'the whole line' through to Croydon.

The first half of the following year was to some extent taken up with seeing the plans through Parliament, and Barry was to be available to answer questions from a committee examining the soundness of the project. It was not until 25 August 1877 that he was officially appointed Engineer of the company, a position he had held in all but name since the venture was first mooted. The remuneration of the Engineer was to be 5% on the cost of the railway and works, but this was not to include the preparation of the working plans for use of the solicitors in the purchase of the land.

The latter subject was to prove a sore one, with reverberations that lasted through to the very final meeting of the LEGR Co. The nub of the problem largely stemmed from the fact that, while the LBSCR was willing to take over the LEGR, it was not so willing to take over the latter's engineer or accept his decisions without questioning them. As their two directors appointed to the LEGR board had considerable powers, backed by friends to sway decisions, they succeeded in appointing their own engineer, Frederick Dale Banister, to oversee Barry's work and vet it before authorising funding. The Brighton Company called the tune and would, if it could, have dispensed with Barry's services then and there.

The confrontation was set off when the LEGR board read a letter from Mr Barry at its October meeting, regarding payment of £2,000 on account of engineering. They forwarded this application to the LBSCR, which, considering this on 6 November, noted he was also asking £150 for balance of preliminary expenses, justified by virtue of his official appointment and above-mentioned terms of remuneration. The Brighton board stalled, stating: 'the contract with Mr Barry is one to which the assent of the company was required . . . and is not one to which this board can agree but it will be prepared to confer with the East Grinstead board and Mr Barry, so as to place his claim for professional remuneration on a fair footing.' They advanced the £2,000 on the 'distinct understanding that the company is not bound by the contract made without their consent with Mr Barry.' They viewed Barry's LEGR contract as unacceptable, and to be treated as a question in dispute. By 22 October they were able to forward a 'Memorandum of arrangement with J. Wolfe Barry relating to his position as engineer of the LEGR' for submission the following month.

Portrait and autograph of Frederick Dale Banister, the LBSCR's appointed Chief Engineer to the line.
Courtesy Michael Banister

While all this to-ing and fro-ing had been going on, Wolfe Barry had perforce to continue with his work while awaiting events. Having completed the initial survey, he had been further instructed by the LEGR to proceed with the necessary plans for the northern extension, only to find that Banister was also working over the same ground for the Brighton company as to some preliminary works considered necessary. Though the LEGR deputation had shown themselves agreeable to employing the LBSCR's contractor, they insisted he was to take all his instructions from the LEGR board and its engineer. Following the takeover, Barry found it difficult to move with the LBSCR's engineer on his back, so to speak. The new paymaster called the tune. However, so much of the original plans and designs were Barry's that Banister must have been spared heartache. It was Barry's idea of a high- and low-level platform arrangement at East Grinstead which was accepted by the Brighton company when it came to the line north of the town.

By 1880, when the construction was in full swing, Barry had found it necessary to appoint a resident engineer who could permanently supervise the works on site. This Mr J. Robinson was granted possession of an empty residence at Kingscote for a nominal rent of five shillings a year and to take care of land on behalf of the company. The question of outstanding payment continued to rumble on, for, as the work expanded, so did the financial outlay. There followed a further fracas over the doubling of the section south of Horsted Keynes. Barry, out of pocket, sent in pleading letters, but the Brighton board was tough and heartless; on 20 September 1882, after the line had opened, Barry's extra claims, approved as 'fair and reasonable' by the LEGR board, were

forwarded to and rejected by the LBSCR board, which refused to alter the terms.

The idea of two engineers, each responsible to his own board of directors, proved to be a ludicrous and frustrating arrangement, and not just for Barry. Banister was hauled over the coals, being taken to task by the LBSCR Engineering Committee on 30 April 1883 regarding an excess over estimates. Large outstanding claims for work done and not paid for were mentioned, for permanent way materials delivered and not charged up, besides very large claims for land and compensation. 'It is perfectly true', said Banister in his defence, 'that I was appointed to act with Mr Barry as engineer of this line, but as the execution of the works was entrusted to Mr Barry and his staff, I was necessarily in his hands as to the cost of works, measurements etc.' He added that Mr Barry employed a very competent staff, saying so much not out of charity but to prop up his own case. He gave the reasons for extra costs: doubling work from Horsted Keynes to Barcombe, the Leamland Viaduct, the strengthening of Sharpthorne Tunnel, the additional tunnel at Lywood Common, the extension from Copyhold Cutting to Haywards Heath comprising 1¼ miles of double railway, the cost of 10 stations and, for good measure, the additional work rendered necessary by slips and difficulties. 'Bearing in mind the nature of the country through which the line passes,' Banister submitted, 'it will be found that the cost for works has not been very materially in excess of what might have been expected in the circumstances.'

Barry's claim went to the line, for as late as 10 July 1883 the Brighton board was reported as refusing consent to refer Barry's claim to arbitration. On 17 September the LEGR board resolved 'that Counsel's opinion be taken as to the means to be adopted', in order to enforce settlement. Possibly the Brighton board was expecting the imminent winding-up of the LEGR Co now that Railway No 3, the branch to Haywards Heath, had been completed, but 1884 arrived without solution. Eventually, after conferring with his chairman, Mr Banister had prevailed on Mr Barry to accept £705 in settlement of £905 for extra engineering services on the LEGR, on the understanding that £105 thereof was to be accepted by him as a retaining fee. At the start of February, Edward Easton was informed by Mr Barry that his claims had been satisfied.

Perhaps the rather shabby treatment he had received during his involvement with the LEGR scheme was responsible for Barry's firm's diversifying into the field of dock consultants in the mid-1880s, operating in a big way at home and abroad, with a formidable list of works at major dock complexes. However, close ties with the Metropolitan Railway, on which he contributed a paper in 1905, led him back into railways, such as the Glasgow Underground and the Caledonian Railway. With the age of major railway construction drawing to a close, he turned to bridges and his *chef d'oeuvre*, the construction of Tower Bridge in 1894, being responsible for the engineering work but not for the architectural detail or for the staircases in the towers. Barry went on in the next reign to build the King Edward VII Bridge across the Thames at Kew. Among his other notable achievements was the founding of the Engineering Standards Commission and his reduction of the number of patterns for tramway rail from 70 to nine. He became Chairman of the City and Guilds of London Institute and followed such notables as Thomas Telford and Robert Stephenson as President of the Institution of Civil Engineers. He received the ultimate accolade of a knighthood and a portrayal in a nave window in Westminster Abbey. Satisfying as these honours must have been, he must have derived singular pleasure on learning in 1897 that his name had been inscribed on the LBSCR's new 'B2' class 4-4-0 No 209, designed by Robert Billinton. The Brighton company had made just amends. He died as an octogenarian in 1918, and his eldest son became the senior partner in the firm which still continues in the City to this day.

The Contractor

It was on 23 July 1877 that the word 'Contractor' first appeared in the LEGR board minutes, where mention was made of the Brighton company's taking over construction of the line, 'through a contractor of their own nomination'. In December it was agreed to employ 'the contractor of the Brighton Co,' provided he take his instructions from the LEGR board and its engineer. It was only in June 1878 that the secretary was instructed to write to Mr Firbank that the directors wished him to attend the next board meeting, of which he would receive due notice.

Joseph Firbank was one of the most spectacular Victorian entrepreneurs, beginning work in a coal-mine and finishing up as a rich railway contractor and High Sheriff of Monmouthshire. He was the 19th-century ideal of the self-made man, a life story well documented in Frederick McDermott's biography, written in 1887, in which the claim is made that Firbank 'built single handed — that is without partners — more railways in this country than any other contractor'. McDermott adds: 'His was a simple tale of manful and honest labour reaping its due reward of success, and of a young miner raising himself, by industry and pluck, to a position of wealth and influence.'

Born in 1819 at Bishop Auckland, in County Durham, by the age of seven he worked a 14-hour-day, six-day week in the local mine to help the family budget. When 14, with other aspiring fellows, he sought to make up for his lack of schooling by attending a night school at Easington, paying the fees out of his own wages. With a quick eye to a chance, he changed his occupation in 1840, to work on the construction of the Bishop Auckland and Weardale branch of the Stockton & Darlington Railway. His biographer states: 'In the work he saw on this line, he recognised a type of labour for which he felt himself well qualified. Accordingly he made enquiries on his own behalf as to railway works in progress, and, having a high character with his employers for energy and integrity, was fortunate at the age of 22 to secure a subcontract on the great Woodhead Tunnel. From mining to tunnelling proved an easy transition.'

Firbank proved successful and from here his career took off, having by this time accumulated a small capital which enabled him to undertake larger subcontracts, even for George Hudson, 'the Railway King', on the Midland Railway when railway mania was at its height. The panic and collapse of 1845/6 was followed by three years of depression due to public reluctance to invest further capital for new railway undertakings. By good fortune Firbank was not caught with a contract in harness, and was able in 1846 to secure a contract under George Stephenson, one of the few fresh ones let at this time. He forged ahead despite experiencing bankruptcy on the Rugby & Stamford undertaking for the LNWR, when he nearly lost the whole of his hard-earned savings but secured his predecessor's contract to save the day. From 1854 to 1857 he secured large contracts in Monmouthshire, from which time Firbank made Newport his headquarters and bought himself a fine Victorian neo-classical house on its outskirts. Henry Elliott became his right-hand man — a lifelong and faithful assistant.

Joseph Firbank was appointed contractor for construction of the new railway. A self-made man, he became the leading contractor of the late Victorian period and was responsible for building most of the LBSCR's secondary and branch lines. *From McDermott's* Life of Joseph Firbank

In 1859 he forged his first links with Sussex, the county which provided him with more opportunities for railway construction than any other. The first contract placed by the LBSCR was from Shoreham to Horsham, soon followed by the Mid-Sussex line between Pulborough and Arundel and the branch to Littlehampton. The collapse of 1866 affected him gravely and he had to forgo many of his claims. In part payment of his work Firbank took a large sum in stock at par, which in a few months' time fell to 38%. Undaunted, he refused to sell and was ultimately rewarded by seeing it quoted at a high premium. He moved on to several contracts in South London and the Midland Railway's Bedford to London extension, where there was another financial collapse in mid-contract. In 1870 he was awarded one of the four sections of the Settle & Carlisle line, an epic saga of railway construction. Again in financial straits through a virtual trebling of the cost of coal, he was advised by his friends to give up and face the inevitable loss of £100,000, but Firbank remained unshaken: 'My word is my bond, and I've given my word to carry through this job, and through it shall go, whatever may be the consequences.'

Contracts now came Firbank's way with ever increasing rapidity. Noteworthy in the 1870-5 period was the widening of the King's Cross Tunnel beneath the Regent's Canal, where he introduced 'an unsightly machine called the "steam navvy" which not only saved labour costs, but those of victualling the human labourer.' From 1876 Firbank had a succession of contracts over the next decade with the LBSCR on various rural lines in different parts of Sussex, starting with the Eridge-Hailsham line, the Cliftonville Spur line avoiding Brighton station, goods stations at Kemp Town, Hove and Cliftonville, and the enlargement of the main one at Brighton. While these works were in progress came the call to 'the contractor of the Brighton Co' to construct the LEGR.

This somewhat unfortunately came at the juncture where the two companies were haggling over their rights and the LEGR directors were trying to ascertain the exact terms of the contract the LBSCR had entered into with Firbank. The minutes of 13 July 1878 tell how Mr Cope, 'with great difficulty, obtained from Messrs Norton and Co part of the proposed contract with Mr Firbank.' They raised objections to the scope of the contract and specifications, stating: 'the draft as prepared encroaches upon the independence of the LEGR Co, and practically takes control of the undertaking out of their hands.'

Meanwhile Firbank had already been engaged on preliminary work. On 30 October 1878, it was reported that 'the Contractor is now in possession of about five miles of the line,' and Barry was about to authorise a cheque for £10,000. This he did not receive until mid-December, for the Brighton board insisted on receiving a certificate given by both Barry and Banister in favour of Mr Joseph Firbank, but thereafter further payments followed quickly as the work got under way. Meanwhile the solicitors of the two companies had met and had worked out a compromise which sidestepped the issue and passed it on to their respective engineers to effect a working relationship with the contractor. So it was that on 19 November the Brighton board ratified the 'contract for the LEG Railways between the LEGR Co, LBSCR Co and Joseph Firbank for construction and maintenance for 12 months of certain railways and works in the County of Sussex', and Barry produced the contract plans and specifications as finally settled with the contractor.

By mid-1879 the contractor was in full stride, and was requesting a payment, only to be told by the Brighton board that no unavoidable delay had occurred in preparing the cheque, while early in 1882 Barry was taking up Firbank's cause, requesting the board to pay Firbank half the retention money under his contract. In June 1883 the Brighton board questioned a statement of outstanding claims by Firbank and referred additional claims outside the contract to the engineers for their consideration. These were finally confirmed on 22 January 1884.

As regards the supervision of the works, Firbank himself had far too large an empire under his charge to be present with any regularity when so many different schemes were under way. By this time at least three of his sons were working under him. There is mention of Mr Christopher Firbank jr, driving home one evening in March 1879 from the railway works at West Hoathly when his horse shied and he was thrown and his leg broken, while in January 1881 Mr John Brown Firbank, Engineer's Foreman on the new railway, attended the amateur concert in aid of funds for the West Hoathly Reading Room and shared in the provision of refreshments. On Whit Monday 1882 Mr Thomas Firbank, the eldest son, was present at a cricket match for men employed in the construction of the northern extension, at which the Oxted end beat the East Grinstead navvies.

However, Joseph Firbank still kept a firm grip on events. He enforced discipline, for instance, in the case of a *fracas* in one

of the navvy huts at West Hoathly in August 1879. Two women were in one of the huts when two others entered, 'on a friendly scold'. A bottle of port wine was thrown, resulting in a free for all. The *Sussex Express* simpered: 'We may add that all the parties have had notice from Mr Firbank to leave their huts.' Late in 1879, when some of the labour force was already encamped near Ardingly, it was reported that Mr Firbank 'had assumed a plan to stop the pranks of many of the navvies who have been in the habit of absenting themselves from the works and returning at will. He has established a rule that if a man who has not a plea of ill health is missing on a working day, his place is filled up and he sent adrift. There is no difficulty in doing this as numbers are roaming about in search of employ, the works at Cowfold monastery being temporarily stopped.' On the other hand, Firbank was not without great sympathy for the needs of his employees and stepped in briskly with practical help during the terrible winter of 1880/1.

He suffered problems of his own, ranging from a court case, Adams v Firbank, brought against him by one of his navvies who fell from a skip, or wooden basket, used for sending up earth from a shaft, to an occurrence which hit the local headlines: 'Alleged extensive theft by Firbank's cashier'. Thomas Thompson, aged 48, was before magistrate Mr R. Crosskey, charged with stealing £83 from his employer at Newick on 28 June 1879. Both Mr George Holmes, Firbank's head cashier, and Frank Whittle, main cashier at Newick, gave evidence, throwing light on the system. It was explained that a sub-cashier was allowed to hold a balance in hand and debit himself in the next sheet. When tackled about the sheet showing no balance, the accused had quickly disappeared and a letter was returned inscribed 'Gone away'. His house was searched and boxes examined, £15 and some vouchers being found. Thompson was arrested in Staffordshire, saying 'I lost my account book', and was formally committed.

By 1882 Firbank was well under way with the construction of the Croydon, Oxted & East Grinstead Railway, receiving the contract under the joint auspices of the South Eastern and Brighton companies. Major works here included the handsome wrought-iron lattice-girder viaduct at Riddlesdown, the waterlogged 2,266yd Oxted Tunnel and Cooks Pond Viaduct. During the same period, 1881-4, he was engaged on the joint line from Woodside to South Croydon, and almost the last contract before his death was the line from Oxted to Groombridge, with its formidable Mark Beech Tunnel of 1,307yd. Simultaneously, other works were taking place in the Birmingham suburbs, the St Pancras Goods Depot covering 14 acres of Somers Town (a slum district requiring clearance of some 500 houses), various widenings for the LWSR and construction of the Bournemouth direct line via Brockenhurst.

Joseph Firbank died at the age of 67 on 29 June 1886, after only two days' illness, having led an active out-of-door life and hitherto enjoyed the best of health. Samuel Laing, chairing on 21 July the annual meeting of the LBSCR, which Firbank was accustomed to attend, described him as 'an excellent specimen of the class of Englishmen who rise up not so much by any transcendent talents, as by intelligence and energy, and above all honesty and inspiring confidence in those for whom he had to work. I believe he never skimped a bit of work in his life, but in all the contracts he has had with us we have had good honest work for our money.'

Thomas Firbank continued his father's projects and gained many more, including the Great Central Metropolitan Extension. He received a knighthood in 1902, but was not set in the same mould as his father. His last years were dogged by losses and the decline in his fortunes, which his death in October 1910 revealed. He had outlived the railway-building age without finding a successful and profitable niche in the period that followed.

As for the LEGR board, it should have been well content with its 'Brighton contractor', to whose works along the whole of its line the Board of Trade inspector was to pay the highest of all tributes, saying he had 'never seen work better done'.

Land Settlements

Once the Act had been passed, the railway company was entitled to purchase land for the necessary works. The go-ahead came at the LEGR directors' meeting on 1 February 1878, when Cope, the solicitor, Barry, the Engineer, and Sanders, the Secretary, were instructed 'to serve as early as possible notices to treat on owners, lessees and occupiers of the land required throughout the line', and Messrs Hunt, Stephenson & Jones were appointed surveyors to the company for acquiring the lands required for the various lines. The 'Notice to Treat' informed the owner/occupier that the railway company required land for the line described in an attached schedule containing a description and measurements of the area in question and marked in red on a plan. The company gave notice that it was willing to negotiate for the land and pay compensation for any damage that might be incurred by the estate through which the line passed. The landowner was to reply within 21 days with a written statement of the details, charges and value, and make his claim to the company accordingly.

The Notice to Treat was the virtual equivalent of a compulsory purchase order and, if the landowner and the company failed to come to an agreement regarding the price, the issue went to arbitration by means of an inquisition taken before the Sheriffs of the County, in order to assess the value of the property required. On the other hand, if both parties reached agreement without any difficulties, the landowners might execute a normal deed of conveyance, affecting the transference of property to the railway. Such was the case with Lord Sheffield, about which there was naturally no problem, for no one wanted the line in being more than the Earl himself. This the latter arranged to convey in a single sale from the Uckfield Road near Newick to Coneyborough Wood near the foot of today's Freshfield Bank. Fortunately the indenture for this land conveyance, dated 7 January 1880, survives today in the East Sussex Record Office. An indenture was a sealed agreement or contract indented in two halves with a zig-zag line to produce two duplicate halves, so that each party to the agreement was able to retain one half. The half surviving is entitled 'Sale by Lord Sheffield and Others to the Lewes & East Grinstead Railway Co of land in the parishes of Chailey and Fletching for £5,250'. The 'others' referred to a small section of Lane End Common, part of the Manor of Houndean. A description of land and measurements is accompanied by a plan, the central part of which, covering the proposed station area at Sheffield Bridge, is reproduced on below.

Detail from a conveyancing map of the area purchased for the future Sheffield Park station site. Note the road diversion (far left).
Reproduced with the permission of the County Archivist of East Sussex, copyright reserved. Ref ACC 597/2/10

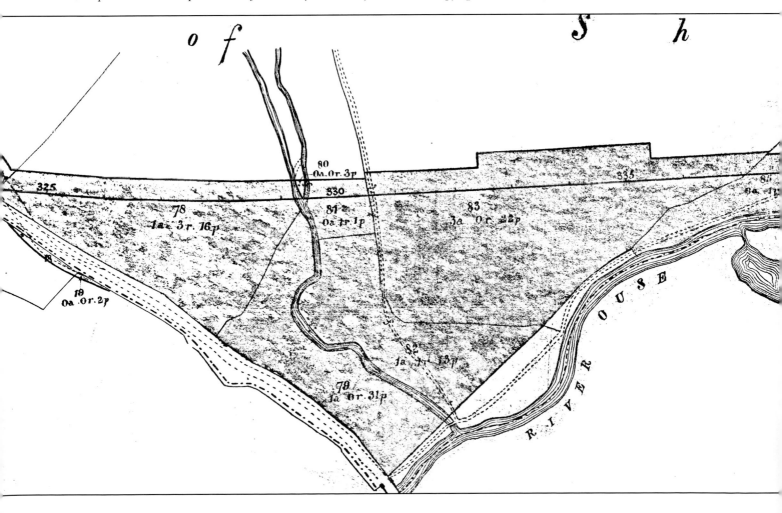

LEWES AND EAST GRINSTEAD RAILWAY COMPANY.

NOTICE TO TREAT.

IN PURSUANCE of the provisions contained in "The Lewes and East Grinstead Railway Act, 1877," and the several Acts of Parliament incorporated therewith, THE LEWES AND EAST GRINSTEAD RAILWAY COMPANY do hereby give you and each and every of you NOTICE that they require to purchase or take the lands and hereditaments specified and described in the Schedule hereto, with the appurtenances, and which said lands and hereditaments so required as aforesaid are reputed to belong to you, or some or one of you, or in which you, or some or one of you, have or claim to have some estate or interest, and which are, for the better description thereof, delineated on the plan attached hereto, and are therein distinguished by a red colour, and which lands and hereditaments the said Company are authorised to purchase or take for the purposes of the Act above mentioned. AND the said Company do hereby further give you, and each and every of you, NOTICE that they are ready and willing to treat with you for the purchase of the said lands and hereditaments so required as aforesaid, with the appurtenances, and of your estate and interest therein, and as to the compensation to be made to you for the damage (if any) that may be sustained by you, by reason of the execution of the works authorised by the said Act, above mentioned. AND ALSO that you, and each and every of you, are hereby required, within twenty-one days from the service of this Notice upon you, to deliver, or cause to be delivered, to Messrs. Cope & Co., the Solicitors of the said Company, at their Offices, No. 4, Victoria Street, Westminster, S.W., a statement in writing of the particulars of your estate and interest in the said lands and hereditaments so required by the said Company as aforesaid, or any part thereof, and of the claim which you make in respect thereof, and to state the charges and incumbrances (if any), to which the same are subject. AND you are hereby also required, within the said period of twenty-one days, to produce to the said Solicitors, at their offices aforesaid, any lease or leases, grant or grants (if any), for a longer period than one year, or the best evidence thereof in your power, under which you have, or claim to have, any estate or interest in the said lands and hereditaments; and, if you make your claim under, or in respect of, any such lease or leases, grant or grants, and fail for twenty-one days from the receipt by you of this Notice to produce the same, or such best evidence thereof as aforesaid, you will not be entitled to compensation as a Leaseholder, but as a Tenant holding only from year to year.

Dated this *twenty-seventh* day of *July* 1880 ~~187~~

To

John Willett Esqre.

Ro Sanders

And to all and every other person and persons whom it may concern.

Secretary to the Lewes and East Grinstead Railway Company.

N.B.—In order to assist you in complying with the provisions of the Acts, a Schedule of Claim, to be filled up and signed by you and returned to the Solicitors at their Offices aforesaid, accompanies this Notice.

By mid-1878 the work had advanced to the point where Sanders was submitting to his directors copies of surveyor's reports of settlements and land compensation which, being approved, were forwarded to the LBSCR in the form of a sealed requisition, a written demand for payment for preliminary expenses and land purchase. It was at this point that the Brighton board established £50,000 in the LEGR Co's account. Following this, major land settlements and the reading of surveyor's reports became a regular feature in the minutes. Each requisition had a number, and those confirmed in September included No 26 F. A. Du Croz £1,581; No 27 Trustees of the late Wm Stenning and others £2,281; and No 31 James Blunt (deceased) £1,926; all in the West Hoathly area including the tunnel site. By May 1879, confirmation had come through of Requisition No 2, the aforementioned sale by Lord Sheffield, and of No 1 J. H. Sclater and No 7 George Grantham, each for £750 and both for land in Barcombe, pointing to early purchase of land being largely on the southern portion of the line. Many landowners agreed to take payment for their land in exchange for shares of the company. But it was not all plain sailing, and problems soon arose. The Guardians of the East Grinstead Union Workhouse ground felt that, the railway having taken virtually all their site, the little that remained was hardly a self-contained entity. They intimated that the railway would be required to purchase the school buildings and site in addition. This was acceded to, with an additional land purchase in July 1881 of £1,250 payable to the Guardians of the Union. In such cases where the railway had to purchase more than it really required, it seems to have sold off its surplus without difficulty. Sometimes there were buyers at hand just waiting for the railway construction to be completed. Such a case was William Uridge of Chailey, regarding land just north of Barcombe, formerly belonging to Sir William Grantham, Lord of the Manor of Balneath. Uridge had to wait until 1887 to gain possession.

The hardest purchase of all concerned the tenancy of a dwelling near East Grinstead called 'Kingscote Cottage'. This had been held by a man called Hopkinson, and the company had been taken to court by one of his daughters, Mrs Peters, and lost. The board resolved to appeal against this decision. In March 1881 Hopkinson's Trustees proposed a settlement by arbitration, but the board instructed its solicitors to proceed with the appeal, which it also lost, and the claim went forward to arbitration. This was held in September when, in order to value the estate, 'the jury walked down the newly constructed line two miles from East Grinstead terminus', and recorded the value at £1,700. By now the matter had dragged on long enough to gain public notoriety and full newspaper coverage. The *North Sussex Gazette* of 27 November had it headlined 'Arbitration Case Peters v LEGR', and told of the action by Catherine Susan Peters to restrain the LEGR Co, its servants and agents, from entering upon or taking possession of or using the dwelling-house known as 'Kingscote', and outlined at length the detailed history of the case. After much legal verbiage the Vice-Chancellor, in delivering judgement, declared in favour of the plaintiff that she would be entitled to one undivided moiety (half). The Brighton directors received the decision with some relief. The verdict had been given for £1,700, the sum being exactly the same as the original farmhouse price offered by the LEGR, and it was decided consequently that Mrs Peters would have to bear her own cost of the enquiry and half of the Sheriff's charges and jury fees,

etc. Again it had been a case where the LEGR was required to purchase the whole property and Mr Cripps, the railway land agent, was authorised to arrange for a sale by auction of 'Kingscote House' and land adjoining the LEGR line. This was bought by a Henry Wm Banks by a conveyance dated 20 February 1884.

Another important compensation case was heard at the beginning of June 1881, over a freehold house in London Road, East Grinstead, required by the railway to carry on 'improvements in the construction of the approach to the new station'. In the end the claimant, a Mr Featherstone, received £2,150. In January 1879, in Gains v LEGR Co, an injunction was served to restrain the company from taking the plaintiff's land for its works, the matter in dispute being that the defendant desired to take part of the land, while the plaintiff thought it ought to take the whole. It was ruled that £4,960, that value of the part of the land required by the railway, be paid into court during an adjournment. A month later it was Mighall v LEGR Co over tenant's compensation for land taken and severance at Wax (today's Vaux) End Farm, north of Horsted Keynes, and for stopping the tenant carrying stones from the mouth of a quarry during construction (the company having taken the mouth of the quarry for its works) and for damage caused to the rest of the farm. The long and short of a drawn-out case was that the magistrate awarded the claimant £35 with costs to the company, a compromise between Mighall's claim for £55 and the company's offer of £25. By the time the LEGR Co was wound up, there was still one outstanding case on the books — Henton v LEGR Co — referred for arbitration, for which an extension of time was given to 14 May 1884.

Returning to the mainstream of undisputed land settlements, by the end of 1879 the major purchases had been completed, concluding with one of £1,927 to the Rt Hon W. B. H. Brand, who held land in the Lindfield Wood area, south of Horsted Keynes, while a payment of £100 to the Commoners of Lywood Common indicated that Railway No 3 was under way through Ardingly. Cope was able to report in January 1880 that 'the contractor is now in possession of the whole of the land required for the lines of the railway, according to notices with the tenants and lessees throughout the whole line with one or two exceptions.' On 11 August the directors heard that the compulsory powers of the company for the purchase of land under the Act had expired the previous day, but notice of the extra lands required had already been served. One of the latter mentioned at the 6 March 1882 meeting spoke of the 'Purchase of additional land at Barcombe'. It is fortunate that the documents involved have survived among the Grantham papers in the East Sussex Record Office. They record the transactions between the LEGR and one John Willett, and through these it is possible to trace successively the railway's dealings with one particular landowner.

Things were set in motion with a formal Notice to Treat on 9 February 1878. The notice no longer survives but the plan does. Entitled 'Plan of land required by the LEGR Co from John Willett', who lived at Handley (today Handlye) Farm at Barcombe, it concerned land for some furlongs either side of Barcombe Cross, and was signed by John Wolfe Barry, Engineer's Office, 23 Delahay Street, Westminster. The indenture for this transaction, dated 20 May 1879, notes that the company covenanted to maintain in good repair a level crossing marked on the plan. This was at the north end of the

Left: LEGR Notice to Treat for compulsory land purchase near Barcombe, the property of John Willett, 27 July 1880.
Reproduced with the permission of the County Archivist of East Sussex, copyright reserved. Ref: GRA 17/45

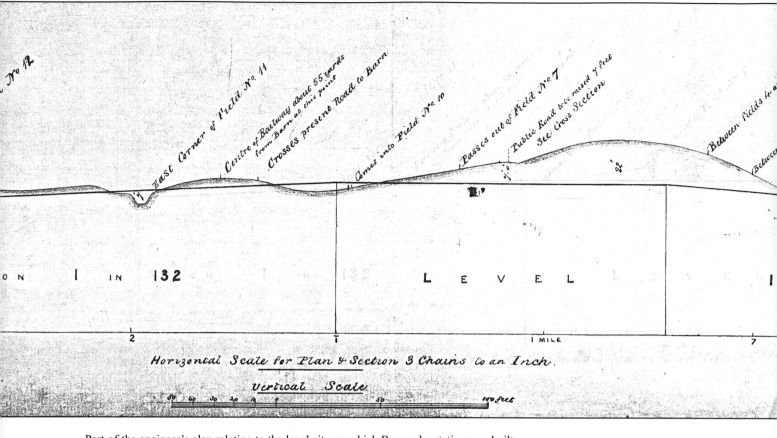

Part of the engineer's plan relating to the level site on which Barcombe station was built.
Reproduced with the permission of the County Archivist of East Sussex, copyright reserved. Ref: GRA 17/48

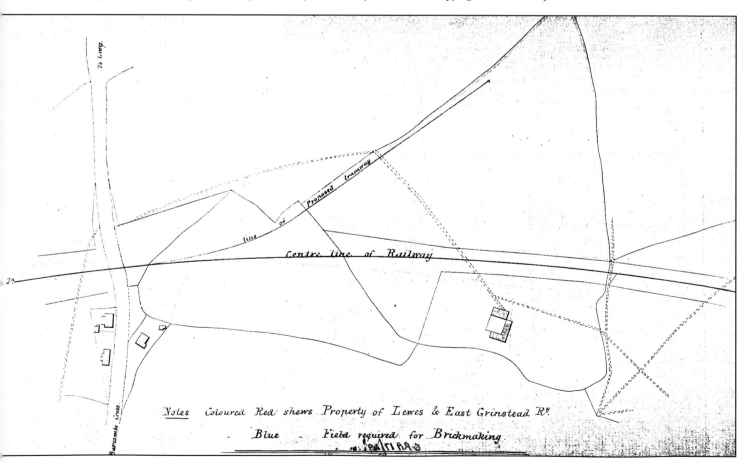

Plan for the proposed temporary brickyard siding opposite the site of Barcombe station for the use of navvies during line construction. *Reproduced with the permission of the County Archivist of East Sussex, copyright reserved. Ref: GRA 17/49*

proposed goods yard, and the track is marked crossing the line of the railway at a right angle. Then on 27 July 1880 a further Notice to Treat (the only one known to survive) was served desiring additional land. This was in two small sections. The first was necessitated by the severe slopes of the cutting on the south side leading up to the bridge by which Barcombe High Street was to cross the line, requiring two small parcels of adjacent land to allow gentler slopes to the cutting. The second was a triangle of land to provide for an enlargement of the future goods yard and an extension of the headshunt. The very next day Willett's solicitors replied, accepting. The conveyance for the additional land (measuring 1 acre 0 roods 22 poles) for £200 included a further map and is dated 7 December 1880.

Among this group of plans, in an envelope entitled 'Barcombe Railway Tracings', is a plan of the inclination and level of the Railway in 1880, Barry's solution with regard to raising the road surface on the railway bridge to the south of Barcombe station by 7ft. But the real find among these plans was a requisition for yet more land from John Willett, this time for a field adjacent to the future station site at Barcombe for a brickyard. To facilitate transport of the bricks manufactured by the navvies for this southernmost section of the line, and Barcombe station and associated bridges in particular, a tramway siding was proposed from the brickworks to the railway line itself, which by 1881 had already been laid for contractor's locomotives and wagons. There is no reason to assume other than that the tramway was of standard gauge, being shown as connected to the centre line of the railway marking the property of the LEGR. This, of course, was just one of several brick kilns along the course of the new railway, nearly all temporary in nature. The sale of the field was conveyed from John Willett to the LEGR for £100 on 3 May 1882 and must presumably have been resold by the railway at a later date, since it reverted to farming use some time after the line opened. John Willett died on 19 October 1889 and in his will the previous year bequeathed his estate to his son Henry, who must have taken the family fortunes much further, since he was resident at Barbican House, Lewes, opposite the castle — the home today of the Sussex Archaeological Society and Museum.

The Memorialists

On 6 March 1882 Sanders was instructed by the board to pass on to the Brighton company the fact that 'three memorials are about to be sent to them, signed by a numerous and influential body of gentlemen and others who are residentially and otherwise interested in the opening of the railway, and have urged upon the company the necessity of using their utmost endeavours to ensure its opening at an early date.' Who were these so-called memorialists? A memorial was a statement of facts as the basis of petition, and was a polite and gentlemanly way of suggesting some action or other to be taken by the company. The three memorials mentioned above were for temporary accommodation to be afforded at the present East Grinstead station, arrangements to be expedited for the line to be opened at the beginning of May, and the third urging the importance of at once constructing the goods warehouses and sidings according to the agreed plans. The two memorials last mentioned were adopted personally by the LEGR board and sent forward with their backing to the Brighton board, who replied stating that the East Grinstead problem would be resolved by construction of a 'junction station'.

Two years previously Sanders had received an impressive memorial from one of his own directors:

'Dear Sir,
I enclose you the memorial to the directors of the Lewes & East Grinstead Railway, which has been numerously signed by influential people residing in the district traversed by the railway, urging the board to use their best endeavours to induce the Brighton Co to prosecute the works of the northern portion of the line. You will be kind enough to present it to the board at their next meeting.
I am yours faithfully
James H. Sclater
Newick Park, Lewes
March 19, 1880

PS. The memorialists have also forwarded a corresponding memorial to the secretary of the Brighton Co for presentation to their directors.'

The LEGR board members sent the memorial straight on to their opposite numbers to add to the earlier one, inserting in brackets: 'many people must have originally subscribed for this'. Laing at his meeting expressed the desire of the Brighton company to make the expenditure it had already incurred on the southern section remunerative as early as possible. He intimated that he had been arranging preliminaries for proceeding with the northern section, that arrangements were in a forward state, and that at least £200,000 had been expended in preliminary works on the old tunnels of the Surrey & Sussex line, and thought they would be in a position very shortly to proceed actively with the construction of the authorised railway from East Grinstead to Croydon. The thing that was holding up the start was that no engineers' agreement had yet been reached with the South Eastern, but south of Godstone the LBSCR had let the contract to Firbank at the schedule price fixed by the LEGR.

Three years later yet another mammoth memorial arrived at 11 Delahay Street, 'from the landowners and residents in the district of the Lewes & East Grinstead Railway calling attention to the great inconvenience, loss and disappointment which will be occasioned to the whole neighbourhood if the northern section of the line is not opened to traffic at the time mentioned in the last Act viz 17 June, 1882.' It also drew attention to the fact that there was a penalty of £50 a day for the non-fulfilment of the undertaking of the Brighton Company to complete the line, and also to the fact that the other section of the LEGR, namely the branch from Horsted Keynes to Haywards Heath, was not yet open, although the time of completion fixed by the Act was 16 April 1882, incurring a similar penalty, and 'finally praying the board will take energetic steps to bring these matters to a conclusion.'

This again the LEGR forwarded to the LBSCR, accompanied by a letter calling its 'earnest and immediate attention to the consideration of the means of remedying the grievances of which the memorialists complain, setting forth also the facts that the agreements with this company are not fulfilled in respect of proper goods accommodation and Sunday trains.' All it got from the LBSCR was a copy of a situation report by Mr Knight, the Secretary. The LEGR directors were in no way satisfied and sent a further resolution on 12 July 1883 to similar effect as the memorial itself, and added a further section regarding through trains and their number. At this stage the matter grew into something far more forceful than a gentle memorial, and almost led to a breach between the two companies and a fiery rearguard action by Edward Easton and his colleagues.

James Henry Sclater, a director of the Lewes & East Grinstead Railway and the line's premier protagonist in its promotion.
Courtesy John Sclater

From the above situations it would appear that the memorials, which were a means of allowing the local populace to make their opinions felt, especially concerning delays in opening the railways and over inconveniences in facilities, were largely used by the LEGR board as a verbal cudgel with which to spur its Brighton paymasters to greater effect. Certainly there were expressions of genuine local feeling which the railway companies could not twist to their own ends, like the one of October 1879 where 'the memorialists urge that, considering the great influx of men employed on the new railway works and the number of lawless characters that abound, another policeman should be granted to the Division.'

But if a memorial was considered too gentle, there were more forceful methods like, for instance, Thomas Cramp's letter in the local paper in June 1879. 'We ratepayers grumbled a short time ago about the damage done to our roads by the railway contractor in moving his material to West Hoathly and other parts of the line; and we gave him to understand through our surveyor, that he would be charged with extra costs for making the roads good.' Another more communal method was actively to organise opposition. In February 1879 the LEGR board received a letter from Mr Arthur Hastie, acting for a committee of inhabitants of East Grinstead, taking exception to the proposed alteration of the railway station in their town. The committee was strongly opposed to its removal from the present site to another, 'two fields beyond the present workhouse', and about double the distance from the town. Some argued that the Bill allowed for deviations and that the alteration had been caused by a landowner's opposition to the line as originally proposed, suggesting instead to route it 'along Glen Vue Road, past the Union Workhouse, through the field beyond it across the road leading from the Old Mill to the Brewery, to near the spot where stands the semaphore signal and where there is a level crossing.' Comments came thick and fast: 'It seems to be a most arbitrary thing for a small body of gentlemen, acting as directors, to have the power of moving a station from one place to another.' 'Go to the Board of Trade and ask them to refuse their certificate.' 'It is likely to injure the trade of the town.' 'A memorial should be presented to the directors, requesting them to retain the station in its present condition with such modifications only as may meet future requirements.' 'It is monstrous that the railway company should propose to move a station without in any way consulting the views and interests of the people chiefly concerned.'

The local paper was rather sceptical of the business: 'We hear that a meeting was held at the Crown Hotel by some few tradesmen of the Old Town, to consider what action should be taken in relation to the removal of the present station to a further distance from the town. We are inclined to think that after the conveners of this meeting have said all they like on this subject, the company will do as they please.' In fact, the press was wrong, for the LEGR board resolved that the above-named committee be invited to meet representatives of both railway companies on the subject on 17 February at 12.30 at London Bridge. The committee must have been well persuaded by what they learned at the meeting, for they were heard of no more, but as late as 4 November 1882 a ratepayer's letter appeared in the press opposing the erection of the station at East Grinstead, then a *fait accompli* and open, 'so far away from the town', and stating that the station approach had not been completed and ought to be carried out. The large potholes and puddles were compared to walking through floods and the letter ended on a sarcastic note suggesting the station be called 'Mudborough', not 'Greenstede'.

3.
The Workforce

The Navvies

The first sign of the arrival of the navvies was in August 1878, when application was made for the appointment of three special constables for the protection of property during the construction of the new railway at West Hoathly, and a sworn affidavit to that effect was put in by three of the leading personages of that village. Provision for special constables was made under an Act of 1837, which allowed them to be paid at the expense of the railway company directors. Firbank as contractor had both to apply for them to be appointed and to be discharged. He was also responsible for their payment: 'Mr Firbank is bound under the general conditions of his contract to pay them.' Close communications were maintained between the LEGR Co and the local magistrates and clerks of the justices. By March 1879 the need was felt to employ special constables at Ardingly and in adjoining parishes, an indication that the workforce had arrived in earnest to commence construction of the railway. In May a local reporter wrote that considerable progress had been made during the past months at East Grinstead and 'the number of men employed made the town all alive!' That same month the issue of special constables produced diverging opinions at opposite ends of the line. A Mr Brewer quoted the number of labourers as 34 at Chailey, 86 at Newick and nine at Barcombe, maintaining that those had conducted themselves very quietly and there was no need for so many constables. He affirmed that notice should have been given to the company and constables, saying it was unfair to call upon them to preserve the peace when the peace had not been broken. Mr Hale, Chairman of the East Grinstead bench, replied that 800 men were employed on the contract and, in view of the very large number of offences committed last year, it was very desirable to increase the number of peace officers. A peak in the workforce appears only to have been reached early in 1880, for that June there was the first reduction in the staff of special constables at West Hoathly, 'the work there being nearly completed with a decrease in the number of navvies'.

The Victorian navvies or navigators, the men who came to build the canals and stayed to build the railways, have been portrayed as 'the giants of British heavy labour'. They earned the reputation as 'the most violent and savage body of men to be let loose on the countryside since Cromwell's wild soldiers. They were nomadic, lawless and ruthless and, as the railway moved, they cut across the country like a horde of driver ants.' Shunned and feared, they lived apart from society and became a herd of men who lived, worked and fought together.

The gangs were not usually brought together by the main railway contractors themselves but by subcontractors, who took a section of the line and engaged foremen called gangers to work a kind of butty or subcontracting system, either by the piece or by the day. Their employ was almost a craft of its own, a set of skills and attitudes which could not be built up overnight nor lightly abandoned once held, and a gang would tend to hang together till the line was done, emptying or filling the ranks on the tramp for fresh work. The work was exceptionally severe, the occupational risks high, the whole way of life reckless, rude and riotous. The work they did was tough and dangerous — blasting, excavating, cutting and tunnelling. Under the best conditions an individual navvy might shift 20 tons of earth a day, removed in small wagons running on rails. In cuttings the work was organised around a series of plank inclines, on which the loaded wheelbarrows and those running them could be caught by those returning for another load. Tunnels were cut from a series of shafts worked by horse-gins, with both men and material being hauled up and down in baskets. The steam shovel did not come into general use before the 1880s and there is no record of one on the LEGR contract. It was small wonder that most navvies were dead before they were 40.

Though there were those that held an opposite view, the navvies, as far as most people were concerned, came with an unenviable reputation, even though the 'dark ages' of the Woodhead and Settle & Carlisle constructions had passed into less disturbed waters. Nevertheless the drink problem remained to a considerable extent, bringing with it an aftermath of unpredictable and violent behaviour, and there were sufficient incidents of note for the wires of correspondence in the local papers to be set buzzing. 'They are quite a harmless set of men before drinking but the very opposite afterwards. Madness and violence follows. Then at no small personal risk our valiant police officers, aided by a staff of specials, have to interfere, and their almost daily duty is to arrest some of the worst of these beer-made madmen and bring them over to our magistrates for punishment. So we are compelled to learn that so much beer carted out to the navvies means so many drunken disorderlies returned. And consider the expense of all this justice involved!' Apart from the few local people who benefited from the presence of the railway construction, the rest of the locality regarded the navvies as a plague temporarily to be endured. Local inhabitants lived in fear, especially at night, and nearly all took particular care to have strong locks and bolts fixed into their house doors, both front and back.

But the great majority of navvies on the LEGR contract did not live up to this reputation and the total of something just

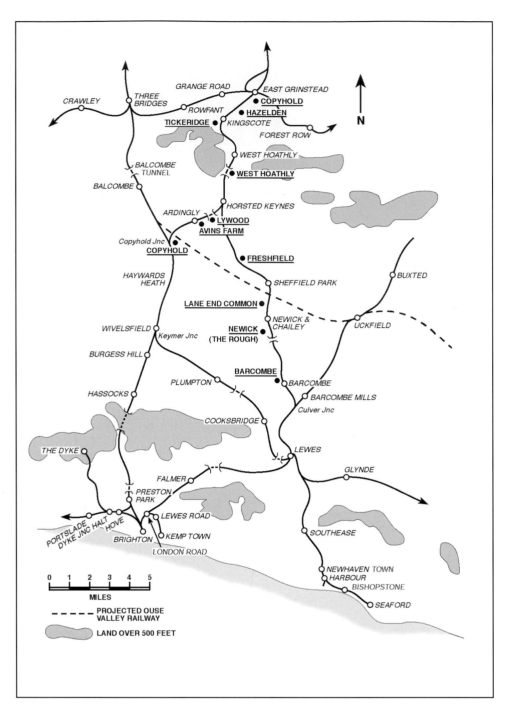

over 100 reported court cases from an estimated workforce of around 2,000 puts matters into perspective. Moreover, several names that occur in reports on the railway indicate that many labourers were recruited locally. Such a case in point was Charles Newnham, born in 1866, whose early days were spent in Horsted Keynes. In those days of limited education the young already sought work before they had entered their teens. At 13 Newnham found himself employment with a local farmer, who set him to task working in a field, picking up large stones which a recent ploughing had exposed. Such labour in the hot sun would become tedious to most people, and Newnham was no exception. His eyes strayed to the bottom end of the field which bordered on the site of the new railway, on which work had already commenced. Soon he was down by the railway fence in search of a new employer and it was not long before he caught the eye of a working ganger named George Thomas. 'Just the boy I want!' he exclaimed, and Newnham was engaged for nine shillings a week — good money for a young lad in those days. He was put to work on

the stretch a mile south of Horsted Keynes, approaching Freshfield, running errands to different parts of the line, more often than not fetching beer for the thirsty navvies from 'Treemaines', the nearest home-made supplier to that section of the line. Newnham distinctly recalled the bridge going up at Holywell, as well as the rows of tents by Freshfield where the navvies made their temporary homes from 1879 to 1880, by which time the greater part of the heavy work had been undertaken and the contractor had begun to reduce the size of the workforce.

Navvy Encampments

Regarding accommodation for this large workforce, times had come a long way from 'living sordid communal lives in turf huts' in conditions where 'shelter was usually shared, imposed, overcrowded and insanitary, run by a kind of concierge'. Those so-called 'shanties' could be constructed

This staged scene at Newick was taken in mid-July 1882, shortly before the opening. The station is almost complete, for some of the new station staff have arrived, including top-hatted stationmaster William Mullinger, while painters are still putting the finishing touches to the footbridge and up platform, where the North signalbox can be seen behind the painting frame. A number of navvies are still busy and the engine crew are beside the contractor's locomotive, the features of which do not match up to any of the photographs of others which have survived, and which sadly remains unidentified. The leading wagon is loaded with coal and the locomotives were hand-coaled on drawing alongside. It belongs to Stephenson Clarke & Co, a firm which held the contract for the LBSCR's coal requirement. The family resided at Borde Hill, just north of Haywards Heath *Miss G Watson/Bluebell Archives*

of turf, wood, brick or stone, according to which was more easily accessible. Some of the men had with them their wives or women, who cooked, tidied beds, washed and mended the navvies' clothes. The navvy's typical working dress was moleskin trousers, double canvas shirts, square tailed coats, hob-nailed boots, with a gaudy handkerchief and light coloured felt hat. Food and drink were often supplied retail by truck shops, run for their own profit by gangers or by subcontractors, less often it appears by a local grocer. Each hut or tent generally undertook its own cooking. Two pounds of beef and a gallon of beer a day was a common diet. It was no small wonder that it came to drinking, swearing and fighting. Since it was the bad news that provoked the local headlines, the reports generally refer to the troubles caused by the navvies but, carefully sifted, these offer valuable details and insights into their lives and employment during the construction. From these, for instance, one can plot the localities of the various navvy encampments.

Copyhold (a common rural word related to manorial tenure) Farm at East Grinstead, long since engulfed by the spread of the built-up area of the town and lying close to Imberhorne Manor, must not be confused with the other farm of that name north of Haywards Heath, where the line through Ardingly branched from the main line. The workload included the vast construction of a completely new two-level station, as well as a lofty 10-arch viaduct just to the south, and the camp continued here through into the Oxted contract. Hazelden, which lies almost halfway between East Grinstead and Kingscote, where an encampment was sited to the southeast of the Imberhorne Lane bridge, was sufficiently distant from the former town, with the steep Imberhorne Valley in between, to put the navvies at a convenient arm's length from the good citizens of the town. Here they were heavily occupied with the deep cutting behind Hill Place and the length of heavy embankment south towards Kingscote. With more than 70 huts, it accommodated something approaching 300 navvies plus families. There is one reference to Tickerage, which is a mere hundred yards west of the site of Kingscote station, and there may have been a camp of short duration to serve during the building of the railway station there.

Next, and by far the largest with accommodation for 600 men and families, was the huge shanty town situated atop the Sharpthorne ridge above today's tunnel. Such numbers were required for the crucial and arduous construction of the tunnel with its five shafts. It was here in 1964 that a 3ft 6in iron crowbar was unearthed by Ganger Harry Wilson in the back garden of his railway cottage, built in the immediate neighbourhood of the former navvy camp, once a mass of numbered wooden shacks where blacksmiths, storemen, engine drivers and the like had their distinctive but temporary dwellings, while the foremen were housed in two specially constructed bungalows. The next encampment southwards was at Lywood, another but smaller tunnel construction, with the workforce also covering the immediate area north and south as well as west of Horsted Keynes. The next camp involved in the construction of the branch was at Avins Farm, just south of Ardingly station, but also called Lindfield. Twenty-five huts housed 200-300 men. To serve the considerable works and widening north of Haywards Heath and the junction with the main line, there was another large encampment known as the Copyhold Huts close to Copyhold Bridge.

Returning to the line to Culver Junction, there are references to a tented camp at Freshfield but nothing directly at Sheffield Park, which appears to have been covered by a camp on Fletching and Lane End Commons. The next was in the Great Rough, adjacent to the site of Newick station, and the southernmost camp was in the fields on the west side of the present Barcombe station. Details from the 1881 census for Newick, by which time the back of the work had been broken, record 33 navvy personnel including wives and children in occupation of the Railway Huts Nos 1-4.

In addition to the huts and tents, each camp would have had stables and stores of timber, coal and other materials, while the larger ones would have had workshops, a complete brickyard with kilns, a canteen and a Navvies' Reading or Mission Room. No detailed description of the navvy encampments on the LEGR have yet come to light, but a visitor to another of Firbank's works wrote: 'We obtain access through the contractor's yard, quite a little town in itself, with its offices, dwellings, workshops and stables. About 150 men are employed in or near the yard, which is the home of above 100 horses. Mr Firbank has about 1,300 men employed on this length, and many portions of the work are prosecuted night and day.' Conditions, nevertheless, were primitive, hygiene much of a lottery — two cases of smallpox occurred in the huts at West Hoathly — and safety precautions were negligible; two navvies died from smoke suffocation, being found dead on a heap of smoking burning ballast, having fancied a warm sleep by the heap for the night, from which they unfortunately never awoke.

But not all the workforce were able to find themselves housed in the encampments, with the advantages of convenience both in facilities and proximity to the line of the railway. In giving evidence in the above-mentioned case of suffocation, James Wood, foreman of the gang to which the two victims belonged, spoke of the difficulties of finding lodging houses. The men would spend their leisure time at public houses until closing time and then, as often as not, sleep anywhere. 'There are huts for the old hands, but not sufficient for the number of men employed.'

A major factor in the unavailability of lodging houses was the dislike by the local populace of the navvies and through them of the railway company which it held responsible for bringing down upon them the dreadful excesses perpetrated by the workforce — ill feeling which it took years to dispel, and elderly people living until recently recalled those fearful days with awe. Predominantly Irish, with many from Scotland, Lancashire and Yorkshire, the wild behaviour and outrages of the navvies were exacerbated by the drink they consumed, and they roamed roaring and brawling through the neighbourhood at night. Many of the extra strengthened door bolts survive to this day in the older dwellings of the district.

Where the navvies encamped at Newick is today still known as The Rough, and there were often real fights with the locals, especially at weekends. One burly bully was on at least one occasion taught a lesson, when a local inhabitant collected a few of his neighbours and saw to it that the offending navvy received a proper drubbing. However, some citizens did manage to come to terms with the navvies, and many were taken in by folks who had room, probably after the main labour force had moved on to other parts. One Newick lady, Mrs Charles Farley, lodged three of them nicknamed Lank, Brumy and Pincher, such nicknames bestowed upon them by their friends and, if they had ordinary names like Smith or Brown, the contractor would give them a nickname. The neighbouring children, who did not like them very much, certainly never heard their surnames mentioned at all.

Navvy Occupations

The numerous newspaper reports provide useful information about the navvies' duties and occupations. Mention has already been made of the contractor and subcontractors and their staff, wide ranging from the engineering to the supervisory, from the administrative to the financial. The highest specific rank appears to have been foreman, and there were foremen in charge of the various working groups — bricklayers, carpenters, ironworkers and miners — as well as many who were 'foremen of the gang'. These working gangs, or squads of a dozen to a score of workmen, were the origin of the later railway term of 'ganger', and the word became interchangeable with 'navvy'. The gangers were of two sorts: walking gangers who controlled considerable stretches of trackbed, and standing gangers who were fixed to a specific location. In addition, there were others simply classified as labourers, and specialists such as horsekeepers and even gardeners. That Firbank should employ a gardener on his contracts may at first appear odd, but, in the sense used, that particular skill was more akin to that of a landscaper. Another prominent group was concerned with the operation of the contractor's sidings and overland railways. The word 'shunter' was not in full usage, and the terms instead were 'ropeman', 'roperunner' and 'uncoupler'. The locomotive crews will be discussed later. There were distinct rigid social divisions between navvies and the other groups mentioned, such as carpenters, brickmakers and bricklayers, who were artisans.

Navvy Crimes

During the period the navvies were working, almost without fail the local press made mention of navvy 'incidents', which are full of rich pickings detailing working conditions, local landmarks and progress of the work. Though it was the horrendous accidents that made the headlines, it was their misdemeanours in their leisure time that gave their image a murky complexion during the construction. The most common crime was theft, and a wide range of objects came up for mention. They stole the contractor's equipment: horse reins, shovels, tools and pails. They pilfered from his stocks of wood and coal, even from as far afield as Forest Row station yard, where Firbank had a store for incoming supplies, particularly during the unseasonable winter, to snatch a fleeting feeling of warmth. They spirited away personal property and belongings, probably for the same reason; a ganger's coat here and an engine driver's cap there, and even a whole bundle of clothes from Ardingly College! They poached livestock to fill their starving stomachs: fowls from a farm, fish from the river, and even a duck from a convent pond. They plucked apples by the bushel in organised gangs, dug up cabbages and turnips and even gathered watercress. Loaves of bread disappeared daily from cottage tables. One wonders what story lay behind John James, a respectably dressed young navvy, who was charged with stealing a toy engine and a squeaking doll from the West Hoathly Club, for which he received 14 days. Money was found missing on numerous occasions — even Firbank's office was broken into and about 16 shillings stolen — for those who blew their week's pay on drink found it exceedingly difficult to last out until the next pay day. Beer and strong drink were illicitly consumed without payment. The range of sentences varied from three months' hard labour to a caution, and in financial terms from £69 10s, the largest fine noted, to a discharge.

Sleeping overnight in a cowshed collected seven days; in fact they slept where they could, preferably under cover, under a haystack or in someone else's bed. In April 1879 Walter Henton of Rivers Farm, Ardingly, had complained that a group of navvies had obtained admission to his farmstead, opened the barn and scattered straw about the place, intending to abide there. They had seriously damaged the premises by stalking about with lighted pipes, and he implied that the special constables who were paid were not doing their work. Frequent cases of begging were cautioned. Two navvies drove off with a horse and cart from Felbridge as a joke. His lordship in discharging them said it was a very foolish 'freak' (whim) and cautioned them not to indulge in such tricks again, as they might perhaps carry their joke too far. One, James Bent, was described as a 'dirty lodger' by his landlord, but was discharged. But most of the rest, the large majority of cases brought before the magistrates, had their origins in just one root evil, that of drink. This was not just a problem associated with the local hostelries that receive regular mention in connection with the navvies: the Rose Beershop, the Railway Hotel, the Ship Inn, the Sussex Arms and the White Lion at East Grinstead, the Fountain Inn, Vinols Cross and the White Hart Inn at West Hoathly. There also existed an extensive spirits-selling racket within the encampments and instances were all too numerous of selling beer without a licence. Seizures of navvies' beer are mentioned at Hazelden and Tickerage but the extent of the navvies' secret organisation is illustrated by the story of a successful coup by the local constabulary at the Railway Hotel, Ardingly, one August day in 1879.

The Police discovered that an illegal sale of beer was going on at the Lywood Common railway huts. The officials wisely judged that, as from 200 to 300 navvies were congregated there at the tunnel and other works, it would be useless to go with a small force. Mustering 24-strong from the Cuckfield and East Grinstead divisions, headed by Superintendents Pocock and Berry, they proceeded to a hut occupied by one of the gangers. Here they found two 18-gallon casks of 'Double X' in tap, one half full and the other nearly empty, and two 'nines'. These, together with a lot of drinking mugs and glasses, were confiscated, the seizure being accompanied to Cuckfield Police Station by a strong escort! The navvies offered no resistance, but treated the capture with an ongoing volley of hard words. On the arrival of the Police, navvy intelligence quickly tipped off the nearby huts at Avins Farm, next to the site of the future Ardingly station, where the same illicit game was being carried on. Consequently the barrels were quietly rolled out and stored away, and a drayload just arrived was sent back post-haste undelivered.

Thus by and large the navvies outwitted the constabulary and beer was plentifully available among the encampments. Being drunk and incapable was the least of the crimes in this category. It was what was perpetrated under the influence of drink that outraged the local Police. There were numerous instances of assault against special constables — Henry Clark received three months for biting a constable's fingers at the Rose Beershop. There was a brutal assault on another by navvies at the Fountain Beerhouse. Landlords too suffered, trying to keep order in their local hostelries — William Mills assaulted Peter Meade, landlord of Vinols Cross Beerhouse. Likewise railway employees and other navvies, where, in one case, the court was told, 'the prisoner caught hold of his whiskers and pulled him down'. Arthur Russell assaulted Henry Lake, a walking ganger on the upper section; he had been discharged only the previous day and now ended up with a fortnight's hard labour. Abuse took place of navvies' wives, such as the case of Henry Chant who used threatening language, but his wife Mary went even further, assaulting Ellen Royal, the wife of another navvy, on the way from her house to the canteen at Horsted Keynes. Though it was reported 'the fight continued in court!', subsequently the charge was withdrawn. But sometimes excesses were even more serious, witness the headline: 'Alleged disgraceful outrage of rape by navvies employed on the new railway works,' when a group of five navvies 'ill used' a local girl. On another occasion two engine cleaners, Charles Fenning and Francis Westlake, 'ravished' Mary Mason. It must certainly have been advisable to lock up one's daughters during such risk-fraught times.

Another whole chapter of crime related to damage done. A local correspondent was not alone when he wrote: 'a great deal of damage has been recently done by the navvies in this neighbourhood'. The most common damage victims were the local taverns, where drunken navvies reacted strongly to requests to leave at (or even before) closing time. When James Scales and Frederick Walker refused to quit the Vinols Cross Beerhouse, they broke open the taproom door and duly got 14 days. On another occasion two miners, Edwin James and John Fletcher, damaged the stable door of the Fountain Inn. The penalty was usually a fine, as in the case of Henry Laidlaw and James Williams, whose damage to a door at the Ship Inn cost them a one shilling fine, a shilling to pay for the damage but also 4s 9d costs. Window smashing was a frequent occurrence among the other cases of wilful damage.

Most of the above cases were the depredations of one or two navvies. Together in any substantial number, a situation could become menacing, especially at the end of an evening's drinking. A regular headline was 'Disturbance at the huts', and the charge made on individuals was 'Drunk and riotous'. Nothing less than a riot took place at East Grinstead on Guy Fawkes Night 1881. Whether this had anything to do with the occasion, some 50 navvies described as 'roughs' battled with the police that evening.

A correspondent quoted previously referred to the number of lawless characters that abounded. The LEGR construction threw up its fair share of these. There was Henry Smith, alias

The original Navvy Mission Room at West Hoathly, situated on the north side of the road through Sharpthorne, lay above the tunnel. Set up at the close of 1880, it survived as a store shed and garage until 1960 and lay in a derelict condition when this photograph was taken in 1965.
Klaus Marx

'Fighting Harry', who was giving constant trouble at West Hoathly when not preoccupied with his terms of hard labour. But perhaps the most colourful character of all was William Brown, alias 'Birdcatcher Bill', a veteran of many railway contracts and a widely wanted criminal, having several times been previously convicted but resuming his black-market dealings after each occasion. He was a sort of hanger-on to the navvies, and whenever new railways were being constructed he quickly became acquainted with the neighbourhood where the navvies committed burglaries and robberies. He was in the habit of 'buying' articles from various workmen. He would then act as agent for the stolen goods and doubtless gained some striking profits. The enterprise developed vast proportions, for the stolen goods were hidden in locations as far afield as a house near Carshalton and Marden Tunnel, Caterham.

It was on the LEGR that 'Birdcatcher' came unstuck, when one of his sale outlets run by a William Morris (formerly a miner and by 1880 promoted to a subcontractor at Lywood Tunnel) who kept a 'shanty' or provision store, was charged with receiving stolen goods, namely some tools, and in March 1882 was allowed bail for £110. During the first week of April Birdcatcher Bill was caught red-handed together with his hidden haul in the tunnel at Caterham, and committed for trial which took place three weeks later. Brown was sentenced to five years' penal servitude, to be followed by three years' Police supervision, his lordship remarking that he was afraid that that was not an adequate sentence for his many offences. As to Morris, it appears he turned Queen's evidence and gave the information necessary for the 'Birdcatcher's' arrest, for he was discharged.

Another case of being caught red-handed was that of Reuben Carver, working at West Hoathly, who was charged with stealing a quantity of coal, property of Joseph Firbank, Contractor. In the prisoner's bedroom at New Coombe, PC Harris found 14 lumps of coal weighing about 15cwt, worth about £1. Carver said he had bought them from a farmer. Mr James Kirby, manager of the tunnel works, identified the coal as the same as that used at the works. The prisoner pleaded guilty and received two months' hard labour.

Another colourful tale under the headlines 'Getting the steam up' concerns Andrew Calvert, an engine driver who assaulted his wife. He had starved her of money, which he spent on booze. They had a real set-to near the 'engine shed' at West Hoathly. Calvert, who had a wooden leg, kicked her on the head. He then knelt on her stomach with one leg and on her left arm with the leather joint of his wooden leg. He held her finger between his teeth and his pocket handkerchief round her neck till her tongue protruded at some length! She asked her husband to have mercy on her. Fortunately two men came, and she escaped by the back door. Blood was lying all over the floor where she had lain. However, this harridan was no angel, having admitted not only to biting her husband but also to throwing a horseshoe at him. This brought neither any luck, for the couple were charged £1 and costs, which left their matrimonial finances in further disarray. The magistrate condemned her conduct as aggravating and her behaviour as anything but proper. Calvert certainly hit the headlines, but occasionally he was on the other side of the bar in the Police court, giving evidence as 'Firbank's engine driver', as in the sad case of an 11-year-old lad who was crushed by a muck wagon and had to have his leg amputated.

Then there was the nameless navvy who committed a 'base robbery' on Thomas Ward of Horsted Keynes, who rented a room at the house of a person called Taylor. At his work this local man became acquainted with the navvy and took him home with him as a lodger, and they occupied the same bed. Wood told his 'chum' that he 'had a nice little sum of money saved up in his base to keep him in his old age'. One morning, after the companions had had a glass together the previous night, Wood got up about the usual time and departed for his work, leaving his 'friend' who said he would not be commencing work till after breakfast. During the day Wood found that five shillings had been abstracted from his money bag. This made him think of his box, and when he returned he found the key in the lock and the money (£34 10s) gone. The navvy had meanwhile gone to the cashier's office on the line and drawn nearly all that was due to him, and made off!

An even more blatant case of literal daylight robbery occurred near Cuckfield. The Police court there had scarcely closed before an aged couple named Wilkinson, who kept a lodging house, came running into the town in pursuit of a navvy who had stolen 1lb of beef off their table, intended for dinner. The fellow, who was casually sauntering down the street, was instantly arrested by a policeman and taken to the lock-up, but too late to have his hearing. Next day the court recorded that William Connor, a navvy of West Hoathly and lodging at Mr Neville's, the Wheatsheaf Inn, ran off with a beefsteak, valued at 1s 10d, for which deed he earned 14 days' hard labour.

Rather more of a stir was caused by the antics of Thomas Jones, an East Grinstead navvy, charged with being drunk and incapable. PC Anscombe said he received complaints from the stationmaster, Mr Mitchell, that the prisoner was drunk and annoying the passengers at the railway station. He refused to go away when requested, lay down on the middle of the road, in front of three or four carriages, and had to be forcibly removed in a cart to the police station. He got seven days.

Perhaps the last word in the motley array of navvy characters should come from Thomas Stevens, who received 14 days for being drunk and using obscene language to the parish clergyman at West Hoathly. His parting retort as he was led away was: 'The railroad would never be finished if navvies will continue to be locked up like this!'

Navvy Welfare

While the majority of citizens complained bitterly about the conduct of the navvies, there were just a few who held to a more sympathetic and positive view. A leading protagonist on behalf of the navvies was Mrs Kingsley, the widow of the late Mr H. Kingsley the novelist, who lived at Cuckfield. Writing to a London contemporary in July 1880, she says:

'I am a constant visitor to the infirmary of the Union for a large number of parishes. Recently men have been brought, mainly navvies, in such an advanced state of disease that they are past human aid. Who is to blame? Surely when railway and other works are in course of construction, some more adequate accommodation than overcrowded huts, or even more overcrowded farmhouses and cottages, ought to be provided by the contractors, and whenever the men are massed together there ought to be at least a bi-weekly medical inspection in order to ascertain whether there are cases of illness or not, and not to be left to the chance of anyone sending for a doctor. When we consider that these men aid us, forming as it were a bridge of their lives, to enable us to reach those whom we love, and hear their dying words and receive their last look, we ought to feel bound to succour them, so far as it is possible, from dying alone and amongst strangers in a workhouse infirmary.'

It was people who thought like this who concerned themselves with the welfare of the navvies. Medical care was the responsibility of the contractor but, all too often, the cost of medical services for the navvies — an amputation cost £5 and there had been three navvy cases during the past week — was carried by the parish. On 31 May 1879, the master of the Union House at East Grinstead complained to his guardians that they should take the matter up with Mr Firbank. At the end of that October the rural sanitary authorities were corresponding with the railway. On 31 December there was an outbreak of smallpox at the West Hoathly works, notices being posted and no children admitted to local schools. Reading through the accident reports gives the impression that it was the local doctors who continued to bear the brunt of health care.

An accepted practice of the time was for railway contractors to provide recreational reading rooms at all large navvy camps. Joseph Firbank certainly shouldered his responsibilities in this respect. A reading room was erected for his employees at West Hoathly and opened in time for Christmas 1878. The cost had been largely borne by a handsome donation of £100 given by Mr Du Croz for its support. On the last day of March 1879 an entertainment of readings and music took place in the new reading room, chaired by the Rev J. Raven. 'The room was densely filled with an appreciative audience. Not less than 350 people were present, and many more were unable to gain admission.' On 23 December the night shift of about 150 men was entertained to a substantial supper, followed by a concert at which several ladies residing in the district assisted. 'Mrs Du Croz takes a great interest in the welfare of the men and their wives and her efforts are highly appreciated.' This interesting building, which survived for storage use until the mid-1960s, is variously described as 'the Sharpthorne Reading Room at the railway works' and the 'West Hoathly Recreation Room'. It consisted of a coffee and a smoking room which, when deprived of the centre screen, made a spacious room for entertainments, many such occasions being recorded. Over the platform was emblazoned the word 'Welcome'. By October 1881 it was being suggested that the railway reading room was no longer required and should be formally closed. A minute records a recommendation by Mr Banister, the LBSCR's Engineer, that the company should purchase for £100 a building erected by Mr Firbank on its land at West Hoathly for a navvies' coffee house, which would for about £50 be made available for three platelayers' cottages. Two were built opposite, on the south side of the lane through Sharpthorne, and remain to this day, though no longer in railway use.

In December 1879 it was reported: 'the local gentry have provided a reading room close to the railway navvies' huts near the high road from Chailey. It will have newspapers etc, and is intended to keep the navvies out of mischief. A chapel has been erected at the Kingshead Road and a coffee and reading room erected beside it will shortly open.' In February 1880 a concert of vocal and instrumental music was held at the national school in aid of funds for the recently built railway reading room. That September a well-attended entertainment was held there for the men employed in constructing the new railway line, with another successful show the following month, and a party held for the Sunday School children of the railway workers, followed by sports. A month later a further entertainment included a handbell performance. Mention is made of other reading rooms at Lane End Common and at Lywood, which were visited by the Bishop of Chichester in July 1880.

If possibly not enough was effected on behalf of the navvies' physical well-being, the same could not be said for those who laboured to save their souls. The earliest report, December 1878, states that 'the spiritual welfare of the navvies is attended to by local clergy, who are ably assisted by the ladies'. Caustically it has been said that 'clergymen, doctors, schoolmasters and magistrates appeared in almost inverse order to the need for them'. The local pastors, though faithful in the ministration of christenings, weddings and burials, seem to have made little spiritual impact on their temporary residents. Far more was achieved by those who called themselves 'navvy preachers' and followed the new constructions whenever they arose, holding special missions. 'On Sunday, 23 February 1879 addresses were given in the Public Hall at East Grinstead to crowded audiences by William Taylor, formerly a navvy. Evening services, conducted by him at Moat Lane and Zion Chapel during the week, have been very successful. On Sunday next special services will be held, on which occasion Taylor will be assisted by his son. All classes are invited. No collection.' — a special navvy-slanted hint. Also on the spiritual scene were so-called 'scripture readers', who appear from time to time in the magistrates' courts, 'putting in a good plea for the defence' of navvies who had fallen into diverse temptations. One clergyman whose services were appreciated was the Rev A. C. MacLaglan, who in January 1881 was presented with a very handsome gold watch by the friends and navvies of Newick for the work he had done over the last nine months in the welfare of the railway workers. He was leaving to do missionary work in Africa. His kind and genial manner would be much missed.

Even the railway company felt a degree of spiritual responsibility, for the Brighton board forwarded a donation of £20 on 20 October 1880 in response to a letter received from Mr Henry R. Freshfield, seeking the company's aid towards the Navvy Mission for the Lewes & East Grinstead line. A navvy mission room was set up above the tunnel at West Hoathly and another set up at the Copyhold (Junction) huts early in 1880. 'On Friday evening 16 April the recently erected Navvies' Mission Room at Copyhold was opened by the Bishop, assisted by several clergymen of the neighbourhood. There was a large attendance and the room was very prettily decorated for the occasion.'

There was one at Lywood whose balance sheets the *Mid Sussex Times* chose to publish. Over a period of 18 months receipts included subscriptions of £76 3s 6d, a sale of work per Misses Rodwill which brought in £2 and a balance from the navvy relief fund of £5 13s 6d, which totalled £83 17s. Expenditure was chiefly for the salary of the resident scripture reader, Mr H. Baker, over nine months amounting to £57 18s 8d, hire of conveyances for long distances £4 12s 6d, and salary for a missionary for Sunday services of £21 9s, total £84 0s 2d, leaving a balance due to the treasurer of 3s 2d. On 28 February 1883 the final report was printed for a period lasting 26 months. The balance that remained was to be handed over for 'Furtherance of the work in the East Grinstead district'.

At East Grinstead there was a longer element of continuity, with the LEGR contract to the south and the extension to Oxted to the north, a period covering six years up to 1884. The hall there was called the Signal Box Mission Room. On the last Sunday in September 1881 a harvest thanksgiving was conducted there by Rev H. D. Barrett, described as 'Chaplain to the Navvies'. On another occasion, a week before Christmas that same year, there was a lecture by Rev C. Whittaker, Secretary to the Navvy Mission, and his talk was illustrated by 'dissolving views'. Regular lectures at the Mission Hall became a feature. Another railway missioner who straddled both contracts was a Mr Varney, who went on to have charge of the mission chapel at Dormans Land and paid regular visits to the Lingfield huts, following the move of the navvy force northwards. Inevitably the congregations at East Grinstead dwindled and at the start of May 1882 it was reported that 'the mission room in connection with the LEGR works is being moved from its present site near the signalbox to the field of the East Grinstead Cricket Club. W. V. K. Stenning intends allowing it to remain there as a gift or loan to the club. This will be a decided acquisition as it will form an excellent luncheon room. *Sic transit gloria!*'

Navvy Relief

A record of the navvies on the LEGR contract would not be complete without a mention of their terrible deprivations during the winter of 1880/1. An early warning of impending conditions came on 20 October 1880 when 'a very heavy snowstorm visited the neighbourhood, doing considerable damage to a great number of fine oak trees which, being in full foliage and heavy laden with acorns, combined with the weight of the snow, crushed many of them down, several of them being rent in twain.' Another more enduring fall of snow fell continuously from 18 to 20 January 1881. 'A very severe snowstorm accompanied by heavy gales commenced early on Tuesday and continued without intermission during the day. The drifts of snow in many places were several feet deep and the roads almost impassable, business being nearly suspended. Railway traffic was greatly impeded, the 5.25 train not reaching East Grinstead till midnight. The mail cart after proceeding a few miles was completely snowed up and left by the wayside.'

Soon the local editorials were full of commiseration for those directly affected by privations during the severest winter for many a year. 'Hardships of a Hard Winter', 'The Weather and the Poor', ran the headlines. 'Large numbers of persons, owing to the severity of the weather, are thrown out of employment, and much distress exists among the poor. To mitigate this, by the arrangement of an influential committee, bread and soup has been liberally distributed twice a week at the Crown Hotel' [East Grinstead]. But what of the navvy poor, isolated in primitive accommodation in the open fields? 'We are glad to state that Mr Joseph Firbank has, although at great expense and loss to himself, again opened his works and found employment for three-quarters of the men who had been thrown out of work in consequence of the late very severe weather. Mr Firbank has also subscribed liberally to the various soup kitchens established in the neighbourhood for the relief of the poor.'

It was indeed a winter long remembered by the countryfolk in these parts. One such was Mrs Sarah Funnell of Barcombe, who in 1960 was aged 92, and even at that age was able to describe vividly the conditions then prevailing. It was one of those very white winters, of snow that never melts but only packs tighter to form a firm bed for later falls. During that third week of January 1881 the falls had been particularly heavy, and icy nights had refrozen any surfaces that had made a pretence of melting during the day. For the perplexed people in village and farmhouse it was more than an extraordinary fall of snow, in some places up to one's neck, more even than a freeze-up; it was total isolation, possibly starvation. True, every cottage in those days had a sack of flour stored in the house but that supply had virtually run out. How to get out, how to transport supplies, when traffic was impossible, how to survive, these were the thoughts on everyone's minds. No amount of shovels would have dug them out; there were no snowploughs as yet, and even they would not have done the job. It needed men, hundreds of them, with sharp picks, but where could such gratuitous labour be found?

Eyes turned down to the low ground north of Barcombe, to the shacks and tents of a veritable shanty town. Wisps of smoke rose into the bleak sky as surly Irishmen slept and drank and gambled. They were idle navvies whom the snow had put out of work on the construction of a railway through Barcombe, where a station was to be built. Suddenly the rough voice of the foreman put a halt to all idle occupations and summoned them out to trudge across the uneven, frozen landscape to various outlying cottages and farms, as well as into the streets of Barcombe, where Mr Funnell was the village blacksmith. He was kept busy all day sharpening blunted tools. Meanwhile, the noise of pick on ice resounded across the hitherto silent neighbourhood and, with everyone working hard, it was not long before the ice-siege was lifted. Had they but known, within a week the ice and snow was to melt, but the ordeal of that January and the unselfish assistance of the navvies was never to be forgotten.

4.
Construction

Staking out the Line

It was in October 1878 that the contractor was reported to be in possession of about five miles of the line at West Hoathly, and on the 19th the first of the contractor's locomotives arrived there. But it would have been two years earlier that the first sign of activity might have been discerned, as surveyors with their theodolites and notebooks took the requisite measurements and levels, with a view to drafting the plans that would eventually go before Parliament. The next point of activity prior to the arrival of the main workforce was the staking out of the line by a team supervised by the surveyors, armed with measuring tapes, wooden stakes and sledgehammers. Wooden pegs were set in the ground at regular intervals to mark the centre line of the railway and the furthest line of deviation. The latter, marked on the deposited plans, allowed the contractor plus or minus 100yd for his works. Within this area he had the right to remove all trees, which accounts for the bare appearance of new lines for many years after opening. Curves were set out using a theodolite, and cross-sectional dimensions set at right angles to denote the width of formation, cutting, embankment and bridges.

Mrs Jared Brooks, who was in correspondence in 1961 at the ripe age of 93, remembers seeing the very first signs of the coming railway construction that was to create a lasting upheaval in her rural community. 'My father William Hart was very interested when he heard the line was coming through Newick where he worked, and every Sunday morning he would take me and a cousin up to see where it was coming through. He was excited when the stumps were put along the prepared track, and the following Sunday the navvy huts were there on the Lane End side of the road to the King's Head.'

The line had to be seen to be believed, for the majority of locals were sceptical. Too often in the previous 40 years the rumours raising expectations had turned out to be a charade to no lasting purpose. The local editor could comment with some reason: 'Apparently railway extensions have nearly reached their limit, and there are now but narrow fields in which projectors can exercise their ingenuity.' Imagine therefore the excitement as the local populace read in the *North Sussex Gazette* of 28 December 1878: 'The construction of this railway is being actively proceeded with in the neighbourhood of West Hoathly.'

West Hoathly Tunnel

It was no surprise that the first set of works in the construction of the Lewes & East Grinstead Railway should commence at West Hoathly, for it was an underlying principle of Victorian contractors to make a start with tunnel construction. It was here that the largest and lengthiest excavations usually took place, and it was from here that the vast amounts of spoil required to embank and fill in other works was obtained, obviating the need to seek materials outside the railway at added expense.

West Hoathly Tunnel was constructed under the Sharpthorne ridge and is 731yd in length. The local press reported at the close of 1878: 'There are 600 men employed, and no accidents have as yet occurred, owing in great measure to the care of Mr Kirby, the superintendent, who is a most experienced tunnel maker. Five shafts have been sunk for the purpose of expediting the work underground and at each shaft is an engine for hoisting and lowering workmen and materials. The preliminary driftway is almost complete from one way to the other. The tunnel passes through a very hard dark blue clay of the Wealden series. When brought to the surface it becomes soft after a little exposure to the atmosphere, although previously it had to be blasted, and there being none of the same description in the immediate neighbourhood, it is of interest to geologists.' The driftway was in fact broken through on 14 January 1879.

It must have been an animated scene that greeted the local reporter at the Sharpthorne Tunnel works. At each shaft head, besides the panting chugs of the steam hoist engaged in bringing up loads of excavated earth, alternating with the lowering of bricks and mortar and lengths of timber, were a number of horses engaged in the conveyance of materials to and from the shaft. A similar procedure would be taking place on the horizontal plane at each tunnel mouth over the rails or tramlines. Wagons, known as skips — incidentally the name also given to the navvies' wooden baskets — loaded high with earth, would emerge one after the other from the dark opening, while others stacked up with bricks were lined up waiting to be pushed or horse-drawn inside, where in the shadows of the oil-lit interior, unseen to the world outside, a vast hive of activity was under way. At the heading, miners or excavators would be working their way with pick and shovel and baskets made from hazel rods, to carry spoil to the nearest skip, and close behind would be the carpenters who stepped in quickly to shore up the newly won territory with temporary wooden ribbing. They would be followed later by highly skilled bricklayers, constructing the portico, retaining walls and roof.

Tunnels were built to last but their period of construction was always fraught with danger, whatever the workman's trade. On the morning of 11 October 1879, while he was engaged on the 'recently constructed' tunnel, some brickwork gave way and fell on a navvy, dislocating his shoulder and breaking one of his legs. On 1 December that same year

The 731yd tunnel at West Hoathly, driven through the Sharpthorne ridge, seen through the north portal, whose parapet records its completion in 1881. The change of gradient at the end of the long climb at 1 in 75 from Horsted Keynes is very apparent and the sparse vegetation points to a date not too many years after construction.
A. C. E. Notley

occurred a far more 'shocking and fatal accident' to a labourer at Sharpthorne Tunnel. The unfortunate man, whose name was Henry Mighal, a native of the village, was engaged as a bricklayer's labourer in one section of the arch work on No 3 shaft, about the centre of the tunnel, when the wooden centres which supported the arches gave way while in the course of being turned, so crushing the victim that he expired before he could be got out of the tunnel. On 9 August 1880 a serious accident befell Mr William Elliot, one of the subcontractors engaged in building Sharpthorne Tunnel. He was about to ascend the shaft in a basket, which by some means collided against the brickwork, and the unfortunate man was precipitated onto a trolley of brick beneath, a distance of about 20ft, breaking his arm and otherwise receiving serious injuries. Another serious accident was the collapse of the huge wooden doors which had been erected at either end of the tunnel after the driftway was finished, in order to prevent the through draught from blowing out all the lamps used in the excavation. This occurred early in February 1881, resulting in a fatality and subsequent inquest. Sorry tales indeed, but they do provide the only first-hand details of the construction of the tunnel.

The final siting of the tunnel was slightly west of what had originally been intended by the surveyors, having been marginally deviated by Wolfe Barry in deference to the opposition of certain landowners, in particular Mr F. A. Du Croz of Courtlands and General Arbuthnot, who resided at Hoathly Hill. They maintained that the alignment as originally intended would have interfered with their hunting and game-shooting. The matter was of such concern that on 5 November 1879 the LEGR Committee passed a resolution that Mr Du Croz should have a right of shooting subject to such conditions as had been agreed with the LBSCR, over the portion of the tunnel at Sharpthorne constructed through his property. The final choice was a bad one, discovered too late, for it was built through some underground springs which ever since have cascaded their surplus water down the vents and through the lining of the walls and roof. There was even a well above the tunnel. The West Hoathly end was the worst and, with freezing northwest winds blowing down through the portal, icicles 'big as human bodies' stretched from roof to rail. It became a routine Sunday duty in wintertime for the platelayers to go in with every kind of long tool, and soon the noise was such as might have been produced by the old Crystal Palace in its dying day. The broken lumps of ice were

carted away on trolleys but beware any reveller returning home of a Saturday night who put his head out in the dark to check whether he was approaching his destination! Engine crews, particularly on the early morning trains, huddled well under the shelter of their cabs. On certain occasions the icicles blocked the tunnel completely and traffic was suspended while a special train of empty wagons and additional permanent way staff with sledgehammers was despatched from the north.

Eventually three of the five shafts were blocked out, leaving two, capped by vast ventilation chimneys, which remain to this day, one on either side of the road through the centre of Sharpthorne up on the ridge. The tunnel was completed in 1881, the date encapsulated in the rectangular block of stone set in the centre of the parapet of each portal, and was described as being built of extra strength, owing to the treacherous nature of the soil, and also affording scope for 'a capital piece of brickwork', according to the local reporter who saw the tunnel in its pristine glory.

Once the tunnel was under way, the spoil would be run off to build up the prepared embankments and, as soon as it became a practical distance, locomotive haulage was introduced to convey the trainloads of skip wagons to the tipping platform out on the partially firmed embankment. Here the wagons were emptied and the earth spread evenly. If the soil was soft, there would be constant slips necessitating widening the base as the foundations sank. There were some considerable embankments to be established north of Kingscote, and these must have been well under way by the close of 1878, for it was reported that 'earthworks within a few miles of East Grinstead are in hand, and also on the branch line to Haywards Heath. Nothing has been done at the south end, where the inhabitants are most anxious for a line of railway.'

The Southern Section

What exactly were the problems delaying a start on the section south of Horsted Keynes is not immediately obvious. The answer could well lie with the land purchases and the diversions of Cockhaise Brook in the neighbourhood of Lindfield Wood, which required further slivers of land to be purchased. There was, moreover, uncertainty whether the track south of Horsted Keynes should be single or double, the latter proposed by Wolfe Barry as late as the summer of 1880. Possibly priority had been given to the really major works of the enterprise: the widening and junction at Copyhold Farm on Railway No 3, the tunnel at Lywood Common, the cuttings at Hazelden and the viaduct at Imberhorne.

Another factor in concentrating the early work north of Horsted Keynes was that that part of the line lay within the High Weald with its strata of sandstone and clay. A particularly tough rock known locally as Ardingly sandstone, belonging to the Tunbridge Wells series, formed the top stratum, leaving weathered outcrops. These can be seen beside the line at West Hoathly and Kingscote, where the valley of Rocks Wood has been cut through the sandstone to the underlying Grinstead clay, resulting in a striking wall of rock each side of the valley. This wall has been separated into units by weathering processes, leaving outcrops of high standing rock, one of which just to the east of the railway at Stone Farm has been named 'Great upon Little'. Similar examples exist at Hill Place cutting. The base of the soils encountered comprises the Grinstead clays, and the whole of this area is a product of the complex geological formation of the Weald, resulting in deep ridges, gentle slopes, fertile soils and deep channels called ghylls.

Priority was given to the branch to Haywards Heath, completion of which was intended to coincide with Railways Nos 1 and 2, though in fact it opened just over a year later than the lines between East Grinstead and Barcombe. The first report on Railway No 3 appears on 8 February 1879: 'The works connected with the construction of the new junction line of rail from the neighbourhood of West Hoathly to Haywards Heath are being busily entered into by a large number of navvies, and on Sunday last a proportion of them were employed in erecting a temporary wooden bridge or 'under shed', to carry over the traffic at Copyhold during the time the addition to the main bridge is in progress, and the widening of the cutting at Copyhold so as to allow room for a double line to pass. The cartage of materials has terribly cut up the roads in the neighbourhood, entailing a heavy expense on the local boards of Lindfield and Haywards Heath. The roadway from the railway arch to Naldred Farm [between the southern end of the Ouse Viaduct and Borde Hill] is in a disastrous condition, being in many places impassable for light traffic from Balcombe, which is somewhat considerable on market and stock sale days.'

It was this latter problem that presented a perpetual headache and legal acrimony with the local authorities and which Firbank sought to ameliorate. The local Ladytide Vestry Meeting had sent a draft agreement to Firbank regarding the repair of roads, for the condition of which they held him blameworthy. Firbank had replied: 'I have put men and horses on to repair the roads referred to, and I have no doubt you will soon find them in their usual condition. There is very little metal on them, and I must not be expected to improve them, as I have to pay rates and taxes the same as other people.' The parochial surveyor postulated that nothing but sundry material was being spread over the roads. The feeling of the meeting was to stop Firbank from doing any more to their roads and leave the surveyor to assess the damage chargeable to the contractor.

Meanwhile at the turn of 1878 it appeared as if the first stirrings were imminent on the southern section. The *Sussex Gazette* reported: 'Last Tuesday [5 January] the preliminary driftway of the tunnel at West Hoathly was completed after seven months' continuous work. In a few days a party of navvies are to be sent to Lane End Common and the land adjoining Earl Sheffield's estate to erect huts for the accommodation of the contractor's employees. The contractors intend to complete that portion of the line which is to run into Barcombe station with as little delay as possible.' The 22 February edition stated: 'On Mr Watson's Farm at Lane End Common a gang of navvies commenced raising earthworks. As soon as the huts are erected at West Hoathly, a large gang of navvies are to be sent to complete the portion of the line to Barcombe. The only hard work on this portion of the line is between Lane End Common and Newick Park, this being a deep cutting from 45-50ft, including a bridge from 50-55ft high. Mr Kenward of Fletching Common has rendered great assistance to the contractors by a generous offer to lend them a team of horses.'

On 1 March 1879, a Chailey correspondent wrote: 'In this parish the preliminary works of the new Lewes and East Grinstead line commences in earnest this week. Boring for clay for making bricks shows a prospect of an abundant supply. Metals are being laid for draught purposes, and when the contemplated building of the huts is completed, we may expect an additional immigration of two or three hundred navvies.' However, the locals regretted it had been necessary to alter the site of the proposed station. The original plan placed it at Reedens, 500yd to the east on the main road between Chailey and Newick, but 'the impracticability of the site for a luggage station on account of the declivity has led to the determination to erect it at Ox Bottom, about 800yd further down from these villages, along a minor road in the direction of Cinder Hill. This change, however, will necessitate the macadamising of the new approach and be a source of great inconvenience to pedestrians.' In fact the station was in the area known as the Great Rough. It was originally proposed that the station building be situated on the road bridge (now the A272 main road), similar in layout to LBSCR stations like Eridge and Holmwood, but when it was realised just how long the connecting stairways would have to be, the idea was abandoned in favour of a site just off the main road and level with the railway, necessitating a three-storey building. Newick station site was a hive of activity, becoming one of the major depot yards during the construction (a scene repeated in 1960/1 when the line south of Sheffield Park was lifted and the yard at Newick & Chailey was stacked high with track panels). It was early in 1879 that a point of access was laid in for the contractor's rolling stock and materials, which entered the line of the railway via a spur curving southeast from the goods yard. The earthworks of this shallow embankment continued to be shown on the large scale Ordnance Survey map until the recent building developments over the site. Local inhabitants clearly recollected these trolley lines in use. (See map page 142.)

The Overland Tramway

The damage caused by the haulage of heavy materials along country lanes never intended for such loads has already been noted, and posed an acute problem for contractors. A partial answer, for it would not cover all route eventualities, was the so-called 'overland route' or 'tramway'. In May 1879 plans were presented by Mr Charles Weston, surveyor, showing the route and level crossings of the overland tramway in connection with the new railway at East Grinstead. Mr Waite on behalf of the contractor undertook that every care would be taken to protect the public by gates at the crossings, which would be locked at night, and that someone should be in

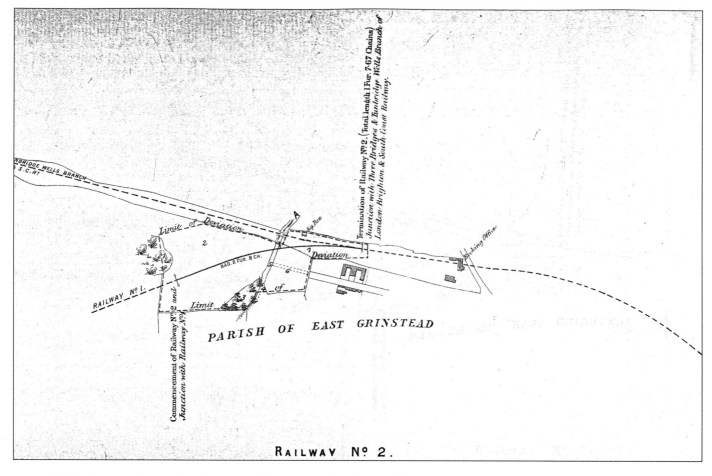

Original plan for the spur line, later amended to connect into the site of the original 1855 station in the High Level yard rather than directly to the Tunbridge Wells line and into the 1866 station shown on the right.

Reproduced with the permission of the County Archivist of East Sussex, copyright reserved. Ref: QDP/EW 428

attendance when traffic was going on. On 6 June it was reported that 'Yesterday afternoon the first trucks passed over the temporary bridge from East Grinstead station down the overland tramway.' The temporary bridge was sited across the steep valley, later to be straddled by the 10-arch Imberhorne Viaduct.

Lest it be misrepresented that the overland railway refers to the huge viaduct itself, references must be made to similar overland routes on the Oxted to Groombridge line, constructed up to the northern and southern ends of Mark Beech Tunnel. By definition an overland route or 'temporary way' is a primitive and severely graded light railway constructed to meet the difficulties of carting materials where roads are inadequate or non-existent.

McDermott, Firbank's biographer, must have experienced these at first-hand since he wrote: 'To those who have never been over a contractor's railway, it is difficult to convey the idea of gradients and curves which are ventured upon; but those who have seen the Atlantic billows will be able to judge what sort of roadway 1 in 7 or 1 in 13 represents, and what are the sensations of the uninitiated on their first ride on a small contractor's engine over gradients of this description. Comparatively few accidents, however, occur on these overland routes, and their aid in assisting excavations and in the carriage of materials is invaluable.'

References to the LEGR's overland routes are so sparse that comparison with the contemporary overland route near Edenbridge, commenced in 1885, will help to portray a fuller picture. The following interesting description comes from Mr

William Stennett, one of Firbank's trusty representatives, under whose direction that line was laid. 'The overland route on the Oxted & Groombridge Railway was one of the first importance, the public roads of the district, with hardly any exception, being little more than lanes with superficial metalling only sufficient for the small local traffic. Without the overland road a single month's wear by the carts and vans which would have transversed them during the construction of the railway, would have undoubtedly rendered all of them practically impassable. Besides, to reach any point of the railway from another by means of the hilly and narrow roads meant miles added to the journey.'

A description follows, commencing with proceedings for the possession of the land required for the railway, its start from a junction with the existing railway, and laid over hill and dale, crossing the SER line by an existing public road bridge and including serpentine curves of four chains and gradients of 1 in 10, crossing the Eden river on timber trestles and baulks with many other similar erections over other streams.

'Throughout, four locomotives were continually employed in the conveyance of materials alone, two on each portion, and when the rails were slippery through rain or sleet, the engines at the southern portion near Ashurst, which had a 1 in 7 gradient and a temporary wooden viaduct over a mill stream and another over the Medway, both formed of timber longitudinally with sills on piles driven in the beds, were worked coupled together as the inclines were too steep for one locomotive to surmount. The cost of maintenance was large, but in haulage alone the temporary road favourably compared with any other possible cartage, and the trans-shipment of materials was wholly saved.'

Returning to East Grinstead, the overland railway made its way southwards out of the town's built-up area, from the station's goods yard located on the site of the original 1855 terminus, along the line of the future spur forming LEGR Railway No 2 and, crossing several small lanes and roads, made off across the Imberhorne dip by a temporary bridge before rising steeply to cross the rocky outcrop near Hill Place and Hazelden, which required a cutting of considerable depth. The gradient into the valley was so steep that the incline was rope-worked, using a steam winding drum on this section of the temporary tramway.

Imberhorne Viaduct

By July 1879 a start had been made on the future 262yd span known variously as East Grinstead, Copyhold, Imberhorne and latterly Hill Place Viaduct. This was a lengthy project both in time and space, as the quantity of bricks must have approached almost half the number used in the construction of the Ouse Valley Viaduct near Balcombe in 1838.

Fortunately an etching exists of the viaduct under construction, showing it emblazoned in wooden scaffolding. The arches at its northern end appear less advanced. Underneath, bricklayers and masons would skilfully set bricks to line the inside of the curved arches. In the centre there appears to be some kind of hoist and blocks of stone and stacks of bricks not yet laid.

Over in the right-hand corner an access path leads down to a store yard, in which lie sundry materials. In the foreground the field portrays the rough aspect of recent upheaval, perhaps as an access area, before being returned to agricultural use. The contractor's private locomotive making a crossing, with its distinctive high cab and square saddletank, is a Manning Wardle 0-4-0ST (Works No 725) built new for Firbank and completed in October 1879, when it was delivered to the line and appropriately named *Grinstead*.

A contemporary account describes the viaduct as of 'a stately length of 10 arches of 60 spans each, crossing the valley of a small stream called the Ouse, which at one point is 93ft below the crown of the arch. The stream a mile or so further on flows into the infant River Medway, which the line itself crosses near Kingscote.'

Work on the viaducts, to all appearances, would seem more dangerous than that inside tunnels. Sure enough, a shocking accident on 26 May 1880 befell a young man of about 20, named Isaac Wickens, of Ashurstwood. He was engaged on wheeling a barrow of planks on the top of the scaffolding erected at the viaduct works when the legs of the wheelbarrow caught against a mortar board that lay on the planks, the result being that both he and the barrow were canted off. He fell a distance of about 45ft but the fall was broken by some planks against which he fractured his thigh, which very probably prevented his being killed on the spot. He was at once removed to the infirmary of the East Grinstead Workhouse close by, where the house surgeons were promptly in attendance and rendered the injured man every assistance. Exactly a month later a young lad of 16 years was found in great pain, hobbling along near the Union Workhouse. He had been working at the new viaduct and while employed underneath, 'a shovel fell from the top a distance of 40 or 50 feet and struck him in the loins, and supposedly injured his kidneys'. Firbank employed his own medical officer who, according to complaints made to the board of guardians, sent all his cases to the Union Workhouse to be looked after at the expense of the parish, while he allegedly pocketed the fees!

A piece of light relief was the visit in July 1880 of Jack the Railway Dog. This faithful old hound arrived on a Sunday morning on his return from Salisbury and during the day paid a visit to the viaduct works on the new railway. Railway Jack was the first and most famous of a long line of railway dogs bearing collecting boxes strapped on their backs and soliciting the travelling public for contributions towards railway orphanages. The dog travelled by itself all round the system, with a certain degree of help from the railway staff. In the evening of his visit, after partaking of a biscuit and a drink of water, he wagged his tail and appeared grateful for the kind treatment shown him by the stationmaster, who then placed

A contemporary etching of the 262yd viaduct at Imberhorne in the final stages of construction, with the contractor's locomotive *Grinstead* making a crossing. *From McDermott's* Life of Joseph Firbank

him in the guard's van of the last train to Three Bridges, to start his homeward journey to Lewes. This affectionate creature became a general favourite with railway officials, having made himself popular by continually travelling to and from nearly every railway station in Sussex.

Only a month previously this well-known canine hero, a favourite at railway balls and parties, had been presented with a silver-plated collar by Mrs J. P. Knight, wife of the respected General Manager of the LBSCR, on learning that Jack's old collar presented to him at Lewes had apparently been stolen. The inscription read: 'I am Jack the LBSC Railway Dog. Please give me a drink and I will then go home to Lewes.' There he was looked after by his owner, Stationmaster Moore. Unfortunately Jack met with an accident at Norwood Junction in 1882, in which he lost a leg, much to the consternation of the general public who followed the progress of his recovery with great interest. Many further Railway Jacks were to take up the cause, and a stuffed 'London Jack' may be seen in the Bluebell Railway's museum today.

Mishaps During Construction

No works like these, where health and safety issues were virtually unknown, could fail to be dangerous and all too often cost lives. The accounts are gory but illuminate aspects of the construction. Back on the overland route an horrific accident occurred when George Wheatley was decapitated. William Greenwood, engine driver, was the first to give evidence.

On 20 August 1879 'at 4pm I was in the engine shed and saw the deceased go past across the points towards the fields, there being no fencing between the line and the field which belongs to Messrs Firbank. The engine is fixed and draws the trucks up and down by a rope.' There was a man on the points 40yd from the engine shed, another at the foot of the incline. Five to ten minutes after the deceased went into the field, there was a signal from both to stop the engine. A truck loaded with six tons of blue brick coping stones was going down and it went another 40yd before it could be stopped, for being halfway down the trucks had considerable speed and could not be stopped in less distance. The trucks were attached to wagons by a wire rope but the momentum was too great. Some trucks had holes and pins to fasten brakes down but not apparently this one. There was a mark on the wire to indicate when it was fully run out and the truck was at the bottom.

On that day the rails were wet and greasy, making stopping even more difficult. Pointsman Thomas Beare had seen someone walking between the rails and, noticing a pair of legs, gave the signal to stop, but the truck went about 30yd before striking the deceased. He ran down and found him, feet on one line, head on the other, quite dead. John Brown, a carpenter, was coming up the line on top of a truck 4ft high and sighted Wheatley walking down, with the truck some 50yd behind him. He waved to him to drop out to the right, the nearest side. He shouted 20 times, jumped off and ran to meet Wheatley who was walking, looking down to the ground. He saw Brown when only 14yd away, looked back behind and jumped to the left! The truck struck him in the back and the coupling wire seemed to roll him over. He fell on the rail and the wheels passed over his left arm, transversely across his face, literally crushing the poor fellow's brains out. Brown saw men at the top waving, and the truck was checked. He intimated that there was a footway employed for men walking the line. The body awaited the inquest in an outhouse of the Railway Hotel, East Grinstead.

The sum total of pain endured by those navvies that survived a horrendous mishap must have been indescribable. On 26 May 1879 George Clifford was working with a party in the cutting between Mill Place and Tickeridge Farm, when a quantity of earth fell on him, breaking his leg below the knee. When released, a deep incised cut was found halfway round his leg, apparently caused by the shovel lying under him. A cut across the forehead also laid bare his skull, and the unfortunate man received severe internal injuries. He was removed to the East Grinstead Workhouse infirmary under the care of Dr Mahoney.

The first mention of the works at Sheffield Park occurred on 16 July 1880, in connection with a strange mishap in which Richard Dawes, 18, met his death at the Sheffield road bridge of the railway which was under construction. He joined two other navvies who were in search of employment and were aiming for the Newhaven Harbour Works. They were going down the railway from Freshfield to Lewes at 8.20pm and arrived at a partly finished bridge over the turnpike road (now the A275), part of which was boarded, and on that side they decided to cross except for Dawes who took the other side and fell about 18ft through the girders. His companions did not think he had had too much to drink because he had been at work all day, and thought he must have missed his footing. They hurried down to him but when they reached him he was dead. They had only met him at 4 o'clock. They had had some drink at the huts but the time between 4pm and 8pm was spent lying down at the side of the railway, as they were tired with the walk from East Grinstead. There had been no quarrelling. However, the countryside was not unpopulated that day for James Martin, a farmer's son, was in a hayfield close by the bridge and noted the group were somewhat excited, spreading their arms and talking loudly, which attracted his attention. He heard a crash and on looking again saw Dawes was missing and his companions turning back to look down through the girders. They could not have come into contact with the deceased during the brief moment his eyes were turned away. A verdict of accidental death was returned.

At the beginning of September there was another inquest at the Crown Hotel, Newick, this time into a fatal accident near Chailey, the evidence of which sheds interesting light on the way shunting was carried out. John Rilet, a walking ganger on the railway and living at Ox Bottom, said that the deceased navvy John Sheppard was his son (!). He was a rope runner on the engine, and it was his duty to get down and uncouple the trucks as required. Rilet said he was about 100yd off at the time of the accident. John Sheen, an engine driver, said that at 6.30am he went up the cutting with 10 wagons. The ganger, Joseph Smith, gave the signal to leave half in the cutting and take half higher up. Sheppard got down to uncouple the first five. He gave the signal to stop and Sheen had worked to his signal. It was uphill all the way. As soon as Sheppard gave the signal, he jumped to uncouple the wagons, and the wagons bumped together and caught him. When he received the signal from the wounded Sheppard, he stopped the engine and put the brake on. Sheppard had got in between the trucks before they had bumped and the buffers caught him. Usually he waited for the bumping, but not always. There was great risk going between the trucks before the bumping had finished. There had been no necessity for Sheppard to go in before the bumping. Joseph Smith confirmed his directions to leave half the train in the cutting. Sheppard had acknowledged that he understood the signal. The engine stopped and, instead of waiting, the lad nipped in. He was quick and nimble but had been told by Smith and others of the danger he was running. There was no reason for hurrying. Smith said to him: 'What made you get up there?'

Sheppard replied: 'I have often done it before, and I thought I had time, but I was caught.' Richard Gravely, surgeon to Newick Cottage Hospital, who lived at Stroods, Fletching, found the deceased in a state of partial collapse, from which he did not rally but died at 4.20 the next morning.

In January of 1881 the scene of inquest changed to Horsted Keynes, where Frederick Jefford was killed by a fall of earth on the 13th while at work on the new line. George Lacy, a navvy living at West Hoathly, said he was at work close beside Jefford on that part called 'Junction [Leamland] Cutting'. They had just filled a wagon when he turned his head round and saw Jefford in a stooping position and some 10 or 11ft above him a lump of earth, which had become detached, falling down. He called to Jefford to get out of the way but before he had time to, the earth fell upon him, striking him across the middle of the back and knocking him face downwards. Lacy assisted in removing the earth, but Jefford died almost immediately afterwards. Robert Prowse, ganger, said he was about 70yd from Jefford when he saw the fall of earth. Jefford and two other men had been filling wagons. He explained that when the men were working in a cutting, it was usual for two to undermine while one watched the earth above. He had been there 10 minutes before the accident but had not noticed any overhanging earth. It was his duty to see that the ground above was safe but, having 70 men under him and a considerable length of work to watch over, he thought he might rely on the judgement of the deceased and his mate, both of whom had been accustomed to the work for many years. The ground that fell had a 'smooth back'. Being clay it would crack with exposure to the sun's rays in dry weather and, when the rain came afterwards, the crack would be filled with water and the upper part close up, so that a slip might easily occur when there was nothing to indicate a loose fall of earth was imminent. Five hundredweight had fallen on Jefford from a height of 6ft and then rolled down a slope of 10ft. Verdict: 'Accidentally killed by a fall of earth'.

Another accident in the area, involving rather more people, took place just before noon on 5 April 1881. It appeared that a ballast train was passing a point between Horsted House and Caisford Bridge when one of the trucks, laden with ballast, ran off the metals, causing several others to shelve over as well. A number of navvies were riding on the trucks at the time and they were thrown off and buried under the ballast. One unidentified man of about 50 years of age died as a result of his injuries and several others were more or less hurt. The deceased was taken to the Crown Inn, Horsted Keynes, for inquest. Mention of navvies riding on the trucks only underlined a commonplace practice, for a quick lift home to base camp might save a mile of more of trudging along the trackbed and in summertime, when longer hours were worked well into the evening, the limited hours of drinking time were an extra incentive.

Progress Reports

The construction was not without its setbacks. In mid-April 1879 New Mill Pond overflowed and, on opening the sluice gates, water rushed furiously down the brook north of Kingscote, filling the channel and fields adjoining, so that the valley between the pond and Cockhouse Mill was one sheet of water. A strip 40yd long and 2yd wide was washed away.

In May it was reported that 'owing to the heavy cost of carting materials by road, the contractors have been pressing forward a train between East Grinstead and West Hoathly. A powerful locomotive engine was on Saturday [3rd] taken from East Grinstead station to run on the track between Hazelden and Mill Place, being drawn by a traction steam ploughing engine. Beyond Mill Place to the tunnel at West Hoathly, the train has been in full work for some time, and in some places discarded for the alternate route in the cuttings, only about 100yd of cutting remaining to be done in that section. There are one or two breaks in the line where engineering difficulties present themselves — as at the Mill Place culvert, and the site of the proposed viaduct at Hill Place, close to the town. A train connection, with a siding at East Grinstead station, will allow trucks to run to the viaduct, and is rapidly approaching completion. Considerable delay has taken place at the Old Coombe culvert, the top brickwork of which had to be entirely rebuilt in consequence of the wagons being run close up to it before it had properly hardened. Considerable difficulty has also been met with at "Watery-Land", and it is anticipated that piles will have to be driven to secure a foundation for the bridge.' (This was the crossing over the upper Medway just north of Kingscote.)

On 30 May, 'Mr Joseph Firbank, accompanied by Messrs Twisle and Elliott, had a trip over the new train route from Hazelden Cross to West Hoathly on the engine *Walsall*. The full connection with East Grinstead station was expected to be made next week, and this will enable through running to the central section to the great advantage of the contractor. Considerable progress has been made with the railway through the Watery Lane embankment and bridges. The stupendous cutting (between 60-70ft deep) at Hill Place Farm, and the construction of the Copyhold Viaduct remain to be done. At the viaduct the overland route is very precipitous, and provision for lowering and raising trucks up and down it is made by means of a couple of steam drums at the crest of each hill. One is nearly completed.'

The labours of making a cutting had advanced somewhat from Bourne's sketches of the work at Tring in the 1830s but the principles and problems remained the same. Baskets and wheelbarrows were still used for removing the spoil to the wagons on the tramline, and horses for shifting material, but it continued to be pick and shovel work, assisted by the occasional blasting with gunpowder. In the closing stages top soil would be brought in and spread evenly on the sides of the cutting. But even simple excavations were not without their hazards. In May 1879 an earthfall was reported in the cutting between Tickerage and Mill Place, south of Kingscote. In that July, when work was well under way at Hazelden, a number of navvies were engaged in removing earth from the side of the cutting there. One man, named John Simpson, had previously been cautioned by his comrades for his reckless bravado, but was unheeding of their warnings. A large stone became detached and before he had time to escape, fell with great force, breaking his leg.

No exact date has so far come to light for the completion of Imberhorne Viaduct, but by mid-September 1880 the two-mile section between East Grinstead and Kingscote was sufficiently complete for the jury of an arbitration case to walk down the newly constructed line from East Grinstead terminus, and materials were being brought in direct from Three Bridges via the spur line at East Grinstead. In November there was an accident at Grange Road between a double-headed goods train and a stationary ballast train destined for the LEGR construction. By 1881, however, special parties were being conveyed in open trucks with suitable seating. The first ride over the newly laid tracks on the upper section of the line was by a private party to attend an amateur concert in aid of funds for the West Hoathly Reading Room, starting from the north end of the new Imberhorne

This photograph of a celebratory inspection party travelling over the newly laid metals of the Freshwater, Newport & Yarmouth Railway, another Firbank contract, gives an idea of the occasion that took place on 24 January 1881, when Joseph Firbank arranged a special party in open 'JF trucks' (seen here with suitable seating) to travel from East Grinstead to West Hoathly and back. *Collection Dr John Mackett*

Viaduct at 6.30pm on Monday 24 January 1881. It had been arranged by Mr E. Elliott, Manager to Firbank, who 'rigged up a couple of JF trucks (as they call them, after Joseph Firbank) which were attached to the locomotive *Portsmouth*. The special steamed comfortably away over the new viaduct, which is an extremely fine piece of brickwork, and in a very few minutes reached Kingscote where, the signal for stopping being answered, a ladder was lowered.' After picking up several of the engineering staff, the train arrived at West Hoathly at 7pm. Shortly after 10pm *Portsmouth* and the two JF trucks started back, stopping at Kingscote to set down and the *Portsmouth* again puffing off, the remaining party arrived at East Grinstead by 11pm, and retired well pleased with the enjoyable evening they had spent.

It appears to have been a traditional contractor's practice that when the line of rails over a whole section was complete and prior to any official inspection and opening, there was some kind of local celebration train for which the contractor provided one of his engines as motive power and, as on the above-mentioned party outing, 'JF trucks' were provided. There seems to be no local press reference, leading one to suspect that this was a private occasion. The scene must have been closely similar to that depicted in the photograph of a party travelling over the new metals of the Freshwater, Newport & Yarmouth Railway on the Isle of Wight, an outing similarly arranged by Joseph Firbank.

Certainly an occasion which took place mid-year in 1881 was remembered by Mrs E. Isard, an aunt of the Watson family of Lane End, who died in 1960 at the age of 92. She described it like this: 'The carriages were all open at the top with seats arranged transversely so that the passengers could look directly at the landscape. I wore a long dress with three rows of braiding at the bottom. I hated the dress because it was too long. A Mr and Mrs Trangmar took me from Newick station to Horsted Keynes.'

Jim Watson, recalling the event and the JF trucks, mentioned that the trucks that got broken were written off and thrown into the permanent way to help build up the line to rail level. Doubtless they remain there to this day! This stretch bridging the Warren north of Newick & Chailey station was one of the last stretches of the track to be completed as 'the heavy embankment between Fletching and Newick on the direct line' was listed as still outstanding in mid-1879.

A report on the progress of the works was made at the end of March 1881, when the chairman asked when the construction of stations on the southern section would commence. Banister reported that plans were well advanced and 'the stations would be commenced as soon as the open weather would permit of it'. This referred, of course, to the

unprecedented grim winter conditions of the first quarter of 1881, when it was impossible to forward the work. Evidence of the recommencement of work comes from an accident which befell George Skinner, 21, of Mayfield, on 22 February. He was working on the line north of Barcombe, underneath a bridge which crosses a stream. Three other navvies were working on top when a large piece of iron, weighing about half a ton, used in stabilising the iron piles of the bridge, fell between the girders, breaking his right leg below the knee. He was taken to Lewes dispensary in a cart, suffering from a compound fracture from which he later fully recovered.

Regarding the stations, a more encouraging note came from Wolfe Barry, stating that the construction of the platforms and subways at the stations was in hand, but that the booking offices and station buildings had not yet been commenced, and that there was now no reason why these should not be pushed rapidly forward. These he estimated would take six months to complete. Confirmation of this is recorded in the Brighton board meeting of 6 May, authorising to Firbank the erection of the station buildings on the LEGR line upon the same schedule of prices as that agreed for the stations on the Tunbridge Wells-Eastbourne (Cuckoo) line, completed the previous year.

The later stages of the work necessitated considerable ironwork for bridge and station construction. Much of this was supplied by Every & Sons of the Phoenix Ironworks, Lewes, whose name could be seen on many of the iron pillars and brackets supporting the platform awnings of stations on the line. In February 1882, when the finishing touches were being put to the stations, two navvies classified as 'ironworkers employed on the new railway, Benjamin Crabtree and Joseph Fenton, were charged with stealing watercresses from part of a bed in Dean Field from the LBSC Railway'. Presumably this was on land bought by the company in the course of construction.

Contractor's Locomotives

No account of the line's construction would be complete without some mention of the contractor's locomotives. From sifting contemporary press reports and an extended correspondence in 1960 with Mr W. K. Williams of the Birmingham Locomotive Club, later the Industrial Locomotive Society, it has been possible to compile the following basic table of those locomotives known to have been employed on the LEGR contracts:

Summary Table of Contractor's Locomotives on LEGR Construction					
Name	*Type*	*Built*	*Builder*	*Builder's No*	*Disposal*
Portsmouth	0-4-2ST	c1860	George England	?	?
Taunton	0-6-0ST	1864	Fox Walker	16	to William Rigby c1900
Henry Appleby	0-6-0ST	1870	Hawthorn Leslie	45	to Charles Wall 1918
Brighton	0-6-0ST	1876	Hawthorn Leslie	162	to Logan & Hemingway c1888
Cliftonville	0-6-0ST	1876	Hawthorn Leslie	165	?
Walsall	0-6-0ST	1877	Hawthorn Leslie	188	?
Sharpthorn	0-6-0ST	1877	Manning Wardle	641	from Charles Deacon/to William Rigby
Grinstead	0-6-0ST	1879	Manning Wardle	725	to William Rigby, 6/1899
Sussex	0-6-0ST	1879	Hawthorn Leslie	221	to Price Wills

Taking them in order of building, a degree of uncertainty exists regarding *Portsmouth*. A locomotive of that name and another named *Brighton* both started as 0-4-0Ts but were later converted to 0-4-2STs and were employed by F. Furniss, contractor for the Hayling Island branch between 1864 and 1867. Furniss No 2 was rebuilt with 3ft 0in trailing wheels added by Furniss, which contrasted strangely with the 2ft 10in driving wheels. This engine also hauled service trains and went to Boulter's sidings in 1871. The name *Portsmouth* acquired around this time may have come through employment on the Portsmouth drainage contract, on which other Furniss engines were used. On the other hand it needs to be borne in mind that it was commonplace for contractors to rename a secondhand purchase when it came into their possession. Whether the *Portsmouth* which hauled the first makeshift passenger trains across the more or less complete Imberhorne Viaduct was the aforementioned veteran or a more recent locomotive remains an open question. In the case of *Brighton* it proved to be the latter.

Taunton was one of at least two locomotives operating the Newick stretch of the line. It was acquired new but the origin of the name is uncertain. There is no record of a Firbank contract in the Taunton area and the best suggestion is that it was named after Lord Taunton, one of Firbank's backers. Dimensions are unfortunately lacking, as Fox Walker's early records were all destroyed, but by way of compensation a priceless close-up photograph of *Taunton* near Lane End Bridge has survived through the Watson family. Its arrival was a dramatic event long remembered by the family, who lived at Rotherfield Farm until 1937. The arrival of *Taunton* to lay the line was recalled in 1961 as if it was only yesterday. 'The *Taunton* was towed from Mrs Gibson's gate across Lane End Common and put on the rails by the Old Barn [now pulled down] near the present railway bridge.' They recalled the engine driver with his wooden leg, together with his mates and their families. After working the sections north and south of Newick — *Taunton* certainly ventured as far as north as Freshfield — the veteran continued in Firbank's hands at least until 1899, as requests for spares were received at the Hunslet Engine Co, Leeds, in June and August of that year. Its final fate following sale to William Rigby is not known.

The large locomotive engine *Henry Appleby* was supplied new to Firbank at Gresley near Burton. It had 12in x 18in inside cylinders and 3ft 1in wheels. On 10 March 1879, it was drawn by a 27-horse team under the supervision of Mr Henry Britchfield, Mr Firbank's horsekeeper, from Forest Row station to West Hoathly via Wych Cross. It became mixed in mud and sank so deep in the ground that it had to be left until more horses had been summoned. Firbank went on to use it on the contract through Oxted and still had the locomotive in July 1899, when on a contract at Basingstoke. In 1918 it was sold to Chas Wall, a dealer of Grays, Essex. Henry Appleby was consultant engineer of the Monmouthshire Railway and supervisor of the Neath & Brecon Railway's locomotives, and this ties in with Firbank's connections with Monmouthshire.

Brighton was the first to arrive on the line, as reported on Saturday, 19 October 1878; a memorable landmark event in the construction. 'The first locomotive to be used by the contractor was drawn from Grange Road station to West Hoathly, a distance of five miles, by 20 powerful horses under the management of Mr Britchfield. The engine which is named *Brighton* was got safely on the works without a single casualty of any kind, under the superintendence of Mr Brown Firbank, engineer to the contractor.' Nearly all Firbank locomotives had place names, and this name was acquired during the construction of the Cliftonville spur, comprising 1½

The contractor's locomotive *Taunton* worked the section south of Horsted Keynes down to Newick. Back in 1961 there were local folk still alive who could remember *Taunton* arriving across Chailey Common pulled by six horses. It was close by, near Lane End Bridge, that this photograph was taken. The group gathered around *Taunton* portrays an interesting cross-section of the contractor's working community — the driver clutching his child at the side of the open cab, an extra workhand standing to his left, and two young navvies below. Standing on the running plate is the driver's mate who has a wooden leg, one arm on the handrail and the other grasping an oily rag, below him the 'teapot' boy, with another navvy and his family. Many of the navvies were lodged in homes in the neighbourhood.
Miss G. Watson/Bluebell Archives

miles from Preston Park, Brighton, to Hove. The contract included the goods stations at Kemp Town and Cliftonville (Hove), together with the enlargement of the main Brighton goods station, and was carried out between 1876 and 1878, dates which fit its delivery to the LEGR in October that year.

Cliftonville served from 1876 to 1879 on the same contract, from which it took its name on arrival new. Based at East Grinstead, it worked first on the LEGR contract with its companion *Grinstead,* with which it moved north to serve on the East Grinstead-South Croydon contract in the company of Manning Wardles Works Nos 527 and 597, which were respectively and appropriately named *Croydon* and *Oxted.* Some were later involved with the construction of the 2½ -mile Selsdon Road-Woodside line of 1881-5 and also the Hurst Green-Ashurst Junction line of 1885-8, which involved some heavy works. *Cliftonville's* disposal is not recorded.

Not much is known about *Walsall*, which took Firbank himself, accompanied by his assistant, on an inspection trip from Hazelden Cross to West Hoathly over the newly laid permanent way. It certainly took its name from a previous service on the Walsall, Sutton Coldfield & Water Orton contract for the Midland Railway, on which it arrived new in 1877.

The first engines to arrive were delivered to West Hoathly, the hub of the contractor's enterprise centring on the excavation of Sharpthorne Tunnel, where an engine shed and workshops are mentioned as being in existence in July 1879. One occupant was a fairly new Manning Wardle built at the firm's Boyne Engine Works, Leeds, for Charles Deacon of Kettering, and originally named *Solomon*. Not much more than a year later it was sold to Firbank and renamed *Sharpthorn*, with no 'e' in keeping with the local spelling of the village in mid-Victorian times. Remarkably, the locomotive survives to the present day. Firbank later sold it to William Rigby of Duffield, who renamed it yet again, *Jessie*. Its fourth owner was C.D. Phillips of Newport, during whose ownership the name may have lapsed. In 1888 it was purchased as one of a batch of four locomotives by Samuel Williams & Sons and became No 4 in its locomotive stock.

For the next 70 years it hauled coal trains over the Dagenham Dock Estate to the main line railway sidings. It was fitted with a radio telephone in 1954 and remained in service until 1958, when it was retired after 81 years of service, but remained on the site in a preserved state sporting the company's blue and white livery. It was later transferred to Alan Bloom's new steam museum at Bressingham, where it was repainted in a dark green and placed out in the open at the end of a quiet siding, for youngsters to climb over. In the spring of 1981 Samuel Williams recalled the locomotive to its Wiltshire depot at Braydon Hill, Minety, from where it travelled the following April by road to Sheffield Park to take part (being hauled out of steam) in the centenary cavalcade of the line it had helped to construct over a century previously. That year, while still on LEGR metals, its owners went into receivership and it was purchased by the Bluebell Railway. No locomotive on the latter's books has a closer link with the line than the old *Sharpthorn*. It even had the distinction of being presented to Her Majesty the Queen in June 1984, at an exhibition at Olympia!

Another Manning Wardle which graced the works was built new for Firbank in October 1879 and delivered to East Grinstead. Naturally named *Grinstead*, it belonged to the maker's Class K and was fitted with 12in x 17in cylinders and 3ft coupled wheels. The etching of Imberhorne Viaduct under construction illustrated in McDermott's biography of Firbank, shows one of the contractor's locomotives crossing the viaduct, and close examination under a glass shows the features to be compatible with photographs and plan drawings of *Grinstead*. The locomotive continued to serve on the northern extension through Oxted, and on later Firbank contracts, for it was not sold until June 1899. The new owner was once again William Rigby, who renamed it *Middleton* and painted it dark blue with red and white lining. Following completion of a contract in Folkestone Harbour, including the new pier, it was sold in June 1904 to the SECR for £400, just £45 more than Firbank's was paid in 1899. It entered Ashford Works at the end of August for repairs and the addition of a

Left: The 0-6-0ST *Henry Appleby* is recorded as coming to the line on 10 March 1879, being drawn through Forest Row to West Hoathly by a team of 27 horses. En route it sank so deep into the mud that a pause ensued until more horses could be obtained. The location is Oxted, indicating that the locomotive moved on to the northern contract after service at West Hoathly. *Bluebell Archives*

Upper right: Sharpthorn in the service of Samuel Williams & Sons as their No 4 at Dagenham Docks on 24 May 1956. The crew pose for a photograph during what was obviously an enthusiast group visit. *Eric Sawford*

Lower right: A later photograph of *Grinstead,* which, having been passed on by Firbank to William Rigby, was sold by the latter to the SECR in 1904. Ashford added a more spacious cab and turned it out in the attractive Wainwright livery in which it is seen standing at Folkestone on 20 September 1910. *H. I. Hopwood/LCGB Ken Nunn collection*

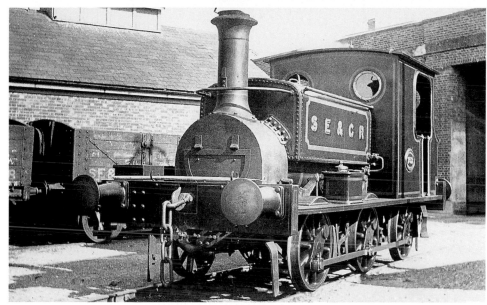

large distinctive enclosed cab and ornamental chimney (removed 1918), to reappear in March 1905 in Wainwright's attractive varnished green livery and, as SECR No 752, was permanently employed at Folkestone Harbour. It gave wartime service at Tonbridge, Maidstone West and Hawkhurst before returning to dock duties at Folkestone in 1917. The SR transferred it to Dover where it acquired the nickname 'Thumper' because of the noise made at speeds above 5mph. Laid aside at Ashford in 1925 and sold in the following March to George Cohen & Sons for £250, it was repaired and resold to the Thames Deep Water Wharf Co Ltd and as *Dolphin* painted dark green. The firm and its successor at Northfleet employed it till 1943. It lay partially dismantled until disposed of for scrap early in 1945.

There was one further locomotive delivered new in 1879, *Sussex,* later sold to Price Wills, but no local details have come to hand. But it might have been the unnamed locomotive which on 5 May 1879 was taken by steam ploughing engine from East Grinstead station to West Hoathly to work the tramline traffic between Hazelden and Mill Place.

And what of the men who worked and attended to these locomotives? They appear to fall into three categories — engine drivers, stokers (firemen) and engine cleaners. The majority of references to these emanate from West Hoathly,

the only contractor's base to receive mention of an engine shed and workshops. Geographically the location was certainly well placed, near the centre of gravity of the enterprise from which, once the rails were joined, they could work in all three directions, with only the Barcombe leg involving any distance, and that under 10 miles. Locomotives remained at their point of work unless called in for urgent maintenance.

Several of the West Hoathly drivers are mentioned, including Andrew Calvert of 'Mr Peg' fame. Could that be he in the Newick construction picture, standing in front supported with a stick, for he has a stump rather than a shoe on his right foot and an unnatural straightness of his trouser leg? Bryan Ratcliffe was in trouble for 'threatening a man's life'. Perhaps the pleasantest of the trio was John Henry Williams, who was on the receiving end, having had his cap stolen, possibly one of those short peaked affairs shown in the navvy illustrations. Thomas Lucas was a driver on the Haywards Heath section, John Shee at Lane End, Newick, while John Morton and Henry Howard were firemen working on the Ardingly line. William Greenwood at Imberhorne Viaduct was an engine driver of a different kind, being responsible for a fixed steam engine housed in an 'engine shed' to work trucks up and down the steep incline by rope.

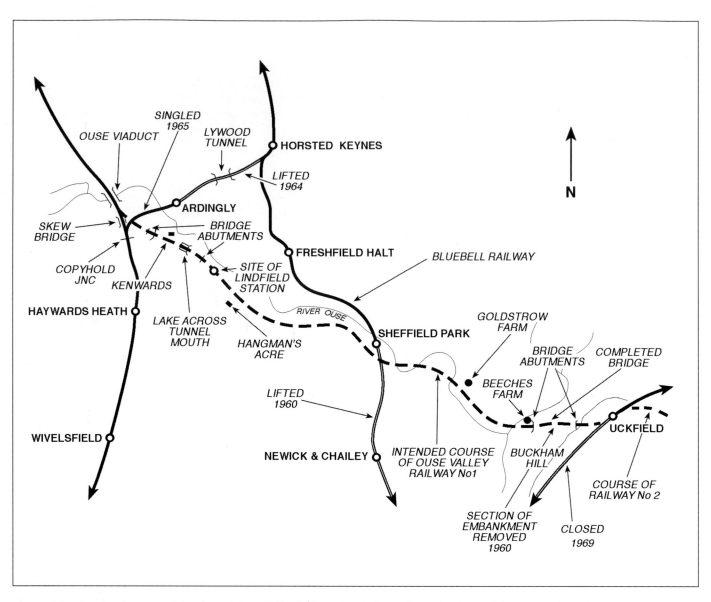

Map showing the route of the planned Ouse Valley Railway in relation to the LEGR line and the proposed junction near Sheffield Park.

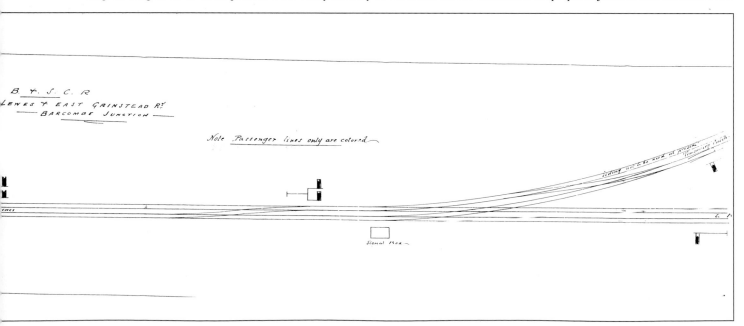

Plan of the proposed Barcombe Junction with indication of 'siding not to be used at present' and reference to a 'temporary catch point' on the LEGR single track just short of the junction. These arrangements were in order to provide the contractor access from the southern end of the line. *PRO MT 6 251/3*

5.

Inauguration

Late Alterations

The deposited plans left considerable scope for alterations in the face of unforeseen problems that were not obvious at the time the Bill was passed. Wolfe Barry's plans were not necessarily to the liking of the Brighton board but after some investigation his proposed arrangement of East Grinstead with high and low level platforms was approved. The same meeting on 30 October 1878 discussed whether the works at Lywood Common should be constructed in tunnel according to the deposited plans, or in open cutting. Barry and his opposite number Banister explained that the tunnel should be made. But in the case of the dipping ground immediately north of Leamland Wood at Horsted Keynes, where a further grand viaduct was proposed, it was changed to a high embankment. With hindsight, this was a costly decision, for throughout the years following the construction, earthslips have frequently occurred and, having been re-established with ash, have resulted in periodic slow-burning fires, causing further collapses. A graphic example of this took place on 8 November 1925 when a slip occurred in the embankment alongside the down main line, half a mile north of Horsted Keynes station, necessitating single line working being established over the up line between Horsted Keynes and West Hoathly, commencing with the 6.38am train from Brighton to London Bridge. The line was cleared and normal working resumed at 8.5pm on 11 November.

In the autumn of 1879 there was a belated attempt to revive part of the Ouse Valley scheme, by turning Sheffield Bridge into a junction and using the abandoned and incomplete trackbed from there to Hellingly. The Brighton company replied that it was heavily over-committed in expenditure and that any such scheme would have to go it alone.

The next matter of some moment to be broached occurred in the summer of 1880, when a letter was read out at the June meeting of the LEGR board, in which Mr J. W. Barry suggested the desirability of making the railway double from Horsted Keynes to Barcombe at a probable outlay of £28,000, exclusive of the permanent way. This was referred to the Brighton board for consideration a week later on 16 June, which referred it to Knight and Banister. They duly reported on 28 July and the meeting resolved that 'the works on the LEGR between Horsted Keynes and Barcombe be constructed for a double line of rails, on the understanding that existing contracts are not affected thereby and that no additional charge or remuneration be made in respect thereof.'

At the LEGR meeting of 11 August, Easton, the Chairman, asked Sir Philip Rose whether the Brighton board had arrived at any decision as to the proposed doubling, and intimated that his company had consented to a double line of rails. Banister was to communicate with Barry and arrange accordingly. On 6 October a letter reached the Brighton board, asking for formal authority in writing, empowering the LEGR to proceed with the aforementioned doubling. A fortnight later a letter was received by the Brighton board from Barry, stating that the proposed widening would cause him considerable extra labour, as well as costs out of pocket for new drawings etc, and suggesting that his remuneration as Engineer of the line should be increased by £800 in respect of such widening. The board replied saying there was nothing to this effect in the original agreement but, if it could be shown that any small additional expense was incurred for plans or otherwise, they would be ready to consider it without prejudice. The result was a compromise, for it was in fact constructed for double track but the second set of rails was never laid. After the Wivelsfield accident of 1899 it was understood among the Brighton enginemen that the doubling would only be a matter of time and that the line would then be used as an alternative to the main line. In 1916 efforts were again made, without success, to persuade the LBSCR to double the Culver Junction-Horsted Keynes section, so that it could be freely used in the event of any obstruction occurring on the main line. For the 1916 project, with the intense wartime Newhaven munitions and military traffic, government assistance would have been forthcoming, but the opportunity was never taken.

The next earthquake of shattering proportions to land upon the table came in 1880, with persistent reports of a new line contemplated, running via Ringmer and Laughton to curve into Barcombe from the southwest, hence the need for a new station west of the point where the LEGR was to turn north and the closure of the Uckfield line's Barcombe station. Evidence of location first comes in an official LBSCR Table of Distances issued in November 1881, which cites a station five chains to the lower side of the junction with the almost completed line to Horsted Keynes. The junction itself is shown on the map and tables as 'Barcombe Junction'. Banister got a quotation from Firbank for £15,000 for laying out the site, which was likely to be designed on a plan similar to Horsted Keynes, with two island platforms.

On 19 April 1882, at a meeting of the Brighton board, 'Mr Banister submitted plans for the junction stations at East Grinstead and Barcombe, the contracts for which he proposed to let to Mr Firbank at the schedule of prices which was agreed with him for the construction of other stations on that line. It was approved at an estimated cost of £17,000 for *each* station.' John Hoare, in his book *Sussex Railway Architecture*, comments on the high cost: 'It is difficult to understand how

LONDON BRIGHTON & SOUTH COAST RAILWAY.

NOTICE TO ENGINE DRIVERS, GUARDS, SIGNALMEN, AND ALL CONCERNED.

Opening of the Lewes and East Grinstead Line.

(Between Culver Junction and East Grinstead)

On Tuesday, August 1st, 1882, the above Line will be opened for Passenger Traffic, and Trains will run as per Time Table given below.

This New Line forms a connection with the Lewes and Uckfield Line at Culver Junction, at a point about three miles and three chains north of Lewes Station, and about forty-one chains south of the present Old Barcombe Station.

The Stations on the New Line will be as under:—

	DISTANCE FROM CULVER JUNC.	
	M.	CH.
Barcombe, New	1	8
Newick and Chailey	4	45
Fletching and Sheffield Park ...	6	30
Horsted Keynes Junction	10	65
West Hoathly	13	10
Kingscote for Turner's Hill	14	78
East Grinstead (Low Level)... ...	17	13

The Line is Single as between Culver Junction and Horsted Keynes Junction, and double as between the latter Junction and East Grinstead.

The Single portion will be worked under the Rules and Regulations for working single Lines by Train Staff and Train Ticket.

The Line will be Up from Culver Junction to East Grinstead, and Down East Grinstead to Culver Junction.

The Train Staff Stations and Sections, as between Culver Junction and Horsted Keynes, will be as under:—

Sections and Staff Stations.	Colour of Ticket, Letters of Staff, and Ticket Boxes.	Shape of Train Staves.
Culver Junction and Newick and Chailey..	Red ..	Handle at end.
Newick and Chailey and Fletching.. ...	Blue..	Handle in centre.
Fletching and Horsted Keynes Junction ..	Red ..	Handle at end.

All Trains going to or coming from the New Line must stop at Culver Junction to receive or deliver the Train Staff or Ticket, and must also call at all Stations.

Opening Notice of the Lewes & East Grinstead line.
Bluebell Archives

case with the Chichester & Midhurst line of 1881 and the line northwards from East Grinstead to Sanderstead, which opened in 1884. When it came to the LEGR, the photographer appears to have been more selective. The standard views across the platform exist for Newick and Horsted Keynes, but at Newick and Ardingly there are shots of details of the platforms under the canopies, and at Horsted Keynes of the exterior of the newly licensed refreshment room and of the station house from the forecourt. In variety they somewhat compensate for the pictures that were apparently not taken at Barcombe, Sheffield Park, West Hoathly and Kingscote.

With the staff in residence, the aspect of the stations on the line must have improved greatly by the time Col Yolland went over the line a second time, accompanied by a large party of Brighton and LEGR officials. They included, in addition to those mentioned as attending the first inspection, J. Wolfe Barry, Mr Elliott (LEGR Manager), Joseph Firbank, Mr C. Hodgson (Saxby & Farmer), Mr Houghton (Telegraph Superintendent) and Mr Cope (LEGR Solicitor).

Those coming from Brighton had left that terminus at 8.30am, and at 9.5am the whole party left Lewes in a special train hauled by three heavy engines for the purpose of testing the underbridges and other works. A reporter for the *East Grinstead Observer*, who travelled with the special train, described the inspecting cavalcade.

'The day proved delightfully fine, the scene along the new route being one that is unsurpassed for beauty of landscape anywhere in Sussex. Going by way of Lewes, the new line was entered at a point marked only by a junction signalbox at a place called Colve.

'From here a careful inspection of the various bridges and permanent way was carried out from a train consisting of a contractor's engine with an extempore raised box seat on the footboard in front of the engine, from which the inspector was able to obtain an excellent open view of the line. An engine and trucks followed with a large party of officials, the rear being brought up with an engine and train of three saloon carriages conveying a large company of the Brighton company's officials and invited guests.

'The first station is Barcombe Cross, four miles from Lewes. The next station reached is Newick & Chailey, both places served by one station. Fletching was the next station, after which came Horsted Keynes, where the connection line with the Brighton main line branches off, and not being ready was not inspected. Here a halt took place for luncheon and the whole party of 70 guests, who had been sumptuously provided for in three saloon carriages, did full justice to an excellent luncheon which mine host of the Railway Hotel, East Grinstead, Mr G. Payne provided. At this station the views to the south are magnificent, the whole panorama of woodland and greensward and the encircling downs in the background spreading as a real panorama. No prettier spot can be found for excursionists after the route is open on Tuesday.

'Having satisfied the inner man, no time was lost making for Sharpthorne Tunnel. Torches were lit to inspect the arches overhead and, on emerging, arrived at West Hoathly station, sheltered close to the steep hill which the tunnel pierces. This station has a very light and pleasant footbridge erected, by which passengers can cross the line. Here all alighted and the Inspection party returned for a second inspection of the work done in the tunnel. They then went on to Kingscote. A subway is formed here, while outside there is scarcely a house to be seen, but two cottages are already begun, for the railway has displaced the Watery Lane, and contractor and engineer skilfully surmounted the difficulties at this spot. Within a quarter mile one foundation has sufficed on which to erect a culvert arch for the road and a bridge for trains. In two places there is a stupendous embankment between which the water is all guided into straight channels.

'Leaving the valley and piercing the high land at Hill Place are some well erected skew bridges, their foundations as firm as the hills, Mr Holden having been subcontractor for the whole of the brickwork. In a rocky cutting 70 feet deep were found some specimens of Derbyshire spar, followed all at once to Copyhold [later Imberhorne] Viaduct 80ft above ground, commanding an extensive view of 20 miles of country, stretching to the Manor of Duddleswell and Ashdown Forest. It was nearly 6pm when the now tired party arrived at East Grinstead, and Col Yolland briefly summarised his findings to the assembled company.

'The Inspector expressed himself well satisfied with the general excellence of the line, and a favourable report to the Board of Trade could be expected. There need be no anxiety with regard to 1st August. The new stations on the line were all built in an ornamental Queen Anne style and were quite a feature of general railway architecture, being very picturesque as well as substantial and durable. The permanent way had been finished off with copious dressings of Eastbourne beach which, when washed by rain, looked exceedingly clean and nice. Security of the sleepers from wet had also been obtained by their being laid up on ballast some two feet on a short,

The LBSCR sent its official photographer to each newly opened line and the LEGR was no exception. Here we see the frontage of the magnificent exterior of Horsted Keynes station with its painted panels and flower patterns, its decorative porch with leaded stained glass windows. Stationmaster William Yeomanson, in bowler hat, poses with four of his initial team: left to right George Daws (porter), Charles Smith (assistant clerk) and John Mills and Walter Coomber (signalmen). Of interest is the poster advertising Brighton Regatta and next to it on the ground the station handbell, rung five minutes before a train was due to warn passengers still on their way to make sure of catching the train, for few people owned watches in those days. *H. M. Madgwick collection*

rough stone wall on either side of the metals. The inspector was reported to have said he had never seen work better done! The train bearing the official party was shunted up the spur line over the new points into the old station on the Tunbridge Wells line, and reversed in order to return to Victoria and Brighton via Three Bridges, leaving about 6.15pm.'

The full report of Col Yolland was presented at the next LEGR board meeting on 9 August 1882, after the opening, and was satisfyingly minuted to the effect that 'it was also intimated to the board that at the inspection Col Yolland stated publicly that it had seldom fallen to his lot to inspect a railway that was so thoroughly satisfactory. Overall, it is a very well finished line.'

The *Sussex Daily News* concluded its report: 'The whole construction is one that will reflect the highest credit on those trusted with its formation,' but in its final sentence stated: 'That branch of the line which runs from Horsted Keynes to Haywards Heath will not be ready for some time.'

Following the final inspection, an East Grinstead correspondent wrote on 29 July: 'The opening for traffic is announced to take place on Tuesday next the 1st of August. The temporary approach to our new station is by way of Glen Vue, a place left for a road some years ago, which at present is repaired with sawdust and ashes; there is another entrance in course of construction opposite the Gas Works, down Imberhorne Lane.'

The Opening

By the standards of the earlier openings of pioneer days, the arrival of the Lewes & East Grinstead Railway upon the mid-Sussex scene was a distinctly modest affair, almost unassuming after the merry junketings of the two inspections. The line was opened for public traffic on 1 August 1882 which fell upon a Tuesday, and the LBSCR, with good taste, trusted to the published announcements and to the public for whatever 'demonstration' the opening night might cause.

Passenger traffic commenced with the first train leaving the new low level station at East Grinstead at 6.57am. A small group assembled to witness the departure and a solitary cheer rang out as the train left the new platform. The local paper reported:

'A fair number of passengers were conveyed during the day, many residents paying visits of a local character, and from the conversations sometimes heard it was evident that some of the passengers travelled by rail for the first time in their lives, the different contrivances, so well known to all who have travelled, having to be explained to them. The day was delightfully fine. The unfinished state of the various station accessories caused but little inconvenience, though should it continue passengers will find a little mud and not much shelter from the rain at East Grinstead. But a short time will suffice at the present rapid pace at which the contractor is pushing on the work, for securing the much needed conveniences and also the through line to London.'

One of the people to travel on the first up train over the line was Miss K. Longley, who was interviewed in 1959 at the age of 84, and was then believed to be the only surviving link with the inaugural train. Born in 1875, she lived at Selsfield Place, Turner's Hill, and vaguely remembered as a child the workmen and activity during the construction of the line and the excitement that spread rapidly at the thought of a line so close at hand. The day of the opening had everyone on their toes. All put on their best clothes and finery and went down to see the first train. The feature that stood out most distinctly in her mind was the fact that her brother was asked to ring the large station handbell. This LBSCR practice was used to warn people that a train was due. There were few enough clocks in a built-up area, in the countryside next to none apart from the odd church tower, and certainly none at Kingscote, 'A railway station without a village', as a guide book of 1887 describes it. Wrist watches had not then come in, pocket watches on the chain were the preserve of the well to do, and the ordinary person relied on a sense of time which could never be wholly accurate. So five minutes before a train was due, a handbell was rung on the platform or station forecourt, which warned people still on their way along the approaching roads and lanes just how much time they had in hand to catch their train. The bell was rung in close liaison with the signalman, who lowered the home signal at the same time. The bell at Horsted Keynes is admirably illustrated in the photograph of the station house and forecourt. Jacob Voice, Porter-Signalman at Sheffield Park 1901-5, recollects: 'I used to play one tune on it five minutes before a train was due to arrive. This is how it

EAST GRINSTEAD TO BRIGHTON.—WEEKDAYS. | SUNDAYS.

Distance M.C.	DOWN	A.M. ARR	A.M. DEP	A.M. ARR	A.M. DEP	P.M. ARR	P.M. DEP	P.M. ARR	P.M. DEP	P.M. ARR	P.M. DEP	Sun A.M. ARR	Sun A.M. DEP	Sun P.M. ARR	Sun P.M. DEP	Sun P.M. ARR	Sun P.M. DEP
	East Grinstead	..	6 57	..	9 55	..	1 20	..	5 45	..	9 10	..	10 15	..	4 0	..	8 0
2 15	Kingscote	7 3	7 4	10 1	10 2	1 26	1 27	5 51	5 52	9 16	9 17	10 21	10 22	4 6	4 7	8 6	8 7
4 3	West Hoathly	7 9	7 10	10 7	10 8	1 32	1 33	5 57	5 58	9 22	9 23	10 27	10 28	4 12	4 13	8 12	8 13
7 48	Horsted Keynes	7 17	7 19	10 15	10 17	1 40	1 42	6 5	6 12	9 30	9 43	10 35	10 37	4 20	4 22	8 20	8 22
9 33	Fletching	7 30	7 31	10 28	10 29	1 53	1 54	6 23	6 24	9 54	9 55	10 48	10 49	4 33	4 34	8 33	8 34
13 68	Newick	7 37	7 38	10 35	10 36	2 0	2 1	6 30	6 31	10 1	10 2	10 55	10 56	4 40	4 41	8 40	8 41
16 13	Barcombe, New	7 46	7 47	10 44	10 45	2 9	2 10	6 39	6 40	10 10	10 11	11 4	11 5	4 49	4 50	8 49	8 50
18 1	Culver Junction	7 50	7 51	10 48	10 49	2 13	2 14	6 43	6 44	10 14	10 15	11 8	11 9	4 53	4 54	8 53	8 54
20 16	Lewes	7 58	8 0	10 56	10 58	2 21	2 23	6 51	6 53	10 22	10 24	11 16	11 18	5 1	5 3	9 1	9 3
24 52	Falmer	..	8 9	11 8	11 9	..	2 32	..	7 2	..	10 33	11 28	11 29	5 13	5 14	9 13	9 14
27 41	London Road	8 15	8 18	11 17	11 20	2 38	2 41	7 8	7 11	10 39	10 42	11 37	11 40	5 22	5 25	9 22	9 25
28 14	Brighton	8 21	..	11 23	..	2 44	..	7 14	..	10 45	..	11 43	..	5 28	..	9 28	..

BRIGHTON TO EAST GRINSTEAD.—WEEKDAYS. | SUNDAYS.

Distance M.C.	UP	A.M. ARR	A.M. DEP	A.M. ARR	A.M. DEP	P.M. ARR	P.M. DEP	P.M. ARR	P.M. DEP	P.M. ARR	P.M. DEP	Sun A.M. ARR	Sun A.M. DEP	Sun P.M. ARR	Sun P.M. DEP	Sun P.M. ARR	Sun P.M. DEP
— —	Brighton	..	7 45	..	10 20	..	2 15	..	5 3	..	7 40	..	8 30	..	2 15	..	6 0
— 53	London Road	7 48	7 49	10 23	10 24	2 18	2 19	5 6	5 7	7 43	7 44	8 33	8 34	2 18	2 19	6 3	6 4
3 42	Falmer	7 55	7 57	10 31	10 32	2 26	2 27	5 14	5 15	7 51	7 52	8 41	8 42	2 26	2 27	6 11	6 12
7 78	Lewes	8 12	8 22	10 47	10 50	2 42	2 45	5 30	5 32	8 7	9 3	8 57	9 0	2 42	2 44	6 27	6 30
11 1	Culver Junction	8 29	8 30	10 57	10 58	2 52	2 53	5 39	5 40	9 10	9 11	9 7	9 8	2 51	2 52	6 37	6 38
12 9	Barcombe, New	8 34	8 35	11 2	11 3	2 57	2 58	5 44	5 45	9 15	9 16	9 12	9 13	2 56	2 57	6 42	6 43
15 46	Newick	8 44	8 45	11 12	11 13	3 7	3 8	5 54	5 55	9 25	9 26	9 22	9 23	3 6	3 7	6 52	6 53
17 31	Fletching	8 49	8 50	11 17	11 18	3 12	3 13	5 59	6 0	9 30	9 31	9 27	9 28	3 11	3 12	6 57	6 58
21 66	Horsted Keynes	9 1	9 3	11 29	11 31	3 24	3 26	6 11	6 13	9 42	9 44	9 39	9 41	3 23	3 25	7 9	7 11
24 11	West Hoathly	9 12	9 13	11 40	11 41	3 35	3 36	6 22	6 23	9 53	9 54	9 50	9 51	3 34	3 35	7 20	7 21
25 79	Kingscote	9 17	9 18	11 45	11 46	3 40	3 41	6 27	6 28	9 58	9 59	9 55	9 56	3 39	3 40	7 25	7 26
28 14	East Grinstead	9 25	..	11 53	..	3 48	..	6 35	..	10 6	..	10 3	..	3 47	..	7 33	..

The Bold Figures (**000**) indicate Shunt.

EMPTY RUNNING.—An Engine will leave Three Bridges for East Grinstead at 5.50 a.m. every weekday.
An Engine will leave East Grinstead for Three Bridges at 10.15 p.m. every weekday.

Timetable for the inaugural train services. *Bluebell Archives*

went: "Look out she's a coming x 3, What ho!" He recalls a letter coming in 1908 from the LBSCR's General Manager, Sir William Forbes, phasing out the ringing of station handbells and most were returned to stores in 1909/10.

The seven-year-old Miss Longley and her family then boarded the first up train from Lewes at Kingscote at 9.17am and travelled to East Grinstead and back. There were good crowds, and she was much impressed with the exciting heights of the new 10-arch Imberhorne Viaduct. Miss Longley was to create a unique record 78 years later, by also travelling on the first train at the opening of the Bluebell Railway on 7 August 1960.

At that date there were still quite a number of people alive who saw the first services on their way that first August morning of 1882. Newick children Timothy Watson and Louisa Freeland were two of those that travelled on the first train from the new station. Mr Fred Marchant, a great character in Newick, recalled as a boy at the local school, that Mr Oldaker, the stern and strict village schoolmaster, for once relented that morning, and lessons went by the board as he marched his class to the fine towering overbridge north of the station to see the first mid-morning train (10.20am ex-Brighton) on its way below. From what motives the children cheered we are left to guess. The paper reported: 'The children from Newick School had a half holiday and enjoyed waving from the bridge.'

With groups of people by the lineside, the new railway was given a send-off with plenty of local fervour. One who saw it all from a strange angle was Mr Will Watson, then a young lad who, on hearing the train coming, ran across the orchard at Rotherfield Farm to see it go by, but caught his foot in some brambles and fell headlong in a ditch. All he saw were the wheels of the passing train, an event he laughingly recalled to his family many times after.

And so it was that the opening of the new line was welcomed not so much by the gentry and landowners who were behind its promotion but by the local country folk to whom it brought fresh-found prosperity and a new mobility into a hitherto isolated section of the mid-Sussex countryside. All classes were to benefit, as well as to contribute their share towards the railway company's receipts, as pointed out by a local correspondent. 'It will be seen by the annexed timetable that a capital service of trains has been arranged. All trains are first, second and Parliamentary Class.' (The last was a throwback to the past, as no such class existed on the railway by this time.)

The Haywards Heath Extension

Following the opening, the local editorial commented: 'The new line will bring East Grinstead and the country beyond in closer connection with Brighton than can be had either by way of Three Bridges or the line via Horsted Keynes and Haywards Heath, which will not be ready for some time.'

The first recorded mention of work being under way on the link line in February 1879 has been noted earlier. The widening through Copyhold Cutting and into Haywards Heath was by far the most difficult and urgent of the enterprise on Railway No 3 of the LEGR Bill, the works having to go alongside a mile-long stretch of the busy Brighton main line. The urgency lay in obtaining access from the latter to the branch trackbed and by the end of May 1879 this had been accomplished. 'The works above Copyhold Bridge are sufficiently advanced to allow of laying down a temporary line of rails as far as the deep cutting opposite Ardingly College, at the mouth of the tunnel passing under Lywood Common. At this the hands were kept busy at work on Sunday to enable an engine to work in removing the muck wagons. But a vast deal remains to be done below at the Copyhold cutting and embankment between that and Haywards Heath station, as well as between Ardingly and West Hoathly.'

The danger of the works at Copyhold alongside the main line took its toll. According to the testimony of John Turner, a guard employed by Firbank, a navvy named Charles Scott was run down by nine trucks pushed by an engine as he was stepping the sleepers towards the train, when his attention was taken by a Brighton train. This was in October 1879. The following April another navvy was run over by a train, also at the new Copyhold cutting, the wheels of the engine passing over both legs and causing a fracture. 'The poor fellow was dreadfully hurt and was put into a Brighton train at once and conveyed to the County Hospital.' Even more gruesome was an accident on 20 August 1879, in which a navvy met with a horrible sudden death. 'The unfortunate man was in search of employment and, walking down the incline on the temporary tramway towards Copyhold Viaduct near the town of Haywards Heath, was knocked down and run over by a truck loaded with bricks, that was being let down by a steam drum. Death was instantaneous and the poor fellow's head was completely crushed and his brains scattered about in all directions.' The mention of Copyhold Viaduct near the town of Haywards Heath remains an enigma. The other Copyhold Viaduct is of course near East Grinstead and certainly used steam drums. The Ouse Viaduct just north of Copyhold Junction was standing since 1841. Sheriff Mill Viaduct is close to Horsted Keynes, leaving the long, high embankment south of Copyhold Cutting as the likely 'viaduct'. An accident of similar nature befell George Keyton on the south side of Copyhold Bridge in August 1882. He was making his usual way home up the track to the Copyhold Huts when he was accidentally killed by a passing train, 'while trespassing upon the line in a state of liquor'.

By the close of 1879 the work was still proving hard going, especially with regard to Lywood Tunnel. 'Considerable difficulty is experienced in carrying through the tunnel below Hapstead (Ardingly village), owing to the influx of water and the slippery state of the soil, but the works at the heavy Copyhold Cutting are progressing admirably by the aid of steam power.' Certainly the building of this section took a more than average toll, or was it that, being on the periphery of a more populous area, there were more witnesses and consequent reports? On 8 January 1881, 'A navvy employed as a ropeman was standing on the hinder part of an engine close to where the tender is attached, when the coupling pin dropped out, causing the tender to part from the engine, which was then going at a moderate speed. The man fell through the opening, his head striking the footboard, and was very badly injured, being sent to the Sussex County Hospital.' This took place at Haywards Heath and, since there is no record of Firbank using tender locomotives on this contract, the reference must presumably be to an LBSCR locomotive bringing in materials to the works. In the last week of 1881 a fatal accident overtook William Taylor as he was walking drunk down the contractor's track towards his house near Ardingly. The report mentioned that 'the railway is not yet completed but an engine is used to take away the trucks containing the earth and other materials.'

On this section were the three previously noted navvy settlements which all receive frequent mention. The 'Copyhold Huts' were in the area near the New Barn just opposite to where the main line and the branch came together, a few yards north of the present Copyhold Bridge. There on Friday, 16 April 1880 a recently erected Navvies' Mission Room was opened by the Bishop, assisted by several clergymen in the neighbourhood. There was a large attendance and the room was reported as 'very prettily decorated for the occasion'. The second camp was in the proximity of the Ardingly station site near Avins Farm. It was here that Firbank sited his main stores, for one Edward Ancock, 'employed since the commencement of the works on the Haywards Heath branch, stole boarding, tools, iron and telegraph wiring from Mr Firbank's stores at Ardingly.' Purloining articles from the stores had been going on for a long time, and Firbank wished an example to be made to deter others employed on the works. Ancock was remanded in custody. The third encampment was 'the Lywood Huts', situated close to the tunnel and mentioned in connection with Arthur May, a labourer and engine cleaner, who in March 1883 stole 50lb of coal from the railway tunnel, for which he received a £1 fine with costs. It was here that the Act of 1877 designated, in addition to Ardingly, a further intermediate station to be called Lyewood, but this never materialised. The proposed station would have been but a mile from Ardingly or Horsted Keynes.

Though the workforce had been engaged on Railway No 3 since the winter of 1878/9, no ripples of complaint had worked their way through to the directors of either board. Only as late as 19 April 1882, following a report by Banister to the LBSCR board, was an expenditure of £18,000 sanctioned for the extension of the LEGR from its junction with the Brighton main line at Copyhold Bridge to Haywards Heath, 'the works of which are being carried out by Mr Firbank in connection with the LEGR contract'. Meanwhile the LEGR board was facing an action commenced against the company by Mr Walter Henton, the lessee of Rivers Farm, Ardingly, to compel it to make good an alleged deficit of water supply to a pond on the farm. This was one of several mentioned in the LBSCR Traffic Committee minutes regarding compensation for land damage by the LEGR extension line. In April 1883 the LBSCR board had before it a plan submitted by Banister for the rebuilding of Haywards Heath station to accommodate the four-track entry from the north, consequent upon the extension of the LEGR line, the estimated cost being £3,100 for platform roofs and signals and £3,684 for remaining works, in a total of £6,784. This was approved, the general works being done by Firbank under his schedule of prices, tenders being invited for the roofs. The rebuilding of Haywards Heath consisted of the provision of bays at the northern end of the platforms, a new signalbox and junction, and the widening of the embankments and the two bridges at the station and at Balcombe Road near Bridges Mill. There were already four tracks running north, two being sidings.

The extension was now well behind time and sure enough, on 21 May 1883, a memorial from local landowners was read out before the LEGR board which drew special attention to the fact that 'the other section of the LEGR . . . has not yet been opened,' and reminding the company of the 16 August deadline for completion and a £50 a day penalty fine. It was not until 8 August 1883 that Messrs Knight & Banister verbally reported that notice was about to be given to the Board of Trade of the intended opening of the line on

Detail of the down platform at Ardingly prior to the opening of the branch to Haywards Heath. There is plenty of carved and panelled woodwork on view. The attractive canopy stanchions with their intricately patterned supporting brackets were manufactured for the line locally and bore the inscription 'John Every, Iron Founder, Lewes'. On the left the stairs lead up to the footbridge and extended covered way to the station house.
H. M. Madgwick collection

1 September. This in fact took place on Monday, 3 September, as the line did not receive its inspection until 31 August.

'The official inspection of the line was made on Friday by Col Rich, one of the Inspectors of the Board of Trade, who was attended on the occasion by the Co's representatives. Mr J. P. Knight, General Manager; Mr F. D. Banister, Engineer; Mr W. J. Williams, Traffic Supt. Messrs Perry, Goldsmith, Berkshire and Woodhead of the Engineers, Traffic and Locomotive departments, Messrs Throssel & Elliot, the representatives of Mr Firbank, and Mr John Saxby, the contractor for the works in connection with the signals, the latter explaining the interlocking of the signals and points on what is generally known as the 'block' system, which is in general use throughout the lines of the London & Brighton Co.'

Col Rich's report of his inspection was read to the LBSCR board at its meeting on 4 September and a timetable was then issued, indicating three trains each way daily but no Sunday traffic. The local press report provides a valuable account of the opening of the branch:

'The opening of this small but important piece of railway, which forms another connection link between the London & Brighton Railway Co's system in the eastern part of Sussex and the main line, took place on Monday, unaccompanied by any demonstration or even formality. The only public intimation of opening was the issue of special timetables, and the first train which left Haywards Heath at 8.34am [another account gives 8.43am], simply ran into the station, received the freight and steamed away on its first business journey.

'The new line is only about 4½ miles long but its importance cannot be measured by its length . . . and when — it is expected that it will be this year — the new line between East Croydon, Oxted and East Grinstead is completed, it will give another route between London and Brighton, furnishing similar accommodation on the east of the main line to that which is given by the Horsham line on the west.

'The Horsted Keynes railway crosses the main line at a point about a quarter-mile distant from Haywards Heath on the north, running between the junction box and the distant signal. [The branch trains ran on independent tracks beside the main line from Haywards Heath North box.] From this point it traverses a very pretty country, a good view of which is obtained as there is only one tunnel, and a short one, just before Horsted Keynes is reached, where it taps the East Grinstead & Lewes line between Fletching and West Hoathly. Nearly midway is Ardingly station, around which a popular district is already springing up, and there is very little doubt the new line is destined to play a still more important part in the economy of the present Co's system. As stated, when the Croydon and Oxted line is finished, another route between Brighton and the metropolis will be brought into use, and the present bay siding into which the Horsted Keynes trains now run on the east side of Haywards Heath station will, it is believed, be ultimately pushed on into Brighton and be available as a goods line, leaving the main line wholly free for passenger traffic!'

There was some wishful thinking here, for Haywards Heath tunnel remains just double track to this day. Also the above account is noteworthy for absence of any mention of Ardingly College, which dates from 1858, surely a major attraction for traffic, and also nothing of the quite imposing Sheriff Mill Viaduct.

There was some local agitation because the goods accommodation at Ardingly was not ready at the time of opening, which filtered through to the LBSCR board. At their meeting on 17 October 1883 a report was read from Mr Knight as to the arrangements rendered necessary by the opening throughout for traffic of the LEGR, and mentioning that Ardingly station would shortly be open for goods traffic. Apart from this matter, unlike affairs on the direct Lewes-East Grinstead line, nothing remained outstanding as a cause of friction between the two boards. It was the Brighton one which had to deal with the matter of Wickham Lane (Farm) bridge. The line from Haywards Heath to Copyhold Bridge was crossed by two footpaths. When the line was opened powers were sought in the LBSCR (Various Powers) Bill, published in November 1883, to block these and replace them with a footbridge. The owners of Wickham Farm protested

Recently come to light is this age-scarred photograph of a ballast train employed on the northern extension, working out of East Grinstead. The contractor's locomotive is *Cliftonville* of 1876, named after its first Firbank contract on the new spur between Preston Park and Hove, from where it moved to the Oxted and Croydon works. Of special interest is the bidirectional signal in the centre, behind it the West Signalbox, while in the distance can be seen the North box and the still incomplete state of the High Level station with its white roof. *N. Stephanakis collection*

and the footbridge was enlarged to carry road traffic. The Bill was passed in 1884 and the bridge was opened later that year or early the next.

The Northern Extension

No account of the LEGR would be complete without some brief mention of its half-brother, the Croydon, Oxted & East Grinstead line. The two lines together had initially formed a unified plan in the minds of the local promoters — neither made any sense without the other. The earlier part of the traumatic saga featuring the collapse of the determined efforts of the local gentry in the face of the powers of the mighty LBSCR, itself influenced by the interests of the South Eastern Railway, has already been related.

On 1 February 1878 it was announced that the LBSCR had deposited a Bill in Parliament entitled London Brighton & South Coast Railway (Croydon, Oxted & East Grinstead Railways), and on 16 June Mr Cope reported that the Bill had passed both Houses and now awaited Royal

Assent, which was expected to be given that night. This duly took place.

From that point on it was a question of trying to move things on, as the LEGR lines would come into their own only when the Oxted line was open. Due to the confrontations and discussions between the various parties concerned, the northern line Bill was almost a year behind the LEGR one and as a result the latter's board continued to chivvy the LBSCR on every possible occasion.

Early in 1880 nothing as yet seemed to be moving and landowners and others in Sussex were enquiring when the northern section of the line would be commenced. They received from Laing an evasive reply about preliminary works on the Surrey & Sussex line and that arrangements were in an advanced state. James Sclater, himself a LEGR director, wrote a covering letter to an enclosed memorial, signed by numerous influential people, urging the board 'to prosecute the work of the northern portion of the line'. The real reason for the delay was that no Engineer's agreement had been drawn up with the South Eastern as yet but by March the LBSCR had let the contract south of Godstone to Joseph Firbank.

The earliest press evidence that the navvies had at long last arrived and made their presence felt comes late in the summer of 1881, with references to 'the Lingfield huts', a Railway Missioner 'at the chapel at Dorman's Land', and a Chaplain to the navvies administering baptism at Oxted. In the autumn of that same year accidents at Cooks Pond Viaduct and a fall down a 218ft shaft at Godstone Hill indicated the progress of the works on the northern section.

In May 1882 the local paper headlined: 'Lingfield navvies assault police: Scripture reader puts in good plea for the defence', but by October there was an application for the removal of two special constables from Oxted by Mr James Crump, Manager to Firbank. 'The works were nearly completed in that district, there were very few men employed, and those remaining were very respectable. They had got rid of the rough element.' The tunnels, cuttings and embankments were completed so that there remained very little to be finished — except the stations, of which it was reported at the beginning of May 1883 that the directors had advertised for tenders for the erection of new station offices with stationmasters' residences, platforms etc, at Dormansland and Lingfield. But the local population were not totally rid of navvies, for they had only gone round the corner to Edenbridge, to work on the Oxted & Groombridge Railway. Following arbitration at the end of 1883, it had been taken over by the LBSCR which had bought out the original company at a cost of £400,000.

Meanwhile the months slipped by, to the growing impatience of the local residents, and in May 1883, 'A memorial from landowners and residents in the district of the Lewes & East Grinstead Railway' was presented to the LEGR board, which urged it 'to take such steps as may be advised to enforce the penalty in the event of the line not being opened by that date'.

The board considered the memorial and 'consulted with its solicitors as to the best method of giving effect to the same'. It was decided to forward it to the secretary of the LBSCR, 'with a letter calling the earnest and immediate attention of the Brighton board to the consideration of the means of remedying the grievances of which the memorialists complain.' All it received from Secretary Allen Sarle was a reply late in June, giving a report of the situation pertaining.

By September it was rumoured that the East Grinstead, Oxted & Croydon Railway would be open for traffic early that November; a week later, more specifically, that the 'new Oxted Railway would have one line open on 1 November from East Grinstead to Oxted, and double from thereon to Croydon. Only five or six navvy huts were left standing [they were removable] and the services of special constables were no longer required.'

But four more months were to elapse before everything was ready. In early October there was a major accident north of East Grinstead, 'on the loop line portion of the Oxted line'. A short workmen's train, comprising an engine and a couple of trucks containing about 30 people, was returning towards the town when it ran at considerable speed into an ordinary railway truck standing on the line. The locomotive was pushing and the standing men barred the full view. The truck's coupling, being higher than those on the contractor's wagons, smashed into the end of the leading one, injuring four men, one seriously.

October passed and, with the closure of the second East Grinstead station as from the 15th (it was eventually demolished in 1908), expectancy was buoyant in the local press. 'So much of this route will be available as will provide a third route from London to Brighton, and a shorter road to Newhaven Harbour whence the Company's continental business via Dieppe is conducted. The advantages of this new route are not confined to the opening up of a fresh district but will be felt in the relief which will be afforded to the traffic over a portion of the main line, which is often more crowded than is desirable in the interests of safety and punctuality.'

On 9 February 1884 it was announced that the Croydon & East Grinstead would be opened on the first day of March. A final inspection was undertaken on Monday, 18 February by Inspector Hutchinson, who pronounced everything satisfactory. The way was now clear for the moment the original LEGR promoters had visualised eight years earlier — that of a through, and for them a direct, railway route to the metropolis — and the gathering of the dignitaries for the occasion was something far in excess of the openings of the original Railway No 1 in 1882 and Railway No 3 in 1883.

On Tuesday, 1 March 1884 a special train from Victoria conveyed a number of directors and officials of the Brighton company, besides representatives of other railways, southwards over the new routes, the special going on to Brighton by the Lewes route and back by Ardingly. The guest list reads like a roll-call of the 'Gladstone' class in person: R. L. Lopes, Hon T. F. Fremantle, C. B. Cardew, J. P. Bickersteth, R. Jacomb Hood, J. P. Knight, Sir Philip Rose and Allen Sarle. The general body of dignitaries included one who must have been well satisfied, the Earl of Sheffield himself, together with the Marquess of Abergavenny, Lord Henry Nevill, Sir Andrew Clarke, Sir George Shiffner, Sir Arthur Otway, Sir Francis Truscott, Sir Benjamin Philips, Sir Arthur Sassoon, Sir Charles Young, Sir John Monckton, Maj Gen Hutchinson of the Board of Trade, besides the mayors of Brighton, Eastbourne, Lewes and Gravesend.

The party on this occasion were able to see the LEGR work in a more complete state than on their earlier tours, including the new East Grinstead double-deck station, described as 'handsome and commodious, as indeed are all the stations, the Old English picturesque style having been adopted'. The report went on to mention Mr J. Firbank from Newport (Mon) as the contractor and J. Wolfe Barry and F. D. Banister as engineers, and the fact that Henry E. Wallis of Westminster supervised the construction of the handsome iron viaducts.

Luncheon was taken at Brighton, followed by several enthusiastic speeches. In particular Mr Lopes said that although the pecuniary advantages of the lines opened that day must be prospective, yet he believed there was a great future open to them. How prophetic these words were to be, judged by the later history of these lines and the fact that the line newly opened a few days later still remains in service today.

Despite earlier predictions, more than a week elapsed before it was announced that 'on 10 March 1884 a local and temporary service of passenger trains will run from East Grinstead low level, with weekday departures at 8.7am, 10.22am, 2.55pm and 8.55pm, Sundays 9.58am and 8.8pm, all first, second and third class'. Why it was a temporary service of trains has not as yet been resolved satisfactorily. The local paper mentions, in connection with the railway route to London, a temporary Sunday service from East Grinstead to Brighton, 'to establish through services for the remainder of this month'. The fact that on 11 March, the day following the opening, a landslip occurred on the new railway at the Croydon end obviously had no bearing on a previously announced temporary service but the fact that the existing service was temporary was just as well. Probably it took some considerable changes in the existing timetables of adjacent and feeder lines to implement a smooth through service between London and Brighton via Lingfield and Horsted Keynes.

The Omissions

As recorded previously, the memorialist lobby had been extremely active, agitating over repeated postponements regarding the belated opening of all three lines being constructed in their area, none of which realised their projected opening dates. They now found that the Brighton company was also selling them short in other respects, with regard to what the plans had originally promised. They made common cause with the LEGR board, whose local members not only felt let down by certain omissions but also considered it a matter of public honour that the original proposals were fulfilled.

The first hint of this appeared on 22 March 1882, before any of the three lines were opened, when James Sclater's letter forwarding three memorials was read before the LBSCR board, the first two regarding the speedy opening of the LEGR lines and the third 'urging the importance of at once constructing the goods warehouses and sidings according to the agreed plans'. This topic rumbled on through to the final days of the LEGR Co.

Other complaints of shortcomings and omissions came in thick and fast over the period. In the forefront was the intrepid Mr Sclater. On 9 August, hardly more than a week after the opening of Newick station, he drew the attention of his LEGR colleagues to the obstruction of the footpath near the station, and the engineer was asked to report as to whether access could be given to the station along the line in lieu! The minutes are silent on the outcome but a map is extant in the East Sussex Record Office, which indicates how this was resolved. Entitled 'Abolition of Level Crossing at Chailey', it is recorded as, 'Lodged in my office in Lewes, 29 November 1884 at 10.15, signed F. Memfield, Clerk of the Peace for the County of Sussex,' and shows how a footpath running from Cinder Hill to Little Cinder Farm and crossing three sets of rails near the neck of the proposed goods yard, was to be stopped for reasons of public safety and operating convenience, and a diversion made along a strip of land, already shown on the plan and parallel to the track but adjoining the railway fence. Several local people, including Miss M. Bessemer, have recalled how it was possible to gain access along the path through a gate onto the up platform. Also in October there had been an earthslip about a mile to the south of Newick station — not a complete surprise, for Colonel Yolland had warned in July that these banks would need to be looked after.

The next problem was in connection with the Sunday train service on the line. The LEGR secretary had written to Mr Knight on 6 October 1882, asking why the Sunday trains had

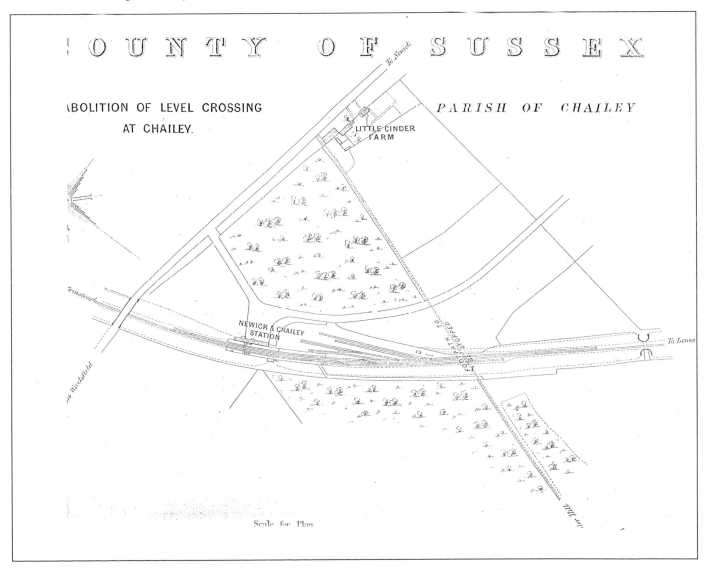

Map indicating the line of the footpath crossing rails on the level to be stopped near Newick & Chailey station for reasons of public safety and operating convenience. *Reproduced with the permission of the County Archivist of East Sussex, copyright reserved*

been discontinued after less than two months. The reply was received that 'it was not considered necessary to run Sunday trains on this line during the autumn and winter months, and that the Brighton Co have simply applied an arrangement which has been in force on other branches of their railway for many years.' Mr Knight further explained that Sunday trains would be run in the summer, and would be resumed as soon as the trains to London were running, giving an extraordinarily optimistic date for probable commencement of April Fool's Day 1883! When that time passed, the LEGR board in July reminded its senior partner of unfulfilled promises regarding through trains and their number.

A further bone of contention between the two boards over this same period was the question of Wolfe Barry's remuneration, mentioned previously, which was not satisfied until early 1884, having filled a regular paragraph in every intervening LEGR board meeting. In view of all these outstanding omissions and, sensing the intense local pressure from the grass roots memorialists, the LEGR board on 10 July 1883 passed the following resolution:

'That this company, in view of the approaching completion of the railway authorised to be constructed by them, wish to draw the attention of the Brighton Co to the fact that the agreement made between the two companies has not been fulfilled in several particulars, the chief being in relation to Sec5 as to goods sheds and Sec12 as to through trains and their daily number.'

The modelling of the letter to the LBSCR was referred to the solicitor, and the secretary was instructed to forward the same as soon as it was prepared. A further resolution embracing questions in dispute between the two companies, which included further correspondence in relation to Wolfe Barry's claim, went so far as to state 'that Counsel's opinion be taken as to the means to be adopted, and as to the procedure for enforcing the agreement existing between the companies, the solicitor setting forth the case to be submitted and the breaches of agreement in various directions complained of.'

The Winding-up

The apparent reaction of the LBSCR board to the dissenting spirit within the LEGR establishment was to fire a formidable and final broadside to require its submission. On 14 December 1883 a letter from Mr Sarle was read to the LEGR board, requesting that all the books, papers and documents relating to the LBSCR be handed over to the Brighton company in accordance with part five of the Railway Clauses Act 1863, and asking for an appointment for that purpose.

However, the LEGR board had no intention of winding up matters until the LBSCR had fulfilled its part to the letter, and the following was minuted: 'After full discussion, at which it was hoped the representatives of the Brighton Co would have been able to assist, the directors came to the conclusion that until the question of Mr Barry's claims, which have been recognised and allowed by this board are settled, the request contained in Mr Sarle's letter cannot be complied with.'

The LBSCR board received this statement on 9 January 1884. It contained the added suggestion that if the LBSCR still declined to admit Barry's claim for extra engineering services, it be referred for the decision of Sir Theodore Martin or any other competent person. This produced no change of mind in the Brighton board, whose solicitors reported the

arrangements they had made for the transfer of the books and papers of the LEGR Co, having been authorised to exercise their discretion as to leaving any small conveyancing matters in the hands of Messrs Cope and Co, their LEGR opposite numbers. But the final dissolution of the LEGR was not likely to come that quickly. Sarle wrote again on 9 and 24 January, further requesting that the documentation be handed over and seeking an appointment.

At the start of February 1884 Edward Easton reported that he had been informed by Mr Barry that the LBSCR had satisfied his claims. However, 'the directors being desirous that certain matters in relation to agreements between the two companies should be recorded, the following memorandum was ordered to be placed upon the minutes:

'That Section 35 of the Act of 1878 confirms Articles 5, 11 & 12 between the Earl of Sheffield and Edward Easton and the LBSCR.

'That as regards Article 5, the agreement is fulfilled except in respect of goods accommodation.

'As to Article 11, the accommodation provided for the reception and delivery of goods is insufficient, there being no goods sheds at any of the stations, and at some of them there is a want of space and means of lifting heavy goods. The bridges for passengers from one platform to another need protection from the weather.

'As to Article 12, for a considerable portion of the year no Sunday trains are provided, contrary to the express conditions contained in this article. These are great complaints of omission, and a considerable loss to the Brighton Co as well as inconvenience to the public results therefrom.'

Edward Easton reported that he had had a long interview with Mr Knight, who took notes of all these matters and promised they should receive attention. Mr Knight added that as soon as the northern line was opened, which it was intended it should be on 1 March, it would be much easier for the Brighton company to comply with the stipulations of the agreements. The following resolution was then passed:

'That the secretary be authorised to hand over the papers, documents and books, together with the seal of the company, in exchange for a cheque for £275 (being the amount of Directorial fees and the secretary's salary for the previous half year) in accordance with Mr Sarle's letter of 24 January.
(Signed)
Edward Easton
4 February 1884'

The return was signed by Easton and Sanders and the minute book was closed with the following memorandum:

'Under the LEGR Act 1877 the company was empowered to raise capital and debentures to the extent of £533,000. These powers were abrogated by an Act of Parliament in 1878, whereby the LBSCR Co find the money necessary to build the railway, which on completion will revert to that company.'

So it was that the LBSCR board meeting on 20 February 1884 heard from their secretary that the seal and books of the LEGR Co had on the seventh instant been handed over to him, in pursuance of the instructions of the board on 23 January. The rearguard action by the LEGR had not achieved all it both desired and demanded, and the broad back of the LBSCR now had to shoulder the constant pressure of local complaints, which, as ever, it continued to take in its stride.

6.
The Route Described

Lewes to East Grinstead

Starting from Lewes, the first three miles made use of the existing line to Uckfield. Originally this exited west from the station, leaving the 'Keymer line' via the Hamsey loop, built in 1858, which remained west of the Ouse to avoid any crossings of the river. However, the Hamsey loop was closed when a new line was cut through the flood plain of the Ouse, involving several crossings of the river and accompanying water channels. This opened on 3 August 1868, enabling a more convenient departure from the station's east end, together with the lines to Newhaven and Eastbourne.

The line to East Grinstead parted company with the Uckfield line at Culver Junction and the single track veered left via a tight curve of some 30 chains, leaving the Ouse Valley to turn northwards through lands belonging to the Parsons family, on a rising gradient of 1 in 80. At the end of

An out of the ordinary photographic subject, showing bridge renewal at 48m 48ch between Hamsey Crossing and Lewes whose outskirts are visible on the horizon. The busy scene of the strengthened permanent way gang contrasts with the leisurely walk of weekend strollers in Edwardian dress along the bank of the adjacent River Ouse.
From the Richardson Collection, courtesy Peter Hay

Above: On a stretch of line rather off the beaten track for photographers, 'K' 2-6-0 No 32342 hauls the first up train of the service restored on 7 August 1956, leaving behind one of the farm occupation bridges in the area of Old Park Wood. *Gerald Siviour*

Left: The icicled interior of Cinder Hill Tunnel, as members of a local family take snaps in the arctic surroundings in the winter following final closure. *Colin Tompsett/Bluebell Archives*

the curve was a road overbridge to the hamlet of Barcombe on the west and 1,000yd further on, the line went under another bridge, carrying the road from nearby Barcombe Cross village on the east to Pounds Corner, then gained a level section and entered Barcombe station.

It then entered a straight section through Sewells Farm Cutting, crossing Beven Brook, an area noted for its wild strawberries, passing an embankment on the east side, the edge of Knowland and Old Park Woods, on land belonging to James Sclater, one of the line's formidable protagonists. Between the woods were situated two farm occupation bridges, the southern one accessing Brickyard Farm. A descent of 1 in 80 now changed to a rise of one of the taxing 1 in 75s met with on this line, followed by a brief level, the site of the proposed station named Markstakes after an adjacent farm

(Masticks in the plan) to the west, situated on a small lane linking Newick with South Street, Chailey. The area here was known as Town Littleworth. A falling stretch of 1 in 600, passing through the now disappeared Shoulders Farm, led to a brief level through the lands of James Ingram, whose homestead lay close by. It passed under an occupation bridge by Tutts Farm to cross the Longford stream, a tributary of the Ouse, by a high level embankment close to Coppers (now Cockfield) Bridge. Across the stream lay the properties of another promoter, T. St Leger Blaauw, the line rising again at 1 in 75 past Cinder Farm (the name recalls association with a former Sussex iron foundry) and Vixengrove Farm, both on the left side, to reach the 63yd Cinder Hill Tunnel, which lay under a road junction that provided two more alternatives between Newick & Chailey . Cut into the rocky sandstone, the

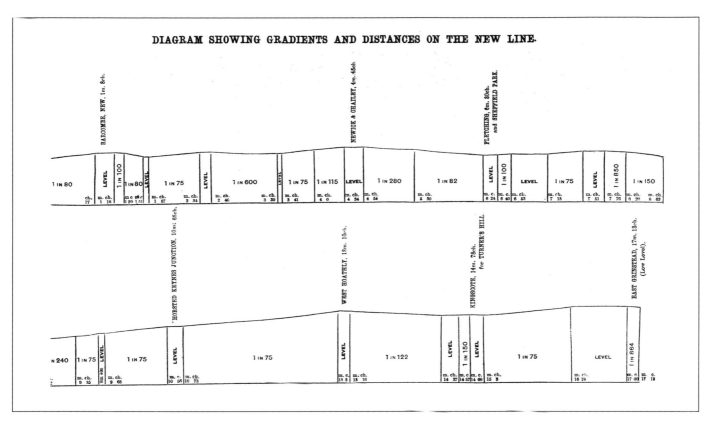

DIAGRAM SHOWING GRADIENTS AND DISTANCES ON THE NEW LINE.

1882 Gradient profile, published at the opening of the line in the 'Notice to engine drivers, guards, signalmen and all concerned.' The diagram shows both distances and gradients, with large stretches of 1 in 75 northward indicating the prevailing incline.
Bluebell Archives

construction incorporated four rows of white brick let into the tunnel wall each side of and at each end 1½ft from the ground. The tunnel lacked a proper face to its portals and was lined with eight rows of red brick with an outermost row of blue ones. Twenty-two feet six inches in width, for some reason it was not built to double track specifications, as were all the rest of the bridges and trackbed. The rising gradient eased to 1 in 115 towards the area of the Great Rough. Near the site of Newick & Chailey station, which was laid on a right-hand curve, lay Ricketts Wood belonging to William Tyler, through whose property the line was destined to go. His objections did not stop the railway and his property must have disappeared in the new station yard complex built on the level.

The line now passed under the Haywards Heath-Uckfield road and, falling for ¾mile at 1 in 280, entered the Warren and the property of yet another promoter, William Hallett, curving northeast past the two Birchland Farms on the right and threatening part of Lane End Common on the west. It ran in a deep cutting past Lane End, under the three-arch overbridge carrying the road from Fletching to Chailey. It ran very close to Rotherfield Farm, and entered Lord Sheffield's lands, descending to the Ouse at Sheffield Bridge on a falling grade of 1 in 82, to first cross over the Wych Cross-Lewes road and then over Warr's stream on an arched bridge with an 8ft span, at the south end of Sheffield Park station by the present water tower.

Crossing the Greenwich Meridian, the line left the station on a short rise of 1 in 100 across the girder bridge over the Ouse, to gain a stretch of level embankment overlooking the valley floor, which has been known to flood occasionally. The line veered to the left between Wapsbourne Wood across the fields to the west and Ketches ('Sketches' on the plan) Farm on the east, whose tenant was a Mr Kenward, who specially

grew spring onions in considerable quantities for the navvies constructing the line. Here was a farm occupation bridge, demolished in 1987. The grade now changed to the 1 in 75 of the ¾-mile Freshfield Bank, at the foot of which lay Coneyborough Wood followed by Round Wood, thick with bluebells in the spring, and halfway up crossing a tiny stream which emanated from Kings Wood by Freshfield Manor. At the top, by Town Place Farm, the line crossed over the road from Freshfield Crossways to Scaynes Hill. Along the road to the west, by the old canal of the Ouse Navigation, stands the Sloop Inn and the remains of a lock.

The line rounded Freshfield by a long, wide, right-hand curve, in the middle of which was an occupation bridge, demolished in 1992, which led to Town House Farm. Now on falling grades of 1 in 850 and 150, the line passed close to Cockhaise Mill as it crossed over the Freshfields-Lindfield road, with Wildboar Wood immediately on the right-hand side. Crossing Danehill Brook at Otye Bridge, where it enters the Cockhaise stream, it twisted its way as it followed closely the course of Cockhaise Brook, which cuts a tortuous course from side to side across its narrow valley. The changing formation of the brook and its oxbow ponds caused a number of alterations to the alignment at a late stage of the line's construction, with fresh drawings having to be prepared. Subsequent undermining of the embankments on this stretch causes the occasional slip to this day. The landmark on this section was the mansion known today as 'Treemaines' but written 'Trimmings' in the plan.

The line now changes to rising grades of 1 in 240 and 75 through Lindfield Wood, to reach Holy Well on the west. This was the source of Lindfield's water, a mineral spring rising in an open basin in a field by the roadside at Horsted Keynes whose 'water is of beautiful clearness, charged with oxide of

The delightful rural scene along the straight past Mill Place, just south of Kingscote, as Fairburn Class 4MT 2-6-4T No 42103 takes the 3.35pm Oxted-Brighton in its stride on 27 May 1955. *Denis Cullum*

iron, which so enters largely into the soil'. A waterworks was built on the site and remains today. It was probably on the short level here that the proposed station named Danehill was to be sited (as was the shortlived Holywell Halt in 1962), just north of the Keysford (Caisford) Lane underbridge.

The line now swung north at 1 in 75 under an occupation bridge towards the deep cutting by the Three Arch Bridge, which spanned the cutting like a great gateway, with Nobles Farm and wood to the west and Great Oddynes to the east. The line curved right in a wide arc to cross New Road Bridge and join Railway No 3 at Horsted Keynes. The land in this area was in the hands of six different owners, including the Rt Hon William Brand and Lindfield Parish Council.

The site of Horsted Keynes Junction lay in Leamland Wood and, once past the set of eight railway cottages high up on the bank on the left, the line passed under the brick-built Leamland Bridge, whose track accessed the cottages and, with Cragg Wood on the right, came to the most taxing part of the line for up trains: just under two miles of 1 in 75 all the way to Sharpthorne Tunnel, lifting the line out of the Ouse Valley and into the hills of the Weald. The line wove its way through several sets of gentle reverse curves, first out on a high embankment (originally planned as a viaduct), another spasmodic trouble spot through slippages over the years, then turning north past Horsted House Farm and its access road's stone overbridge, to curve left round Vaux End and enter Northwood Cutting, named after the mansion of that name on the right. The line followed the valley of one of Cockhaise Brook's tributary streams, which it crossed for the last time between Courtlands and Sloe Gardens Wood, just before entering the tunnel and emerging on the level to run into West Hoathly station. Here it passed through the land of Frederick Augustus du Croz of Courtlands, his mansion being half a mile east on the road astride the Sharpthorne ridge and well clear of the railway.

So on to the property of the Trustees of William Stenning, in the area of Old and New Coombe, over a lane joining the two. The 1 in 132 falling gradient continued past Marl Pit Shaw on the left, Neylands Wood on the right lending its name to the cutting, and on a three-furlong curve northwest, round

Birch Farm on an embankment, with its warning boards for a well-used public footpath with excellent approach ramps and cut stairs either side. Outcrops of rock were visible at this point as the line ran through the properties of Messrs Blunt and Henry Longley at Mill Place, first under an occupation bridge and then crossing its small stream at a breathtaking height at this point, to be followed by the shallow Mill Place cutting. A short stretch of level and a brief rise of 1 in 150 towards South Wood and Tickerage on the left led to the embanked site of Kingscote station for Turner's Hill, two miles to the west. A few yards short of the station, at the back of the semi-detached railway cottages, the lane to Ridge Hill Manor to the east was crossed.

Curving away northeast on bridges, first over the Medway and the road to East Grinstead and then over Watery Lane on a long embankment of 29 chains at its tightest, and avoiding Harley Farm on the west side, the line yet again entered a formidable 1 in 75 rise, first in a cutting past Kingscote House and next Hazelden on the east side. The original Hazelden Farm, lying right in the path of the line, was obliterated. Entering a cutting which led under a skew bridge carrying Imberhorne Lane to the Hazelden Crossroads a few yards east, the line now ran through the deep Hill Place Cutting, where in the years either side of 1970 East Grinstead's local council decided to dump the rubbish and waste of the town. The original plans here intended a tunnel 503yd long but it was subsequently decided to open out the terrain as a cutting. Passing under another occupation bridge, accessing Hill Place Farm, the line opened up onto the level stretch that was to take it to the north end of Imberhorne Viaduct, named after the large estate to the west of East Grinstead. The land here belonged to George Norman and the Trustees of the Pearless family. The viaduct negotiated, the gentle grade of 1 in 864 led into the Low Level platforms.

Railway No 2 commenced a few yards beyond the north end of the viaduct. The original plan envisaged the spur line leading into the second station of 1866, to enable direct running to Tunbridge Wells. What was in the event constructed led to the High Level goods yard and the site of the first East Grinstead terminus of 1855, necessitating a reversal of trains to reach the High Level platforms. Near this point stood the long-vanished Copyhold Farm, while most of the land belonged to the Guardians of the East Grinstead Union (Workhouse). The spur line was to rise first at 1 in 100 and then, after crossing a newly constructed bridge over the road connecting Glen Vue Road to the station forecourt, at 1 in 200 to the High Level junction.

Horsted Keynes to Haywards Heath

The line to Haywards Heath ran from the southern slopes of the Wealden ridge, across the Ouse Valley and then up to the high ground beyond the south end of the Ouse Viaduct on the Brighton main line, and had eight bridges, a viaduct and a short tunnel. Railway No 3 left Horsted Keynes on a curve of 32 chains radius, gently falling southwest at 1 in 500 for half a mile to cross a tributary of Cockhaise Brook and New Lane. This was achieved at one stroke by building the 117yd, six-arch Sheriff Mill Viaduct, named after Lower Sheriff Farm 200yd west up the road beside Cockhaise Brook. The line crossed the latter and fell at 1 in 70 to a level which allowed for a possible station at Lywood, the land here belonging to the Stephenson Clarkes of railway coal fame. It then rose at 1 in 132 towards the 216yd Lywood Tunnel. At this point stood the cottage of Anne Williams, an objector whose dwelling stood right in the line's path. Generally the smaller landowners whose homesteads and lands were threatened by the course of the line were the ones to dissent. Occupiers were much more sympathetic! Leaving the tunnel, the grade changed to fall at 1 in 100 through the land of William Dixon, past Great Lywood Farm and under its occupation bridge on a section of light embankment. Soon another bridge led from Bursteye Farm to the south. There was yet another leading to Avins Farm, just a few yards from the overbridge of the road from Ardingly to Lindfield, at the east end of which the platforms of Ardingly station commenced.

The level section through the station continued till the Ouse was crossed, just beyond the limits of the goods yard headshunt. The line then rose at 1 in 70, 109 and 70 again, onto a 32-chain, left-hand curve past the edge of Rivers Farm to the south, with its occupation overbridge close to the path of the abandoned Ouse Valley Railway near New Barn, to gain the main line at Copyhold, 1¼miles north of Haywards Heath, close to Little and Great Naldry (Naldred today) Farm to the west, passing through Mary Bannister's homestead, which was to disappear despite objections.

A Guide to the New Railway

East Grinstead and its Environs — A short History and Guide together with a Series of Routes and a Guide to the New Railway, published by Farncombe & Co, *Observer* Office, East Grinstead, is a notable surviving publication from those early days. No date of publication is shown but it is clear from the text that it was written soon after the line through Oxted to Croydon was completed and the Oxted-Groombridge cut-off line had been started, narrowing the date to 1885-6. The front cover contains an exquisite etching of the new Low Level station, while on the inside back cover William Miller,

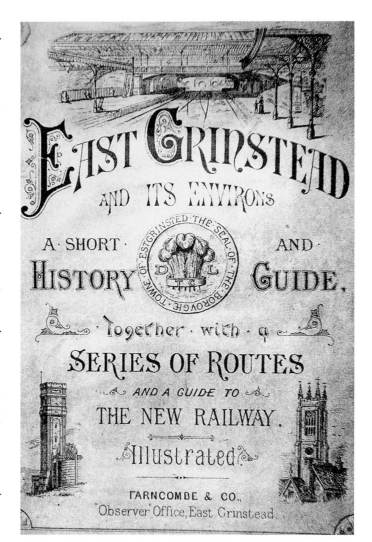

Cover of an 1885 Guide to 'East Grinstead and its Environs' including 'A Guide to the New Railway' [LEGR]. It includes a generously spaced etching of the ornate Low Level station with its intricate ironwork and columns, its valanced canopies, the North signalbox and, above, the High Level platforms. *Bluebell Archives*

proprietor, advertises the Royal Oak Inn, Barcombe ('Near the Railway Station — Lewes & East Grinstead line'). The railway is not described in any detail except scenically, but used as a connecting link between descriptive panegyrics over mansions, churches, villages and plantations. Leaving aside mention of the northern section southwards from Croydon, the guide may be allowed to speak for itself.

'We enter the low level station and here again is a marked improvement in the building of stations. All stations on this part of the line down to Barcombe are built and decorated in the Queen Anne style. They have spacious waiting rooms and offices and lengthy platforms, which in most cases are tastefully adorned with flower beds, rose trees and shrubs . . . East Grinstead is a very commodious and convenient structure, there being high and low level platforms and spacious buildings for the accommodation of both passengers and officials. There are embankments on the outside which, when in full foliage and blossom, present a very showy appearance. The drive up to the entrance is well arranged, a centre clump of plants with lamp forming a useful, and at the same time pleasing, aspect.

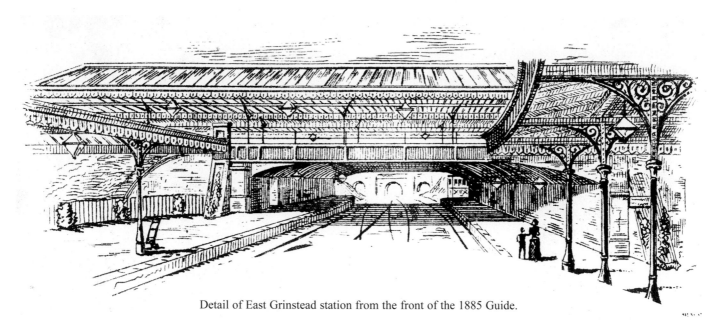

Detail of East Grinstead station from the front of the 1885 Guide.

'Leaving East Grinstead, on our right we get a glimpse of Imberhorne, a large mansion with spacious and pretty grounds. Over a brick built viaduct we come to a cutting of rock of immense thickness. Having glanced at the beautiful scene of a well wooded valley situate on our left, we arrive at Kingscote. There is nothing to particularise in the immediate neighbourhood . . . Our train being again in motion, we get a succession of views of forest, hill, dale and woodland scenery . . . After quitting the railway station at West Hoathly we climb a footpath of rather steep gradient leading to the village . . . We have scarcely resumed our journey before finding ourselves in the tunnel of Sharpthorne.

'Horsted Keynes Junction is one of considerable size for so rural a district . . . Once regaining the station we take a short bye-trip on the loop line and proceed to Ardingly. Having travelled to the 'tether end' of the loop communication between Horsted Keynes and Haywards Heath, we avail ourselves of a return train and again reach Horsted Keynes Junction . . . After passing a plantation of oak, we come to Sheffield Park station. It is well previously to ascertain if there is a cricket match being played on the day selected. As a rule two matches are played each week during a generally extended season.

'Again by aid of the distance-destroying train we proceed further south . . . and after a few minutes' further ride through arable fields, small woods and hop gardens, we arrive at Newick & Chailey station. . . We return, proceeding thither by a road leading through the fields on the platform of the station. There is little to interest us in the journey to Barcombe. The country becomes flat and loses a good deal of its picturesqueness. Hop gardens, pasture fields and woods, with the Downs constantly in view, constitute the elements of attraction.'

The Railway Enthusiast Arrives

We have to wait until 1914 for the first appearance of a brief descriptive account in the railway press of a journey down the line. J. Francis wrote in *The Railway Magazine* in September that year:

'East Grinstead is a somewhat remarkable 'two decker' station. The town is an important one, with a weekly market, local industries and much to interest the visitor. The high level station has two island platforms, and is used by trains between Three Bridges and Tunbridge Wells, as also by trains which use the [St Margaret's] spur, instead of running direct into the lower station. The latter is nearly at right angles, but all the platforms are well connected. There are neat station buildings and refreshment rooms, while in many cases three or four trains are arranged to connect here one with another.

'Proceeding south an interesting viaduct is traversed, followed by a high embankment. Kingscote station is notable for the display of roses in the platform gardens, and at Horsted Keynes one is again in a district remarkable for the beautiful scenery visible from the carriage windows. Here is a four-road, five-platform station, one island used exclusively by Lewes trains, while both can be used by trains towards Haywards Heath. The down Lewes line has platform faces on both sides. The station as a whole is an exceptionally neat and artistic one. To Haywards Heath the branch is only a short one, though it carries a good deal of traffic and is double track. To Lewes the line is single track and passes through very pretty country, as it serves Sheffield Park and Newick & Chailey, before reaching Barcombe station (non-crossing) and joining the Uckfield line at Culver Junction.'

The stopwatch enthusiast also arrived upon the scene, quite remarkably in this relative backwater of a secondary line, where no great speeds could be recorded. J. Pattinson Pearson was an Edwardian railway enthusiast, who in the course of his many travels took in the Lewes-East Grinstead line. His recorded times for his journey the length of the line were unimpressive. He travelled on the 3.24pm train from Lewes behind 'Gladstone' class 0-4-2 No 179 *Sandown* and the 10mile 73ch stretch to Horsted Keynes took 30 minutes against the scheduled 26. The last 6m 26ch north from Horsted Keynes, departing 3.50pm, took 11.3 minutes against the 10 allowed.

However, he was far more impressed with the stations, writing of the 'extremely fine and very tasteful structures at East Grinstead and Horsted Keynes' and concluded: 'Although much praise might unreservedly be awarded to many stations, we think Kingscote, near East Grinstead, with its luxuriant growth of trailing creepers and geraniums, takes pride of place.'

7.
Passenger Train Services

Timetable Services to World War 1

The line opened as a branch line to East Grinstead and the timetable illustrated on page 66, showing five trains each way and three return Sunday trains, was displayed on the opening notice. It was the practice on most railways to show in bold figures 'Shunt' indicating where trains had to cross, as at Lewes or Horsted Keynes. The cessation of the Sunday service in October 1882 has already been noted, being a major point of complaint by the LEGR board to Mr Knight. This was shown in the November timetable, which also showed a newly

introduced goods service from Brighton at 7.15am, with over an hour's shunting time at Lewes and no stop at New Barcombe, arriving at East Grinstead at 11.40am and returning at 2.50pm. It also registered several alterations to the passenger services, such as a long stopover for passengers on the 1.20pm from East Grinstead at Lewes, from 2.21pm to 3.15pm. A Sunday service of just two trains was introduced in May 1883 for the summer season, leaving Brighton at 8.25am and 6.10pm and East Grinstead at 10.35am and 8.15pm.

The opening of the Ardingly link line on 3 September 1883, with a service of three trains each way, augmented to five in November, brought further changes to the evolving timetable, but there was no Sunday service over the branch because of very strong local objections, not overcome until the end of

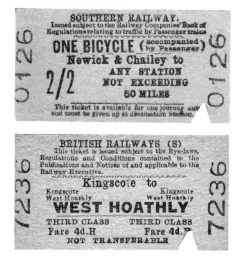

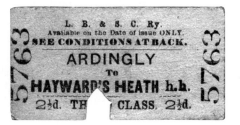

The scene showing the Brighton platforms of Lewes's second station of 1857. In the bay under the train shed stands 'Terrier' No 84 *Crowborough* of Newhaven shed, waiting to depart with a local service to Seaford. On the right is the distinctive chalet-style station building. The date is April 1887, shortly before the third and present station was constructed a short distance to the south, enabling the bay to be turned into a through platform. In the initial timetable all LEGR line services ran through to Brighton but after the new station came into use on 17 June 1889, a number of trains terminated at Lewes. *Alan A. Jackson collection*

1945. At the same time the service to East Grinstead via the single line section was further augmented, providing six trains between Brighton and East Grinstead via Sheffield Park and a 6.55pm working just to Horsted Keynes, returning at 8.20pm. The day started with the 6.5am Brighton-Horsted Keynes via Ardingly, closing with the 9pm from East Grinstead, which reached Brighton via Sheffield Park at 10.17pm.

The opening of the route north through Oxted to London on 10 March 1884 caused a major expansion, to include three Brighton-London through trains via Sheffield Park and a 7.44am Haywards Heath-London Bridge via Ardingly service. 1886 saw considerable fine-tuning to the service, with small alterations of some 2-10 minutes to certain trains, the day now starting with a 6am Brighton-Horsted Keynes via Ardingly and closing with two trains from Brighton, the 7.15pm via Sheffield Park and 7.35pm via Ardingly, which joined at Horsted Keynes to reach London Bridge at 10.12pm. These two services were much too early for a night out on the town and small wonder the people of Newick & Chailey complained. In June 1887 the local paper reported 'The LBSC has responded to the petition by agreeing to add an extra train in the evenings.'

In May 1898 an approach was made to the LBSCR to achieve a better service in the winter, and in November the company agreed to run a late train from Brighton on Thursday nights, terminating at Newick & Chailey at 11.39pm and returning e.c.s. to Brighton. The following March the LBSCR made it known that the late evening train had had a fair trial but was not proving remunerative, 'carrying an average of 11-12 passengers'. The local response was a plea to continue the

late train on Saturdays in winter, to which the company consented in September 1899.

The timetable for 1890, now incorporated into 'Main Lines — Brighton and Eastern District', shows nine daily trains each way via Ardingly and six via Sheffield Park, reduced to five by 1900. By the time the century had turned the line had already seen its best days. The LBSCR directors gave it low priority and the stock which ran was always in want of repair or eking out its last days in this rural backwater. Local inhabitants noted the dirtiest trains were always running over this section and that the services did not really cater for the public, arguments heard again over 50 years later. These complaints may have caught the ears of Earle Marsh, Locomotive Superintendent, and his colleagues, for the line was earmarked for the introduction of his 'Rail Motor' system, using 'A' class 'Terriers' with an outsize 'Balloon' coach. Introduced in October 1905, they appeared on Lewes-East Grinstead line services from June 1906, advertised in the public timetable as 'Motor, Third Class only', and provided an economical means of augmenting the service. The 'Terrier'-hauled balloon coaches were not trailers in the accepted sense of the word, because they had a driver's compartment at the end. There were 17 of these and each coach had 52 seats divided into two sections, one of which accommodated 28 non-smokers. Later a trailer coach was used to strengthen the train. From 1911 purpose-built intermediate trailers were introduced, permanently coupled to the driving trailer.

Photographs of the 'Terrier'-hauled motor trains on the line show just a single balloon coach but, as the 'D1M' tanks took over shortly before the 1923 Grouping, a two-coach motor set

The challenge of the motor car and falling receipts soon after the turn of the century led Earle Marsh, the locomotive superintendent of the LBSCR, to experiment with rail motor services on selected branch lines. Introduced in 1906, three years later motor train services commenced over the southern part of the LEGR line. This view, from which a coloured postcard was made, shows 'Terrier' No 81 (formerly *Beulah*) at that time running as a 2-4-0T, standing with its outsize balloon coach at Newick & Chailey. The stationmaster is William Marshall, who arrived in October 1903 and remained through to the Grouping. *Bluebell Archives*

Fairburn Class 4MT 2-6-4T No 42081 leaves Newick & Chailey on the 8.3am London Bridge to Brighton train on 16 April 1955. *Colin Hogg*

became standard practice. The motor services wove an intricate web on top of the normal pattern of trains. These units were economical, versatile and time saving, involving no run-rounds and ensuring a system of quick reversals. Indeed, such was the flexibility that not only did they fill in on adjacent lines but the locomotives ran several duties of mixed passenger/rail motor turns in the interwar years.

Quite a number of other changes took place in the early years of the century, and not merely fine-tuning, for several trains were axed to be replaced by others. In June 1906 Sunday trains were recast to leave Brighton at 9.3am and 8.35pm, and East Grinstead at 12.15pm and 9pm. The 1913 timetable showed half a dozen services daily, run chiefly for schoolchildren travelling to Lewes and Brighton, and services ran only as far as Newick & Chailey or Sheffield Park. There were now nine trains each way over the single line, and a similar number via Ardingly. The two Sunday trains via Sheffield Park left Brighton at 8.35am and 6.42pm, London

BRIGHTON AND EAST GRINSTEAD
(via Haywards Heath, via Three Bridges, and via Lewes and Sheffield Park).

STATIONS.					WEEK DAYS.															
	a.m.	a.m.	a.m.	¶ a.m.	a.m.	a.m.		a.m.	¶ a.m.	a.m.	a.m.	a.m.	a.m.		p.m.	p.m.	p.m.		p.m.	
BRIGHTON dep.	6 15	6 20	6 30	7 6	7 23	...	7 35	8 55	10 8	...	1030	1130	...	1 20	1 25	1 45	...	...		
London Road "	...	6 24	...	...	...	...	7 38	8 58	...	...	10 33	...	...	1 24	...	...				
Falmer "	...	...	...	...	...	...	...	9 4	...	...	10 41	...	...	1 31	...	...				
LEWES { arr.	...	6 40	...	7 25	...	...	7 53	9 14	...	...	10 51	...	...	1 41	...	...				
{ dep.	...	6 41	...	7 30	...	7 35	8 8	9 22	...	10 54	11 0	...	...	1 43	...	...		Saturdays only.		
Barcombe "	...	6 55	...	7 41	...	...	8 21	9 34	...	...	11 13	...	...	1 55	...	...				
Newick and Chailey "	...	7 4	...	7 48	...	...	8 30	9 41	...	...	11 21	...	...	2 6	...	...				
Sheffield Park "	...	7 10	...	7 54	...	...	8 37	9 46	...	...	11 27	...	...	2 13	...	...				
Preston Park dep.	...	...	6 34	...	7 27	...	...	...	10 12	...	...	11 34	...	...	1 29	...				
Hassocks "	...	...	6 47	...	7 38	...	...	...	10 24	...	...	11 47	...	...	1 41	1 57				
Burgess Hill "	...	...	6 53	...	7 44	...	...	...	10 30	...	...	11 54	...	...	1 47	2 3				
Wivelsfield "	...	...	6 57	...	...	...	...	...	10 34	11 23	...	11 58	...	...	1 51	...				
HAYWARDS HEATH { arr.	6 37	...	7 4	...	7 51	7 56	...	...	10 41	11 30	...	12 5	...	...	1 57	2 11				
{ dep.	6 39	...	7 5	...	8 12	8 20	...	...	10 42	11 31	...	12 7	...	...	1 59	2 13	...	2 25		
Balcombe "	6 48	...	...	...	8 21	...	...	...	10 51	...	...	12 16	...	...	...	...				
Three Bridges { arr.	6 58	...	...	...	8 30	...	...	...	11 0	...	...	12 26	...	...	2 27	...				
{ dep.	7 10	...	...	...	9 0	...	...	...	11 10	...	...	1 3	...	...	2 35	...				
Ardingly dep.	...	...	7 10	...	...	8 26	...	...	...	11 36	...	...	...	2 5	...	2 30				
Horsted Keynes { arr.	...	7 23	7 16	...	...	8 32	8 45	9 55	...	11 42	11 38	...	...	2 24	2 11	...				
{ dep.	...	7 23	7 23	...	...	8 33	8 50	9 57	...	11 44	...	...	...	2 25	2 12	...				
West Hoathly "	...	7 30	7 30	...	...	8 39	8 57	10 4	...	11 51	...	...	...	2 32	2 18	...				
Kingscote "	...	7 37	7 37	...	...	...	9 3	10 9	...	11 57	...	...	...	2 39	2 24	...				
EAST GRINSTEAD arr.	7 28	7 44	7 44	...	9 19	...	9 9	10 15	11 26	...	12 4	1 22	...	2 46	2 31	2 54				
EAST GRINSTEAD dep.	...	7 53	7 53	...	...	...	9 15	9 30	10 27	...	12 12	...	...	2 58	...	...				
East Croydon arr.	...	8 43	8 43	...	...	...	...	10 20	11 10	...	1 1	...	...	4 10	...	...				
LONDON BRIDGE "	...	9 1	9 1	...	...	...	10 7	...	...	...	1 42	...	...	4 32	...	...				
Clapham Junction "	...	9 0	9 0	...	...	...	...	10 39	11 26	...	1 19	...	...	4 27	...	...				
VICTORIA "	...	9 8	9 8	...	...	...	...	10 46	11 34	...	1 26	...	...	4 35	...	...				

¶ Motor, Third Class only.

Passengers are only conveyed between Victoria and Clapham Junction and between London Bridge and New Cross by Local Suburban Trains. For Local Line Time Tables see pages 48 to 99.

This Spread: The last LBSCR timetable of 1922: Brighton and East Grinstead — East Grinstead and Brighton.

BRIGHTON AND EAST GRINSTEAD
(via Haywards Heath, via Three Bridges, and via Lewes and Sheffield Park).

STATIONS.	WEEK DAYS.												SUNDAYS.				
	p.m.	p.m	p.m.	p.m.		p.m.	p.m.	p.m.	p.m.	p.m.	p.m.		a.m.	a.m.	p.m.	p.m.	
BRIGHTON dep.	3 5	3 25	3 57	5 5	...	5 6	5 9	6 5	6 25	7 20	7 45	...	8 30	8 25	6 40	7 35	...
London Road "	...	3 28	...	...	...	5 6	...	...	...	7 23	...	...	...	8 28	6 43	...	...
Falmer "	...	...	...	...	...	5‡13	...	...	...	7 30	...	...	...	8 35	6 50	...	...
LEWES { arr.	...	3 42	...	...	...	5 23	...	...	...	7 40	...	...	...	8 45	7 0	...	...
{ dep.	...	3 55	...	...	...	5 36	...	...	...	7 58	...	...	...	8 46	7 1	...	...
Barcombe "	...	4 6	...	...	...	5 48	...	...	...	8 9	...	...	...	9 0	7 14	...	...
Newick & Chailey "	...	4 13	...	...	...	5 58	...	...	...	8 17	...	...	...	9 10	7 24	...	...
Sheffield Park "	...	4 18	...	...	...	6 8	...	...	...	8 22	...	...	...	9 15	7 33	...	...
Preston Park "	3 9	...	4 1	...	...	...	5 13	...	6 29	...	7 49	...	8 34	...	...	...	...
Hassocks "	3 22	...	4 13	...	...	...	5 24	...	6 42	...	8 0	...	8 47	...	...	...	...
Burgess Hill "	3 28	...	4 19	...	...	...	5 29	...	6 50	...	8 5	...	8 54	...	...	...	...
Wivelsfield "	3 32	...	4 22	...	...	...	5 32	...	6 53	...	8 8	...	8 58	...	...	...	...
HAYWARDS HEATH { arr.	3 39	...	4 28	5 25	...	...	5 38	6 25	6 59	...	8 14	...	9 5	...	7 57	...	...
{ dep.	3 41	...	4 29	5 26	...	...	6 5	6 55	7 2	...	8 22	...	9 8	...	7 58	...	...
Balcombe "	...	...	...	...	...	...	...	...	7 12	...	...	...	9 19	...	...	...	...
Three Bridges { arr.	...	...	4 43	5 41	...	...	...	...	7 23	...	...	...	9 29	...	8 14	...	...
{ dep.	...	...	5 5	5 53	...	...	...	...	7 38	...	...	...	9 34	...	8 35	...	...
Ardingly dep.	3 47	...	...	...	...	...	6 10	7 0	...	...	8 27	...	...	...	...	...	...
Horsted Keynes { arr.	3 53	...	...	...	...	6 19	6 16	7 6	...	8 31	8 34	...	...	9 29	7 44	...	...
{ dep.	...	...	...	...	...	6 23	6 23	...	...	8 36	8 36	...	...	9 32	7 45	...	...
West Hoathly "	...	...	...	...	...	6 30	6 30	...	...	8 42	8 42	...	...	9 40	7 53	...	...
Kingscote "	...	...	...	...	...	6 36	6 36	...	...	8 48	8 48	...	...	9 47	7 59	...	...
EAST GRINSTEAD arr.	...	...	5 24	6 13	...	6 43	6 43	...	7 58	8 55	8 55	...	9 53	9 53	8 5	8 55	...
EAST GRINSTEAD dep.	...	...	...	...	...	7 2	...	...	...	9 15	...	...	10 0	...	8 7	...	...
East Croydon arr.	...	...	...	...	...	7 54	...	...	...	10 3	...	...	10 52	...	9 0	...	...
LONDON BRIDGE "	...	...	...	...	...	8 46	...	...	...	10 25	...	...	11 19	...	9 26	...	...
Clapham Junction "	...	...	...	...	...	8 19	...	...	...	...	...	...	...	...	9 34	...	...
VICTORIA "	...	...	...	...	...	8 27	...	...	...	11 15	...	...	...	...	...	...	...

‡ Does not Call at Falmer on Thursdays.   ¶ Motor, Third Class only.

Passengers are only conveyed between Victoria and Clapham Junction, and between London Bridge and New Cross, by Local Suburban Trains. For Local Line Time Tables see pages 48 to 99.

Bridge at 8.20am and 6.25pm, both pairs of trains crossing at East Grinstead. By the time the LBSCR published its last timetable in 1922, train times had lengthened slightly, having perceptibly slowed during the war years. Apart from very minor alterations, the timetable saw no radical changes until the first closure. The Sheffield Park line saw eight down and nine up workings, and that through Ardingly 10 down and eight up, and an extra one each way on Saturdays.

Mention will be made later of the milk traffic, much of which travelled in the brake compartments of passenger trains. At certain times of the day extra minutes were built into the timetable to allow for the loading of churns — a halt of eight minutes' duration, for instance, being allowed at Sheffield Park on the 5.10pm from Brighton for what 'Curly' Lawrence, a Brighton fireman at the turn of the century, termed 'the milk churn stunt'.

EAST GRINSTEAD AND BRIGHTON
(via Sheffield Park and Lewes, via Three Bridges, and via Haywards Heath).

STATIONS.		WEEK DAYS.														Not Sats.	Sats. only.	p.m.	p.m.
		a.m.	a.m.	a.m.	a.m.	a.m.	a.m.	a.m.	a.m.	a.m.	a.m.	p.m.	a.m.	noon.	p.m.			p.m.	p.m.
VICTORIA ....dep.		...	...	...	...	...	...	7 23	9 10	...	...	...	10 40	12 0	...	...	1 20	1 25	...
Clapham Junction "		...	...	...	...	...	...	7 29	9 17	...	...	...	10 47	12 7	...	...	1 27		...
LONDON BRIDGE "		...	...	...	...	...	...	8 7	9 6	...	...	...	10 35	11 50	...	...	1 38	1 38	
East Croydon "		...	...	...	...	...	...	8 32	9 39	...	...	...	11 6	12 26	...	...	1 58	2 1	
EAST GRINSTEAD arr.		...	...	...	...	...	...	9 24	10 33	...	...	...	11 56	1 20	...	...	2§54	3§0	
EAST GRINSTEAD ...dep.	6 40	...	...	7 57	...	9 36	9 38	10 41	...	...	12 7	12 15	...	1 30		3 03	3 7	
Kingscote "	6 45	...	...	...	...	...	9 43	10 47	...	...		12 21	...	1 35		3 6	3 12	
West Hoathly "	6 51	...	...	...	8 48	...	9 49	10 53	...	...		12 26¶	...	1 40		3 11	3 18	
Horsted Keynes { arr.	6 57	...	...	...	8 53	...	9 55	10 59	...	...		12 32	...	1 45		3 17	3 24	
{ dep.	6 58	...	7 40	...	8 54	...	9 58	11 1	...	11 50		12 32	...	1 46		3 18	3 25	4 10
Ardingly "	...	...	7 46	...	8 59	...	...	11 8	...	11 55			...	2 45		3 23	3 30	4 15
Three Bridges { arr.	...	...	...	8 16	...	9 56	...	...	...		1226	...						
{ dep.	...	...	...	8 45	...	10 5	...	...	...		1247	...						
Balcombe "	...	...	...	8 56	...	10 14	...											
HAYWARDS HEATH { arr.	...	...	7 53	9 5	9 5	10 22	...	11 15		12 1			...	2 50		3 29	3 37	4 22
{ dep.	...	...	8 20	9 7	9 20	10 23	...	11 26	112c	12 4			...	3 11		3 31	4 0	3 44 5 5
Wivelsfield "	...	...	8 26	...	9 25	10 29	...		1126							3 37	4 5	3 50
Burgess Hill "	...	...	8 29	9 15	...	10 32	...	11 32								3 40	4 8	
Hassocks "	...	...	8 36	9 20	...	10 37	...	11 37								3 45	4 14	
Preston Park "	...	...	8 49	9 32	...	10 48	...	11 48		12 22	1 15					3 56	4 25	
Sheffield Park "	7†13	7 59	...	...	...	10 9	...					12 43		1 54				
Newick and Chailey "	7 20	8 4	...	...	10 15	...						12 49		2 3				
Barcombe "	7 30	8 10	...	...	10 23	...						12 57		2 13				
LEWES { arr.	7 43	8 23	...	9 48	...	10 36	...	1150		1 11¶				2 25			4 12	5 25
{ dep.	8 13	8 31	...	...	10 44	...				1 14				2 30				
Falmer "	8 25	8 41	...	...	10 55	...				1 24				2 41				
London Road "	8 32	...	...	11 3	...					1 30				2 48				
BRIGHTON arr.	8 37	8 48	8 54	9 37	...	1053	11 7	11 53		1227	1 20		1 34	2 52	3 30		4 1	4 30

§ Rail Motor as between Oxted and East Grinstead.   ¶ Motor, Third class only.   † Arrives Sheffield Park 7.8 a.m.

Passengers are only conveyed between Victoria and Clapham Junction and between London Bridge and New Cross by Local Suburban Trains.   For Local Line Time Table see pages 48 to 99.

EAST GRINSTEAD AND BRIGHTON
(via Sheffield Park and Lewes, via Three Bridges, and via Haywards Heath).

STATIONS.		WEEK DAYS.									Not Sats.	Sats. only.			SUNDAYS.			
		p.m.	p.m.	p.m.	p.m.	p.m.	p.m.	p.m.	p.m.	p.m.			p.m.	p.m.	a.m.	a.m.	p.m.	p.m.
VICTORIA ....dep.		...	...	4 0	...	...	...	...	...	5 48	6 50	7 15	...	...	8 10	...	6 33	
Clapham Junction "		...	...	4 8	...	...	...	...	5 12		6 57	7 22	...	...	8 18	...	6 40	
LONDON BRIDGE "		...	...	4 10	...	...	...	...	5s41		7 0	7 38	...	...	8 30	...	6 46	
East Croydon "		...	...	4 30	...	...	...	...	6†7		7 21	8 0	...	...	8 57	...	7 12	
EAST GRINSTEAD arr.		...	...	5 21	...	...	...	...	6 56		8 10	8 51	...	...	9 46	...	8 5	
EAST GRINSTEAD ...dep.		4 10	5 34	...	...	...	6 52	...	7 6	8 20	9 5	9 5	...	7 52	10 0	6 22	8 15	
Kingscote "		...	5 40	...	...	...	...		7 12	8 25	9 10		...	10 6		8 21		
West Hoathly "		...	5 46	...	...	...	...		7 18	8 31	9 16		...	10 12		8 27		
Horsted Keynes { arr.		...	5 51	...	...	...	...		7 24	8 37	9 22		...	10 18		8 33		
{ dep.		...	5 52	6 35	...	...	...	7 18	7 25	8 50	8 50	9 23	...	10 19		8 34		
Ardingly ....dep.		...	...	6 40	...	...	...	7 23		8 57	8 57	9 20						
Three Bridges { arr.		...	4 28	...	...	...	7 10	...	...				9 23	8 11		6 41		
{ dep.		...	4 53	...	...	...	7 26	...	...				10 12	8 27		7 18		
Balcombe "		...	5 0	...	...	...	7 36	...	...				8 37		7 25			
HAYWARDS HEATH { arr.		...	5 8	...	6 47	...	7 44	7 30	...	9 3	9 3	9 37	10 25	8 45		7 36		
{ dep.		...	5 23	...	...	6 51	7 4	7 45	7 45	9 4	9 4	...	10 26	10 35	8 46		7 37	
Wivelsfield "		...	...	...	...		7 45	7 51	7 51	9 10	9 10		10 40	8 52		7 43		
Burgess Hill "		...	5 30	...	...		7 9	7 55	7 55	9 14	9 14		10 43	8 57		7 48		
Hassocks "		...	5 36	...	...		7 16	8 1	8 1	9 20	9 20		10 49	9 4		7 55		
Preston Park "		¶	5 47	...	...		7 27	8 13	8 13	9 33	9 33		11 0	9 17		8 6		
Sheffield Park "	4 28	6 §9	...	...				7 36	...	...			10 29		8 45			
Newick and Chailey "	4 33	6 18	...	...				7 42	...	...			10 35		8 50			
Barcombe "	4 41	6 27	...	...				7 50	...	...			10 43		8 58			
LEWES { arr.	4 53	6 39	...	7 10				8 2	...	...			10 55		9 10			
{ dep.	5 3	6 45	...	...				8 7	...	...			10 57		9 18			
Falmer "	5 13	...	...										11 9		9 31			
London Road "	5 19	7 0	...					8 22	...	...			11 16		9 36			
BRIGHTON arr.	5 23	5 52	7 4	...		7 32	8 18	8 18	8 27	9 38	9 38		1047	11 5	9 22	11 21	8 13	9 42

s On Saturdays leave London Bridge 5.21 p.m.   § Arrives Sheffield Park 6.2 p.m.   † Calls to take up passengers

Train Services in the Interwar Period

This section relies heavily on Dick Kirkby's detailed notes of train workings over the line from 1919-39, of which the following paragraphs are an abstract, commencing with the down passenger services.

6.40am East Grinstead-Lewes

This train had been in the timetable since the line opened, although the departure time had varied by up to 25 minutes. In the opening years it was worked by the East Grinstead-based 'D' Tank No 233 *Handcross*. In about 1887 the working was transferred to Three Bridges. At first the engine ran light but by the 1890s it first worked the morning goods from Three Bridges to East Grinstead. From July 1925 until 1927 it was worked by a Redhill engine, possibly a 'C' or 'O1'

The only known photograph taken from this viewpoint, showing 'E5' 0-6-2T No 32399 climbing up to the Brighton main line (seen in the background), towards Copyhold Jct with the 8.52am West Hoathly to Haywards Heath train on 14 April 1952. *David Duncan*

class 0-6-0. After reversion to Three Bridges, a 'C2' was usually turned out and the late J. Truss recorded Nos B527 and B531 many times on this working in 1928-9. From January 1933 the train was extended from Lewes to Brighton and the locomotive ceased to work the 8.10am from Lewes. Prior to July 1925 and after January 1933 an 'E4' or 'E5' radial tank was the normal motive power for this train.

7.59am Sheffield Park-Brighton (Rail Motor)
Apart from a few minutes' variation in the departure time, this train remained unchanged throughout the period and was worked by a Brighton 'D1M'. The stop at London Road was deleted in May 1920 and restored in July 1931.

8.7am London Bridge-Lewes
This service also dated from the 1880s. For many years, after arrival at Lewes it continued on to Horsted Keynes via Haywards Heath, returning via Haywards Heath to Brighton. This working ceased on 14 May 1924, after which the train terminated at Lewes, continuing on to Brighton on Wednesdays only. During the summer timetables of 1925 and 1926 it ran on to Brighton daily. From 10 July 1927 it was diverted from Horsted Keynes to Brighton via Haywards Heath, and ceased to call at Kingscote and West Hoathly, a very rare case of an LEGR line train being timetabled to omit intermediate stops. These stations and the Sheffield Park line were served by a new rail motor working, which left East Grinstead at 10.15am. In the following summer timetable dated 17 June 1928, the new rail motor started from Horsted Keynes, and the stops at Kingscote and West Hoathly by the London Bridge train were restored. The next change was at the start of 1933 when, as a result of the electrification to Brighton, the train reverted to the Sheffield Park route and so remained well into the BR era.

8.18am East Grinstead to Haywards Heath
During the life of the LBSCR there was until October 1922, no southbound train from East Grinstead between the 6.40am departure and the 8.7am from London Bridge at around 9.30am. In the last LBSCR timetable, dated 22 October 1922, however, the 6.45am Victoria to Tunbridge Wells via

Lingfield was diverted to Brighton via Ardingly, leaving East Grinstead at 8.20am. This arrangement lasted only one year and in the first SR timetable, dated 9 July 1923, the 6.45am reverted to its original route via East Grinstead High Level to Tunbridge Wells and a new train left East Grinstead for Brighton via Haywards Heath at 8.18am. From 1 January 1933 this new train terminated at Haywards Heath, then from 7 July 1935 it terminated at Horsted Keynes, returning to West Hoathly to form the 8.51am thence to Haywards Heath.

The 6.45am from Victoria was a Battersea turn but the 8.18am from East Grinstead was worked by a Brighton locomotive, generally a radial tank, except from July 1925 to July 1926 when it was hauled by a Tunbridge Wells engine, which worked over light. From 7 July 1935 it was worked by a Three Bridges radial in winter and a Brighton radial in summer.

8.45am West Hoathly to Haywards Heath
This service first appeared in the early 1900s and was formed by the 8.20am Haywards Heath-West Hoathly. On arrival at Haywards Heath it ran into the down bay platform, to connect with the 7.25am London Bridge-Brighton, later continuing on to Lewes and Seaford. The departure time varied over the years from 8.45am to 8.53am. From 1 January 1933 until 7 July 1935 it was worked by an Eastbourne rail motor but, as stated above, it was then formed by the 8.39am ex-Horsted Keynes.

10.12am Oxted to Brighton via Haywards Heath
Originally worked by a Tunbridge Wells 'D' tank and a three-set, this became part of a new Brighton rail motor working (see 6.45am Haywards Heath-Oxted) from 2 October 1922. From 14 July 1924 it was retimed to leave at 10.3am and connected at Haywards Heath with the 10.5am Victoria-Brighton express. From 1 January 1933 it was diverted to run from Haywards Heath to Seaford and from 7 July 1935 it was again diverted, this time to Lewes via Sheffield Park.

10.15am East Grinstead to Lewes (Rail Motor)
This train was relatively short lived. Introduced on 10 July 1927 when the 8.7am from London Bridge was diverted via

Coasting down towards Barcombe on 30 June 1950 is the 12.3pm Victoria-Brighton with 'U1' 2-6-0 No 31892 in charge of a rake of four Maunsell coaches supplemented by a van just behind the engine. *Pamlin Prints*

Ardingly, it started from Horsted Keynes at 10.5am. A year later on 1 January 1933, when the 8.7am reverted to the Sheffield Park route, it in its turn was diverted to Lewes via Haywards Heath. It ceased with electrification on 7 July 1935. Throughout its eight years of existence it was worked by a 'D1M' based at Newhaven.

12 noon Victoria to Brighton via Sheffield Park

Prior to the turn of the century this train started from London Bridge but for most years it had started from Victoria at times varying between 11.55am and 12.5pm. From 1914 to 1923 it terminated at Lewes, while on Mondays to Fridays during the period of engineering work in Limpsfield Tunnel it terminated at Woldingham and started up again at Oxted at 1pm. Its locomotive working has varied. Prior to World War 1 it was worked by an 'I3' based at Brighton, first going up the main line with the 9.45am Brighton-Victoria express. After the war it remained a Brighton turn, more often a 'B2X' or an 'I1'. From 10 July 1927 it became a St Leonards turn, worked off the 8.25am Hastings-Victoria, and so it remained for the next eight years. Initially St Leonards used a 'B2X' and as they were scrapped, and particularly after Hastings and St Leonards sheds were combined, an ex-SECR 'F1' was the more usual motive power. From 7 July 1935 it became a

Brighton working again, this time usually a 'B4', until July 1938 when it became a Stewarts Lane diagram, invariably an ex-SECR locomotive, either 'B1', 'D1' or 'E1'.

12.15pm East Grinstead to Brighton via Sheffield Park (Rail Motor)

This train was one of the earliest rail motor workings, introduced in the years just after the turn of the century and remaining unchanged until World War 2, when it was withdrawn. Working up from Brighton to East Grinstead around 9am, it transferred to the High Level station via the single-line connecting spur and ran to Three Bridges and back before returning from East Grinstead Low Level at times varying between 12.7pm and 12.15pm. It was always a Brighton working and during the period of this survey up to 1938, a 'D1M'. After 1938 a motor-fitted 'D3' made occasional appearances.

3pm East Grinstead to Haywards Heath

The departure time of this train varied between 3pm and 3.7pm. Formed of a 3-set (see 1.25pm ex-Brighton) it remained unchanged until 7 July 1935, when it was diverted to Lewes via Sheffield Park. Immediately after World War 1 it was worked by a St Leonards 'D1' but from 1921 until 1935

The 3.35pm, headed by BR Standard Class 4 No 80016 in mint condition, having recently emerged from construction at Brighton Works, and seen here on 24 September 1951 on the straight stretch south of Cinder Hill Tunnel. *S. C. Nash*

After the lifting of weight restrictions in 1943, the famous Brighton Atlantics put in regular appearances on the line. The doyen and last survivor of the class, 'H2' No 32424 *Beachy Head* rolls into Horsted Keynes with the Saturdays-only 4.18pm service from London Bridge to Brighton on 26 July 1952. *Colin Saunders*

The 4.20pm London Bridge-Brighton, behind 2-6-4T No 42104, heads down from Imberhorne Cutting towards Kingscote on 23 May 1955. *John Head*

it became a Brighton working, first a 'D1' and later a radial tank, while from July 1935 until 1939 it was worked by a Three Bridges 'E4' or 'E5'.

4.35pm Sheffield Park to Brighton (Rail Motor)
This was a Brighton rail motor working and was withdrawn from 2 October 1922, when its path was taken by the 3.33pm ex-Oxted (see below). In February 1921 it was retimed at 4.28pm.

3.33pm Oxted to Brighton via Sheffield Park
Introduced from 2 October 1922 as part of the extension of rail motor working based on Brighton, it was retimed in July 1923 to leave Oxted at 3.36pm. From 8 July 1934 it ceased to be a rail motor working and was worked by a 'D3' or 'E4' based at Tunbridge Wells West. From 4 July 1937, however, it was restored as a Brighton rail motor working, although in the 1930s it was not uncommon for a rail motor set to be hauled, particularly on this working, by a non-motor-fitted

locomotive. In these circumstances a variety of locomotives appeared on this train.

4.10pm London Bridge to Brighton via Sheffield Park
One of the longer-established services in the timetable, its departure time varied between 4.8pm and 4.20pm and it usually left London Bridge at a slightly later time on Saturdays. During part of the period of engineering work in Limpsfield Tunnel (20 May 1920 to 2 February 1921) this train terminated at Woldingham on Saturdays and restarted from Oxted at 5.3pm. This train was a Brighton working from World War 1 until September 1926, when it became a New Cross turn, returning with the 8.50pm stopper up the main line. During this period a great variety of locomotive classes appeared on this train. From 6 July 1930 it became a Brighton working again on Mondays to Fridays but remained a New Cross Gate turn on Saturdays. Then in January 1933 New Cross Gate again took over the Monday to Friday working while a Three Bridges engine worked it on Saturdays,

returning light from Brighton to Three Bridges shed up the main line. From 7 July 1935 it again reverted to being a Brighton turn, usually a 'B4' but an 'I1X' would sometimes be used. When New Cross Gate had the working, ex-LBSCR engines were the norm but ex-SECR 'B1s' and 'F1s' made occasional appearances.

7.7pm East Grinstead to Lewes

This train was formed by the 5.5pm Victoria to East Grinstead, which sat in the down Low Level platform from 6.39pm to times varying between 7.7pm and 7.16pm. In 1921 the stock was half a divisible suburban six-wheeled set, which remained overnight at Lewes and next morning worked the 7.45am Lewes to Brighton, returning to suburban work via Horsham and Sutton. In 1922/3 this suburban set was replaced by Set No 73, formed of two bogie third brakes at either end of a bogie composite and a bogie lavatory composite, which was based at Lewes. Its day started on the 8.8am from Lewes to London Bridge via Sheffield Park.

At East Grinstead Low Level this train passed the 5.6pm Brighton to Victoria and by an intricate shunting move the two trains changed locomotives. A Battersea engine worked from Victoria to East Grinstead and back, while a Brighton engine worked from Brighton to East Grinstead and back. The 7.7pm from East Grinstead remained a Brighton turn until the winter of 1927/8, when it became a Newhaven turn, remaining so until January 1933, when once again it became a Brighton working. Following electrification to Eastbourne and the East Coast lines from 7 July 1935, the practice of changing engines at East Grinstead ceased. The 7.7pm was then formed by the locomotive and stock of the 5.40pm ex-London Bridge on Mondays to Fridays and the 5.10 ex-Victoria on Saturdays, both Brighton 'B4' workings.

7.23pm Sheffield Park to Lewes (Rail Motor)

This train was first introduced from 6 July 1930. Originally an Eastbourne 'D1M' working, it became a Brighton rail motor working from 7 July 1935. Formed by the 6.52pm motor ex-Lewes, it continued to run after the outbreak of World War 2.

7.22pm SX East Croydon to Horsted Keynes (later 6.50pm ex-Victoria)

Introduced on 2 February 1921, this train was worked by a West Croydon locomotive and ran empty from East Grinstead to Horsted Keynes, where the stock was attached to the 8.50pm Horsted Keynes to Brighton via Haywards Heath and the locomotive returned light to West Croydon. From August 1921 it ran as a passenger train between East Grinstead and Horsted Keynes. With the termination of engineering work in Limpsfield Tunnel from 1 December 1921, the train started from Victoria at 6.50pm, worked by a Brighton locomotive which ran light from Horsted Keynes to Brighton — which route was not specified. From 9 July 1923 this train was worked by a Three Bridges engine and the stock was returned empty from Horsted Keynes to East Grinstead, except on Wednesdays when it carried on as a passenger train to Lewes via Sheffield Park. From the same date the Saturday 6.50pm ex-Victoria, which previously terminated at Oxted, was also extended to Lewes via Sheffield Park and likewise worked by a Three Bridges engine, which ran light from Lewes to Three Bridges. From 12 July 1925 engine and stock returned with the 9.30pm WSO Lewes to East Grinstead. From 10 July 1927 the train did not run beyond East Grinstead except on Wednesdays and Saturdays and the 9.15pm NWS empty stock train from Horsted Keynes to East Grinstead was withdrawn. From 3 July 1938, however, the train ran through to Lewes

daily during the summer service and Wednesdays and Saturdays only during the winter service.

8.55pm Horsted Keynes to Brighton via Sheffield Park (Rail Motor)

This train was the back working of the 8.5pm Lewes to Horsted Keynes. Prior to 7 July 1935 it returned to Brighton via Haywards Heath but from that date it ran via Sheffield Park and was worked by a Brighton 'D1M' (Duty No 735). From 5 July 1936 it terminated at Lewes, running on to Brighton later.

9.5pm East Grinstead to Haywards Heath

This train was an extension of the 7.38pm London Bridge to East Grinstead and ran on Saturdays only until 9 July 1923, from when it ran daily. Up to August 1921 it terminated at Horsted Keynes. It was worked by a Three Bridges locomotive. After July 1923 it became a Brighton turn and remained so until September 1925, when it became a New Cross working, the locomotive returning up the main line with the up mail from Brighton. Both Brighton and New Cross Gate used a great variety of locomotive types — 'B1', 'B2X', 'B4', 'C2X', 'E5', 'H1', 'I1', 'I3' & 'I4' classes have all been recorded, together with occasional 'F1s'. From 17 June 1928 Eastbourne shed took over the working, the locomotive generally continuing on to Eastbourne, either with the Eastbourne portion of the 10.5pm Victoria to Brighton, or sometimes going through to Brighton, returning with a local to Haywards Heath to work the Eastbourne/Hastings section of the down mail (10.35pm ex-London Bridge). Except for a short period in the latter half of 1932, it remained an Eastbourne working until 7 July 1935, when Three Bridges took over. It remained a Three Bridges duty until the war. Eastbourne put out 'B4Xs', 'Us' or 'U1s' for this train until 1933, when 'J' or 'L' class tanks became the norm. Three Bridges used mostly 'E5s' or 'I1Xs' and occasionally a 'Vulcan' 0-6-0.

Up Passenger Services

6.20am Brighton to London Bridge via Sheffield Park

Introduced well before World War 1, this service remained a through train to London until July 1923 The newly formed Southern Railway, in a fit of enthusiasm for amalgamation, then introduced a new train worked by a Tonbridge engine and men, which left Tonbridge at 6.59am and ran via Tunbridge Wells, Forest Row, Lingfield and East Croydon to Cannon Street. From East Grinstead it took up the path of the Brighton train, which then terminated at East Grinstead, the stock forming a new train from East Grinstead to Haywards Heath at 8.15am. This latter arrangement lasted for 12 years until 7 July 1935, when once again the 6.22am ex-Brighton, as it then was, was extended through to London Bridge. Always a Brighton turn, in 1914 the locomotive, after arrival at London Bridge, ran light to Victoria to work the down 'Southern Belle' at 11am. From 1923 to 1935, except for a short period in 1925/6, the locomotive returned with the stock at 8.15am. During that short period, on arrival at East Grinstead at 7.44am, it ran smartly back light engine to Haywards Heath to work the 8.22am to West Hoathly. The only record of this train during the 12 years indicates it was worked by a 'D3'. After 1935 it was generally a 'B4'.

6.45am Haywards Heath to Oxted (Rail Motor)

Introduced from 2 October 1922, the motor set for this train was berthed overnight at Haywards Heath, having previously worked the 10.20pm Brighton to Haywards Heath. The locomotive, a Brighton 'D1M', worked up with a three-set on the 5.50am ex-Brighton and then continued on with the rail motor working. On arrival at Oxted a trip was run to Tunbridge Wells and back, before returning with the 10.12am (later 10.3am) from Oxted — see under down passenger services. After electrification to Brighton in January 1933, the locomotive and stock ran empty from Brighton to Haywards Heath at 6.1am. The working was discontinued at the outbreak of World War 2.

7.30am Lewes to Sheffield Park (Rail Motor)
A Brighton rail motor working, which originally worked first to Seaford and back to Lewes. From 1 December 1921 it started back from Brighton at 7.6am. After this date, apart from some variation in the departure time between 7.6am and 7.10am, it remained unchanged.

8.8am Lewes to London Bridge via Sheffield Park
This train was due at London Bridge around 10.40am, having sat in the Low Level up platform at East Grinstead for some 20 minutes. By changing at East Grinstead passengers could pick up the 8.30am from Tunbridge Wells West, which, for a number of years, ran non-stop from Lingfield to London Bridge, arriving at 10.8am. This connection was severed from 1 January 1933, when departure from Lewes was put back to 8.16am, then 8.21am. For one year, July 1935 to July 1936, the train started from Brighton at 7.53am then reverted to its 8.21am departure from Lewes. Until 1 January 1933 this train was worked by the locomotive off the 6.40am from East Grinstead to Lewes, for most of the time a Three Bridges working, except for two years as a Redhill working (see 6.40am ex-East Grinstead down). From January 1933 it became a New Cross Gate working, off the 4.5am vans London Bridge to Lewes. In due course this train was terminated at Three Bridges and the 8.21am ex-Lewes reverted to a Brighton working, usually a 'B4' or 'I1X'.

8.20 am Haywards Heath to West Hoathly
This train had been in the timetables since the early 1900s and was worked by a Brighton local passenger engine. Apart from the departure time varying between 8.17am and 8.22am, it remained unchanged until electrification to Brighton on 1 January 1933, when it was worked by an Eastbourne 'D1M' and rail motor off the 6.15am Eastbourne to Haywards Heath. Following electrification to Eastbourne on 7 July 1935, this train started from Horsted Keynes at 8.39am, formed by the 8.15am East Grinstead to Horsted Keynes, a Brighton working in summer but Three Bridges in winter.

8.55am Brighton to East Grinstead via Sheffield Park (Rail Motor)
One of the earliest Brighton-based rail motor workings, this train remained almost unaltered until withdrawn on the outbreak of World War 2. Its previous working was 7.59am Sheffield Park to Brighton and in some timetables the turnround at the latter point was as short as three minutes. On arrival at East Grinstead it ran a trip to Three Bridges and back, returning from East Grinstead at 12.15pm. From 4 July 1937 it made a third sortie up the Sheffield Park line with the 1.20pm Brighton to Oxted and return.

8.46am Seaford to East Grinstead via Haywards Heath (Rail Motor)
This train, which for many years had run between Seaford and Haywards Heath, was from 10 July 1927 extended through to East Grinstead, calling only at Ardingly and Horsted Keynes. This was an arrangement which lasted less than one year and

from 17 June 1928 it terminated at Horsted Keynes to form the 10.5am thence to Brighton via Sheffield Park.

10.30am Brighton to Victoria via Sheffield Park
Another service dating from the 1880s. During the period of engineering work in Limpsfield Tunnel (May 1920 to December 1921), this service terminated at Oxted and restarted up from Woldingham, except on Saturdays when it went through on the single line. Otherwise the train ran unchanged through the whole of the period of this review, except for some minor variation in the departure time, between 10.30am and 10.48am. Just prior to World War 1 this train was a Brighton Atlantic turn, the locomotive subsequently working the 5.20pm from Victoria to Eastbourne and back to Brighton. It remained a Brighton turn after the war, usually returning with the 3.45pm ex-Victoria via Eridge, until April 1925 when it became a New Cross turn. The full working was:

7.20am	London Bridge to Brighton via main line
10.35am	Brighton to Victoria via Sheffield Park
3.45pm	Victoria to Brighton via Eridge
8.50pm	Brighton to London Bridge via main line

From 1 January 1933 to 7 July 1935 it reverted to a Brighton turn. After that, although worked by a Brighton 'B4' on Saturdays, from Mondays to Fridays it was worked as far as East Grinstead by a Three Bridges radial tank off the 6.40am ex-East Grinstead. On arrival at East Grinstead this engine ran light to Upper Warlingham to work the local goods to Oxted, serving the Lime Siding, and was replaced by a Norwood 'E5' which had worked the 10am goods from Three Bridges to East Grinstead.

1.20pm Brighton to Oxted via Sheffield Park
In LBSCR timetables up to October 1922, a few weeks before amalgamation, this train usually returned from Oxted to East Grinstead and formed the 4.8pm thence to London Bridge. Usually a 'B1' or a 4-4-2T, the locomotive returned with the 7.20pm London Bridge to Brighton via the main line. From October 1922 it became a Brighton rail motor working and returned with a new service, the 3.33pm Oxted to Brighton via Sheffield Park (see 4.35pm Sheffield Park to Brighton). Apart from three years from July 1934 to July 1937, when the train was worked by a Tunbridge Wells West engine ('D3', 'D3X' or 'I1X'), it remained a Brighton rail motor working until withdrawn at the outbreak of World War 2.

1.25pm Brighton to East Grinstead via Haywards Heath
Altered in July 1924 to start from Haywards Heath at 1.48pm, this train remained at about that time except for a six-month period from January to July 1933, when it left at 2.12pm and ceased to call at West Hoathly or Kingscote. These stops were restored when the departure time reverted to 1.45pm. Originally a St Leonards turn, it became a Brighton working in 1921 and remained so until 7 July 1935, when it became a Three Bridges radial turn, worked (except on Saturdays) off the 12.13pm vans Newhaven to Haywards Heath.

3.7pm Brighton to London Bridge via Ardingly
Introduced in the last LBSCR timetable of October 1922, this train had previously run only as far as Horsted Keynes and was extended through to take up the working of the 4.8pm East Grinstead to London Bridge (See 1.20pm Brighton to Oxted via Sheffield Park). From July 1924 it started from Haywards Heath at around 3.48pm. From October 1922 to

In the early BR period Stewarts Lane Depot was the regular provider of 'U1' 2-6-0s, one of which, No 31900, in charge of the 11.2am Brighton-Victoria, approaches the three-arch road bridge by Lane End Common on 16 April 1955. The train is formed of Bulleid three-set 799 and an added Maunsell corridor coach at the rear.
S. C. Nash

July 1924 it was a Brighton turn, returning down the main line with the 7.20pm ex-London Bridge. From the latter date it became an Eastbourne main line turn, starting out with the 1.30pm Eastbourne to Haywards Heath stopping service and finishing with the 7pm London Bridge to Eastbourne express. From June 1928 it returned with the 7.38pm London Bridge to Haywards Heath via East Grinstead. (See 9.5pm East Grinstead to Haywards Heath.) From July 1935 it became a Three Bridges duty and remained so until July 1937, when it became a New Cross Gate job Mondays to Fridays and Three Bridges on Saturdays. From 1 January 1938 it became a New Cross turn daily. From Brighton shed 'B1', 'B2X', 'C2X', 'E5' & 'I3' classes were noted. Eastbourne shed used 'B4X', 'I3', 'U' and 'River' classes until January 1933, when 'J' or 'L' tanks were more usual. Three Bridges used 'E5s' or 'I1Xs', while New Cross Gate used 'B4X,' 'H1' and ex-SECR 'B1' & 'E' classes, and an occasional 'I3'. Both Three Bridges and New Cross Gate occasionally provided a 'K' class Mogul, particularly on a Saturday.

3.55pm Lewes to Sheffield Park (rail motor)
The return working of this service was the 4.35pm ex-Sheffield Park. When in October 1922 this last service was altered (see under down trains), the 3.55pm ex-Lewes was

retimed to 4.5pm and extended to Horsted Keynes, returning to Brighton via Haywards Heath. From July 1932 it started from Brighton at 3.44pm, until 7 July 1935 when it again started from Lewes, this time at 4.7pm, formed of the three-set off the 3pm ex-East Grinstead instead of a rail motor.

Originally a Brighton rail motor, it was worked from Eastbourne from July 1924 to July 1925, from when it again became a Brighton working. From July 1930 Eastbourne took over once more, until July 1932, from when it is thought Tunbridge Wells West worked it until 1 January 1933. Brighton then took over again. From July 1935, when rail motor working ceased, it was worked by a Three Bridges 'E4' or 'E5'.

5.6pm Brighton to Victoria via Sheffield Park
The departure time of this train became 5.15pm from October 1922 and from then on varied by only a minute or two, except for the summer of 1925 when it left at 4.55pm and spent 20 minutes at Lewes. At East Grinstead the train was booked from 6.43pm to 7.10pm and even with a 5.15pm departure it was a very slow train, taking over three hours to reach Victoria. During the early part of the engineering work in Limpsfield Tunnel (May 1920 to February 1921) the train terminated at Oxted on Saturdays and started up again at

The 2.58pm Brighton-London Bridge has Bricklayers Arms 'N' 2-6-0 No 31824 at its head as it passes by Mill Place on its way to Kingscote.
S. C. Nash

Woldingham. Until July 1925 it was worked as far as East Grinstead by a Brighton engine but from then until the end of 1932 it became a Newhaven turn, reverting to Brighton on 1 January 1933. In July 1935 it became a New Cross Gate turn, working throughout from Brighton to Victoria, and was usually worked by an ex-SECR 'B1' or 'E' class 4-4-0. Finally from July 1938 it became part of Stewarts Lane Duty 503, which worked down with the 12 noon from Victoria and was usually an ex-SECR 'D1' or 'E1' 4-4-0.

6.35pm Brighton to Sheffield Park (Rail Motor)

First introduced on 6 July 1930, this train was worked by an Eastbourne 'D1M' and rail motor set. From 7 July 1935 it started from Lewes at 6.52pm and became a Brighton 'D1M' job.

7.45pm Brighton to London Bridge via Ardingly

This train was shunted at Haywards Heath from 8.14pm to 8.28pm and waited at East Grinstead from 8.56pm to 9.20pm so, like the 5.6pm, it took nearly three hours to reach London Bridge at around 10.40pm. During the engineering work in Limpsfield Tunnel it terminated at Oxted at 9.57pm, ran round its train and returned to East Grinstead High Level, where another run round enabled it to reach London Bridge via Three Bridges and East Croydon. On Mondays to Fridays in summer only, commencing in July 1925, it started from Brighton at 8pm and ran non-stop to Haywards Heath. From 1 January 1933 as a result of electrification to Brighton, it started from Haywards Heath at 8.35pm and the waiting time was reduced to 13 minutes. Apart from a short period in 1935, after electrification to Eastbourne, when a Three Bridges engine

Left: Marsh's rebuilt 'I1X' 4-4-2Ts were seen on occasions in the interwar period. No 2002, still in late SR livery, was the ultimate survivor and is leaving Barcombe on the 4.3pm Lewes-Horsted Keynes on 14 May 1951. It made regular appearances that spring on the 1.20pm Brighton-Oxted, before succumbing three months later on 12 August. *J. J. Smith*

Below: The 8.36am (Sun) London Bridge-Brighton crosses Every's Bridge on the approach to Lewes on 9 August 1953. John Every & Sons was the local firm of iron founders, whose workmanship was to be seen all over the line, from girder bridges to station fitments. Ivatt 2-6-2T No 41307 hauls an unusual formation consisting of two three-coach sets of pre-Grouping stock. *S. C. Nash*

worked the train from Haywards Heath to East Grinstead where engines were changed, a New Cross Gate locomotive worked throughout. A great variety of locomotive types have been recorded on this train, varying from 'C2Xs' and 'E4s' to Atlantics and 'K' class Moguls.

7.58pm Lewes to Horsted Keynes via Sheffield Park (Rail Motor)

Although the departure time varied between 7.58pm and 8.5pm, and it became a rail motor working from 2 October 1922, this service remained otherwise unchanged throughout the period of this survey. Its purpose was to connect at Horsted Keynes into the service mentioned above. For many years a Newhaven 'D1' working, it became an Eastbourne turn from 1 January 1933 and a Brighton working from 7 July 1935.

9.10pm WSO Lewes to East Grinstead via Sheffield Park

Introduced by the Southern Railway in July 1923, this was one of a pair of late trains between these two points, running on Wednesdays and Saturdays only. The down train passed the up one between Lewes and Culver Junction. Both were worked by Three Bridges engines. From July 1925 the up train was put back to 9.30pm, so that it could be worked by the engine and coaches of the down train. Although this resulted in keeping the signalboxes open another 20 minutes, it also afforded a later connection from Brighton, leaving at 9.5pm. It was further retimed to 9.37pm from July 1932 and 9.43pm from July 1935. From July 1938 it ran daily during the summer timetable period.

Sunday Services

Down 8.30am London Bridge to Brighton via Sheffield Park
6.42pm London Bridge to Brighton via Sheffield Park

Up 8.25am Brighton to London Bridge via Sheffield Park
6.40pm Brighton to London Bridge via Sheffield Park

These four trains comprised the booked Sunday service throughout the whole period from 1919 to 1939. The only change was in the morning up train from Brighton, which from 17 June 1928 was diverted to Victoria. Equally there was little change in the locomotive working. A New Cross Gate locomotive worked the 8.30am down and 6.40pm up and until 1 January 1933 was used on various local services around Brighton during the middle of the day. Another New Cross Gate locomotive worked the 6.42pm down and returned via the main line with the 10.40pm from Brighton to London Bridge, which after electrification became a van train. A Brighton locomotive generally worked the 8.25am up, returning via the main line with the 1.10pm stopping train from London Bridge. After its diversion to Victoria in 1928, it returned with the 1.10pm express from Victoria to Brighton via the main line. Following electrification to Brighton, it returned down the main line with a van train, initially from Victoria, later from London Bridge. Occasionally, prior to 1933, the New Cross Gate locomotive which had worked the 5am newspaper train from London Bridge to Brighton returned with the 8.25am up via Sheffield Park, instead of the 8.30am stopping train up the main line, which was its normal working.

From 1932 onwards a number of regular and dated Sunday excursion trains began to appear in the working timetables.

One such which ran for most of the summer period was the 10.15am Selsdon Road to Brighton via Sheffield Park. Usually worked by a 'Vulcan' 'C2X', it left with the empty coaches from New Cross Gate at 9.51am. The return left Brighton at 7pm. (For fuller details, see under 'Special Traffic'). From July 1939 these trains ran to and from New Cross via the Mid-Kent line and were worked by a Bricklayers Arms 'C' class 0-6-0.

Van Trains

For most of its history milk and parcels traffic on the Lewes-East Grinstead line was conveyed by passenger trains and it was not until 17 June 1928 that a milk train — the 7.42am Polegate to Tulse Hill — was routed via Sheffield Park and Oxted, leaving Lewes at 8.22am. It lasted until March 1930, when it was re-routed via Uckfield and Edenbridge Town. This was worked by a New Cross Gate engine which worked down with the 3.20am milk train from New Cross Gate to Polegate via the main line.

In July 1933 a new 10.35am vans Brighton to New Cross Gate was routed via Lewes, Sheffield Park, Horsted Keynes (11.43-11.51am), thence to Haywards Heath (12.1-12.9pm) and so up the main line. This did not appear again in the 1934 timetable.

Motor Train Workings

While the rosters of most of the through services were uncomplicated, those for the motor trains were quite the opposite. These sets proved most versatile and in a day's rota provided the services over a number of adjacent lines. The following duty rosters for one vehicle a day were issued by the LBSCR in 1906:

Brighton Duty No 3

Time	Route
6.30am	Brighton-Seaford
7.20am	Seaford-Lewes
7.52am	Lewes-Sheffield Park
8.21am	Sheffield Park-Lewes
9.28am	Lewes-East Grinstead (in place of ordinary train)
10.35am	East Grinstead-Three Bridges (in place of ordinary train)
11.20am	Three Bridges-East Grinstead (in place of ordinary train)
12.30am	East Grinstead-Brighton via Ardingly (in place of ordinary train) Crew change

At East Grinstead incidentally, the set was timetabled to transfer from Low to High Level, to run to Three Bridges, the move being via the ground frame at East Grinstead South and the connecting spur, but on one occasion J. R. W. Kirkby recalls the transfer was made via St Margaret's Junction in order to get to High Level Platform 1.

Afternoon turns leaving Brighton at 2.55pm took the set in turn to Uckfield, Seaford, Uckfield and Seaford, before returning to Brighton at 8.45pm.

In 1910 the timings were altered to:

Time	Route
7.48am	Lewes-Newick & Chailey
8.11am	Newick & Chailey-Brighton

A fine portrait of a motor train at Barcombe with 'Terrier' No 673 (formerly *Deptford*) provides a close glimpse of the advertisement panels and station furniture and goods under the canopy of the single platform.
F. Burtt/L. G. Marshall collection

9.5am	Brighton-East Grinstead

From 1921 the duty started with:

7.10am	Brighton-Sheffield Park
7.59am	Sheffield Park-Brighton
8.55am	Brighton-East Grinstead

Brighton Duty No 5 (1910)

9.5am	Brighton-Seaford
9.55am	Seaford-Lewes
10.37am	Lewes-Seaford
11.10am	Seaford-Lewes
11.50am	Lewes-Seaford
12.50pm	Seaford-Lewes
1.18pm	Lewes-Uckfield (non-stop)
1.40pm	Uckfield-Brighton
2.40pm	Brighton-East Grinstead via Sheffield Park
4.12pm	East Grinstead-Brighton via Sheffield Park
6.10pm	Brighton-Kemp Town
6.30pm	Kemp Town-Brighton
7.20pm	Brighton-West Worthing
8.8pm	West Worthing-Brighton

Dick Kirkby has provided some details of the changing face of these workings, as follows:

July 1928

Brighton Duty

7.10am	Brighton-Sheffield Park
8.2am	Sheffield Park-Brighton
8.56am	Brighton-East Grinstead
12.12am	East Grinstead-Brighton via Sheffield Park

Brighton Duty

1.20pm	Brighton-Oxted via Sheffield Park
3.36pm	Oxted-Brighton via Sheffield Park

Brighton Duty

4.5pm	Lewes-Horsted Keynes via Sheffield Park
4.50pm	Horsted Keynes-Brighton via Ardingly

Newhaven Duty

7.58pm	Lewes-Horsted Keynes via Sheffield Park

8.50pm	Horsted Keynes-Brighton via Ardingly	

July 1933

Three Bridges Duty 653

5.27am	Three Bridges-East Grinstead (Goods)	6.2am
6.40am	East Grinstead-Brighton via Sheffield Park	8.3am

Three Bridges Duty 660

6.40am	Haywards Heath-Oxted	7.38am
10.3am	Oxted-Seaford via Haywards Heath	12 noon

Eastbourne Duty 803

6.15am	Eastbourne-Horsted Keynes via Haywards Heath	7.36am
7.42am	Horsted Keynes-Haywards Heath	7.53am
8.22am	Haywards Heath-West Hoathly	8.39am
8.51am	West Hoathly-Lewes via Haywards Heath	9.37am

Brighton Duty 744

7.5am	Brighton-Sheffield Park	7.49am
8.3am	Sheffield Park-Brighton	8.49am
9am	Brighton-East Grinstead via Sheffield Park	10.09am
12.10pm	East Grinstead-Brighton via Sheffield Park	1.22pm

Brighton Duty 742

1.28pm	Brighton-Oxted via Sheffield Park	3.23pm
3.38pm	Oxted-Brighton via Sheffield Park	5.17pm

Brighton Duty 745

3.48pm	Brighton-Horsted Keynes via Sheffield Park	4.40pm
4.46pm	Horsted Keynes-Lewes via Ardingly	5.35pm

Eastbourne Duty 807

6.33pm	Brighton-Sheffield Park	7.17pm
7.22pm	Sheffield Park-Lewes	7.43pm
8.2pm	Lewes-Horsted Keynes	8.33pm
8.40pm	Horsted Keynes-Lewes via Ardingly	9.17pm

September 1938
(After the 1935 electrification between Haywards Heath and Horsted Keynes)

Brighton Duty 735

7.7am	Brighton-Sheffield Park	7.43am

Motor trains call on opposite platform faces at Horsted Keynes on Saturday, 3 March 1934. The train in the centre of the picture with set 763 is the 1.45pm Haywards Heath-East Grinstead. That on the right headed by motor-fitted 'D1M' No 2284 is the 2.1pm Horsted Keynes-Haywards Heath. Note the bare westernmost platform and the 'Tommy Dod' ground signal between the lines. *H. C. Casserley*

8am	Sheffield Park-Brighton	8.39am
9.6am	Brighton-East Grinstead via Sheffield Park	10.11am
10.33am	East Grinstead (HL)-Three Bridges	10.48am
11.25am	Three Bridges-East Grinstead (HL)	11.41am
12.7pm	East Grinstead (HL)-Brighton via Sheffield Park	1.14pm
3.5pm	Brighton-Crowborough	4pm
4.10pm	Crowborough-Lewes	4.48pm
6.52pm	Lewes-Sheffield Park	7.14pm
7.23pm	Sheffield Park-Lewes	7.44pm
8.8pm	Lewes Horsted Keynes	8.34pm
8.55pm	Horsted Keynes-Brighton via Sheffield Park	9.42pm

Brighton Duty 736

| 6.40am | Haywards Heath-Oxted | 7.31am |
| 10.6am | Oxted-Lewes via Sheffield Park | 11.20am |

As will be seen from the above workings, the line through Ardingly also had its share of motor workings prior to electrification. With electrification, most steam-hauled passenger services were lost but one that survived was the much-photographed 3.28pm from Haywards Heath. Prior to 1933 it had left Brighton at 3.5pm but was now cut back to start at Haywards Heath, at first with a set of three coaches, with another four attached at East Grinstead. However, in postwar days it took all seven from Haywards Heath, arriving at London Bridge at 5.20pm, the stock forming the 5.40pm to East Grinstead, frequently an Atlantic turn.

Later Events and Changes

The line led a placid existence except at times of emergency. Such an occurrence took place in 1920, when part of a goods train came off the road at Wivelsfield and the Brighton Pullman

had to be re-routed via Oxted and Sheffield Park. This was particularly remembered by that well-known Brighton driver George Washington, who fired *Gladstone*, Battersea having substituted one of that class because of engine restrictions south of Horsted Keynes.

A different kind of emergency was the exceptionally cold and severe weather with deep snow just before Christmas 1938. Six inches fell on 22 December, with a temperature of 30°F. By next day it had frozen, with 28°F recorded, resulting in traffic chaos round Lewes, with no down trains on the main line for two hours. Trains were stuck, especially by ice affecting the electric services, and up trains were stopped and warned under Block Working Rule 11 ('Train unusually long time in section'). The Horsted Keynes-Seaford electric trains were running two or more hours late, and doubtless the more hilly Lewes-East Grinstead route was severely affected.

When the branch through Ardingly had been electrified, the general pattern of working was as follows: There were five up trains from Brighton to London via Sheffield Park (two to Victoria and three to London Bridge) and only three down (one from Victoria), with one each way between Haywards Heath and London Bridge via East Grinstead. The seemingly unbalanced timetable was evened out by all-station services between Oxted and East Grinstead to Lewes and Brighton, six down and two up. The other services were purely local ones from Lewes, terminating at Sheffield Park (7.49am), Horsted Keynes (4.38pm) and Newick & Chailey (7.20pm). The last had ceased to terminate or start from Newick during World War 1, but was reintroduced in 1930 to run to and from Sheffield Park. (More detail of these is given in the chapter on locomotive workings.)

Special Traffic

The earliest category of special excursion over the line comprised theatre traffic. As early as October 1888 a popular excursion to the International Fisheries Exhibition at South Kensington was advertised, 96 tickets being issued at Newick & Chailey for the cheap Thursday train. Theatre outings to Brighton or the metropolis featured strongly in the years up to World War 1. Excursions of a religious nature were also a feature of those times. In July 1893, an annual treat for 30 members of the Newick church choir was the visit to Crystal Palace, while the following June, 300 scholars and teachers from Brighton had their summer outing to Newick. 'They marched from the railway station with their banners and had tea and recreations at the Home Field.' In 1924 Mr Bessemer chartered a special train for his staff at Burchetts and parishioners, to go to Sudbury to see the British Empire Exhibition at Wembley. This was provided free, as most of the villagers would not have had the chance, owing to the expense.

Another whole category of specials was associated with the great occasions held at Sheffield Park. In May 1891, when Lord Sheffield's team were playing an MCC XI including W. G. Grace, special trains were laid on to bring the visitors from all around. But the grand military displays at the Park were far more demanding, not just in bringing the public but in transporting 5,000 volunteers with their respective equipment in specially dedicated workings, carrying single or several units according to their size. The first volunteer occasion was in July 1890, followed the next year by an even larger display. The mock battle would take place between a southern force disembarking at Newick, which would march up through Fletching Common and Rotherfield Wood to temporary bridges over the River Ouse, to engage the northern army which had started from Sheffield Park station, the mock hostilities using cavalry, infantry and 16 pounder guns making 'much noise'. At the huge volunteer gathering in July 1894 it is recorded that 1,154 soldiers arrived at Newick & Chailey and 1,165 at Sheffield Park. How all these extra trains were timetabled and stabled to await their return journeys in the evening has not been fully ascertained, nor how these were integrated into the normal passenger service carrying the general public. An interesting and amusing episode occurred in July 1894, when one group of 35 (Lewes Company of 1st Cinque Ports Volunteers) mistakenly continued in their train towards Sheffield Park, into the heart of enemy territory. Amid consternation the train came back to Newick, the inept volunteers were detrained and then double-marched to catch up with the rest of their battalion! This incident does imply

that all specials came up from Lewes, resulting in long periods of one way working to Horsted Keynes. Sets would have been stabled there in the west sidings and even as far north as East Grinstead, where engines not 'escaping' via the line through Ardingly, could have been turned via the spur lines, similar to the arrangements for Lingfield race special locomotives. In July 1895, there was another review with 2,500 men, four special trains bringing participants to Newick & Chailey with their artillery, ammunition wagons and baggage. The report for the review at the end of July 1903, at which 4,900 troops took part, speaks for itself.

'The presence at the review of close on five thousand troops necessitated most careful arrangements being made at Sheffield Park station, where the bulk of the force detrained. Mr Barkshire, the District Superintendent, was in attendance, and the station staff, which had been considerably augmented for the occasion, worked splendidly. Mr G. W. Sellwood, the Company's agent at Sheffield Park, performed his arduous duties with great ability and tact. Some idea of the magnitude of the task which had to be performed will be gathered from the statement that there were 21 special trains. The 1st Sussex Royal Engineer Volunteers were the first batch to arrive. One train which left Hastings at 8.20am and arrived at Sheffield Park about half past ten, brought 600 men of this fine force and they were promptly marched to the Park . . . From one o'clock till past three, troops simply poured into the station and as quickly poured out into the road leading to the Park . . . The unloading of the guns was no easy matter but the Artillery knew their work and they soon had the horses hitched to the heavy field pieces . . . Owing to the excellent organisation the detraining of the troops was carried out in good time, and, despite the limited amount of space at the station, everything was done in a remarkably orderly manner.'

The line south of East Grinstead was also used for seaside excursions, to avoid congestion on the Brighton main line. Mr J. W. H. Kent mentions some pleasant memories of journeys in the late 1920s:

'The route from New Cross (SER) to Brighton was via Catford Bridge, Selsdon Road, Oxted, East Grinstead, Horsted Keynes and Lewes. Journey time was about three hours, so one had time to enjoy the pretty autumnal scenery. Rolling stock was mainly LSWR and the family made sure to select

	am		*pm*
New Cross	9.46	Brighton	7.6
Selsdon	10.9-10.15	Lewes	7.23
Sanderstead	10.19	Culver Jct	7.29
Upper Warlingham	10.31	Newick & Chailey	7.41
Woldingham	10.36	Sheffield Park	7.46-7.48
Oxted	10.43	Horsted Keynes	7.58/8.1
Crowhurst Jct	*10.48*	West Hoathly	8.8
Lingfield	10.53	East Grinstead	8.20-8.25
Dormans	10.59	Dormans	8.31
East Grinstead	11.5-11.10	Lingfield	8.35
West Hoathly	11.22	Crowhurst Jct.	8.39
Horsted Keynes	11.32	Oxted	8.46
Sheffield Park	11.42-11.43	Woldingham	8.54
Newick & Chailey	11.50	Upper Warlingham	9.0
Culver Jct	*12.1*	Sanderstead	9.7
Lewes	*12.7*	Selsdon	9.9-9.11
Brighton	12.22	New Cross	9.31

(Note times in italics are passing times)

first class compartments, as it was one fare only — about 3s 6d per person return. Motive power consisted of Stirling 'O1' class 0-6-0 goods locomotives. Their narrow tenders needed replenishing at both Oxted and Horsted Keynes, this being a far from level route, while on the return trip the firework display from the tall chimney dimmed the harvest moon and cinders rained down seven coaches back. In 1929 the engine noted was No A438, on another occasion No A434 was concerned.'

The Sunday excursion from Selsdon to Brighton and return (Empty to & from New Cross Gate) first appeared in the summer timetable of 1932, but for only three Sundays, and continued until the war. The excursion from New Cross via the Mid-Kent line first appeared as a Q (Conditional) timing in July 1931. From July 1932 to July 1937 it was booked to run on nominated Sundays, three in 1932, while in 1937 on every Sunday between 4 July and 26 September. From 1938 it seems to have been diverted to Dover or Margate via Crowhurst Junction. It also appeared in Bank Holiday notices and probably ran on some Sundays in May and June under special traffic notices. The 1937 timings are shown below left.

On relatively few occasions specials ran over the line in the night hours. Though the special traffic notice for the Coronation and Naval Review of 1911 had specials scheduled either to Victoria or London Bridge between the hours of 2am and 4am over most LBSCR branch lines, the Lewes-East Grinstead Line was an exception, but amends were made in 1953 when an excursion on Coronation Day ran up the line to the following booked timing:

	am
Brighton	4.6
Lewes	4.15-4.16
Culver Junc.	*4.22*
Barcombe	4.26
Newick & Chailey	4.33
Sheffield Park	4.38½
Horsted Keynes	4.48
West Hoathly	4.59½
East Grinstead	5.5/5½
Dormans	5.17
Lingfield	5.21
Hurst Green Halt	5.29½
Oxted	5.36½
Woldingham	5.44½
Upper Warlingham	5.49½
Riddlesdown	5.54½
Sanderstead	5.59
Selsdon	——
South Croydon	*6.2*
East Croydon	6.4-6.5
Windmill Bridge Jct	*6.6*
Victoria	6.21

(Note times in italics are passing times)

History does not relate how many passengers used this train.

During World War 2 there was a large military camp at Sheffield Park, used principally by Canadians. It finished up as a repatriation centre for German prisoners of war. In connection with this a number of special military trains were dealt with at all hours of the day and night.

'C2X' No 32540, having departed from East Grinstead over Imberhorne Viaduct, curves round towards Hill Place Cutting. The train is the 12.28pm unofficial 'football special' to Lewes on Saturday, 7 May 1955, whence intending visitors to the Goldstone Ground changed onto a train for Brighton. *Colin Hogg*

There were several other categories of excursion traffic, which stayed with the line to the bitter end and even beyond. The first two were connected with sporting venues. As early as November 1899, the Council for Newick & Chailey petitioned the LBSCR that they 'would like to see special excursion fares for villagers attending Brighton United FC games'. In Southern Railway days there was a motor train from East Grinstead, variously timed at 12.10 and 12.15pm, all stations via Sheffield Park to Brighton, arriving at 1.34-35pm in good time for the traditional 3pm kick-off. After the war, there was a football special on match days which left East Grinstead at 12.28pm and ran all stations to Lewes, connecting through to Brighton. Posters advertising Brighton's home games, with timings of the special, were prominently displayed on the platforms of the intermediate stations. By choice the 1956 basic timetable ran the interval service 12.28pm, arriving in Lewes at 1.12½ pm but on Saturdays it was allowed an extra two minutes, presumably because of the fractionally longer times taken for the larger number of supporters to board the train at each station. After 1958 those at East Grinstead travelled via Three Bridges. Those around Horsted Keynes still had five years more of electric services, but the rest, left to their own devices, soon turned to the car.

The other type of sporting special was to Lingfield Races. The majority of excursions came down from London, but there were some from Brighton and the South Coast that used the line over the years. When the end came for the Sheffield Park line, these specials continued to run up through Ardingly, usually with Maunsell Mogul haulage, but

Left: A Lingfield race special passes Ardingly in 1951, on its return journey to Brighton. The locomotive is 'N' No 31815, still carrying its unchanged SR number on its buffer beam.
S. C. Nash

Below: Class 4 2-6-4T No 42103 is captured passing Horsted House Farm on the 11.15am Brighton to Lingfield Race special of 13 November 1954.
Colin Hogg

members of the South Eastern's 'L' class 4-4-0s were in charge of specials from the south on weekends in March and November 1958. These ceased with the branch closure in October 1963. Special services were also run on 5 November for Lewes Bonfire Night celebrations, certainly as late as the 1940s and 1950s.

From 1932 and for the next 30 years the Ramblers' Association was closely connected with the line. The very first Ramblers' Excursion was in fact arranged by the Great Western Railway on Good Friday, 1932. It was billed as a 'Mystery Ramble' and some 250 ramblers were taken from Paddington to Pangbourne, where they were left to plan their own day's walking with inevitable results, but these teething troubles were rectified on subsequent excursions. In those days competition was keen, and the Southern Railway, with its much wider network, was quick to realise the possibilities of this traffic. For Whit Sunday, 15 May 1932, it proudly announced:

'GRAND PICNIC RAMBLE

Among the Woodlands and Rock Scenery of Lovely Sussex

(Note: There is no mystery whatsoever about this)

CORRIDOR EXPRESS TRAIN TO EAST GRINSTEAD, KINGSCOTE AND WEST HOATHLY

The parties will be led by Mr S. P. B. Mais, the famous novelist, journalist and broadcaster on England's Countryside, and Mr H. E. Page, Hon Transport Secretary of the Federation of Rambling Clubs, and other experienced leaders.'

Most of these leaders were actually members of the Federation, which subsequently became The Ramblers' Association as we know it today. Some 600 ramblers were carried in three trains and introduced to organised rambling with a varied choice of itineraries, each under expert leadership, a pattern which has proved popular and so has successfully stood the test of time.

On this occasion no one was quite sure what the response would be and the SR handbill made a pass at the less energetic family man, inviting him down to the 'joyous Sussex Countryside' and adding, 'Give the wife and kiddies a day in the Country — no crowds — no noise. You don't have to ramble — just sit and enjoy life.'

What proportion of sedentary family picnickers went down that Whit Sunday will never be exactly known but the overall response was sufficient to fill three trains. The main train was timed to leave Victoria's Platform 12 at 10am and, with stops for picking up passengers at Clapham Junction (10.7am) and East Croydon (10.23am), made East Grinstead in the good time of 11.2am, Kingscote 11.10am and West Hoathly 11.16am. The advertised return timings were West Hoathly 5.30pm, Kingscote 5.35pm, East Grinstead 5.40pm, reaching Victoria at 6.50pm, but passengers were also given the option of returning by the ordinary train, leaving West Hoathly at 7.53pm, Kingscote 7.59pm, East Grinstead 8.5pm, reaching London Bridge at 9.30pm. Another feature of the trip, and quaint to our modern habits, was the footnote that, 'Special Lunch Boxes, price 1/-, will be on sale in the Special Train on the Down Journey'.

Unfortunately, among the 600, few of whom survive today, there does not seem to have been either a railway enthusiast or a photographer and nothing seems to have come to light about the motive power etc. Only in more recent years has the railway enthusiast realised the interesting possibilities of making use of such excursions in furthering his hobby. In 1935 *The Southern Railway Magazine* reported, 'Ramblers' specials still hold high favour. On Sunday August 11th the two specials to Horsted Keynes were well patronised, 483 people taking advantage of this popular trip.'

However, in 1939 clouds were gathering. One last excursion actually ran on Sunday, 27 August, and by a remarkable coincidence the destination stations included Kingscote and West Hoathly, which had been visited on the very first excursion some seven years earlier. Although this was the last excursion to operate, it is of interest to note that the stencils were actually printed for rambles in the Meon Valley on Sunday, 3 September, the day war was declared.

During the period preceding the war, Ramblers' excursions ran down the line on the 11 occasions listed in the table published below. It will be noticed that fares remained constant for five whole years and went up by only tuppence for the rest of the period. Another feature that will stand out at once is that on no occasion before 1939 did a Ramblers' excursion run to Sheffield Park or to the other two stations on the single track section. Some leading ramblers had been heard to say that the country round there was not attractive enough (!) but the more plausible reason seems to be that these areas were more easily covered from such destinations as Plumpton and Uckfield.

Prewar Ramblers' Excursions				
Date	*London Terminus*	*Destination*	*Fare*	*Loading*
15 May 1932 (Whit Sunday)	Victoria	E. Grinstead, Kingscote West Hoathly	3s	app 600 (3 trains)
25 Feb 1934	Victoria	E. Grinstead, West Hoathly Horsted Keynes	3s	672
2 Sept 1934	Victoria	as above	3s	526
11 Aug 1935	Victoria	as above	3s	483
1 Mar 1936	Victoria	Kingscote, West Hoathly Horsted Keynes	3s	390
23 Aug 1936	Victoria	as above	3s	664
17 Jan 1937	Victoria	as above	3s	not known
15 Aug 1937	Victoria	as above	3s	517
4 Sept 1938	London Bridge	as above	3s 2d	826
5 Feb 1939	Victoria	as above	3s 2d	615
27 Aug 1939 (last to run)	London Bridge	as above	3s 2d	380

Of the postwar trips to the line, the first four ran to West Hoathly, Horsted Keynes and Sheffield Park (incidentally none has at any time run to Newick & Chailey or Barcombe). The first, on 2 April 1949, was hauled by 'N' class No 31816, and the load was 10 bogies. It made heavy weather of the ascent of Dormans Bank, more reminiscent of a coal train than anything else, so a certain amount of time was lost. The last of Mr H. E. Page's efforts down this particular line ran on 24 June 1951 (motive power not known). The next, on 22 March 1953, perhaps because of previous experience of the inadequacies of the Maunsell Moguls with such loads, was hauled by Bulleid light Pacific No 34071 *601 Squadron* and consisted of 11 bogies carrying just over 500 passengers, a load that must have made the use of something really powerful imperative. There was a further excursion on 16 May 1954, of which no details are to hand regarding the motive power.

Meanwhile, before the next excursion could be arranged, the withdrawal of passenger services had been effected and the subsequent excursions served only Horsted Keynes and Ardingly, because, though four of them ran via East Grinstead and were steam operated, the Southern Region was never willing to permit the use of Kingscote (entirely closed), nor West Hoathly and Sheffield Park (reopened under duress for a period, as is well known).

On three occasions following the first closure, electric Ramblers' trains were run to Ardingly and Horsted Keynes via Haywards Heath, but these are of less interest as they did not traverse the Lewes-East Grinstead line proper. However, in the course of negotiating the excursions for the summer of 1957, the organisers found that because of the temporary reprieve, the way south of East Grinstead was open again, so steam-hauled excursions by this route were resumed once more. The first of these trains ran on 8 September 1957, with 'Battle of Britain' No 34068 *Kenley* hauling 11 coaches with a full complement of passengers.

The next, though not strictly a Ramblers' excursion since it was privately organised, proved a most interesting venture. This was the 'Bluebell special' on 11 May 1958. Consisting of eight coaches (seven BR open saloons plus one particularly rough-riding ex-GWR corridor coach) and just under 400 passengers, it started its journey at Greenford (Middlesex) and ran via Perivale and Viaduct Junction to Kensington (Olympia), and onwards to East Croydon, hauled by No 3440 *City of Truro*, the only occasion when this engine penetrated the Central Section of the Southern Region. Mr G.R. Lockie

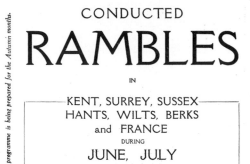

SOUTHERN RAILWAY

South for Scenery !

CONDUCTED

RAMBLES

IN

KENT, SURREY, SUSSEX
HANTS, WILTS, BERKS
and FRANCE

DURING

JUNE, JULY
and AUGUST

Organised by

Mr. H. E. PAGE
Hon. Transport Secretary of the
Ramblers' Association
(Southern Federation),
7, Buckingham Palace Gardens,
S.W.1

CORRIDOR SPECIAL TRAINS

C.X. 1388/—60/25537   Printed in Great Britain by McCorquodale & Co. Ltd., London—31042.

Another comprehensive programme is being prepared for the Autumn months.

tried his best to get agreement for this engine to haul the train right through to its destination but the Western Region would not hear of it and he was lucky to get the 'City' beyond Clapham Junction. It may be that the SR civil engineer was worried about inadequate clearances beyond East Croydon; at all events a 5mph speed restriction was imposed on the return journey through the up local platform at Selhurst. The engine ran with tremendous gusto between Clapham and Norbury on the outward journey and gave the quickest start from Clapham Junction ever recalled with steam traction. After Norbury it was before time, and signal checks spoiled the rest of the run. On the return journey it was given no chance to show what it could do. *City of Truro* spent the day at Norwood Loco.

Above: Extract from *South for Scenery! Conducted Rambles* for excursionists on 5 August 1937. *Dick Kirkby collection*

Left: The Victoria-Sheffield Park Ramblers' excursion of 22 March 1953 brought super motive power down to the line in the form of 'Battle of Britain' Pacific No 34071 *601 Squadron*. It is photographed storming through Three Arch Bridge just south of Horsted Keynes. *S. C. Nash*

Above right: The Ramblers' special of 24 June 1951, 9.50am Victoria-Sheffield Park, hauled by 'N' No 31411, continued from the latter as the 11.30am empty coaching stock working down to Lewes and is seen here on its way south near Newick. *J. J. Smith*

The plea t
'urging th
warehouse
already be
yards were
that the
Brighton,
passenger
hour at Fle
that most
there were
return jou
Keynes ha
down jour
It will l
omitted fr
passing ti
intention
opinion th
Uckfield
memorial
with the s
in the dist
railway ar
persuaded
company t
was prepai
they 'only
more or le
General M
had at last
dock,' and
show the
opened,
remunerat
afforded a
meeting h
shelved q
somewhat
on 3 Marcl
meeting
Constructi
reported f
inspection

Between East Croydon (10.18am dep) and Ardingly (11.14am arr) the train was hauled by 'K' No 32342, recently out-shopped, which put up an excellent performance. It made a phenomenally rapid ascent of the three-mile bank of 1 in 70 between Lingfield and East Grinstead, and gained something like 10 minutes on the schedule between East Croydon and Horsted Keynes (arr 11.4am). The return journey (Ardingly dep 7.38pm) was equally vigorous and it arrived at East Croydon well before the scheduled time of 8.35pm. Looking at the matter in retrospect, a certain element of rivalry entered into it between the WR and SR crews on this inter-regional Ramblers' excursion.

The usual optional arrangements for conducted rambles existed, but for the family man, more interested in paddling on the South Coast, it was suggested that by rebooking at Ardingly on to the 11.20am regular service train, he could avail himself of cheap day ticket facilities to many of the Sussex Coast resorts. But the main incentive, according to the heading of the handbill, was to go 'Down to the Bluebell and Primrose' line for spring flowers amid the tumbled woodlands, rock scenery and old-world atmosphere of North Sussex. The Bluebell motif was specially displayed on the

engine headboard and this excursion not only helped further to popularise but virtually sealed the hitherto tenuous association (originated by the press) of this particular wild flower with the Lewes-East Grinstead line.

With the section north of Horsted Keynes still open to special traffic after the closure of the single-track portion, there followed, on 7 December 1958, a further excursion of 10 coaches behind 'Battle of Britain' No 34077 *603 Squadron*. Finally, on 27 September 1959, the last steam-hauled Ramblers' Special ran down this particular line, with No 34068 *Kenley* once again in charge of 11 coaches. The leading coach of the train had been reserved for members of the newly formed Bluebell Railway Preservation Society, who used these facilities to get down to a special rally day at Sheffield Park, to which they were taken by coach. This train was the final run over the East Grinstead-Horsted Keynes section by a public service train before its closure to all traffic. As a result, the three final excursions reverted to electric haulage via Haywards Heath, on the last of which a large number of the rambling clientele availed themselves of the opportunity of taking the train from Horsted Keynes to pay a visit to Sheffield Park. The wheel had come round full circle once more!

Postwar Ramblers' Excursions

Date	London Terminus	Destination	Fare	Loading
2 April 1950	Victoria	West Hoathly, Horsted Keynes Sheffield Park	5s 9d	562
24 June 1951	Victoria	as above	5s 9d	391
22 March 1953	Victoria	as above	6s	504
16 May 1954	Victoria	as above	6s	481
9 Oct 1955	Victoria	Ardingly, Horsted Keynes (Electric)	6s	440
8 July 1956	Victoria	as above	6s	412
27 Jan 1957	Victoria	as above	6s 3d	540
8 Sept 1957	Victoria	Horsted Keynes, Ardingly (Steam via East Grinstead)	6s 3d	548
11 May 1958	Greenford via Clapham Jct	as above	6s (from CJ)	391
7 Dec 1958	Victoria	as above	6s 3d	440
27 Sept 1959	Victoria	as above	6s 9d	500
10 July 1960	Victoria	Ardingly, Horsted Keynes (Electric)	6s 9d-	336
23 July 1961	Victoria	as above	8s	720
9 Sept 1962	Victoria	as above	8s 6d	not known

line actually opened, through the stationmasterships of George Harmer, James Rawlins, John Holden, Charles Horn, Stephen Sellwood and George Fossey, to 1908. The papers would appear to have been put up in the loft soon after, in the time of George Reddish (1910-15), who earned a reputation for keeping his stations spruce and tidy.

In the intervening period these documents have not lain fallow. The goods register and accompanying bills were closely studied by Jonathon Abson, Carriage & Wagon Steward of The Brighton Circle. His findings, which follow, provide a cameo portrait of a typical rural station goods yard 100 years ago and an insight into the life and needs of the local community.

Goods Stock Proportions

Among a host of rather dirty relics was a goods register for Sheffield Park, covering some four months from 30 November 1899 to March 1900. This is an exciting find, as one can determine precisely what was going into and out of the yard over this period. This sort of information is almost priceless, as so little is known about Brighton line goods traffic. There are no doubt other goods registers in private or public ownership somewhere but this is the only one that has surfaced from the company's 200 or so goods yards.

Table 1

Railways Delivering to Sheffield Park

	Number	%
LBSCR	634	90.3
Private Owners	25	3.6
MR	18	2.6
LNWR	10	1.4
GNR	6	0.9
SECR	3	0.4
NER	2	0.3
GCR	2	0.3
NSR	1	0.1
GER	1	0.1
Total	702	100%

The first surprise, for what is after all a tiny village community, is the number of goods wagons handled each day. There are entries for 1,548 vehicles on 98 separate days, giving an average of all but 16 wagons in the yard on each and every day. In fact 661 loaded wagons were delivered during the four months; and if they averaged only 6 tons capacity each, then a surprising 1,000 tons of rail-delivered capacity arrived each month, not a bad figure one would imagine for a station that opened less than 20 years earlier without a goods yard.

Table 2

Wagons Delivered (by type)

	LBSC	Others	Total	%
Merchandise	217	6	223	31.7
Merchandise and Sheet	228	3	231	32.9
Single Bolsters	82	0	82	11.7
Empty Goods for loading	41	0	41	5.8
Coal	1	53	54	7.7
Box Vans	37	5	42	6.0
Double Bolsters	13	0	13	1.9
Coke Wagons	5	1	6	0.8
Cattle Trucks	5	0	5	0.7
Machinery & Road	5	0	5	0.7
Totals	634	68	702	100%

The second surprise is that one gets at least a glimpse of the habits of the local population from mere lists of data in a record book. The village of Fletching is two or three miles away from the station and separated from it by the Park itself and the circuitous access road. In 1900 beer was certainly brewed in Lewes and Tunbridge Wells and perhaps more locally, but there was enough demand for a wagonful of beer to be delivered every two weeks. For some reason not immediately obvious, the Midland Railway delivered beer from Burton in open wagons, whereas the SECR sent beer from Canterbury in box vans. It all amounts to a steady consumption of pints at very regular intervals.

A sharp contrast with the flourishing conditions described at Sheffield Park at the turn of the 20th century, as regular 'C2X' No 32539 leaves Sheffield Park with the afternoon goods to Lewes on 5 May 1955. The end of goods services is near, and no wonder with traffic down to a mere three wagons. *Geoffrey S. Robinson*

Table 3

'Foreign' Railway Deliveries by Type and Railway

	GCR	GER	GNR	LNWR	MR	NER	NSR	PO	SECR
Merchandise	1				6	1			
Goods and Sheet						1			
Box Van		1		1					3
Coke					1				
Coal	1		6	9	11		1	25	

The goods register seems to have been kept by a goods clerk or perhaps a porter, since for long periods at a time the handwriting is unchanged. However, the hand of Mr Fossey, the station clerk (ie stationmaster) of the time is seen in the regular ticking of all entries and the occasional correction, such as the time the goods clerk entered the day following 31 December 1899 as 1 January 1899 — a common enough mistake in a normal year, but in a new century?

There are no entries for Sundays, the Brighton being a God-fearing line, but modern railwaymen might be a trifle put out to find that they worked on both Boxing Day and New Year's Day in those days. Apart from their weekly day of rest, very occasionally the staff had an easy day, often, for some reason, on a Tuesday, when there were no deliveries or despatches. On a typical day, though, they had seven or so wagons coming into the yard to join about nine left over from the previous days. Wagons seem to have averaged two to three days in the yard, with LBSCR vehicles being turned round slightly quicker than private owners' or other railways' wagons. No doubt it was deliberate policy to favour one's own wagons provided one did not run into paying demurrage on others.

Only 10% of arrivals were from other companies, of which private owners made up by far the biggest chunk at over a third of the balance, with the Midland Railway making the next largest and the rest just about nowhere. The almost complete lack of foreign vehicles leads one to suppose that, both for the sophisticates at Sheffield Park and the rural community in Fletching, the local community was all but self-sufficient and when Lewes could not provide what was wanted, 'Lunnon' could.

Several curiosities were thrown up by the goods register. Most of the box vans came from Kemp Town and it has been suggested that this might have been biscuit traffic. Similarly all the cattle wagons came from Willow Walk. Were they tired cows from the city dairies, sent off like hop-pickers to Sheffield Park for a holiday before returning to their duties, or were cows from the north brought round to Willow Walk for transhipment into LBSCR vans to save payments on foreign vehicles? And how ever did Lewes have all those loaded trucks sent to Sheffield Park?

The reason for so many timber bolsters and so much timber consigned from Lewes to Turner's Timber Mill at Sheffield Park, since Lewes is not known for its forests, is fairly obvious. Len Tavender has suggested that the loaded wagons were held at Lewes to await capacity at the mill to convert into sawn timber. Martin Pettinger has added, 'The railways did not then (and do not now) operate in isolation from other forms of transport. At that time, Lewes was an active port, albeit in decline, and quite able to accommodate seagoing trading ships. One of the main commodities carried was timber from Scandinavia. The ships used the River Ouse at high tides to reach Lewes. After discharge from the ship, the cargo would have been stacked near the quayside and moved away by rail as soon as possible, the speed of delivery probably limited by the availability of such specialist items of rolling stock as timber bolsters, as much as by the storage capacity of Turner's yards.'

The increasing use of the railway spelt the end of small ports such as Lewes, taking goods such as coal and grain that would previously have formed the bulk of the port of Lewes's trade. However, timber and other goods of overseas origin continued to move by sea, although Lewes was eventually excluded from the trade by reason of the navigational restrictions of the narrow River Ouse. The increasing size of coastal vessels meant that they were unable to reach Lewes and were forced to turn to other ports, such as Newhaven at the river mouth.

Table 4

Private Owners

Bestwood
Birley
Cardiff Navigation Colliery
CRC (Cannock Rugeley Collieries)
Lamont Warner
Linby
Newington
Parry
Pelsall
Roundwood (Old Roundwood Colliery?)
Rickett Smith
Staveley
Talk o' the Hill Colliery
Wigan Coal & Iron

Details of the timber sawmills at Kingscote and Sheffield Park appear in the chapter dedicated to those stations.

Milk Traffic

This has already been alluded to when mentioning the added time allowed for in the timetable for loading churns, especially at Sheffield Park which had a dairy close to the station and incorporated a narrow gauge trolley line, to wheel the loaded churns destined for the metropolis to the up platform. Almost every posed photograph of station staff in the 1920s shows a fine array of milk churns displayed in groups on the platforms. Incidentally, should the loading of churns on to the train take more time than allotted on the timetable, it was noted down in the guard's notebook. These 17-gallon churns were carried either in the passenger brake van or, if of considerable quantity, in milk vans attached to a passenger train. At Sheffield Park the most prominent was the 8.10am weekdays Lewes-London Bridge.

The 1921 timetable shows that the vans of empty churns were moved daily, mostly via East Croydon. The 12.8pm New Cross joined with a Clapham Junction portion and the combined train went forward at 2.45pm to Three Bridges, whence the vans were distributed throughout the southern half

An Edwardian postcard photographer has chosen to feature Ardingly with a goods train in the down platform. A Stroudley 'D' tank is being used for the branch pick-up goods bound for Hayward's Heath. *Bluebell Archives*

BR No 32547, propels the weekly pick-up goods from Norwood Junction up the spur line from Low to High Level yards at East Grinstead on 9 June 1954. *R. C. Riley*

of the system by both passenger and goods trains. On Sundays it was the 8.25 Brighton-London Bridge that served the line, the empties being returned on the 1.14pm milk train from London Bridge to Lewes, conveying some 14 vans of empty churns for various destinations.

There are surviving details of the arrangements for the empty vans for 1925. The 12.8pm returns from New Cross Gate contained the empty 'Cans for Ardingly' in the centre section of the fifth van in the formation. In the ninth van the front section was for Barcombe, Newick & Chailey and Sheffield Park, the centre for the Oxted area and the rear end for Kingscote, West Hoathly and Horsted Keynes. The 12.22pm followed as a separate train from Clapham Junction. In the sixth van's front section were empty cans for Oxted-East Grinstead and Kingscote, centre Edenbridge-Ashurst, and rear Barcombe-Horsted Keynes. Ardingly received back its churns on the 1.10pm from East Croydon, in the centre section of the fifth van. Thus did the vast and growing population of London receive its fresh milk daily throughout the year.

The traffic really took off in the 1880s and 1890s with the switch by the local farmers from mostly arable farming to dairying, leading to rail-carried milk. Individual farmers or cooperatives like the Mid-Sussex Dairy Co delivered to local stations, where the clerks then filled in the necessary forms, of which milk traffic returns are possibly the most common surviving document. Their introduction, in many instances, marked the beginning of non-passenger traffic at country stations. Some concerns owned creameries adjacent to the station, for instance the Mid-Sussex Creamery at Sheffield Park. The volume of milk continued to increase after the Grouping and the return-empty movement was transferred to the night hours.

The advent of the Milk Marketing Board resulted in the introduction of more concentration, milk tankers replacing churns, and the change to movement by road resulted in most of the above-described workings ceasing in the early 1930s. Some idea of the decline can be gleaned by a comparison with Fittleworth on the Midhurst line. There 1,000 gallons were moved a day, with 18 different milk carts coming in day and

Above: The versatile mixed traffic 'E4s' were on occasion assigned to the line's goods workings. Slowing for the curve into Culver Junction, No 32494, already displaying the BR number but apparently no crest, is in charge of the 1.20pm goods from Kingscote on 30 July 1949. *Pamlin Prints*

Right: Class C2X, including the trio of unrebuilt 'C2s', had a virtual monopoly of the line's goods services from the 1923 Grouping through to the very end. No 32437, displaying 'British Railways' on its tender, takes the 8.32am up working through open countryside south of Sheffield Park on its way from Lewes to Kingscote on 18 February 1950. *Pamlin Prints*

night. The 1926 strike caused farmers to turn to motorised transport, taking the milk direct to the big depots and cutting out the railway as an unnecessary middleman.

Some other categories of goods were peculiar to a particular station on the line and are mentioned in the respective chapter devoted to each station.

Goods Traffic in the Postwar Years

For the last 20 years of the line the one and only goods train serving the Sheffield Park section intermediate stations was the daily pick-up goods. The summer 1937 working timetable shows the following timings:

Lewes East Sidings		8.35am
Lewes Station	8.37	8.41
Culver Junction	8.51	8.52

Barcombe	8.56	9.13
Newick & Chailey	9.23	9.55
Sheffield Park	10.0	10.32
Horsted Keynes	10.44	11.17
West Hoathly	11.25	12.20
Kingscote	12.27	
Kingscote		1.0pm
West Hoathly	1.6	
Horsted Keynes	1.14	1.30
Sheffield Park	1.42	2.25
Newick & Chailey	2.33	3.40
Barcombe	3.50	4.2
Culver Junction	4.8	4.9
Lewes Station	4.20	4.32
Lewes East Sidings	4.36	

The timetable for 1947 shows almost identical timings but leaving Lewes East at 8.32am and arriving at Kingscote at 12.43pm. But it was not the sole goods working, for the

Freight Train Working Timetable for the summer of that year also shows a fast goods train down the line timed as follows:

Norwood Yard	7.25pm	
East Croydon	7.30	
South Croydon	7.34	
Oxted	8.4	
Hurst Green Junc	8.9	
East Grinstead	8.34	
Horsted Keynes	9.0W	9.8
Sheffield Park	9.20	9.21
Culver Junction	9.41	9.42
Lewes Station	10.5	10.10
Lewes East Sidings	10.15	11.0
Polegate		11.30

W — Calls for water only

This train ran Mondays to Fridays. On Saturdays it was routed via Redhill and the main line (not via Quarry). Note that it was booked non-stop from Norwood Yard to Horsted Keynes. By 1949, however, the train was running via Ardingly and at some point between 1947 and 1951 the 7.25pm became part of alternative steam working No 2, only brought into operation when an electric locomotive (a 'Hornby' Co-Co) was not available for the 7.48pm Norwood-Polegate via the main line.

After 1955, with the cessation of the Lewes-Kingscote goods, the only opportunities were at Ardingly and Horsted Keynes and, at irregular periods, the arrival and departure of trainloads of condemned wagons, which were stored on the up line between Horsted Keynes and Imberhorne Viaduct during 1959-60. The goods facilities at Ardingly and Horsted Keynes eventually closed in March 1962, when at the end of the month the infant Bluebell Railway began running directly into Horsted Keynes station.

Left: No 32437, obviously a regular on this working at this period, running tender-first, brings the 1.20pm from Kingscote to Lewes towards Culver Junction on 30 June 1950.
Pamlin Prints

Below: An unusually busy goods scene at the end of April 1960 at East Grinstead Low Level yard. 'U1' No 31890 stands ready to leave with the final batch of condemned wagons for Lancing, having shunted its train back onto the down line, while 'C2X' No 32521 has arrived with the local goods from Oxted. *Derek Cross*

9.
Locomotive Workings

The Brighton Period

One of the factors that has undoubtedly popularised the Lewes-East Grinstead line for enthusiasts has been the great variety and range of motive power, in which steam remained unchallenged to the very end. There were several reasons for this, quite apart from the rich mixture that lay inert at Horsted Keynes from 1905-8, for upon a rural branch line there was superimposed the services of a secondary main line and, indeed, until the quadrupling north of Balcombe Tunnel, a regular route for excursions from London to Brighton and Eastbourne was until 1910 via Oxted, East Grinstead and Ardingly.

Discounting the previously mentioned small group of contractor's engines used by Firbank during the construction of the line from 1878-82, the first regular locomotives to run the line's services from the outset were Stroudley's 'D' tanks, for which there is evidence photographic and otherwise. The engine chosen for the first of the two inspections of the line, which took place six weeks prior to the opening, was No 266 *Charlwood* which, with William Stroudley himself on the footplate, hauled a three-coach train containing 'the Government Inspector and a number of Directors and other gentlemen,' from Lewes up to East Grinstead. No 265 *Chipstead* was the locomotive involved in the accident at Newick on 4 January 1883. Both were new and allocated to Brighton the previous May, and were regular performers on the line. Another of the class involved almost from the start was No 233 *Handcross,* allocated new in 1883 to East Grinstead, an intriguing posting, becoming the resident of the tiny one-road shed which lay tucked away, almost a lean-to, at the side of the larger goods shed in the High Level yard. Up to its arrival the 5.30am goods from Three Bridges was double-headed as far as East Grinstead, to provide an engine for the first train from the Low Level terminus to Brighton. By 1883 the supply of an extra engine from Three Bridges had ceased, indicating *Handcross* taking over the 6.45am to Brighton.

The full working of No 233 while allocated to East Grinstead in 1886 was:

	East Grinstead	6.45am
8.4am	Brighton	10.35am
1.20pm	London Bridge	5.18pm
5.54pm	South Croydon	6.10pm
	via Crystal Palace	
6.54pm	London Bridge	7.27pm
8.43pm	East Grinstead	

Sister engine No 234 *Rottingdean's* tally of 1,050 miles run between Sunday, 6 February and Saturday, 12 February 1887 is recorded in *The Southern Railway Magazine* for February 1929. Driver H. Barber and Fireman H. R. de Salis each worked a week of 95 hours 50 minutes. On the Monday their day included the 1.25pm Brighton-Horsted Keynes and 2.35pm back to Haywards Heath, and on Wednesday the 7.10am Brighton-Horsted Keynes and 8.30am back to Brighton. On Tuesday, coming on duty at 5.20am, they worked the 6.5am Brighton-Horsted Keynes, 7.15am Horsted Keynes-Lewes, 8.28am Lewes-East Grinstead, 10.30am East Grinstead-Haywards Heath and 11.5am on to Brighton. At the end of the day they worked a special train for Haywards Heath cattle market and after shunting there, returned with the train to Brighton, coming off duty at 8.45pm.

Saturday's morning timetable was a repeat of Tuesday, and only on Monday 14 February did locomotive and crew earn a well-merited shed day. In 1890 this first working was terminated at Lewes. Two years later the shed at East Grinstead was closed and No 233 departed to Three Bridges, but as late as 1896 it was reported as working the 8.8am ex-Lewes via Sheffield Park.

Until R. J. Billinton's 'D3' bogie tanks entered general circulation in the mid-1890s, the sturdy and hard-working Stroudley 'D' 0-4-2Ts took almost complete charge of the passenger services. Between 1890 and 1910 the following are on record as having worked for periods over the line, based on Brighton and Eastbourne sheds:

14 *Chelsea*	26 *Hartfield*	267 *Maresfield*
18 *Stockwell*	27 *Uckfield*	270 *Warnham*
23 *Mayfield*	28 *Isfield*	296 *Osborne/Peckham*
24 *Brambletye*	265 *Chipstead*	297 *Bonchurch*
25 *Rotherfield*	266 *Charlwood*	362 *Kidbrooke*

The Eastbourne duties included Brighton-Horsted Keynes via Haywards Heath, returning with the slip portion off the 4.30pm Victoria-Brighton, also the 5.10pm Brighton-East Grinstead via Sheffield Park and back to Lewes, finishing with the Eastbourne carriages off the 'Grande Vitesse' express.

At the turn of the century, the pattern was very much what one might expect, the sad but nevertheless interesting spectacle of what, when new, were the latest designs for main line express trains, now working out their final mileages on secondary train duties. The local services were invariably powered by tank engines but the locomotive department never quite made up its mind about the use of tender engines on the four daily through trains. The 'D2' 0-4-2s from New Cross and Brighton, ousted by the spate of Billinton 4-4-0s,

Left: The Southern Railway soon realised the sparsity of passenger traffic as the car came into its own in the 1930s, and 'D' tank workings with two- or three-coach sets became the norm. Here No 2226 has just arrived at Lewes with a working from East Grinstead on 23 October 1934. *H. C. Casserley*

Below: Though there are no photographs of Stroudley 'D2s' working on the line, several members of the class were stored at Horsted Keynes prior to their withdrawal. No 309 *Splugen* stands at the end of the long pump house siding by the finely constructed water-tower with the pump house chimney protruding in the background.
M. P. Bennett/Bluebell Archives

Left: During the Edwardian period the line's through services rested in the capable hands of William Stroudley's famous 'Gladstone' class 0-4-2s, by then downgraded to secondary services by more modern motive power. No 178 (formerly *Leatherhead*) stands at Barcombe with the late morning through train from Victoria to Brighton in 1910. This resplendent locomotive was scrapped not long after, in 1912.
Bluebell Archives

No 468 belonged to a class of 0-6-0s built for the LBSCR by J. Slaughter & Co in 1868 and known as the 'Standard Craven Goods', which served as the crack goods locomotives on the Brighton system until Stroudley's 'C' class arrived in 1873/4. Relegated to secondary duties, members of the class worked goods services over the Lewes-East Grinstead line during the early years, based at Newhaven. No 468 was the final survivor of the class, lasting until August 1898.
David Green/Bluebell Archives

performed for some years on the Haywards Heath, Horsted Keynes, East Grinstead and Oxted services, on which Nos 303 *Milan*, 304 *Nice*, 305 *Genoa*, 308 *Como*, 311 *Rhone* and 312 *Albion* were noted. With the practice of changing engines at East Grinstead, as happened on the 1.20pm and 5.8pm ex-Brighton via Lewes, the turning via St Margarets Junction and the goods spur not only took five minutes but gave frequent headaches to already hard-taxed sets of signalmen. Gradually the 'D3' 0-4-4 tanks assumed these duties, but only in relatively rare instances did the problem of water shortage arise. However, before the Grouping it was usual to fill up at Sheffield Park in either direction.

With the arrival of the Marsh Atlantics on express services the 'Gladstone' 0-4-2s began to appear on the line but not habitually until 1909, by which time the scrapheap had rendered extinct both the 'D2s' and the slightly longer-lived Stroudley Singles, which seem to have seen little service on the line other than on excursion trains. Among the 'Gladstones' recorded on the line, which regularly worked the 10.30am Brighton-London Bridge and 4.5pm Victoria-Brighton were:

173 *Cottesloe*	185 *George A. Wallis*	199 *Samuel Laing*
178 *Leatherhead*	192 *Fremantle*	219 *Cleveland*
179 *Sandown*	194 *Bickersteth*	

In June 1906 the famous 'Terriers' made their first appearance on the line. Marsh had turned to the idea of a steam rail motor service using 'A' class 0-6-0Ts with one balloon coach. As part of the experiment he adapted two of the class, Nos 81 *Beulah* and 82 *Boxhill*, as 2-4-0 tanks by replacing the leading coupled wheels with a pair of 2ft 9in diameter carrying wheels, and with cylinders lined up to 9in diameter. These appeared in October 1905 and were introduced on the Bluebell line the following summer. Besides these two, other 'Terriers' commonly turned out by Brighton shed for these rail motor duties were Nos 643 *Gipsyhill*, 647 *Cheapside*, 655 *Stepney*, 667 *Brixton* and 673 *Deptford*, all engines with a considerable record of service! However, when Marsh came in the old names went out and all but one arrived on the line nameless and in the new umber livery. The exception was *Boxhill*, which at the time was painted in 'experimental' goods green, still retaining its name.

The era of motor-fitted duties by the 'Terriers' was, however, short lived for the first 'D1s' converted for push and pull work were so fitted in 1905 and their increasing numbers soon caused the disappearance of the 'Terriers' by degrees. During 1919 and 1920 the latter came off and the veteran 'D1s', often with an extra non-driving piped trailer inserted between the engine and the balloon coach, returned to monopolise these duties to the end.

The complicated variety of turns has already been touched upon, the 1906 service bringing the Seaford branch engine up the line. There was a 12.30pm motor train working (11.20am ex-Three Bridges) which ran from East Grinstead to Brighton via Haywards Heath, but by 1910 had been retimed to form the 12.15pm departure via Sheffield Park. Afternoon trips took this set to Uckfield, Lewes, Seaford and Brighton.

Turning to goods workings, some of Craven's mixed assortment of locomotives may have made sporadic appearances but the only regular performers on record were a batch of his goods engines based on Newhaven, which came up the line on freight trains from the coast, chiefly with 'sea coal' for the southern Home Counties. Hence the up freight traffic, coming onto the line via the Ardingly branch, was always the heavier. Extra goods workings up from Lewes were frequently laid on when required during winter coal shortages, up to a permitted 35 wagons, and the Lewes pilot, a Brighton engine, was often commandeered for such a duty. This, however, lapsed after World War 1.

The engines, soon known locally as the 'Newhaven Goods', a class of 0-6-0 goods engines, appeared in October 1868, and were put to work on the main line. The last six, built by Slaughter & Co of Bristol, carried the numbers 468-473. These goods engines, says Burtt with conviction, the last of Craven's designs, were without exception the finest, which may account for their lengthy survival into the Billinton regime. John Pelham Maitland, who was later based at Newhaven shed, has recorded three of the class as working on the line: No 468, the last to survive, still prizing a copper-capped chimney to the end, and Nos 471 and 472. They were replaced on their duties from Newhaven by members of Stroudley's first goods design, his Class C 0-6-0 tender engines, which when they were built were the most powerful and up-to-date design for ordinary traffic in the country. Nos 403, 405 and 409 were the new arrivals, replaced by one of a similar class from Brighton, when one of the others was under repair, Nos 401 and 402 being among those recorded.

When these were withdrawn in 1902, their place at Newhaven was taken by Billinton's 'C2s' Nos 530, 538 and

Above: 'Vulcan C2X' No 32539 brings the 8.32am up goods from Lewes past MP9½, crossing Allen's Bridge in the vicinity of 'Treemaines', on 30 April 1955. *J. J. Smith*

Left: 'D3' Bogie tank No 373 (formerly *Billingshurst*) pauses at Barcombe with steam to spare on an up stopping train to East Grinstead. This class replaced the Stroudley 'D' tanks on some of the heavier workings. *Bluebell Archives*

555. Stroudley's 'E1s' in their earliest days had some share in this traffic but, as they left the country branches and were concentrated in the suburban area and as shunters in the larger marshalling yards, they were replaced by the Billinton radial tanks. Until 1911-12 these predominated on the one goods train which went right through from Lewes to East Grinstead. The 'C2s' and their Marsh rebuilds then came into their own on the local goods for the next 40 and more years, though 'E4' tanks were frequent performers right up till 1955. But while the traffic lasted the 'Vulcans' remained the most efficient performers on the none too easy grades.

The earliest recollections available in some detail come from A. L. Maycock, 'a small boy who was mad on trains',

who lived at Horsted Keynes from 1909-15. 'With no buses and knowing no acquaintance who had a car, and with a steeply undulating mile and a half from the village, to get anywhere the family either walked or bicycled to the station or, if taking luggage, hired the village cab, which was kept by the proprietor of the Crown Inn. To get to Brighton over either route, the 17-mile journey took just short of 50 minutes. Actually it was sometimes possible to get into Brighton a good deal more quickly. By taking the 8.53am via Haywards Heath, one might sometimes, as the train came up from Ardingly to Copyhold Junction, see the white plume of an express approaching on the main line from Balcombe. Then the race was on, and if fortune favoured it was possible to nip

'E5' 0-6-2T No 574 (formerly *Copthorne*) takes a breather at East Grinstead Low Level station in 1921, before returning southwards. In the background stands the palatial double-winged station house in keeping with such an important rail centre, while on the left a group of milk churns stand on the up platform awaiting delivery to London *Kenneth Nutt*

out of the local train at Haywards Heath and board the main line express, with a non-stop run into Brighton and a saving of 20 minutes.

'Most of the traffic in those days was handled by the LBSCR's wide variety of tank engines — Stroudley's "D" class, Billinton's 0-4-4s and 0-6-2s, and later Marsh "I" series 4-4-2s. The London trains were often hauled by "Gladstones" or the "B" class 4-4-0s and, on rare occasions, by a Marsh Atlantic. By this time Stroudley's splendid golden-ochre livery had almost disappeared, to be replaced by Marsh's neat but unexciting dark umber.'

A detailed survey of motive power during the closing years of the LBSCR era relies upon the recollections and photographs of Kenneth Nutt, who lived all his life in Station Road, East Grinstead. He took photographs with an old Box Brownie from 1919 as film became available in the shops, and continued through to 1921 with a larger camera. Locomotives photographed in the High Level station did not necessarily perform south to Horsted Keynes and must be discounted, and it needs to be noted that some of the heavier types recorded would have travelled via Ardingly due to the weight restrictions on the single line section to Culver Junction.

Taking first the Stroudley survivors, rapidly thinning out, this was the period in which the 'D1s' were quickly ousting the 'Terriers' from the motor train duties. Nos 662/3/7/77 were frequently seen but, as the 0-4-2Ts took over, on occasions an additional coach was added to the balloon trailer. Among the performers were Nos 245/8/79/352, No 248 freshly painted

and fitted with new square tanks, following extensive damage sustained in a collision at Streatham Junction in 1919. Members of the 'Gladstone' class were still around, particularly Nos 173/81/94. Turning to Billinton's locomotives, the 'D3' 0-4-4Ts continued to perform regularly, Nos 372 & 380 being photographed, but they were being replaced by the more modern 'E5' 0-6-2Ts, cascaded from main line duties. These included Nos 403/567/72-4/83. On the goods side the 'E1' 0-6-0Ts had virtually disappeared from the countryside and 'E4' 0-6-2Ts were beginning to arrive, a class used on passenger trains as well. 'E3' 0-6-2Ts were rare, but the larger 'E6' counterpart No 418 was photographed in the Low Level station. Billinton 4-4-0s appeared rarely in the eyes of the camera but the odd 'B2X' and 'B4' did appear at Low Level.

The silhouette that was most to be seen, however, and indeed right through to 1950, was that of the Marsh Atlantic tanks in their various classes and batches: the 'I1s' frequently, the 'I2s' unfailingly (in 1929 members of the class based at Littlehampton shed were regulars through Ardingly), together with the occasional 'I4', but the highly-prized 'I3s' performed rather more sporadically over the secondary route. Routed via Ardingly were the LBSCR's most powerful types, the Marsh Atlantics and his pair of large 4-6-2Ts, together with Lawson Billinton's Baltic (4-6-4) tanks. But even this was not the complete story, for the Lingfield Race traffic brought many foreign locomotives into East Grinstead Low Level station, to water and turn round via the spur to the High Level.

Unrebuilt Billinton 'B4' 4-4-0s took over the main through services from the declining number of 'Gladstones' from the late 1920s into the years of World War 2. No 2042 is seen in 1933 at one of the line's very popular photographic locations immediately south of Horsted Keynes on the single line section, on the 8.3am London Bridge-Brighton. At this period severe restrictions were in force on this section, precluding the Marsh Atlantics and L. Billinton's 4-6-4Ts.
Dr Ian C. Allen

Locomotive Restrictions

In order to understand the nature of the motive power recorded on the line, one needs to be aware of ongoing changes in weight restrictions. Sid Nash has made these a special study interest and the paragraphs that follow comprise a summary of his notes. The idea of excluding a class of locomotive from certain lines is a relatively modern one. Although light railways were coming into vogue at the end of the Victorian period, and in odd places, (particularly in mining country where the word pitfall came into common usage) our ancestors gave no thought to the problems of weight/rail ratio. Taking the weight of the engine alone in 1900, the most powerful tender engines on the LBSCR, the Billinton 'B4' 4-4-0s, were 49 tons, and only his 'E3' topped the 50-ton mark. Within 14 years his son L. B. Billinton turned out from Brighton his first Baltic tank, which weighed 98 tons 5cwt, and it was not long before several types exceeded the 100-ton mark! The question of large scale restrictions does not appear to have arisen until the middle of World War 1, when, with manpower sadly depleted, track maintenance fell below par in most places and available workers were channelled to the busiest lines. Thus before 1914 it was possible to see at Horsted Keynes the 89-ton Marsh tanks *Abergavenny* and *Bessborough*, which came up on the 3.18pm from Brighton via Ardingly as part of their trial trips, and Nos 327 and 328 may have done likewise. According to the SR's engineers, it was axle weight rather than gross weight which was the governing factor, together with the 'hammer blow' of piston-connected driving wheels.

The double-track section north of Horsted Keynes and down through Ardingly was always more of a main line than the single line section to Culver Junction. In 1917, however, there was published a list of engine restrictions which included among its prohibitions the banning of the Baltic and Pacific tanks and the 'K' class Moguls over the entire route from Oxted to Lewes, and also the Horsted Keynes-Haywards Heath section. But by the time the next working appendix was issued, in 1922, these classes were permitted from Oxted to Haywards Heath (though not on the Sheffield Park route) and the double track section was thus free of any restrictions.

In early SR days, too, it remained almost unrestricted, only the 4-6-0s being barred. Until the Eastbourne electrification in 1935 there used to be a 1.51pm Eastbourne-London Bridge via Haywards Heath and East Grinstead, regularly worked by one of the Baltic or Pacific tanks (for many years a monopoly of *Bessborough*) and on very rare occasions by a 'Schools' class 4-4-0. In July 1935 it was altered to start from Haywards Heath at 3.35pm (later 3.28pm), in which form it continued to provide East Grinstead with its biggest engine of the day, New Cross Gate Atlantics or 'B4' 4-4-0s being used for many years.

After the war Eastbourne 'Ks' were used for a year or two and then Bricklayers Arms got the job and 'L1s' and 'Ns' appeared. The most interesting period was the summer of 1949, when the same depot began using 'WD' 2-8-0s on the turn — one of the very few passenger duties they worked on the Southern and the only one to run into London — and a very rough ride it proved. This working ceased in the autumn, as the 2-8-0s had no steam heat fittings. In its latter years the 3.28pm was usually Mogul-hauled, but the Oxted-Haywards Heath route was passed for use by much heavier engines, including Class 5 4-6-0s (BR and LMS) and 'Britannia' Pacifics, though there is no indication that any of these classes ever availed themselves of the opportunity.

The Sheffield Park line was much less favourably placed. In 1917, and again in 1922, Atlantics were permitted, as indeed they were on virtually all LBSCR lines. Mr John Glandfield can distinctly remember as a boy, travelling up from Lewes to Newick & Chailey round about 1921 or 1922 behind Atlantic No 39 *La France*. 'The incident,' he writes, 'is clear in my mind as I remember my father remarking, 'You're behind a big one this time,' and I was taken forward to see the engine after alighting from the train at Newick.' It was during this period that the Marsh Atlantics performed regularly over the length of the Bluebell line on the Sunday London-Brighton through services.

These liberties were soon reversed by the Southern after the Grouping, when more engine restrictions were gradually imposed, culminating in the very drastic 1937 *Engine Restriction Book*, which barred Maunsell 2-6-0s (the Billinton ones were of course forbidden anyway), 'B4Xs' and even the modest 'I3' tanks; this last embargo caused much inconvenience to the operating department, and it meant that 'D1' and 'E1' 4-4-0s had to be borrowed from the Eastern Section to work some of the heavier trains, since no suitable Central Section class was permitted. However the Sunday excursion from Selsdon to Brighton via Sheffield Park was normally given to a Norwood 'C2X' which, with the 'I1X', 'I2', 'I4' and 'B4' classes were the largest Brighton engines allowed at this period.

World War 2, unlike the First, saw a general easement. 'B4X' engines were already using the line by the summer of 1940, 'I3s' were readmitted in 1942, and by the summer of the following year all classes of 2-6-0 and also the Atlantics were permitted, and returned to daily use on the main through trains to and from London. Later even the 'WD' 2-8-0s were authorised, and after the war, about 1947-48, they had a regular evening job on the 6.56pm Norwood-Polegate freight, which then ran via Sheffield Park and reversed in Lewes station. By 1949, however, this train was running via Ardingly, usually Mogul-hauled.

A Bulleid Pacific appeared on the line on 21 June 1945 when No 21C101 *Exeter* worked the 12.3pm Victoria-Brighton on its first day in traffic. Soon afterwards this class was prohibited on the single line and the ban continued until early 1953. On 22 March that year No 34071 *601 Squadron* celebrated its lifting by working a Victoria-Sheffield Park Ramblers' excursion. In the last year or so previous to the 1955 closure, there was often one of this class on the 11.18am Brighton-Victoria via Sheffield Park, though it returned to Brighton via Uckfield from Victoria at 3.45pm.

And so the wheel of route restrictions had come full circle just two years before the closure of the line. 'K' class Moguls and Standard 2-6-4 tanks were the largest classes to appear during the brief reopening between 1956-58. Although a section of concrete sleepers had been laid to the north of Sheffield Park in the early 1950s, no major work was put in during the last years of operation under British Railways, and there were several speed restrictions and permanent way slacks in operation at the close, a particularly severe one of 15mph over a bridge north of Barcombe.

Locomotive Duties

The locomotive depots responsible for workings over the line are listed in the following tables, using sample years as snapshots during the line's history, assembled by Dick Kirkby. The use of abbreviations to save space should be self-explanatory, using initials for starting and terminating stations and the old LBSCR shedcodes or an equivalent for the depots. Trains run via Sheffield Park unless otherwise stated.

1886			Depot
Down	6.45am	EG-B'ton	EG
	8.15am	LB-B'ton	N+
	10.30am	EG-B'ton via HH	B'ton
	12.27pm	V-L	BAT
	4.10pm	LB-B'ton	BTN
	7pm	EG-L	EBN
	8.20pm	IIK-L	B'ton
Up	6.35am	B'ton-LB	B'ton
	8.22am	L-EG	B'ton
	10.35am	B'ton-LB	EG
	3.10pm	L-LB	BAT
	5.10pm	B'ton-EG	EBN
	7.15pm	B'ton-HK	B'ton
	7.33pm	B'ton-LB via HH	N+
Sundays			
Down	8.40am	LB-B'ton	N+
	6.50am	LB-B'ton	B'ton
Up	8.30am	B'ton-LB	B'ton
	6.40pm	B'ton-LB	N+

1896			Depot
Down	7.5am	EG-L	3B
	8.11am	LB-L	N+
	10.10am	O-B'ton via HH	TW
	12.3pm	LB-L	B'ton
	2.10pm	EG-B'ton (Goods)	B'ton
	4.9pm	LB-B'ton	N+
	7pm	EG-L	EBN
	9pm	EG-HK (SO)	3B
Up	6.45am	B'ton-LB	B'ton
	8.23am	L-LB	3B
	9am	L-EG (Goods)	B'ton
	10.35am	B'ton-V	BAT
	12.18pm	B'ton-N+ via HH	N+
	1.20pm	B'ton-O	N+
	5.10pm	B'ton-EG	EBN
	6pm	NHN-NOR via HH (Goods)	NHN
	6.28pm	B'ton-BAT via HH (Goods)	BAT
	7.49pm	L-HK	B'ton
	7.35pm	B'ton-LB via HH	N+
	9.22pm	HK-EG (SO empty)	3B

1914		Depot	Duty			Depot	Duty
Down	6.54am EG-L	3B	1	*Up*	6.45am B'ton-LB	B'ton	M5
	8.7am LB-L	N+	M8		7.48am L-N+C	B'ton	RM4
	8.11am N+C-B'ton	B'ton	RM4		8.15am L-LB	3B	1
	8.45am WH-HH	B'ton	L1		8.20am HH-WH	B'ton	L1
	10.12am O-B'ton via HH	TW	9		8.50am L-EG (Gds)	NHN	1
	12.5pm V-L	B'ton	M17		8.56am B'ton-EG	B'ton	RM4
	12.15pm EG-B'ton	B'ton	RM4		10.35am B'ton-V	B'ton	M20
	2pm EG-L (Gds)	NHN	1		1.20pm B'ton-O	B'ton	M24
	3pm EG-HH	StL	8		1.25pm B'ton -EG+ via HH	StL	8
	4.10pm LB-B'ton	N+	M1		4.55pm L-SP	B'ton	RM5
	4.35pm SP-B'ton	B'ton	RM5		5.8pm B'ton-V	B'ton	M4 (to EG)
	5.3pm V-L	B'ton	M4 (from EG)		7.43pm B'ton-LB via HH	N+	M2
	7.39pm LB-B'ton	N+	1(to EG)		7.58pm L-HK	B'ton	L21(Rtn HH)
					9.5pm L-EG MX	??	
					9.15pm L-EG MO	??	

'E4' No B491 (formerly *Hangleton*) enters Haywards Heath with a local train off the Ardingly branch on 19 July 1930. Haywards Heath North box was brought into use when the line through Ardingly was opened on 3 September 1883 and closed on 12 June 1932 in connection with the electrification of the Brighton main line. *H. C. Casserley*

July 1926

Down		Depot		Up		Depot
	6.40am EG-L	RED			6.20am B'ton-EG	B'ton
	8.2am SP-B'ton	N+			6.43am HH-O	B'ton
	8.7am LB-B'ton	TW			7.10am B'ton-SP	B'ton
	8.15am EG-B'ton via HH	B'ton			8.10am L-LB	RED
	8.47am WH-HH	B'ton			8.20am HH-WH	B'ton
	10.3am O-HH	B'ton			8.35am L-K (Gds)	NHN
	11.57am V-B'ton	B'ton			8.55am B'ton-EG	B'ton
	12.12pm EG-B'ton	B'ton			10.34am B'ton-V	N+
	12.47pm EG-K (Gds)	3B			1.12pm K-EG (Gds)	3B
	1.5pm K-L (Gds)	NHN			1.20pm B'ton-O	B'ton
	3.3pm EG-HH	B'ton			1.48pm HH-EG	B'ton
	3.36pm O-B'ton	B'ton			3.48pm HH-LB	N+
	4.10pm LB-B'ton	B'ton			4.5pm L-HK	B'ton
	7.7pm EG-L	B'ton			5.15pm B'ton-V	B'ton (to EG)
	7.38pm LB-B'ton via HH	3B			7.48pm B-LB (SO)	N+
	8.15pm EG-HK (NWS)	3B			8.0pm B-LB (NS)	N+
	8.15pm EG-L (WSO)	3B			8.0pm L-HK	NHN
					9.15pm HK-EG (NWS empty)	3B
					9.30pm L-EG (WSO)	3B

The R. Billinton 'E5' 0-6-2Ts were the mainstay of local workings during the interwar period. Not resoundingly successful, the widespread presence of the Marsh 4-4-2Ts saw them cascaded onto light secondary duties like this East Grinstead-Lewes stopping train consisting of a birdcage three-set entering Hill Place Cutting (the site of East Grinstead's rubbish tip for the last quarter of a century) behind No 2402 (formerly *Wanborough*). *Lens of Sutton*

		Depot	Duty				Depot	Duty
Down	6.40am EG-B'ton	3B	649		*Up*	6.22am B'ton-LB	B'ton	701
	8am SP-B'ton	N+	735			6.40am HH-O	B'ton	736
	8.3am LB-B'ton	N+	547			7.7am B'ton-SP	B'ton	735
	8.13am EG-HK	B'ton	730			7.53am B'ton-LB	B'ton	703
	8.51am WH-HH	B'ton	730			8.35am L-K (Gds)	NHN	773
	10.6am O-L	B'ton	736			8.39am HK-WH	B'ton	730
	12.3pm V-B'ton	B'ton	705			9.6am B'ton-EG	B'ton	735
	12.7pm EG-B'ton	B'ton	735			10.48am B'ton-V	3B	649 (NS to EG)
							B'ton	706 (SO to V)
	12.47pm EG-K (Gds)	NOR	587 (NS)			1.12pm K-EG (Gds)	NOR	587 (NS)
		BAT	524 (SO)				BAT	524 (SO)
	1pm K-L (Gds)	NHN	773			1.20pm B'ton-O	TW	632
	3pm EG-L	3B	650			1.45pm HH-EG	3B	650
	3.35pm O-B'ton	TW	632			3.35pm HH-LB	3B	641 (NS)
							3B	645 (SO)
	4.9pm LB-B'ton (SX)	B'ton	703			4.7pm L-HK	3B	650
	4.14pm LB-B'ton (SO)	B'ton	703			5.18pm B'ton-V	B'ton	729 (to EG)
	5.48pm V-L (WO)	3B	640			6.52pm L-SP	B'ton	735
	6.53pm V-L (SO)	3B	647			8.5pm L-HK	B'ton	735
	7.7pm EG-L	B'ton	729			8.35pm HH-LB	3B	650 (to EG)
	7.23pm SP-L	B'ton	735			9.43pm L-EG	3B	640 (WO)
							3B	647 (SO)
	7.40pm L-HH	3B	641 (NS)					
			645 (SO)					
	8.55pm HK-B'ton	B'ton	735					

Locomotive Headcodes

A year prior to the line's opening, the LBSCR introduced its scheme for 'Head Boards and Lights' under an instruction commencing 4 April 1881. A copy has been made available by Gerald Collins and is repeated below:

Engine Head Boards and Lights

Commencing April 4th, 1881

The following is a list showing the number and description of Engine Head Boards to be carried by Day, and Lamps to be carried by Night, and the position of each.

All the Boards will be round, fifteen inches in diameter, and of the following patterns, viz:

Double Diamond Board carried by Special Trains White Board with Black Cross White Board with Black Centre White Board Green Board with White Rim

The Lamps will show White or Green Lights.

All Trains not shown in the Service Time Book must be considered as Special Trains, and carry Head Boards or Lamps accordingly.

When necessary to divide an ordinary train, the first Train is to be considered the ordinary, and carry the 'Special to follow' Tail Board or extra Red Light, The following Train or Trains to carry Special Head Boards or Lamps.

In some cases it will be necessary to change Head Boards or Lamps during the journey, and Drivers must be careful to make the proper changes.

Break Down Tool Vans

Immediately the Message is received ordering out the Tool Van, the person to whom such message is addressed must cause the information to be at once given to the Signalman on duty, who must Telegraph, if on Speaking Instrument, to each Signal Box to destination, giving as near as possible time it will leave, and when it starts, Signal it on Block Instruments.

Station Masters, Inspectors or other persons in charge, must see this is properly carried out, and give all possible dispatch to the Break Down Tool Van Train.

When the Break Down Tool Van Train is returning home it must carry the Special Head Boards or Lights, as per route.

Empty Trains

Engines Working Empty Trains must carry same Head Boards and Lamps as ordinary Trains, if not otherwise ordered.

Ballast Trains

The Engines of these Trains to carry the ordinary Head Board and Lights, if not otherwise ordered.

Single Lines

Engines running on Single Lines must carry Head Boards and Lights as shown in Rules and Regulations for working Single Lines by Train Staff and Ticket.

The Opening Notice of 1882 contained the following designations:

Engine Head Boards and Lights Between Brighton and East Grinstead Via Lewes

By Day — One Board with Black Cross, each end of Buffer Beam.

By Night — One White Light near side of Buffer Beam, and one Green Light off side end of Buffer Beam.

When carrying the Train Staff on the Single Line, the above will be the Head Signals throughout as between Brighton and East Grinstead, but when carrying the Train Ticket over the Single Line the following alteration must be made at the Train Staff Station, where the ticket is issued.

By Day — The Board with Black Cross on off side end of Buffer Beam must be changed to a White Board.

By Night — The Green Light off side end of Buffer Beam must be changed to a White Light.

In the Headcode section of the Rules and Regulations Book for 1888 the instructions were as follows:

45

Brighton and East Grinstead
Via Haywards Heath and Horsted Keynes

Day Ordinary
One Board
One white board with Black Cross, near side end of Buffer Beam.

Day Special
Two Boards
One double diamond, top of smoke box. One white Board with Black Cross, near side end of Buffer Beam.

Night Ordinary
One Lamp
One Green Light, near side end of Buffer Beam

Night Special
Three Lamps
Two Green Lights, one at each end of Buffer Beam. One White Light, centre of Buffer Beam.

89

Brighton and East Grinstead via Lewes
Day Ordinary
Two boards
(When carrying Train Staff by day between Culver Junction and Horsted Keynes)
One White Board with Black Cross each end of Buffer Beam.
(When carrying Train Ticket by day between Culver Junction and Horsted Keynes)
One Board with Black Cross on near side end of Buffer Beam. One White Board on off side end of Buffer Beam.

Night Ordinary
Two Lamps
(When carrying Train Staff by night between Culver Junction and Horsted Keynes)
One White Light near side end of Buffer Beam. One Green Light on off side end of Buffer Beam.
(When carrying Train Ticket by night between Culver Junction and Horsted Keynes)
 One White Light near side end of Buffer Beam. One White Light on off side end of Buffer Beam.

In the 1901 Appendix for the route via Ardingly, instructions remained unchanged but contained the following footnote:

'Up Trains, Special and Ordinary, East Branch to East Grinstead, via Haywards Heath and Horsted Keynes, to carry the same boards and lights from Lewes as Brighton to East Grinstead Trains via Haywards Heath.'

'Down Trains for East Branch to carry from East Grinstead or Horsted Keynes, the same boards as Trains for East Branch via Main Line.'

The section for the route via Sheffield Park appeared much simplified.

107

Brighton and East Grinstead via Lewes
No Boards
No head signal

Two Lamps
One White Light near side end of Buffer Beam. One Green Light on off side end of Buffer Beam.

In the book for June 1910, smokebox diagrams with the relevant boards were given for each headcode:

Between
80
Brighton, Haywards Heath and East Grinstead, via Horsted Keynes. Also Up Trains from East Branch to East Grinstead. Note — Down Trains East Grinstead or Horsted Keynes to East Branch carry Boards or Lights as per section 8.

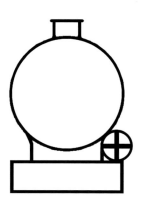 

Day Ordinary   **Day special**

Between
101
Brighton and East Grinstead (Via Lewes)

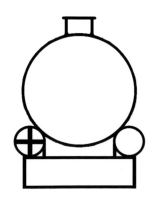 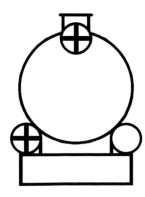

Day Ordinary   **Day special**

By 1917 it was down to single headcodes for each route.

Between
56
Brighton, Haywards Heath and East Grinstead, via Horsted Keynes. Also Up Trains from East Branch to East Grinstead. Note — Down Trains East Grinstead or Horsted Keynes to East Branch carry Boards or Lights as per section 8.

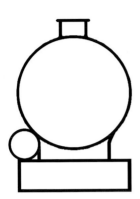

Code

Between
78
Brighton and East Grinstead (via Lewes)

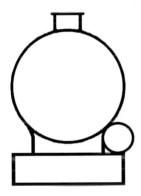

Code

These codes continued through to the Grouping at the end of 1922.

The 1922 LBSCR headcodes continued in use on the Southern Railway until 1934 when completely new ones were introduced as under:

Oxted to Brighton via Sheffield Park

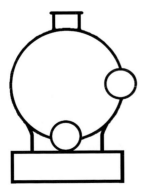

Oxted to Brighton via Haywards Heath

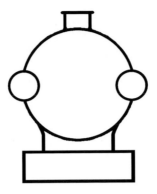

Oxted to Lewes via Haywards Heath

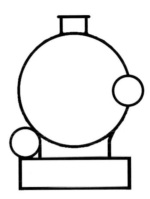

Through London trains changed discs at Oxted — or were supposed to but sometimes forgot!

After nationalisation new three-disc codes were introduced to cover London workings throughout:

Victoria to Brighton via Sheffield Park

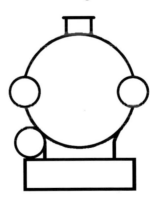

London Bridge to Brighton via Sheffield Park

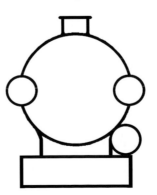

119

Rail motor services covered almost half the workings on the former LEGR lines until much reduced by electrification of the branch from Haywards Heath, the destination of 'D1M' No 2221 in August 1934. Horsted Keynes's fine oil lamps, shortly to go over to electricity, are visible, together with a row of flat wagons of LMS and LNER origin in the siding beyond Platform 1.
H. F. Wheeller

The 3.35pm Oxted-Brighton was a much-photographed train. Here, with 'I3' 4-4-2T No 32076 heading a birdcage set and van, it passes under the bridge at Culver Junction on its way to Lewes on 26 August 1950.
S. C. Nash

The Southern Period

The rail motors continued to remain very much part of the scene until the end of World War 2 and the workings continued to ring the changes, in timings, route and shed responsibility. In 1924 there was a Lewes-Horsted Keynes working via Sheffield Park, returning via Haywards Heath to Brighton and its home shed Newhaven. Three years later the 2.27pm from Seaford to Brighton left the latter at 5.18pm for East Grinstead via Sheffield Park, forming the 7.7pm back to Lewes and 9.3pm Lewes to Seaford.

Brighton was responsible for the 8.8am Lewes-London Bridge via East Grinstead and 5.40pm return (on Saturdays from Victoria at 5.9pm) but then became a Three Bridges turn (except from 1925-7 when it was a Redhill working) until 1933 when Brighton again took over. Three Bridges shed was also responsible for the cut-back 3.35pm Haywards Heath-London Bridge via East Grinstead.

John Hull, who stayed for long periods at East Grinstead during the interwar period, regularly visited the station and took photographs, and noted that the prevalent performers at Low Level were members of classes 'D1', 'D3', 'E4', 'E5' and 'C2'/'C2X'. Anthony Notley, during a stay at West Hoathly in the late summer of 1938, made some detailed notes of the locomotive workings. Since he was on holiday he saw neither of the first two trains of the day: 6.38am East Grinstead to Brighton and 6.15am Brighton to London Bridge. After breakfast came the arrival of the 8.13am from East Grinstead behind 'E5' No 2405. This engine had, for the line, an intensive diagram, for on arrival at Horsted Keynes it returned to West Hoathly to work the 8.51am to Horsted Keynes. This was a curiosity in the timetable for so many years, being surely too late for school children and office workers to reach Haywards Heath. Hardly had the latter's smoke finished eddying out of Sharpthorne Tunnel before the 8.4am Brighton to London Bridge arrived, hauled by a 'B4' 4-4-0 (an exception being the appearance of 'E5' No 2574 on one day). This engine may have been balanced on the 4.20pm London Bridge to Brighton, which was worked by 'B4s'. Nos 2042/44/62/63 could all be seen at West Hoathly during late August and early September 1938.

The first down through train left London Bridge at 8.3am for Brighton, reaching West Hoathly at 9.47am, and was the prerogative of the rebuilt 'B1' 4-4-0s, James Stirling's last design for the SER. Nos 1018/1101/1440/59 were seen on this working at various dates. Then followed an Up train — which disappeared from the postwar timetable — worked by one of Stroudley's delightful and diminutive but sturdy 'D1s', which returned from East Grinstead at 12.7pm, and featured Nos 2221/53/75/2627. Just about to leave his vantage point for lunch, the 10.48am from Brighton to Victoria would emerge from the portals of the tunnel with an 0-6-2T at the head. This could be 'E4' Nos 2465/84 or 'E5' Nos 2405/2594, although on the last Saturday of the summer service 'B4' No 2044 was the train engine. The only working other than the 8.3am for London Bridge which was regularly entrusted to an ex SECR 4-4-0 was the 12.3pm ex-Victoria, this engine returning on the 5.18pm from Brighton. This was a job for one of Maunsell's handsome 'E1' rebuilds, Nos 1019, 1165 or 1511. An unusual visitor on 7 September was an unrebuilt 'E', No 1547, working an excursion from East Croydon.

In the afternoon two up trains followed within half an hour. The first was worked by a radial tank, which returned from East Grinstead at 3.10pm ('E4' Nos 2493, 2559 and 'E5' No 2589), but the second provided more varied fare: Marsh 'I1X' 4-4-2Ts Nos 2006 and 2602 or 'E4' Nos 2498 and 2512, but the *pièce de résistance* on 7 September was the appearance of 'D3' 0-4-4T No 2370. During the afternoon came the pick-up goods for East Grinstead behind a 'C2X', usually No 2441 with No 2538 taking a turn, as did 'E4' No 2492. There are no records of late evening trains except the 5.50pm Victoria to Lewes, which was due at West Hoathly at 7.18pm. A miscellany of engines worked this turn: 'B4' Nos 2044 and 2063, 'I1X' No 2599 and 'E5' No 2567.

The Sunday service was scant. On 21 August 'B1' 4-4-0 No 1013 worked the 8.36am from London Bridge, returning on the 6.48pm from Brighton. The corresponding down train (6.40pm from London Bridge) was worked by 'B4' 4-4-0 No 2063, which may have worked the 8.32am Brighton up. A 'Vulcan' goods, 'C2X' No 2536, appeared in the evening on an unidentified up passenger train, no doubt one of the returning Brighton-Selsdon excursions. Certainly the line in those days did not lack variety in motive power.

From the middle 1930s and beyond the war years we have the travelling records of E. F. Mildenhall. He relates:

'My first trip on the line was entirely unpremeditated. In 1937 my father and I decided to go on a Whit Sunday excursion from Streatham Common to Lewes, mainly because the return journey was advertised as starting from Lewes and would, therefore, not be filled with passengers returning from Eastbourne and Hastings. The down journey was made in uncomfortable suburban electric stock, which we expected would be used for the return journey.

'When we arrived at Lewes station in the evening, we were surprised to be directed to Platform 4, used for eastbound trains. Standing there on a train of ex-LSWR non-corridor carriages was SECR 'B1' 4-4-0 No 1440, which I believe was then stationed at New Cross. Many of this class were working ex-LBSCR services.

'As seems to happen so often on bank holidays, the evening had turned out wet, and the combination of wet rails, sharp curves and the steep gradient on the viaduct over the old main line proved most unsuitable for the 7ft driving wheels, and No 1440 only just escaped stalling. After we turned onto the single line at Culver Junction the progress was scarcely more rapid, although in 1937 there was no restriction of speed required apart from that inseparable from single-line working. At Sheffield Park we passed Stroudley 'D1' 0-4-2 tank No 2227 on a southbound auto-train. When we reached the double track at Horsted Keynes I had hopes that matters would improve, but speed continued to drop, and when we reached the short tunnel at West Hoathly we stopped for nearly a quarter of an hour, while the engine crew managed to raise sufficient steam to get under way again. As the rails in the tunnel were dry, we were able to start without difficulty, and got going reasonably well. We stopped at East Grinstead Low Level to take on water, after which there was little of interest to report. This was my last journey behind a 'B1' on any part of the old LBSCR, although I have a note that No 1013 of this class was on the through afternoon train from Haywards Heath to London Bridge via Ardingly, East Grinstead and Oxted on 2 November 1940.

'Although that was my first trip on the line, I find I had made notes of some of the trains using that line on previous occasions, and the following workings may prove of interest in showing that LBSCR engines were almost exclusively used. I am confining this list *(below)* to those trains which actually worked to Sheffield Park, as the East Grinstead-Horsted Keynes-Ardingly-Haywards Heath line trains usually worked to and from London, and were therefore entrusted to much larger types of engine, including practically all the classes used on the main line except the 'King Arthurs'.

'On journeys to Eastbourne in 1938 I used to see the 6.52pm to Sheffield Park at Lewes, and noted the following 'D1' tanks on this working: Nos 2605 on 26 March 1938; 2215 on 11 June 1938; and 2227 on 24 September 1938; also on Whit Monday, 6 June 1938, No 2227 at East Grinstead (Low Level) on the 4.7pm from Lewes. As I was on the down platform at the time, I was able to get an excellent photograph.

'My second trip on the line was on August Bank Holiday, 7 August 1939 when war was imminent and there was a feeling to make the most of what might be the last holiday for an indefinite period. I saw in the special holiday timetable that there was a through pull-and-push train from Oxted to Lewes at 10.3am, which I could conveniently catch by travelling

Date	Engine	Type	Class	Train
14.5.32	B274	0-4-2T	D1	1.46pm Lewes to Horsted Keynes
11.8.32	B386	0-4-4T	D3	3.44pm Brighton to Horsted Keynes
7.8.33	2450	0-6-0	C2X	8.7am London Bridge to Brighton via Barcombe
28.9.34	2237	0-4-2T	D1	6.35pm Brighton to Sheffield Park
28.9.34	2627	0-4-2T	D1	3.46pm Brighton to Horsted Keynes
28.9.24	2062	4-4-0	B4	4.9pm London Bridge to Brighton via Barcombe
20.4.35	2374	0-4-4T	D3	6.35pm Brighton to Sheffield Park
19.10.35	2625	0-4-2T	D1	10.6am Oxted to Lewes via Barcombe

The 3.32pm RCTS special ex-Lewes on 4 October 1953 is seen behind rail motor-fitted 'D3' No 32390, the last member of its class, hauling an ex-LBSCR two-set through the wooded glades on its way from Newick & Chailey to Sheffield Park. *Colin Saunders*

The 4.3pm Lewes-Horsted Keynes working in the capable hands of 'I3' No 32079 eking out its last days on this humble duty, and seen approaching Barcombe on 7 August 1950. It was withdrawn three months later in November. *J. J. Smith*

Foreign motive power in the form of ex-SECR Wainwright 'E' 4-4-0 No 31491, easing the 4.18pm London Bridge-Brighton down the curve into Culver Junction on 4 August 1951. *J. J. Smith*

down to Oxted in a Victoria to Tunbridge Wells train which called at Streatham Common. Hence my first trip down the line was behind one of my favourite class of engine, Stroudley's 'D1' 0-4-2 tanks. That morning the engine was No 2699, already 63 years old. I little imagined that about five years later I was to see the same engine shunting carriages at Inverness, over 500 miles away. No 2699 gave me a very fast run, and the contrast between the 'holiday abandon' of this trip and the funereal pace of the up run behind No 1440 was most striking. As I had not a stop-watch I was unable to do any accurate timing, but from passing times at the mileposts I calculated that we probably reached the mile-a-minute rate passing Crowhurst North Junction. The weather was ideal, and although it was too late in the year for bluebells and primroses, the full beauty of the 'Weald Countree' beloved by Rudyard Kipling made a lovely rural setting for the old-time train, the carriages being ex-LBSCR stock of about 1912.

'In October 1941 I was called up for the RAF, and the Air Ministry during my four and a half years of service posted me to all parts of Britain except the Southeast, so it was not until 1947 that I once again travelled on the single line from Horsted Keynes to Culver Junction. After World War 2 broke out, I made more use of the line, as much for convenience as for pleasure. At that time my father was in Eastbourne. I was still working in the City but tried to spend as many weekends with him as possible. The restricted wartime service from London Bridge usually involved changing at East Croydon and Brighton on Saturday afternoons, and the crowded state of the main-line electrics, which usually had to pull up twice at every station, made it much more pleasant, and very little slower, to travel via Oxted. On some occasions I would catch the 1.42pm from London Bridge, which ran to Tonbridge via Oxted, Ashurst and Tunbridge Wells. I changed at Oxted into the 2.34 pm pull-and-push train to East Grinstead High Level, invariably a 'D1' 0-4-2 tank from Tunbridge Wells shed, and proceeded to Lewes by the 3pm from the Low Level platforms, which was usually worked by an 'E5' 0-6-2 tank. On at least one occasion (30 March 1940) when I finished work later than usual, I travelled down from Victoria to Oxted by the 2.30pm Tunbridge Wells West train and changed into the 3.36pm from Oxted to East Grinstead Low Level and Lewes, consisting of 'E5' No 2572 and an ex-SECR 'birdcage' set. I remember on other occasions about this period seeing the same train worked by 'D1' 0-4-2 tank No 2244. I believe that the last time I saw one of the class on the line was on 9 July 1947, when No 2215, after working the 5.11pm Lewes to Seaford and the 5.49pm return — a steam working which lingered on for years after the electrification of the coast lines — prepared to take the evening trip to Sheffield Park.

'I spent most of my spare time in the latter part of 1947 travelling over as much of the Southern Railway as possible before it ceased to exist. On Whit Saturday, 24 May, I included the Lewes area, travelling from Victoria to Brighton by a circuitous route, then to London Bridge via Ardingly, during which I recorded:

Train	Journey	No	Type	Class
3pm	East Grinstead to Lewes	2405	0-6-2T	E5
4.53pm	Lewes to Brighton	2076	4-4-2T	I3
8.35pm	Haywards Heath to London Bridge via Oxted	2076	4-4-2T	I3

'Unfortunately, 1947 is one of the years for which I am unable to find complete records, so apart from Nos 2405 and 2076 I have no record of what engines were running on the line that

Date	Engine	Type	Class	Train
11.8.32	2052	4-4-0	B4X	8pm Brighton to London Bridge
7.8.33	B486	0-6-2T	E4	(Approx 8pm) East Grinstead to Haywards Heath
26.8.33	2596	4-4-2T	I1X	3.38pm Haywards Heath to London Bridge
29.3.34	2247	0-4-2T	D1	6.41pm Haywards Heath to Horsted Keynes
26.9.34	2365	0-4-4T	D3	4.58pm Seaford to Horsted Keynes
28.9.34	2274	0-4-2T	D1	4.58pm Seaford to Horsted Keynes

day. The same applies to 5 July, when I travelled right through from London Bridge to Brighton via East Grinstead and Lewes on the 4.18pm behind 'I3' No 2088. My last run on the line as part of the Southern Railway was on Saturday, 27 December 1947, which was treated as a bank holiday, and a through train was run at 1.20pm from Brighton to Victoria via Lewes, East Grinstead and Oxted, the normal Brighton to Oxted train being cancelled. The engine was the pioneer 'I3' No 2021, which in spite of its 6ft 9in driving wheels, appeared to have no difficulty in making the grades. Unfortunately, this engine's career came to an abrupt end on the climb from Lingfield to East Grinstead, when the firebox burst and scalded the engine crew in 1951.

'For 1948 my records are more complete. The 4.18pm from London Bridge was now being worked by Atlantics, and the afternoon Oxted to Brighton train by 'I3s'. It was not until 26 September 1953 that I again travelled from London Bridge to Brighton in the through train, which now left at 4.16pm. The engine was the 'H2' Atlantic No 32422 *North Foreland*. This was my last journey on the line by ordinary train.

'On 4 October 1953 the RCTS ran a special tour of the East Sussex lines, from Three Bridges via East Grinstead, the Ashurst Spur, and the 'Cuckoo Line' to Polegate, thence up to Lewes and up the line to East Grinstead and so to Three Bridges. The engine was No 32390, the last survivor of R. Billinton's 'D3' class 0-4-4 tanks, (the last LBSCR engine to be fitted for motor-working). The next special trip was that by the 'Wealden Limited', hauled from Lewes to New Cross Gate by the 'H2' Atlantic No 32426 *St Alban's Head*. Finally came the 'Southern Counties Ltd' on 24 February 1957, when 'C2X' 0-6-0 No 32437 took over at Horsted Keynes from the 'H2' Atlantic No 32424 *Beachy Head* which had worked the train from Kew but developed big-end trouble.

'Although double-track, the line between Horsted Keynes and Ardingly had a very infrequent train service before the electrification. In LBSCR days, and for many years after the Grouping, the service was mainly given by pull-and-push trains. A few through trains to and from Brighton, mainly London Bridge services, used this line. The most interesting was the 3.8pm from Brighton to London Bridge, a 'running-in' turn for main line engines ex-Brighton Works. When there were no ex-Works engines, a 'Gladstone' or perhaps one of the various classes of 4-4-0 or 4-4-2T was the usual engine. On the electrification of the main line to Brighton in 1933 this train was diverted to start from Eastbourne at 1.51pm, involving a long wait at Haywards Heath.

'By 1934 the 'D1' tanks were distributed all over the Southern System from Exmouth Junction to Ashford (Kent). Hence the motive power on the Ardingly line became less varied. The usual engine was a Baltic or Pacific tank, which returned to Eastbourne on the 7.5pm semi-fast from London Bridge. I have a note that 'U1' 2-6-0 No 1907 was on this working on 16 February 1935 and as Eastbourne had about half a dozen of that class at the time, as well as one or two of

the unrebuilt 'B4' 4-4-0s, it is probable that most of Eastbourne's main line passenger engines appeared on the train at one time or another. 'B4' No 2049 was the engine on 11 August 1934 and an SECR 'B1' 4-4-0 on 2 November 1940, I believe No 1013 but this may not have come all the way.

'Other engines I noted on Ardingly line trains in the 1930s were as under [see table above]:

'The electrification of the Eastbourne line and the introduction of a regular electric service between Horsted Keynes and Lewes robbed the Ardingly line of most of its interest. The through afternoon train from Haywards Heath to London Bridge still ran but the engine now ran up light from Brighton. The same arrangement applied to the former 8pm from Brighton, which now started from Haywards Heath at 8.35pm, and it was on this train, on Whit Saturday, 24 May 1947, that I made my first journey by this route. My engine was 'I3' 4-4-2T No 32076.

'I had little occasion to use the Ardingly line and the only occasion I travelled on it was when the steam service was about to be withdrawn consequent upon the closure of the East Grinstead-Horsted Keynes section. I was unable to visit the line during the war years, but from my occasional visits to London Bridge or East Croydon I used to see that the through afternoon train, which still left Haywards Heath at 3.28pm and arrived at London Bridge about 5.20pm, was almost invariably worked by the 'K' class 2-6-0s.

'At various times between 1947 and 1955 I saw the following engines of this class on this particular working: Nos 32338-42/4/8/9/51-3. The remainder were mostly Three Bridges engines, whose duties were mainly freight trains on the Mid-Sussex Line. On my last journey I had No 32339 hauling a mere 'birdcage' set. This was on 14 May 1955. All the same I had a compartment to myself for the whole journey to London Bridge, except for one other passenger from East Croydon. In the circumstances it is hardly surprising that the service was withdrawn. When the East Grinstead to Horsted Keynes section was temporarily reopened, from 7 August 1956 to 16 March 1958, all the trains ran via Sheffield Park and the Ardingly line was left to the electrics.'

Dick Kirkby was another recorder of workings over the line in the period 1935-9, with just the odd sighting in the war years before resuming for 1946/7. What is of particular interest is to compare the locomotive workings either side of the divide in 1943, when restrictions were lifted. There is a marked change to the rosterings involving heavier or more modern classes, such as the Brighton Atlantics, Classes I3, B4X and K, Maunsell 2-6-0s and 'L1' 4-4-0s. The list below covers those timetable workings seen but with the numerous rail motor workings extracted, motive power for these being invariably a 'D1M', of which the following were noted: Nos 2215/21/7/9/53/99/2625/31.

Down		*1935-39*	*1940-47*
8.3am	LB-B'ton	B1 1013/101/440 E5 1516	B4X 2056 H1 2038 I3 2079
8.13am	EG-HK		E5 2572
12.3pm	V-B'ton	B4 2042/4/6/51/4/63/8	D1 1494 H1 2037 I3 2028
		B1 1101 D 1730 D1 1492	K 2344 N 1813/51
		E1 1165 F1 1196	
1pm	K-L (Goods)	E4 2490	C2X 2438
3pm	EG-L	E4 2464/519 E5 2400/2	E4 2516 E5 2405/585
3.35pm	O-B'ton	D1 2275 D3 2386/97 E4 2564/80	D3 2397 I3 2083
4.20pm	LB-B'ton	B4 2042/4/51/4/62/3 E 1491	B4 2042/56 E 1036 H2 2424
		I1X 2006/595/7	L1 1759/82/7
6.48pm	V-L (WO)	C3 2300	N 1414
6.53pm	V-L (SO)	I1X 2599/602/3	
7.7pm	EG-L	B4 2042/4/7/51/4/62-4 E 1587	B4X 2045/55 E 1159 H2 2422
		I3 2084 N 1843/54	
7.40pm	LB-HH via EG	E5 2572 I1X 2600/1/4	I1X 2599

Up			
6.22am	B'ton-LB	B4 2044	N 1843/51/4
7.53am	B'ton-LB	B1 1440 B4 2042/63 I1X 2595	B4X 2067 I3 2086 N 1826/58
		U1 1891	
8.35am	L-K (Goods)	C2X 2529	
10.48am	B'ton-V	B4 2044/54/62/3/8 D3 2388	H1 2038 I3 2076/83 N 1854
		E 1514 E4 2515/9 E5 2402/571/80	
1.20pm	B'ton-O	D1 2253 D3 2398 E4 2488/564/80	E4 2515 I3 2077/8/91
1.45pm	HH-EG	E4 2519 E5 2400/2	E4 2520 E5 2405/572
3.35pm	HH-LB	B1 1013/1440/54 E4 2579	B4X 2072 K 2338/42/3/8/9
		E5 2405/575/89/93/4	N 1839
		I1X 2603/4 I3 2030	
4.7pm	L-HK	E4 2519 E5 2585	
5.18pm	B'ton-V	B1 1101/440 E 1514 E1 1163	N 1854/8
		E5 2571/2	
8.35pm	HH-LB	H1 2037/8 I3 2078/80	H1 2039

Sundays			
8.35am	LB-B'ton	B1 1013	H1 2039
8.32am	B'ton-V	B4 2062	U1 1900

Several special workings were noted on Bank Holiday Mondays and Lingfield race days.

Bank Holiday Excursions			
17.5.37	10.52am	LB-B'ton (via SP)	E 1515
18.4.38	10.52am	LB-B'ton (via SP)	E 1516
2.8.37	8.44pm	B'ton-LB	C2X 2544
18.4.38	9.13am	EG-B'ton	E4 2478
18.4.38	9.58am	Selsdon-B'ton	C2X 2550

Summer Sunday Excursion			
28.3.38	10.15am	Selsdon-B'ton	C2X 2450

Lingfield race specials			
17.4.37	- pm	Lingfield-B'ton (via HH)	U1 1890
9.7.38	12.10pm	B'ton-Lingfield (via HH)	U1 1909

Of interest is the solitary recording of 'C3' No 2300 on 21 June 1937 and a double-headed working on 2 June 1937 on the 3.35pm Haywards Heath-London Bridge with 'C2X' No 2444 leading 'E5' No 2594. The 'C2X' was detached at East Grinstead, a Norwood engine being worked back to its home shed without taking an additional path light engine.

Over the war period a record of locomotive working was compiled by Sid Nash, who used the line frequently in his journeys up to London from the South Coast. The large sample taken (for example the 4.5pm Lewes-Horsted Keynes was noted on 52 occasions) is summarised, together with coach set numbers noted in the table as follows.

TIME	JOURNEY	TIME AT HK	DUTY	LOCOS NOTED	STOCK (SET NO)
6.22	B'ton-LB	7.16	Brighton (usually 4-4-0) 702	B4X 2052/5/67 E 1515 I3 2025	3-7 coaches, most (535) frequently 6 non-corridor
6.40	EG-B'ton	6.54	Three Bridges E4		6 coaches
7.7	B'ton-SP (749) (schoolchildren's)		Brighton 734		Pull-and-push set
8.0	SP-B		D1,later D3		Pull-and-push set
8.0	B'ton-LB		Brighton 707		(This train of 6 coaches was double-headed to Lewes, where the [537] front 3 non-corridors went up via Sheffield Park, the rear 3 corridors via Uckfield with one engine apiece)
8.20	alias L-LB	8.58	Brighton 708 B4, later B4X	B4X 2042/54/63 E1 1157	3 non-corridor (537)
8.15 8.51	HH-WH WH-HH	8.23 8.57	Three Bridges E4 or E5	(E4 2519/59/77 (E5 2403/2585/9/93	3 set 3 sct (680)
8.3	LB-L	9.53	New Cross Duty 534/5/46/9 1942 on, I3	1940 E 1157/9 1941 B4 2062(2) onwards (534) 2030/83/5/8/91	6 coaches to East Grinstead, 3 set
10.3	O-L	10.43	Brighton 683/706 D1, later D3		Pull and push set
9.6 12.7	B'ton-EG EG-B'ton	11.03 12.26	Brighton 685, 735 Brighton 685, 735		Pull and push set
10.50	B'ton-V	11.41	Brighton 669 705 E5 Three Bridges 630 Norwood 576,586 New Cross 533, 602 after 1944 regular Atlantic turn	E5 2587/94 I3 2080 H1 2037-9 H2 2421-3/6 (2426 noted 7 times)	Varied from 3 or 4 weekdays (186-7/90 219/24/38/388) to 6 or 7 on Saturdays (524/ 78/92)
12.3	V-B'ton	1.47	Brighton 703 Stewarts Lane 503,514	E1 1179 D1 1494 B4 2045 I1X 2596 H2 2423-6 (2425 noted 5 times)	3 set (229) (591) (634) (796)
1.20	B'ton-O	2.15	Tunbridge Wells West 632 Brighton 685, D3 soon changed to E4	D3 2372 E4 2496	Pull and push set changed to 3 set
1.45	HH-EG	1.53	Three Bridges 641/9/54	E4 2465/97/2518 /20/59/77 E5 2400 /3/5/2572/84/5/9/93 (2405 noted 6 times)	3 set (223/4/ 6-31/8) (535) (634/79/80)
2.34	O-L (1939)	3.14	Three Bridges E4		3 set
3.0	EG-L		Three Bridges 641/9/54	E4 2520 E5 2589	3 set (632/4)

TIME	JOURNEY	TIME AT HK	DUTY	LOCOS NOTED	STOCK (SET NO)
3.35	O-L	4.16	Brighton, Tunbridge Wells West 612, 632 (2599 4 times in 1945)	E4 2496 I1X 2597/9	3 set (595/619/50) 3 set + 1 corr on occasions
3.35	HH-EG later extended to London Bridge	3.43	Three Bridges 641 New Cross Gate 535, 548 (4-4-0s till 1942)	E1 1159 B4 2054 H1 2039 Q 544 K 2342/3/50/3	Varied from 3 (230) to 6 coaches, (506/32 /52) often just 5
4.5	L-HK via Sheffield Park (schoolchildren's)	4.38	Three Bridges 649 E4 or E5	E4 2465/84/97 2518-20/77 E5 2400/3/5/2572	3 set (551) (610/31/901/1)
4.55	HK-B'ton (via Sheffield Park)			/3/82/5//9/93 (2585 6 times)	
4.20 (4.18 Sat)	LB-B'ton	5.49	Brighton 668, 705 Generally B4X	B4 2054/74 E 1159 New Cross Gate 537 /2/5/6/67/70/1 H1 2038 H2 2421/4 K 2339/47 U1 1902 I3 2026 (2067 8 times)	3 set (536/7) /1516 B4X 2043/50 (530) (580)
5.18	B'ton-V	6.17	New Cross Gate 546 Stewarts Lane 503 later Brighton	D 1742 D1 1741/5/9 E 1516 E1 1179/1506 H1 2038 H2 2424-6 K 2347 B4X 2067 I3 2027	3-6 coaches (229/30/8) (503/18) (655)
7.5	L-N&C (7.20)		Brighton D3	D3 2368/73 /85/90/3/8	p&p 721/56
8.29	N&C-L		Brighton D3	D3 2368/73 /85/90/3/8	p&p 721/56
7.7	EG-L	7.26	Brighton 666/701/7 New Cross Gate 538	B4X 2050/5/67/71 I3 2084	3 set (238) (535)
8.5	L-HK	8.47	Brighton 734	D3 2366/83/5	push and pull (667)
8.51	HK-L		D3	/6/9/90/3/8 (2366 & 2393 each 5 times)	(756)
7.42	LB-HH	9.32	Three Bridges 620 Brighton	I1X 2598/2604 I3 2023 H2 2422	3 set (226) (738)
8.35	HH-LB	8.43-8	New Cross Gate 534, 536, 540	K 2348/9 B4X 2050 I3 2029 H1 2037/40/1	3 set (537) (559)

Sunday had its two 'Victorian' through trains each way, but the records are sparse.

Time	Journey	Time at HK	Duty	Locos Noted	Stock (Set No)
8.32	B'ton-V	9.29	Brighton 665, Stewarts Lane 501		
8.34	LB-B'ton	10.15	New Cross Gate 532	B4X 2055	6 non corridor
6.40	LB-B'ton	8.29	New Cross Gate 531	B4X 2055	6 non corridor
6.50	B'ton-LB	7.43		B4X 2070	6 non corridor (531)

The fireman of 'B4' 4-4-0 No 2068 collects the single line token from the signalman at Culver Junction as his train swings onto the single line section to Horsted Keynes on 18 August 1934. *H. F. Wheeler*

A photograph taken from the gallery of the down starting signal at Horsted Keynes of an unidentified 'B4X' running into the double-sided platform road. A tender-first working in Southern days was something of a rarity and could well have merited wartime film if connected with the 1943 closure of London Road Viaduct outside Brighton, services being curtailed at Lewes where there were no turning facilities for locomotives. *D. Bowley/S. Baker collection*

On 10 October 1943, due to bomb damage to London Road Viaduct outside Brighton, the last-mentioned train ran as the 7.7pm from Lewes behind 'E4' No 2482, comprising four non-corridor coaches. Local goods remained in the hands of 'E4', 'C2' and 'C2X' locomotives. 'C2X' No 2438 was noted on the up working at Sheffield Park on 3 April 1943.

The British Railways Period

R. C. Riley lived at Lewes in 1950-1 and made regular journeys up the line to London, noting representation by the following classes: 'B4X', 'C2' (No 2533 of Newhaven on the Kingscote goods), 'C2X', 'C3' (No 2302), 'E4', 'E5', 'E5X', 'H1', 'H2', 'I3' and 'K' (all ex-LBSCR), 'E1' and 'L1' 4-4-0s, 'Q1' (No 33002), 'N', 'U', 'U1' Moguls and 'WD' Austerity 2-8-0s. Incidentally Bill Howe mentions the small boilered 'C2' No 2533 from Newhaven shed as the last engine he can remember shunting on Turner's Siding at Sheffield Park, shortly before it was withdrawn in March 1950.

Dick Riley has written a number of articles on the line covering the postwar period. While on military service stationed at Brighton, he recalls a footplate journey in July 1943 on the 5.18pm from Brighton behind 'U1' No 1908, just after the 2-6-0s had been permitted to work on the single line section. 'B4X' No 2071 on the 4.20pm down was crossed at Sheffield Park and No 2056 on the 5.40pm down at East Grinstead. Regular journeys on the line did not commence until 1949, when he noted Bricklayers Arms 2-6-0s (Duty 540) on the 3.28pm up from Haywards Heath. These came down on the 12.8pm freight from Norwood Junction and in that summer were also employing 'Austerity' 2-8-0s which were not always filtered out by the Three Bridges foreman and continued south, to return on the 3.28pm. Those used at the time when the class was being renumbered included Nos 77205/26/31/56 and 90552/3/8.

Dick often returned from the City on the 5.40pm from London Bridge, frequently cadging a footplate ride for part of the journey once the suburbs had been left behind, and even helping with the firing. He noted with a smile that some of the footplate crews were keen to partake of the refreshment facilities during the long pause at East Grinstead, and then hot-footed it to Horsted Keynes — 'After all it was an event for anyone to board or leave the train at Kingscote' — to gain a few extra minutes in the buffet there, leaving Dick in full possession of the footplate, waiting to receive the single line staff from Bill Moon with a friendly gasp, 'So it's you again!' While waiting, Dick had time to reflect upon the notice by the water crane: 'Water to be taken by enginemen only when absolutely necessary.' Leaving late from Horsted, the crew ensured Lewes was reached on time after a lively ride.

On a Sunday journey with the 6.50pm from Brighton with 'E1' No 1511, travelling just the Lewes-East Grinstead section, a distinct scarcity of passengers was noted. Apart from a just over two-minute stop at Barcombe, the rest were all well under a minute, with West Hoathly hosting the train for just 14 seconds and Kingscote for 17. The return trip was with 'E5X' No 32576.

O. V. S. Bulleid's experimental 0-6-6-0T 'Leader' class No 36001 is recorded or having traversed the line on 5 September 1949. Having failed on a trial trip at Oxted, it

'K' Mogul No 32340 storms out of West Hoathly with one of the heaviest trains over the double track section, the 3.28pm Haywards Heath-London Bridge on 21 May 1955. *R. C. Riley*

An unusual choice for the inter-closure service is Maunsell 'Q' 0-6-0 No 30540, a Norwood Junction engine, with the 10.28am East Grinstead to Lewes. It is seen on 1 April 1957 in the steep-sided cutting south of East Grinstead, variously known as Hill Place, Imberhorne and Saint Hill Cutting. *J. C. Beckett*

limped down the line light engine to Brighton, taking water at Sheffield park where a garden hose was borrowed from the timber yard and connected to a tap ion the pump house. People have often supposed that the line remained steam to the end but that was not quite the case. In August 1952 the LMR's experimental diesel locomotive No 10800 was transferred to the Southern Region, which carried out a series of test runs on the Central Section to Brighton via Dorking and Horsham, and via Oxted and Eridge. It did pass through East Grinstead on a trip to Tunbridge Wells but no running over the Lewes to East Grinstead line was included in the official rosters. However, on 30 March 1954 it failed at Balham on the 3.52pm Victoria-Brighton, involving serious damage to the diesel engine. It was taken off at Streatham Common and towed to Norwood shed, and on 6 April was hauled by a 'C2X' to Brighton Works via Oxted and East Grinstead, calling at Sheffield Park to pick up the SR-built diesel shunter No 15203, which had failed there several days previously while running light to Brighton Works, pointing to the use of the line for locomotives, including diesel shunters, to reach Brighton Works that way. Mention of Brighton Works is also relevant in connection with the running-in of new locomotives constructed there in the years following the war.

One of the aims of Nationalisation was to provide a modern fleet of standard type locomotives to take over workings still undertaken by veteran pre-Grouping types. This appeared as an urgent priority on the Central Section and, to fill the gap until the new standard types began to emerge in sufficient

numbers, a fleet of LMR Fairburn 2-6-4Ts was sent in 1951 to help out on the Eastern Section. By 1953 these had also gravitated to the Central Section, soon to be followed by LMR Ivatt 2-6-2Ts, both classes taking over a large number, but by no means all, of the Lewes-East Grinstead line's workings. From July 1951 Standard Class 4 2-6-4Ts began to come off the production line at Brighton Works, and many were noted on running-in turns over the line. The Southern Region received only 23 of the original build (Nos 80010-9/31-3 and 80145-54). These were first based at Tunbridge Wells West but soon worked a range of Central Division passenger services from London to the coast and also cross-country routes, the Southern allocation being split between Tunbridge Wells West and Brighton. By the time of the final withdrawals, 60 of the class had been allocated to Southern metals, many coming from elsewhere in the country, such as the Tilbury line, so that the array of members of this class hauling away condemned wagons south through Horsted Keynes early in 1960 was very varied indeed. Nos 80011/31/2/41/88/138/40 were all recorded on this duty. Also seen on these workings were 'Ks' Nos 32343/50, 'U1' No 31890 and, a surprise for this line, Class 4 2-6-0 No 76055.

In the final years up to the 1955 closure, former LBSCR locomotives were still to be seen on a regular basis. Analysing the photographs in the Bluebell Archives relating to the years 1948-55, the following gives a representative cross-section of the different motive power used during the period:

The most modern of motive power to be seen on the line came right at the end, on 9 April 1960; BR Standard Class 4 2-6-0 No 76055 sets back with its train of condemned wagons at the south end of Horsted Keynes, while the 11.16am electric service to Seaford, unusually comprising a 4LAV unit, leaves for Haywards Heath. *W. M. J. Jackson*

The switchback nature of the line north of Barcombe is apparent as on 25 May 1955, just three days before the first closure, the 5.18pm Brighton-Victoria is hauled in the soft evening sunshine by 'T9' 4-4-0 No 30718 of Nine Elms. This working was used to bring spare vehicles back to London and on this occasion a Pullman car is attached at the rear. *Savona* had on 7 April been given trial runs, being formed in the 11.33am Lancing-Redhill and 2.45pm Redhill-Brighton en route to Preston Park shops. *S. C. Nash*

Engine changeover at East Grinstead Low Level during the 'sour grapes' service. The usual 'C2X' on the 11.30am from Lewes has been replaced by ex-SECR 'C' 0-6-0 No 31725. 'E4' No 32494 has backed on to form the 12.28pm to Lewes. The 'C' meanwhile has to go on to collect the 12.40pm goods to Norwood. *R. Hobbs*

A delightful shot of the single-coach 12.28pm ex-East Grinstead in the lunchtime sunshine at Lewes, behind 'C2X' No 32449.
Denis Cullum

C2X	32437/8/40/42/7/2528/36/9/40/7 (10)	
D3	32390 (1)	
E4	32471/5/94/2504/8/16/7/9/20/77/82 (11)	
E5	32585 (1)	
H1	32037 (1)	
H2	32421/4-6 (4)	
I1X	2002 (1)	
I3	32076/86 (2)	
K	32339/40/2/4/5 (5)	
N	31815/24/53 (3)	
U1	31892/4/1900/2/4 (5)	
BB	34071 (1)	
E (SE)	31273 31491 (2)	
T9 (SW)	30718 (1)	
LMR Cl4	42080-2/7/8/90/9/101-5 (12)	
LMR Cl2	41299/1302/6/7/12/13/16-9 (10)	
BR Cl.4	80012/5-7/31-3/105/145/53 (10)	

The final period of running to a very basic 'four trains each way' interval timetable took place from 7 August 1956 to 16 March 1958. Confirmation of engine workings comes from Geoffrey Robinson, who lived at Felbridge and closely monitored the services. He writes:

'At first the line was worked from the Lewes end by one 'C2X' from Brighton all day from 9.30am up to the 5.17pm arrival or later at Lewes. However, about October 1956, there were complaints by engine crews about so much tender-first running in winter, so to avoid this, four engines were employed on the service instead of one, as follows:

9.30am	up	E4	ex-Brighton
10.28am	down	C2X	ex-Norwood
11.30am	up	C2X	ex-Lewes Yard pilot
12.28pm	down	E4	(from 9.30am)
1.30pm	up		⎫
2.28pm	down		All Std Cl4 2-6-4T
3.30pm	up		ex-Brighton
4.28pm	down		⎭

'The 'E4' was replaced by a 'C2X' ex-Norwood, which had brought down the goods to East Grinstead, arriving about 10.5am. The 'E4' then shunted upper and lower yards and in doing so got a fill-up at the water crane in the High Level Platform 5. It then assembled the up goods to Norwood and left this in the Low Level siding. Meanwhile the 'C2X' reached Lewes. There being no time to water and turn, the Norwood engine became Lewes Yard Pilot and the previous pilot returned to East Grinstead, picked up the Norwood freight (waiting ready assembled) to get away about 12.40pm. As the 'E4' could not run to East Grinstead and back without water, it was replaced for the afternoon. The standard tank would not do for the morning because no spare engine of this class was available then, except Sundays. Indeed there were times when the 'E4' carried on in the afternoon and then water had to be taken at Horsted Keynes (which apparently was something to be avoided at all costs if possible!). Lest it be assumed that BR Class 4 tanks virtually monopolised the 'reopening' workings, they only did so on Saturdays and Sundays, classes 'C2X' and 'E4' taking a hand on the other days. The fact that enthusiastic photographers generally came at the weekends led to this impression.'

In February 1957 *The Railway Observer* reported: 'The afternoon trips on Mondays to Fridays are now worked by a Stewarts Lane 2-6-4T on duty 508.'

During the brief reopening period the photographic breakdown of locomotives represented was:

C2X	32434/7/8/40/2/3/6/9/521/36/49 (11)
E4	32467/8/84/5/94/504/8/12/62/71 (10)
K	32342
C (SE)	31724/5
H2	32424
Q	30540
BR Class 4	80010/1/31-3/140/5-7/9/51-4 (13)

From photographic records the following locomotives are known to have been involved during the period January- April 1960: Standard Class 4 2-6-4 T Nos 80011/31/2/41/138/

The rail-strike-delayed final railtour up the line, or so people fondly imagined, was the RCTS 'Wealden Limited', which contained a Pullman car in its formation for the sustenance of the participating enthusiasts. The specially chosen engine is Brighton shed's splendidly turned out Atlantic No 32426 *St Alban's Head*, here seen between Newick & Chailey and Sheffield Park on 14 August 1955. *R. C. Riley*

In the 1950s, trains which had emanated from London and terminated at East Grinstead Low Level were turned for their return journey by running forward onto Imberhorne Viaduct, then reversing up the goods spur into the High Level goods yard, before running forward into the High Level platforms, thus leaving the locomotive facing London. Here Fairburn 2-6-4T No 42105 is carefully propelling its Maunsell four-set past the tall LBSCR signal controlling the exit to the Low Level line on 13 March 1958. It was rarer for this procedure to take place in reverse from the High to Low Level station. *R. C. Riley*

140/ 153, 'N1' 2-6-0 31890 and 'K' 2-6-0 No 32343, the latter two hauling the final trains as they are portrayed just north of Imberhorne viaduct with their respective rakes of condemned wagons.

A final word on locomotive practice and performance. By its very nature, the line was not one to produce any sensational running, so next to nobody considered taking any timings. However one who did, though towards the very end, was A. G. S. Davies, who relates:

'My very first memory is of a golden day in August 1955, when Marsh Atlantic No 32426 made her stately way up the line with the RCTS 'Wealden Ltd' special train. Many people will recollect the sight of *St Alban's Head* glinting in the evening sunlight at Horsted Keynes — a real Brighton vignette if ever. My own railway *metier*, the art of train timing, was still very much in the development stage at that time, and the only record I have of that occasion is a speed of 40mph after West Hoathly. No record, alas!, of how the Atlantic tackled the 1 in 75 of Freshfield Bank with eight carriages.

'My first run on the line in fact was in April 1955 behind 2-6-4T No 80033 on the 11.2 Brighton-Victoria, load four carriages. On this occasion speeds of 42 and 45mph were recorded before and after the Newick stop, and No 80033 climbed Freshfield Bank at 30-31mph. A week later, on 7 May, I travelled on the 3.28pm Haywards Heath-London Bridge, one of those 'out-of-the-ordinary' Southern trains that was often worked by a 'K' class Mogul. I was unlucky that day, for 'U1' 2-6-0 No 31900 worked it — there was a 'K' shunting at Haywards Heath at the time! The load was seven carriages as far as East Grinstead, where four carriages were detached. At London Bridge the ECS was worked out to Rotherhithe Road. This was on a Saturday. On Mondays-Fridays the stock of the 3.28pm formed the 5.40pm back to Lewes.

'My final BR run over the line was during the Bessemer period, in November 1956, when I had a run with No 80019 on the 12.28pm East Grinstead-Lewes, coming back at 1.30pm with No 42071, load one carriage. I recorded 45mph down Freshfield Bank, and 35-33mph uphill.'

While serving a pupillage in the Locomotive Department of the LBSCR, Charles Hodgson formed a friendship with John Saxby, and joined him and J.S. Farmer when their factory was opened at Kilburn, occupying various administrative positions there. At the time of the LEGR contract, Hodgson personally supervised the installation of the line's signalling. On the incorporation of Saxby & Farmer Ltd in 1893, he became managing director and later chairman of the board, holding these offices until his death in 1912.
Westinghouse Brake & Signal Co

Below: Twin photographs showing the Webb & Thompson electric train staff for the Culver Junction-Horsted Keynes section. The small extension beyond the embossed name is the Annett's key to open and lock relevant ground frames. *Courtesy Peter Hay*

10.
Signalling

Saxby and Farmer

The story of the Lewes to East Grinstead line is inextricably linked with the firm of Saxby & Farmer. Born near Hurstpierpoint in 1821, John Saxby had entered the service of the LBSCR at Brighton, becoming eventually the foreman of one of the shops at Brighton Works. He developed an interest in signalling and had in 1856 installed a locking frame, in which signal and point levers were made to control one another, which he duly patented. From 1863 he was joined by John Stinson Farmer, Assistant Traffic Manager of the railway from 1849-62, with whom he executed a deed of partnership and left the railway service. They set up their signal works close to the line at Haywards Heath. Together they were responsible through to 1900 for effectively supplying mechanical signalling equipment to the LBSCR. By virtue of being given a monopoly, the LBSCR was way ahead of other companies with interlocking in the 1860s and achieved the 100% figure in 1880. As such, Saxby & Farmer installed the signalling for the LEGR, and John Saxby himself attended the inspection of the Haywards Heath-Horsted Keynes line on 31 August 1883, 'explaining the interlocking of the signals and points on what is generally known as the "block system".

But at the inspection of the Lewes-East Grinstead line over a year previously, Saxby & Farmer was represented by a Mr Charles Hodgson, an apprentice who had started in the locomotive workshops in Brighton in 1858. While serving his engineering pupillage he had formed a good working relationship with Saxby, who had persuaded him to undertake his early patent drawings, and in 1860 Saxby invited him to become his partner. However, Hodgson had not reached his majority and his father remained adamant — 'No equal partnership, none of the capital of £2000!' The opportunity was passed to Farmer. However, Hodgson was invited to become Works Manager at their factory at Kilburn. On the incorporation of Saxby & Farmer Ltd in 1893, he became Managing Director and later Chairman of the board, holding the offices until his death in 1912.

At the inspection at which Hodgson was present, Colonel Yolland from the Board of Trade had a special word of commendation for Saxby & Farmer. 'The terms of unqualified approbation which were expressed in the Inspecting Officer's certificate are highly creditable to Messrs Saxby & Farmer, the signal engineers. His commendations referred particularly to the perfected signalling arrangements, especially for their ingenious application of electrical agency in their union of lock and block, points and signals, the single-line section

being worked on the electric train staff system.' The line was perhaps fortunate to become both guinea pig and showpiece for these revolutionary and successful experiments, which soon spread to other portions of the Brighton system.

Fortunately the opening 'Notice to Engine Drivers, Guards, Signalmen and all concerned' survives today in the Bluebell Archives, stating: 'The electric block signalling of trains on this new line will be to the union of Lock and Block (Saxby & Farmer's system)', and refers to separate instructions. The single portion of the line was to be worked under rules and regulations for working single lines by train staff or train ticket. It goes on to detail the location of every signalbox and signal on the line, allotting a whole page to 'the Junction Station of Horsted Keynes, with its main South box and a smaller North box on the down side of the line, about 60 yards north of the platform,' but, according to the notice, 'will not be brought into use at present', presumably awaiting the completion of the branch to Haywards Heath. Newick & Chailey had a signalbox placed at the south end of the up platform, with a small shunting box placed at the north end of the same platform, controlled from the main signalbox. Likewise the South box at Sheffield Park provided a close view of the goods yard opposite, though here the shunting box was at the north end of the down platform.

East Grinstead Low Level started as a temporary terminus and at the outset its future South and later 'C' box was located at the south end of the up platform. The spur line to the old High Level goods yard was classified as a siding rather than a spur, being provided with catch points at the south end near the viaduct, the points leading to the siding being fitted with an Annett's Lock (named after J. Annett, Signal Superintendent of the LSWR, who invented the key in 1875). Basically, it unlocks ground frames which control access to the sidings remote from a signalbox. The key can only be removed from the ground frame when it is locked with the points in position for trains running on the main line. The key is usually kept in the signalbox and cannot be released from there unless the signals protecting the ground frame are locked at danger and cannot be moved until the key is replaced.

'Culver Junction, late Barcombe Junction' box had a full set of distant, rear and starting signals for each of the three directions, and specific instructions regarding recognition of engine whistles, one toot for Uckfield line trains and two for East Grinstead line trains.

The line between Ardingly box and East Grinstead South box was the only section of the LBSCR equipped with Saxby & Farmer Union Lock and Block system, invented in 1871 by Charles Hodgson. The boxes on this section had the special instruction that 'The "Train entering section" signal must be

INSTRUCTIONS FOR WORKING
UNION OF LOCK AND BLOCK INSTRUMENTS
(SAXBY AND FARMER'S SYSTEM).

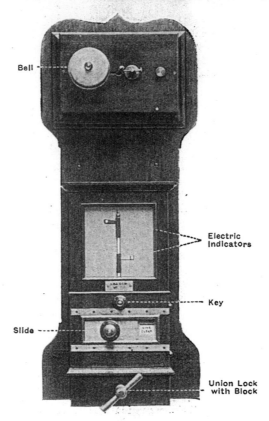

Saxby and Farmer's Union of Lock and Block Instrument.

(*a*) **A, B,** and **C** represent three consecutive Signal Boxes, each provided with the Union of Lock and Block Instruments.

(*b*) When a Train is approaching or about to start from **A** (if the **Train out of Section** signal has been received for the previous Train), it must be signalled on to **B,** and if the Line is clear **B** must set his Points, as necessary, in the proper position for the approaching Train ; having done this, the handle of his instrument becomes unlocked. He must then turn the handle so as to unlock the Sliding Plunger, move it to the left, and then give the **Line Clear** Signal to **A.**

(*c*) The giving of the **Line Clear** Signal by **B** releases the Electrical Slot on the Starting Signal at **A,** which Signal **A** can then lower for the Train to proceed.

Note.—To lower this Signal it is necessary to pull over, replace, and again pull the lever.

(*d*) When the Train has passed the Starting Signal, **A** must signal it out again to **B,** who must move his Sliding Plunger to the right, acknowledge the Signal to **A,** and block the Line by putting the Instrument to **Train on Line** which will put the Starting Signal at **A** to **Danger** (if **A** has not already done so), and lock the instrument at **B,** so that no further **Line Clear** Signal can be given to **A** until the Train has arrived and passed over the Treadle at **B.**

(*e*) The Train in passing over the Treadle at **B** unlocks the Slide Plunger, also the handle in that Signal Box, and the **Train out of Section** Signal (Three Beats) can then be sent to **A, B,** still keeping the instrument at **Line Closed** until the **Warning** Signal for a following Train is received from **A.**

(*f*) **B** must in like manner signal the Train on to **C,** and the same process of signalling must be carried out between each two Signal Boxes as described above.

Note.—These Instruments are in use between East Grinstead South and Ardingly Signal Boxes.

sent after the train has passed the advance starting signal.' A new 57-lever box was also installed at Haywards Heath North. It has been suggested that the overall arrangements for the line were rather more elaborate than seemed necessary, for between Culver Junction and East Grinstead inclusive, there were no less than 11 signalboxes.

Signalboxes

It was on the LBSCR that the signalbox as we know it was developed by John Saxby. The group of LBSCR lines opened between 1880 and 1883 (Hailsham-Eridge, Chichester-Midhurst and East Grinstead-Barcombe/Haywards Heath) had signalboxes designed to correspond with the station buildings and were designed by the same architect, T. H. Myres, who sought to match the signalboxes with the elaborate half-timbered station buildings, to form a harmonious ensemble. Known as LBSC Type 1 in the notation of the Signalling Study Group, 27 of these boxes were built, several stations boasting a pair. They were constructed by the same building contractors as the station buildings, the small 'crosses' in the panels above the windows being the only decorative feature. The boxes were constructed of brick up to operating floor level, with timber above. The operating floor windows were three panels deep. The only remaining box of this type is the large 40-lever example at Horsted Keynes (South), which was built slightly larger than the rest to accommodate the additional levers controlling extra platforms and the junction.

East Grinstead South was a Type 2 timber box, which category also first appeared around 1880, having frames of a new design developed by Saxby & Farmer. This type was hipped, square in appearance with horizontal lapped boarding and square panels, two-panes-by-two. There were wide variations into sub-types but East Grinstead South box had no valancing. The signal cabin at the north end of the down Low Level platform was built over a year later as part of the extension north to South Croydon and it fits in with the Type 2 pattern of boxes on that line, which displayed attractive brackets supporting the eaves.

Signals

These have been classified into three general categories, all to be found in use on the line. The first and most well known were the running signals, namely the stop signal (consisting of an arm with a red face and a white stripe on the front, while the reverse was white with a black stripe), including home and starter signals according to their location, and the caution or distant signal, usually fish-tailed and (after about 1920, before which the fronts were red with white) painted yellow with a black stripe on the front and white with a black chevron on the reverse. When a signal's arm was horizontal it was said to be 'on' and when either raised or lowered it was said to be 'off'. The signals originally installed on the line lowered to the off position and were known as the lower quadrant type. A weight to counter the weight of the signal arm was later introduced, to ensure that if the wire were to break the signal would remain at danger. Under the SR the days of Brighton lower quadrant signals were numbered, though the replacements by upper quadrants were gradual and some remained to the bitter end. Coloured glasses were fitted into a cast-iron spectacle,

the weight of which balanced the arms. The glasses thus moved in unison with the arm and were illuminated at night by a stationary lamp. At some points the distant signal, which indicates that the driver must be prepared to stop at the next stop signal, was fixed; the distant advising the approach from Ardingly towards the junction at Horsted Keynes was a prime example, where the metal arm was in fact permanently fastened to the post. Incidentally the Sheffield Park down distant signal, at 1,520yd, was one of the longer 'pulls' on the system.

The second category was shunting signals, which took many forms. When 'off', it permits the driver to pass, but only for as far as he can see the line to be clear. The most common type on the LBSCR was the 'Tommy Dod', a disc which rotates horizontally, thereby showing two faces towards the driver. When at danger it exhibits a red target with a white hand pointing towards the line to which it applies, in the direction of an approaching movement. When pulled to clear, the target turns through a quarter-circle and the green face, with a white cross painted thereon, is shown towards the shunt movement. One restored working example can be seen at Sheffield Park today. Later rotating devices were either white with a red stripe or yellow with a black stripe.

The third sort were 'information' signals with regard to speed restrictions, sounding the whistle, gradient and mileposts, and stop boards, which required the driver to stop his train and call the signalman, to obtain the latter's permission to proceed. Examples of wooden whistle boards, gradient and mileposts survived to the end.

A classic feature of Brighton signalling was the solid, square-section wooden post, tapered towards the top. The Lewes-East Grinstead line was noted for several extremely tall starting signal posts, which enabled train crews to sight the arms above the station canopies at a comfortable distance ahead. The last one of these was the up starter at Horsted Keynes which survived until the mid-1960s, later to be reused on another portion of the reopened line. Such signals were also for the benefit of the signalman, for instance at West Hoathly, where the footbridge linking the platforms blocked out a good part of the signalman's view south, and at Horsted Keynes South box, where the signalman needed to operate points and control movements at the north end of the station. This problem became so acute that it was decided to remove all the buildings in the west island platform to clear the view.

The LBSCR used its own method of block working, quite different from that used by most other railways. There was no 'Is line clear?' bell signal, the first signal for a train being known as the 'warning', which was acknowledged by exact repetition whether the signalman in advance could accept a train or not. If he could, he replied with one extra beat, and lowered the arm of the block instruments. The 'Train out of section' signal was called the 'arrival' and consisted of three consecutive beats on the Tyers and Harper's instruments prevalent throughout the company's non-suburban lines.

Rationalisation

During the years the line was open, the signalling arrangements at each station underwent a continuing process of change. Sheffield Park is an example, as related by John Hemsley, being originally controlled from two signalboxes. It was the policy in those days to have the box overlooking the

Left: Instructions for working Saxby & Farmer's Union of Lock & Block instruments. *Courtesy Peter Hay*

A quartet of LEGR signalboxes

Left: Signalman T. J. Lamminan looks out of his box as the 1.25pm ex-Brighton via Haywards Heath arrives at East Grinstead at 2.31pm behind 'I1' 4-4-2T No 598 and enters the Low Level station. The box started life as East Grinstead South, became East Grinstead C in Southern days, back to East Grinstead South during the early BR period and finally plain East Grinstead after the abolition of the High Level lines in the summer of 1968. *Kenneth Nutt*

Centre left: A glimpse of East Grinstead Low Level North signalbox with Signalman 'Juggy' Wren on the balcony, carefully eyeing an 'I3' 4-4-2T, which has run round its train, gently easing into the down platform. *Kenneth Nutt*

Lower Left: The scene at Culver Junction as the signalman prepares to hand the staff for the East Grinstead line to the fireman of 2-6-4T No 42087. The signalman normally gave the staff from the box side. This special arrangement was made through the station inspector at Lewes, who duly advised the driver. *R. C. Riley*

Upper right: A pre-1915 view of the North box at Horsted Keynes, just prior to the outbreak of World War 1. The LBSCR undertook a rationalisation of the signalling at the station. The North box was relegated to a shunting frame and later demolished. Signalman F. Simmons proudly stands on the boarded walkway outside.
Roger Resch collection/ Bluebell Archives

Kingscote, photographed on 28 August 1953. Prominent in this picture stands the lower quadrant down starting signal with its tapered wooden post. Its opposite number at the north end of the up platform has already succumbed to renewal but is an interesting lattice post upper quadrant example. Both signals are 'off', suggesting that the box at the north end of the down platform is switched out. *Pamlin Prints*

Horsted Keynes up starting signal, one of the most impressive of the original examples on the line, lasted right through to the late 1960s when the Bluebell Railway decided to utilise the post at a new location. Ex-LMS 2-6-4T No 42102 runs into the station with the 2.34pm from East Grinstead. *R. Hobbs*

Barcombe down distant signal, an original 1882 recessed post. The photograph was taken in 1928; the signal was replaced in 1933. *O. J. Morris, ref 14389*

Etching of LBSCR dummy or 'Tommy Dod' ground signal. *Bluebell Archives*

goods yard where possible; having the South box in such a position rendered the points at the north end of the station too far away to be worked mechanically from that box. To overcome this, the North box was provided, the sole purpose of which was to work these points. It was in fact a covered ground frame, being released in nearly everything it controlled by the South box. This arrangement was in existence for the first 50-odd years of the life of the line, and is depicted in the diagram dated circa 1925 (*right*).

The actual procedure for signalling trains through the station is of some interest, in view of its somewhat complicated nature. If an up train was to pass through the station, for example, the North box signalman would have needed to release his No 6 points. In order to do this, he first had to obtain a release from the South box, which he did by pulling 'asking' lever No 4. This changed an indicator in the South box from blank to 'want' (up points). The signalman in the South box then pulled his No 9 release lever, which changed an indicator in the North box from (up points) 'locked' to 'free', at the same time removing a physical lock from the North box points connections. This enabled the

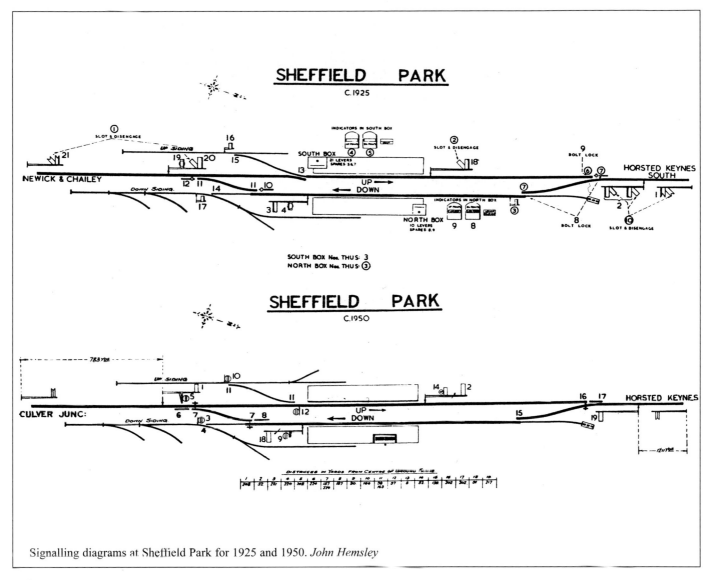

Signalling diagrams at Sheffield Park for 1925 and 1950. *John Hemsley*

North box signalman to actually reverse No 6 points, followed by Nos 1 and 2 slot and disengagers on the up home, starter and distant signals. The signalman in the South box then pulled Nos 20, 18 and 21, whereupon the signals cleared. Either box could replace the signals at any time, and the North box if he did so could restore his points to normal. Crossing trains would appear to have been rather laborious.

With the economic decline of the railways after World War 1, the saving of manpower was obviously a primary consideration, so the Southern Railway duly replaced the two boxes with the present platform level ground frame. It was surrounded by an 'unclimbable iron fence', the staff instruments being transferred from the old South box to the booking office. The same track layout was retained, although obviously renumbered, but minor signalling changes were effected, such as the provision of a shunt-ahead signal beneath the up starter.

Newick & Chailey box was abolished, being replaced by a ground frame in September 1938 and Sheffield Park to Culver Junction became one staff section. This arrangement lasted until after the first closure in 1955 and is depicted in the diagram dated circa 1950. The old Brighton ground signals were replaced with the Southern pattern after World War 2; also the old Brighton up home signal was struck by lightning in the early 1950s and replaced with a rail-post upper quadrant with a side-mounted dummy (now at Horsted Keynes). Just prior to the reopening of the line in 1956, Sheffield Park box was put out of use, the signal arms being removed and the points clipped and padlocked for the down line, which became in effect part of the single line. The line from Horsted Keynes to Culver was worked as one staff section.

The rather more major alterations made at Horsted Keynes, together with accounts of the workings of the box there and at Ardingly, are included in the chapters on the respective stations. As has been hinted, the lavish state of the signalling arrangements installed at the line's opening soon came to be rationalised, first by the LBSCR in the years either side of World War 1 and then by the Southern Railway's pruning of the stations in the 1930s. Both boxes at Newick & Chailey and at Sheffield Park were removed and replaced by platform ground frames operated by porter signalmen, and with access from the booking office. Horsted Keynes North box went in 1914, the signalbox at Barcombe was abolished in 1932, and Kingscote box was used for goods shunting only. Today the only original box surviving is at Horsted Keynes (South), while the platform ground frame at Sheffield Park has been rebuilt for today's more extensive traffic.

The scene after closure in 1958 was a desolate one on the section south from Horsted Keynes, with the signalling dismantled and rusting arms buried in the undergrowth, but much of the equipment on the five-mile stretch south to Sheffield Park was salvaged and reused by the Bluebell Railway.

Above: The open signal frame located at the centre of Sheffield Park's down platform on 18 April 1955. It had replaced the original North and South boxes in 1934. *R. C. J. Day/ Peter Winding collection*

Left: Veteran Signalman at Horsted Keynes, Bill Moon, was photographed in the South box on 9 September 1950, and provides a close look at the equipment housed within. *R. C. Riley*

11.
Incidents

Newick

The line had its fair share of relatively minor mishaps and it is strange that the most notable one, and the only one of sufficient concern to be referred to the Railway Department of the Board of Trade for investigation and a full report, took place soon after the line was opened. The *Sussex Express* for Tuesday, 9 January 1883 reported, under the heading 'Newick/The New Railway/Accident', 'As the 9.10pm train from East Grinstead was leaving Newick station on Thursday evening, the train was turned into the siding instead of the main line and ran into the buffer stops with some considerable force. It is stated that the fireman was injured and a passenger somewhat shaken by the concussion.'

The report identified the locomotive on the train as 'D' tank No 265 *Chipstead*, hauling bunker first a local train consisting of five coaches (Third class brake, Second, Third, an unidentified coach and a passenger brake van.) The report lists the somewhat shaken passenger as the sole paying occupant on the train, a telling statistic despite being the last down train of the day, though it must be borne in mind that the line had only been open for a little over five months and all services terminated at East Grinstead Low Level which, till 10 March 1884, made it just a branch line compared to the secondary line it became when the line was opened to South Croydon. For the signalling enthusiast, the reader is introduced into the intricacies and levers of the South box, and into the practices and malpractices of the station staff.

The report of the accident was submitted by Colonel W. Yolland, Railway Inspector for the Board of Trade, none other than the man who only half a year previously had certified the line's fitness to operate a public service in more than ordinary commendatory terms, having, 'never seen better work done'.

On 17 February 1883 he presented his report:

'The result of my enquiry into the circumstances which attended a collision that occurred on the 4th January between a passenger train and the buffer-stops at the end of a siding at the Newick & Chailey station of the East Grinstead and Lewes branch of the London, Brighton and South Coast Railway. No passenger was injured, but the fireman of the engine was somewhat seriously hurt. The engine was a good deal damaged, the foot plating broken, and the break-rods, back tool box, lamp irons, and hand rail broken. The third-class break-carriage, which was next to the engine, had one headstock, one end panel, three buffer-facings, one step-

board, and one end-rail broken; also one door-light, two buffers, one draw-bar and two step irons broken. No 293, second-class carriage, had two headstocks, two buffer-castings, one buffer-facing, and one quarter-light broken, and one sole-bar slightly damaged. No 305, third-class carriage, had one buffer-casting broken, and the buffer-stops at the end of the siding were smashed.

'Description
The East Grinstead and Lewes Branch is a single line, with loop lines at most of the stations which are used as passing places. There is such a loop at the Newick & Chailey station, with sidings on each side of the line. The signalbox is situated at the south end of the up platform at the south end of the station, and there is a pair of facing-points about 40 yards south of the signalbox on the down line, which points are properly interlocked with the signals and worked from the signalbox. These facing-points lead to the single line on the right hand, and to a siding about 400 yards in length, and terminated by buffer-stops on the left hand. Before the down starting-signal, moved by No 3 lever, can be lowered for a down train to leave the station, levers No 9 & 10, which shift the facing-points and locking bar, must be pulled over to ensure that the points are in their proper position for a down train to proceed.'

Col Yolland then quoted extracts from the Appendix to the LBSCR Working Time Book, showing, 'what a signalman has to do when anything is wrong with the facing points or starting signals', in particular the paragraphs under the heading, 'Signals controlling facing points'. These stressed in the event of finding anything wrong, the signalman must send out hand signalmen to act under his directions, and check the correct setting of the points and immediately inform the stationmaster. Then followed the evidence:

'First to be heard was William Notley, who made a clean confession: 'I was in the signalbox at Newick station on the night of the 4th January doing duty as a signalman. I went in at 6.30pm, and I was to remain there until the last train had passed a little after 10pm. I had been in the habit about one week in three of taking the signalman's duty in the evening. There had been an up train passed through the station, before the accident occurred to this down train, after I went into the box. A down train from East Grinstead arrived here at 10.1pm, the proper time. I gave the signal for the train to leave the station by a hand lamp. I gave this signal by a hand lamp because I thought the semaphore starting-signal was hung up. I tried to pull that signal, but was unable to do so. It is pulled

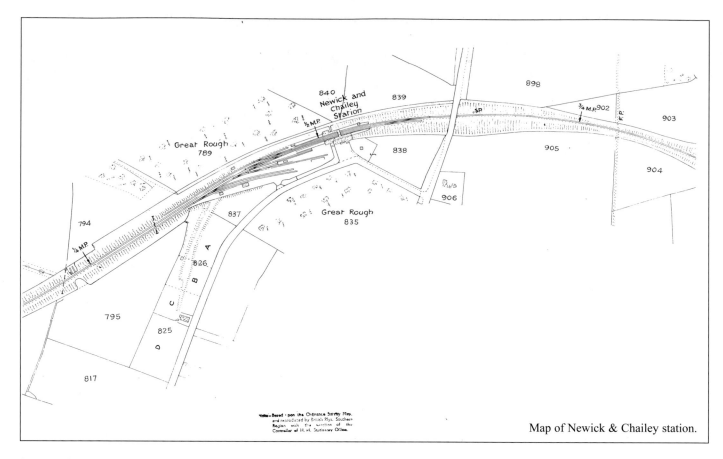

Map of Newick & Chailey station.

by No 3 lever. I told the driver that I could not pull it off. I did not attempt to move the lever that shifts the facing-points. I thought those facing-points stood right for the main road at that time. I had never had any instruction as to the mode in which the levers should be worked; nothing more than I had learnt myself. I am not aware that there was any rule forbidding trains to be started by hand signals. The train started and ran into the siding, and was pulled up by running into the stop-blocks. I did not try the levers that same night after the accident happened, to ascertain whether the starting-signal could be taken off or not. The accident happened from my mistake, and I have no reason to believe that the signalling apparatus was out of order.'

'Jesse Marshall, engine-driver between seven and eight years, states: "I was driving tank-engine No 265 in front of the 9.10pm train from East Grinstead to Brighton on the 4th January. It consisted of five carriages altogether, including a break-van and one break-carriage. It was fitted throughout with the Westinghouse automatic break. We reached Newick about 10pm, the proper time. We were running with the chimney behind. The stationmaster and guard gave the signal to start, after a delay of about one minute. The starting-signal was not taken off for us to leave. I started the train, and stopped at the signal, which was on danger against me, and the signalman put his head out of the window, showed a green light, and said he could not pull the starting-signal. He said, 'All right, — right away.' It was a very dark night. I then started again, and I thought I was running on the right road until my mate called out, 'Hold hard,' and we struck the buffer stops just as he called out. I had shut off the steam as we struck the buffer stops. I think we might have been running about 20 miles an hour when we struck the buffer stops, which we knocked down. The engine got off the rails, the carriage-break next the engine also got off the rails, and the front wheels of the carriage next to it also got off the rails, but no other vehicles. My mate was seriously hurt and off duty for a fortnight. I was not hurt."

'Joseph George, fireman to Jesse Marshall, states: "We reached Newick about 10pm and stopped there about a minute. We then started and stopped at the starting signal, which was on at danger. We received a green light from a hand lamp from the signalbox. The signalman said the lever or the rod of the starting signal was broken, and he could not pull down the signal. We then started again, and I was not aware that we were running on the wrong line until I saw the reflection of the light on the lamp on the buffer-beam of the engine on the buffer-stops, when we were not more than about two yards from them. We were then running about 30 miles an hour. As soon as I saw the light on the buffer-stops I told my mate to stop. I do not know what my mate did, as I was struck on the head as the engine came into collision with the buffer-stops. I was taken to the hospital and was a good deal hurt."

'Walter Hunt, guard a little more than two years, states: "I was guard of the 9.10pm passenger train from East Grinstead to Brighton on the 4th January last, and rode in the last vehicle, a break-van. We reached Newick at the proper time, stopped about a minute, and then started, but we stopped at the starting signal, which was on at danger against us. The signalman showed a green light from a hand-lamp, and we then started again. I was not aware that we were travelling on the wrong road until after the accident had occurred. I think we were travelling at from 16 to 20 miles an hour when we were suddenly stopped. There was no whistle previous to the stoppage. I was not hurt. There was only one passenger on the train; he did not complain of being hurt. I was not aware that anything was wrong until the stoppage took place."

'William Mullinger, stationmaster for about four years, and six months at Newick, states: "The train arrived about one minute past 10 o'clock, and I handed the driver a staff ticket, and I turned to assist some passengers with their luggage. After that I went into my office. About five minutes after this, porter Notley came in, saying that there had been an accident, and I at once went down with Notley and saw the train at a standstill in the siding. The three men in charge of the train and the passenger were together. The passenger said he was not hurt at all; the fireman said he was hurt, but not much. About half an hour afterwards I went into the signalbox; Notley was with me. I noted that only No 7 lever was pulled over. I tried none of the levers. Notley told me that he could not take off the starting-signal, and had given a hand-signal to the driver. We have two regular signalmen at this station, one from 6.45am till 6.40pm, and the other from 9am until 10pm. There is only one porter, Notley. I do not know whether the signalling arrangements were out of order when the accident happened or not."

'EXTRACT from Inspector Barkshire's report of the 6th January 1883 as to the 9.10pm East Grinstead passenger train being turned into Overshot siding at Newick & Chailey station, 4th January.

'On going to signalbox with Mr Mullinger and Notley, I found No 7 lever only over, all the others standing in their normal position. No 7 lever releases the gear in small cabin at the north end of station. I inquired of Notley what levers were over when the 9.10 train came in, and he replied 1, 2, 9 and 10. No 1 is the distant; No 2 the home; No 9 the facing-points; and No 10 the bolt, and these two latter levers must be got before the starting signal No 3 lever can be lowered.

'I asked Notley how it was 9 and 10 were not then over, and he replied he put them back directly train had left, as is usual; in this he was very persistent, although both I and Mr Mullinger explained to him that if his statement was correct the train would not have been where it then was, as the points were properly connected and in good working order. I then instructed Notley to set the road exactly as he had done before the train arrived; he pulled over levers 1 and 2, but, to his surprise, he could not get 9 and 10, although they had not been touched since he had put them back after train had gone.

'After making several unsuccessful attempts to get them, he was told to see if all the springs were right, and in looking through them found No 12 lever spring was not out, and directly he rectified that he was able to get 9 and 10.

'I have no doubt, in my own mind, that Notley could not get 9 and 10 levers when driver whistled for starting signal, and, getting confused, gave the hand-signal and told driver he could not get the signal.'

'*Conclusion*
'From the preceding statements it will be seen that the collision with the buffer-stops was produced by the porter (Notley) acting as a signalman, having started the 9.10pm down passenger train from East Grinstead to Brighton from Newick & Chailey station, by means of a hand-signal from the signalbox, without having ascertained that the facing-points, which are about 40 yards from the signal-box, had been set right for the train to travel on the single southwards.

'The train, which consisted of a tank engine and five carriages, then started, passed into the siding instead of travelling on the single line, and ran along it until it came in contact with the buffer-stops at the end of the siding and smashed them, the train travelling at the time at a speed estimated at from 16 to 30 miles an hour. The engine and the vehicle next to it, and the leading wheels of the next vehicle, got off the rails and were damaged. Neither the engine-driver, fireman, nor the guard of the train were aware that they were travelling on the wrong road, and I do not consider that, as regards the driver and fireman, a proper look-out was kept, especially as the train was started by means of a hand-signal.

'The collision resulted from the porter acting as signalman having improperly started the train; but this man had only been employed five months, and from his statements it does not appear that he had been properly instructed in the duties of a signalman. The porter had varied his statements as to what he had actually done in the signalbox when endeavouring to take off the starting signal, but these statements clearly showed that he was not properly qualified to act as a signalman, inasmuch as he did not understand the working of the apparatus for taking off the starting signal. The person most to blame, in my opinion, was the stationmaster, who had only been six months at this station, in having authorised the porter (Notley), during one week out of three, to take the signalman's place in the signalbox from 6.30pm till after the last train had passed about 10 o'clock. The stationmaster appears to have done this without having apparently obtained the sanction of the superintendent of the line.

'Fortunately the consequences were not very serious, as there was only one passenger in the train when it left the station.

I have, &c.,
W. Yolland *Colonel.*

The Secretary
(Railway Department,)
Board of Trade.'

Allocation of Staff at Newick & Chailey Station, 4 January 1883

In	Position	Name	From	Joined LBSC	Age	Wage	Out	To
13/7/82	Stationmaster	William Mullinger	Cooksbridge	7/66	30	£1 12s 6d	21/8/88	Bexhill
2/12/82	Assistant Clerk	Frederick Briggs	Amberley	6/82	14	12s 6d	10/9/83	Eastbourne, Parcels Clerk
1/8/82	Signal Porter	George Stevens	Crowborough	12/81	21	18s	29/9/83	Cooksbridge, Signalman
25/11/82	Signal Porter	James Potter	Barcombe	7/82	21	18s	24/5/84	Keymer Crossing, Signalman
28/7/82	Porter	William Notley	-	7/82	25	16s	17/10/83	Dismissed, using bad language

Note: By this date two of the staff appointed at the opening had moved on

In	Position	Name	From	Joined LBSC	Age	Wage	Out	To
1/8/82	Assistant Clerk	Frederick Sparkes	Forest Row	5/81	16	12s 6d	4/12/82	Brighton, Parcels Clerk
1/8/82	Signal Porter	Robert Patching	Forest Row	1/82	25	18s	17/11/82	Resigned

On the right, by the nameboard of the station which opened a day or so after this photograph was taken as plain 'Newick', stands top-hatted William Mullinger; next is his clerk, Frederick Sparkes, sporting a pocket watch chain. The remaining three station staff, all wearing identical buttoned uniform, are James Potter, George Stevens and the perpetrator of the 1883 accident, William Notley, who is probably the figure closest to the edge of the down platform, his porter's cap slanted saucily across his head. Workmen on the up platform are still in a rush to get the station spick-and-span in time. *H. M. Madgwick collection*

Comment

The outcome of this enquiry that is really surprising is that no heads rolled. The locomotive crew were reprimanded for not keeping a proper look-out, especially as the train was started by a hand signal. But the crux of the matter was allowing an inexperienced porter with only five months' experience to assume a signalman's duties for which he had not been 'properly instructed'. In his favour, he did confess that 'the accident happened from my mistake'. He continued to serve at Newick until the following October, when an incident involving the use of bad language brought about his dismissal. He was obviously 'quite a lad', and his conduct at the time of the accident could be said to be in keeping with his character.

'The person most to blame' continued to hold his post for another five years, until promoted to the far more imposing station at Bexhill. He had entered into a private arrangement for his porter to take the signalman's place in the box for the evening turn without sanction from above. William Mullinger was given the benefit of the doubt and went on to Bexhill, where he was involved in a scandal over a misplaced sum of money. His health was broken and he was invalided to quieter and less demanding Petworth. Despite these setbacks he went on to greater things at Uckfield, Kemp Town and Worthing before retirement in 1923, serving over 40 years with the company, despite his narrow squeak and rap on the knuckles when he was in charge at Newick.

Sheffield Park

The root trouble of most of the incidents here was the 38 chains of 1 in 75 down from Freshfield to Ketche's Farm, which lies nearly half a mile north of Sheffield Park station. As a result, there were many overshoots in the down direction after descent of the grade at speed, and especially on occasions when the driver was giving his fireman practice in stopping the train. But the station staff were prepared for such emergencies. Since there was no up escape siding beyond the station, it was laid down by the LBSCR's General Manager, Finlay Scott, upon the advice of his chief engineer that the up train should be held for five or six minutes at the home signal, a wise ruling, though once or twice it was not unknown for late running from East Grinstead to result in the up train waiting 20 minutes or more at Sheffield Park until the down train was safely anchored in the opposite platform.

Exchange of the staff token usually kept the trains to the right order over the single sections but on one occasion one was lost at Sheffield Park. The driver declared he had failed to pick it up from the arms of the signal porter. A search was made everywhere at the station, quite in vain, and eventually the locomotive was allowed to proceed. It was later found on the footboard of the first coach.

Another curious mishap occurred in 1914. The crew of an engine running through the station became engrossed watching a low-flying aeroplane, a rare sight in those early

Ivatt Class 2 2-6-2T No 41307 with the 3.35pm Oxted-Lewes would have slowed to a gentle canter before negotiating entry into the platform loop at Sheffield Park. It was common practice to lower the home signal (seen behind the last coach) at the last moment, when the train was almost at a standstill, as a safety precaution.
R. Hobbs

days of World War 1. The locomotive ran the length of the overshoot line and went down the embankment beyond the now-demolished roadbridge. Details of casualties etc were not made public in the veiled records of that war period.

Similar written evidence is lacking for an accident that occurred about 1915 but several old members of the station staff have confirmed its authenticity. The train was the 10.8am to Brighton. The driver, shunting an extra van on, proceeded from the goods yard gaily up the Newick siding, forgetting he was on a single line route. Fortunately the train did not fall into the road, though the guard did not apply the brakes. At the enquiry he admitted losing his head — and lost his job in consequence. Though there were no human casualties, it required a crane to put all the pieces together, and the goods engine shunting at the time at Newick was detailed to fetch it from Brighton.

The only record of a derailment between the wars was an occasion when an engine described as a 'Goods Tank', probably an 'E1' or 'E4', was derailed coming out of Turner's siding. The engine ended up on its side and was the cause of some altercation between the Railway Co and the siding owners as to the responsibility for its upkeep. It was the liability of the Sheffield Park Estate, and Turner's, though holding the sawmill on a 99-year lease, were not liable for the maintenance of the siding.

The last group of incidents came close upon each other in the final year before the first closure, and the details are vouched for at first hand by Mr T. W. Southon of Lewes, who for years was a Relief Signalman and was often at Sheffield Park on duty up to the time the line was closed. Later he served as a Relief Stationmaster.

The first occurred on the Saturday of Christmas week in 1954. The train involved was the 9.43pm Wednesdays and Saturdays-only Lewes-East Grinstead train. The train came down the 1 in 75 from Newick at some speed and went right through Sheffield Park without stopping or changing the staff. The guard, Sam Isaacs, eventually caught the attention of the oblivious engine crew who brought the train to a stand up by Freshfield Lane and then reversed it as far as Sheffield Park down distant whence the guard walked back to obtain permission for it to come back to the station.

The other occurred early in 1955, for Mr Mitchener was stationmaster at the time and he was away at a staff meeting in Brighton that day. Mr Southon was the signalman on duty, and the train was the 11.18am Brighton to Victoria, headed by a Bulleid Pacific No 34067 *Tangmere*. As the train drew into the station, the engine and cab were enveloped in clouds of steam, and as Mr Southon took the staff from the driver, the latter shouted that he had dropped a plug and would have to come off and drop his fire. In all probability it had not in fact been filled before leaving Brighton, and by the time Sheffield Park was reached the boiler was almost empty. The driver had just enough steam left to draw off the train over the bridge and then reverse past the down platform into the goods yard, where the crew shovelled out the fire as best they could. Mr Southon had telephoned Horsted Keynes, where the pick-up goods was waiting to return down the branch to Lewes with its 'C2X', and asked for this to come down and take the 11.18 forward. The 'C2X' came down light to the down home, he piloted it onto the train standing at the up platform and the 'Vulcan' then went up to Victoria with it! The Pacific stood in the yard at Sheffield Park for a couple of days and was then hauled dead back to Brighton.

Finally there was the incident involving the derailment of the 4.20pm London Bridge-Brighton, date uncertain, but it was shortly before the 1955 closure and in winter, for it was dark by 6pm. The 4.20 down crossed the 5.20pm Brighton-Victoria at Sheffield Park, and it was always the custom for the signalman to keep both home signals on and to bring these two trains to a stand outside the station in case of over-running. On this occasion the signalman had according to custom kept both signals on, and just for a minute left the frame to put a label on a parcel in the office. While doing this he was amazed to hear the 4.20pm rumble across the girder bridge over the river in spite of the down home being on. The driver, realising he had passed the home signal, came to a stand with the train, an ex-SECR three-set with the birdcage guard's compartments, partly over the bridge and partly on the bridge. He then rather unwisely started to reverse back to the down home, which is what led to the mishap. Just over the bridge there was a spur leading into a sand-drag close to the down home. With a train reversing as he was doing, the points

'A large quantity of fruit is grown in the district, particularly strawberries, raspberries, currants and gooseberries. Large quantities of manure are received by rail for the fruit growers during the months of April and May, but beyond that parcels traffic is small and inward goods is chiefly confined to coal, coke and stone. Outward traffic of parcels and goods is heavier during the spring and early summer, owing to the despatch of small rock plants to various parts of the country from the Alpine nurseries at Newick.'

A letter survives from this nursery firm:

'We have recently had settled a claim made on the Company for 3s 6d for the loss of small consignment of alpine plants. Whilst thanking you for this settlement, we would like to say how much we appreciate the care taken with the many small consignments the Company handle for us, no less than 678 in the half year since June (1935), many in quite small boxes. When we consider only one claim has had to be preferred, it speaks very highly for the care taken. We have not received any complaints from our customers this year and as all the packages contain live plants that speaks well for the handling.'

Goods traffic was largely what might be expected from a country station, an intake of flints for road building, of farm equipment, racehorses, coal and packages of groceries.

Out of the ordinary passenger traffic included a special morning train for schoolchildren which, during the middle period of the line, actually started from Newick & Chailey, with a return working from Lewes late in the afternoon. There were monthly excursion trains to London; the going party rate was 6d per child to London and back, and adults could go for 1s 6d return. The train arrived back at around 10pm. Later special arrangements were made for the children of 'The Heritage Craft School for Cripples' which was founded by Mrs (later Lady) C. W. Kimmins. The school was often visited by Royalty and other distinguished persons. A common sight was to see the children being wheeled or carried onto the up platform, along which they were all carefully laid out, having come down the little side path on that side from the main road.

In both wars Newick was used as a local centre for the reception and return of London children, this being done latterly through the work of the Children's Country Holiday Fund. The 8.15am up train would have one or two of its carriages specially reserved.

Recession and Decline

Recession in the 1930s and the breaking of the railway's previous transport monopoly when the internal combustion engine passed its initial experimental stage and became more generally available, opened the floodgates to lorries and private cars, and called for incisive sharp economies leading to considerable operating changes. The North signalbox had already been closed on 26 June 1914 by the LBSCR but it was over the weekend of 10/11 September 1938 that the SR's hatchet men finally came to turn their attention to the station. The remaining South box was abolished, likewise all signals previously worked from it, together with the greater part of the station footbridge, leaving just the east side set of steps to descend from the entrance hall to the platform below. The up platform buildings were demolished, as all trains were now to work over the down loop line, the up one becoming a 'loop siding' which could only be used by means of an intermediate staff instrument provided in the down platform. The latter controlled the ground frame which operated points leading to and from the loop siding at either end of the station. By this means goods trains etc could work into the station and be held there clear of the single line section Sheffield Park-Culver Junction.

Prior to the box's demise the cabin had boasted a unique simple, home-made barometer which functioned very helpfully for nearly 40 years, possibly longer as no one could recollect who first put it there and when. It comprised a glass jam jar, three-quarters filled with water, with an old type olive oil flask inverted in the jar. The water rose into the flask when fair weather was pending and left it when wet conditions were imminent.

It was a small compensation for all this marring of an attractive station that it was announced, in March 1938, that at

The end is near in this overview of the station taken on 26 March 1955. A solitary wagon is seen in the goods yard. The wartime white stripes on the canopy supports still remain, while the bank from which this picture was taken shows signs of recent attention.
Denis Cullum

The south end taken the same day as the previous picture shows, in the left foreground, the small lever frame controlling access into the former up loop siding, the brick lower level of the former signalbox, used as a store, and on the far left the access gate to the up platform, put in at the Bessemer family's request. Across the way, the roofing to the set of stairs from the booking office to the down platform is seen above the canopy, then an open staircase from the forecourt down to the goods yard, the very attractive white-boarded coal office, the cattle dock with its pen and behind it the goods lock-up. *Denis Cullum*

the start of the summer season, 'Camping coaches will be stationed at Newick & Chailey and Ardingly'. The new move was but short-lived and died with the war.

In the autumn of 1941 *The Southern Railway Magazine* reported a farm removal at Newick & Chailey, commenting that in the stress of wartime conditions it was somewhat refreshing for the staff to deal with a typical peacetime job when a farm removal was undertaken, consisting of livestock, wagons, implements, etc conveyed to Eastbourne by a special train of 27 wagons. The consignor subsequently wrote in, 'I feel I must thank you and your staff for the efficient way in which the loading of my implements, machinery and cattle was organised and carried through. The cooperation of all concerned resulted in the complete success of a big undertaking.'

The loop siding fell into disuse after World War 2 and traffic fell into a steep decline. By 1950 the local porter estimated that there were but 38 passengers joining or leaving trains on weekdays, and these were shared between a service of 16 trains! The end was near and it came with finality when in the winter of 1959/60 BR decided to remove the track between Culver Junction and the roadbridge just south of Sheffield Park station. The firm of Pittrail was awarded the contract, and made their base in the station area and yard at Newick & Chailey where track panels were dismantled prior to removal by road. Several years later the station building was demolished, the cutting and station area completely filled in and over it a modern affluent housing estate constructed.

Ivatt 2-6-2T No 41299 stands at Newick & Chailey with the 3.35pm Oxted-Brighton train on 2 April 1955, the up platform bare and bereft of all but the 4½ milepost and, at the end of the platform, a warning sign to those who would cross the line. *Colin Hogg*

CERTIFIED COPY of an ENTRY OF BIRTH.

ursuant to the Births and Deaths   Registration Acts, 1836 to 1874.

Registration District   *Lewes*

1883. Birth in the Sub-District of *Chailey* **in the County of** *Sussex*

Columns:— 1	2	3	4	5	6	7	8	9	10
No.	When and Where Born.	Name, if any.	Sex.	Name and Surname of Father.	Name and Maiden Surname of Mother.	Rank or Profession of Father.	Signature, Description and Residence of Informant.	When Registered.	Signature of Registrar.	Baptismal Name, if added *after* Registration of Birth.
3	Twenty first march 1883 Sheffield Park Railway Station Chailey, R.S.D.	George Frederick	Boy	George Carey Harmer	Ada Ellen Harmer formerly Gatrell	Railway Station Clerk	Geo. C. Harmer Father Sheffield Park Station Chailey	Fourth May 1883	James Foster. Deputy Registrar.	

I, *Harold John Tilton*, Superintendent Registrar for the District of *Lewes*, in the County of *Sussex* for the above-named Sub-District, and that such Register Book is now legally in my custody.
do hereby certify that this is a true copy of the Entry No. **3**. in the Register Book of Births No. **15**

WITNESS MY HAND this *6th* day of *December*, 19*27*.

Superintendent Regist

George Henry Harmer was Sheffield Park's first stationmaster, from 13 July 1882 to 16 February 1890. During his stay a son, George Frederick, was born in the station house on 21 March 1883, making for this interesting birth certificate. *Reproduced by courtesy of Gill Price of the Harmer Family Association.*

The famous cricket match on the ice by permission of Lord Sheffield, whose mansion in the background surveys the scene. The photograph, by Hawkins of Brighton, appeared in the *Boys' Own Paper* of 1902. *Bluebell Archives*

14.
Sheffield Park

The First Stationmaster

As has been told earlier, few stations on any railway produced as much controversy over its naming.

The first stationmaster was George Harmer, a Sussex man, many of whose relatives were to serve the railway. Harmer was a young man of 28 leading a team of his own age range, which he had to settle in prior to the opening. Quite a number were first appointments and they were very much a mixed bag. Two resigned from the railway when leaving Sheffield Park, another went absent without leave. Harmer started with two signal porters and an assistant clerk, the latter's successors all being booking clerks, while in 1884 there was a need for an extra appointment of a porter. Harmer proved himself a remarkable man of diligence with the will to progress his work. In each of the places where duty had taken him, he had achieved great popularity, for he was the most courteous of railway gentlemen.

The Cricket

The station staff certainly had their work cut out, for the mansion and grounds at Sheffield Park were in Lord Sheffield's time one of the country's most celebrated attractions, the Alton Towers of their day. Sheffield Park mansion was described as a picturesque domain of 700 acres, celebrated for its well-grown timber, ornamental water and charmingly situated cricket ground. The public were admitted free on high days when Lord Sheffield held court at the Park. The attractions were most varied.

The earliest reference to cricket there goes back to 1846. The young Viscount Pevensey soon cultivated a deep interest in the game. Though he declined the presidency of the MCC, of which he was a member, he enjoyed two long spells as president of the Sussex County Cricket Club, which owed its secure financial position to his active interest and generosity. He encouraged young talent and engaged as coaches several renowned former players. On inheriting the estate in the spring of 1876, he laid down over the next five years, at considerable expense, under the expert supervision of the great Charles Ellis, one of the finest grounds. The area eventually occupied 11 acres and was surrounded by mature oak trees. It contained a bandstand, a hexagonal pavilion — 'His Lordship's', an ornate ladies' pavilion and a timber-structured players' pavilion complete with central clock. The bandstand, where the Chailey Heritage Boys' Band were a regular feature, and two pavilions were made at the same

Phoenix Iron Works in Lewes that supplied Joseph Firbank. The cricket ground was used by local teams from 1877 to the outbreak of World War 2.

It is remembered most, however, for hosting the visiting Australian Test teams of 1884, 1886, 1890, 1893 and 1896, which all opened their tour with a fixture against a more or less representative English XI. Lord Sheffield's team featured the famous cricketing stars of the day and the captain was frequently the immortal W. G. Grace. In 1885 5-6,000 people came to see him; in 1893 the match against the Australians brought a crowd of 10-12,000, standing 10-12 deep. It was in the 1896 match that Ernest Jones fired a bouncer right through W. G.'s beard, which elicited the retort, 'Whatever ye at, young fellow?' Grace was also a member of Lord Sheffield's team of 1891-2 which visited Australia at his sole expense under the management of Alfred Shaw. These were the early days of Test cricket and the Earl's enterprise served to greatly stimulate Australian interest and confidence in the game, to encourage which he presented a silver trophy, the Sheffield Shield, to be competed for annually between the state teams there.

Interest in the matches at Sheffield Park soon spread beyond the county boundaries, and spectators from far and wide began to create transport problems in the neighbourhood. The local reporter wrote in 1890:

'The assemblage of spectators was extraordinarily large and indeed in the early morning the keenest excitement was everywhere visible at the principal railway stations, especially at Lewes. The scene outside the pretty little station at Sheffield Park was a very animated one. There were numerous vehicles to pick up passengers and carry them to the ground for a consideration, and they were largely patronised.' Traffic receipts rocketed by £800 over the preceding year, causing a rise in the price of the company's shares. *The Times* confirmed this was owing to the Australians' cricket match there. 'Therefore the thanks of the shareholders of the railway company, as well as the general public — to whom the gates of the Park were thrown open on all three days — are due to the noble earl for his generosity.'

In 1893 it was reported that 'the special train from Brighton was simply crowded, and the number of people at Lewes station was so large that some had to wait till the ordinary train. This again was fully occupied by passengers, and extra carriages were obliged to be put on. The down trains likewise conveyed hundreds of people.' Still the crowds came. Locals walked or drove over in dog carts, the daring among them on early bicycles. Most, however, came by train, and horse cabs

Territorial volunteers disembark their horses at Seaford station. A dozen or so horseboxes stand in the bay platform and the formation's brake van is on the run-round loop, which was put in shortly after the turn of the last century. No photograph exists of the volunteers detraining or entraining at Sheffield Park but this fascinating photograph gives some idea of the activity which took place.
Dick Shenton collection

stretched solidly far beyond the station drives. The peak years were 1902-5, when the Earl, in keeping with his nationwide recognition as patron of cricket, let it be known that people were welcome and that entry to his cricket ground was free, on the principle of the more the better.

After the great match of 1896, attended by 25,000 people, the opening match of the Australian test tours moved to Arundel, as still pertains today, because the local magistrates refused to grant a drinks licence to Lord Sheffield after that date. The cricket ground was used for a wide range of events, including football matches (Nottingham Forest FC played there in 1894, beating Sussex Martlets 8-3). The Earl hosted local produce competitions and entertained local schoolchildren with fetes and picnics and a tea party at Christmas time, and used to bring up to 2,000 children from the East End of London for a day in the country to be entertained with displays of swimming and diving in the lakes, all at his expense.

After the war years, spent as part of a Canadian army division garrison and then a POW camp, the ground became derelict and the buildings were removed as they had become unsafe. The area was planted over with trees upon acquisition by the National Trust in 1955.

During the luncheon and tea intervals visitors had the opportunity to stroll through the gardens which employed 20 men, seven of these fully occupied on the cricket ground. The gardens were a great show, as they still are. The Earl took a very personal interest in them and, with his contacts abroad, was able to introduce many new and exotic blooms into this country. He was very keen that all should look spick and span, but even in those days there were litter bugs, so on occasions to chasten them he closed the grounds for a short period. The grounds were a dreamland overlooked by the massive, castellated mansion, the gaily decorated pavilions and bandstands, the ornamental waters and cascades, all lit up with hundreds of fairy lamps. In the severest of winter conditions on 2 February 1895, a celebrated cricket match on the ice took place on the new lake.

The Territorial Volunteers

Lord Sheffield was also a patron of the Military and that on a national scale too. He had soldiered in India in his younger days, and his diplomatic service during the Crimean War had brought him into close contact with the War Office. He encouraged the Volunteer Movement, which had grown up in the years preceding the Boer War, to the extent of allowing the army the virtual freedom of his estate. They came often and encamped in his grounds. Most years there was always a monthly spell at the Park in which a full programme of drill and artillery was carried out, sometimes even a military review. Mock battles took place. The Engineers were particular favourites of his and tried their new cordite and first gun cotton on his expendable oak trees.

In the 1890s the War Department developed an interest in the use of armoured trains. In July 1894 as part of one of the Volunteer Field Days, a special siding to house an armoured train was constructed beyond the road bridge south of the station, which curved round on land forming part of Rotherfield Farm. Lord Haldane, Secretary for War, and Lord Kitchener, then CiC for India, were among the many notables in attendance. Lord Sheffield had on this occasion not only invited every volunteer corps in Sussex but detachments from neighbouring counties, and this large army came by train, involving special traffic arrangements on no mean scale. Six military specials brought 2,000 officers and men with their horses and guns to Newick & Chailey to form one army, four brought a similar number to Sheffield Park. The Northern Force at the Park lured the Southern Force into a surprise trap. There was a big puff of white smoke from the direction of Ketche's Farm. A galloper tore across the hill to see what it was and returned with the astounding intelligence — 'It's an armoured train!' The train consisted of 'D3' 0-4-4T No 375 *Glynde*, the locomotive regularly designated to operate this train, which consisted of two armoured carriages, one of which contained the limber for the gun, and the other the armour-plated gun tracks. It had crept up the main line from Brighton and then through Ardingly, being given possession of the line between Horsted Keynes and Newick stations from 3.30 to 4.30pm. R. J. Billinton, who played an important part in designing the armoured gun truck and turntable, joined at Haywards Heath. In the battle the Southern opposition took a battering as the train moved into the shelter of the cutting just beyond Lane End bridge, midway between Sheffield Park and Newick & Chailey, blowing the bridge down (figuratively speaking). One of the lessons learnt from the experiment was that the firing of the big gun, described as 'hot work', did not have the slightest effect on the permanent way. The armoured train turned up on several further occasions, but the element of surprise had gone.

Finally all adjourned to the Park for the march past, the public having been admitted by this time. The pavilions and refreshment tents plied a roaring trade. One corner was an officers' field mess where to this day old champagne bottles are often ploughed up on the site. There was a vast indoor picnic for the troops, and bullocks were roasted by the lake. Tenants and villagers from miles around were invited. Special trains carrying sightseers from Brighton came up in the evening for the great firework display run by Brocks. There were roundabouts, model elephants and swans on the lake and all over the place gaily coloured balloons floated in the wind. Lord Sheffield spent literally thousands on these displays which lived in the memories of all those who attended.

The atmosphere at the station was a little livelier on the return. However, the railway arrangements were as near perfection as the exigencies of the single line would permit. There was very little delay in the arrival and departure of trains, supervised by the district superintendent from Lewes and the relevant stationmasters. On the first day of August 1903 the Grand Military Display, involving close on 4,000 troops, necessitated the most careful arrangements being made at Sheffield Park where the force detrained. It was reported that 'Mr G. W. Sellwood, the company's agent, alias the stationmaster there, performed the arduous duties with great ability and tact. On top of the ordinary trains there were 21 specials. Considering that the line is a single one between Culver Junction at Barcombe and Horsted Keynes, the celerity of the traffic was remarkable.'

In August the Earl made available part of his estate for the volunteers' annual summer camps. The weekly notice of the 1st Sussex RE Volunteers, giving the regimental orders for 5 August 1899, are illuminating:

'HQ Co A Eastbourne will depart by 5.30pm train. B Co depart Newhaven 5.50pm, C Co depart Seaford 5.40pm D Co depart Bexhill 4.30pm, ditto Pevensey 4.40pm, ditto Berwick 5.5pm . . .

'Item 4. Members attending camp are informed that the LBSCR will issue cheap Volunteer tickets from these stations to and from Sheffield Park on any day between 2nd and 15th August inclusive.'

A week later the *Gazette* gave the report of a day's activity at camp:

'5.45am Reveille, 6.30am Early drill followed by breakfast. 9.30am several groups involved in different activities. Sergeant Major Trydell RE and 30 men engaged in constructing a railway including points and crossings (presumably narrow gauge, as at 12.15 the group dismissed for dinner). Other groups connected the railway station and camp by telegraph wire, built a trestle bridge across a reservoir, built floating rafts, and others still erected fortifications.'

The camp itself was situated a quarter-mile south of the mansion, not far distant from the station, and the total number in the camp was 270.

Royal Visits

Another factor that caused a stir amongst the local community was the frequent visits of the Prince of Wales, later King Edward VII. The Earl, when Viscount Pevensey, had become close friends with the Prince at Eton and they travelled

Stationmaster in the mid-1890s was Charles E. Horn, whose responsibility it was to handle the special traffic engendered by the cricket matches, the high days at the Park and the many traffic movements related to the manoeuvres of the Territorial volunteers. Mr Horn was much respected at Sheffield Park and when he moved on in March 1898 after five years, he was presented with a glowing testimonial, and this photograph was taken. *Bluebell Archives*

together on the so-called 'Grand Tour' of Europe in their holidays. The Earl later entertained the Prince, both to inspect the volunteers and to watch the cricket. Incidentally, the Prince fancied himself at the game and was often in Lord Sheffield's team, but he never made a high score, 'usually one or two,' said locals who could still remember. His visit in 1896 was the greatest of these occasions, when 30,000 came to Sheffield Park to witness his arrival and thronged the roadside to watch his carriage make its way to the entrance gates of the mansion in which he overnighted, a bedroom after this being designated 'The Prince's Room' by a plaque on the door. There was a double bonus for the crowds, for W. G. Grace was to play cricket in the Prince's presence.

The stationmaster at the heart of these halcyon days was Charles Horn (21 February 1893 to 5 March 1898). His son recalled life at the station in the mid-1890s:

'We lived within a small community for, apart from the railway cottages, there were only seven cottages and a dairy anywhere near — all nice people. A great day for the locals was 12 May 1896, especially for the station staff, including my father as stationmaster. Lord Sheffield arrived at the station before 11 o'clock, and he was offered, and did accept, the privacy of our sitting room, which looked out on to the platform, until the royal train was due to arrive. At 11.30 the train steamed in bearing the Prince's emblem on the locomotive. Immediately on alighting, His Royal Highness went forward and heartily shook hands with Lord Sheffield,

Left: The main signalbox stood at the south end of the up platform, opposite the goods yard. This group of staff, photographed in 1894, include (beginning at the platform's extremity): Charles Horn (Stationmaster), Reggie (his son), Tom Stedman (Porter), Louis G. Ford (Booking Clerk, aged 15). At the top of the stairs is Len Witcher (Signalman) and at the cabin window his colleague George Sharp.
Louis G. Ford/Bluebell Archives

Lower left: The station staff in 1912 (left to right): Walter Turner (Porter), Harry Edmonds (Signal Porter), bow-tied George Reddish (Stationmaster) extrovertly brandishing the train staff, Harry Winder (Signal Porter, who also filled in as Senior Clerk), and Len Sewell (Junior Clerk). The picture was taken on the up platform, at a time when Turners timber yard had not grown to its later extent.
Bluebell Archives

Right: Stationmaster George Reddish certainly stood on ceremony. The interest in yet another posed photograph centres round what he has managed to arrange among his staff to present an impressive flavour of his domain. To his left is his youthful booking clerk, an early bicycle (looking quite modern) is wheeled along the platform by a carrier lad, a signal porter attends to the oil lamp, the porter does what he does so well, and two dairymen display their skill in rolling milk churns. Note the cobbled section on the up platform opposite the milk trolley shed with its gates ajar.
Bluebell Archives

who stood, hat in hand, to welcome him. This unforgettable moment was witnessed by my mother, myself, and my brother, from our sitting room windows, and I shall always remember it. Then after some introductions, the Prince and Lord Sheffield moved to the carriage, drawn by four fine grey horses. The bands played the National Anthem, while the Guard of Honour presented arms. The decorations, both inside and outside the station and along the roads, were also something to remember. Sheffield Park had never seen anything like it before.'

Station Life

Life and conditions at Sheffield Park station are more fully recorded than any other on the line, thanks to it being the initial focal point when the Bluebell Railway set up its headquarters there, and many former staff made a point of visiting it and sharing their memories. Charles Horn's hobbies were gardening and keeping chickens but he also kept a

fishing rod to dip into the adjacent River Ouse, a cricket bat (for he was often picked to play for the locals) and a gun to deal with uninvited foxes. On 7 August 1893 a newly appointed booking clerk reported for duty at the station. His name was Louis G. Ford, who later became head of one of the largest firms of ironmongers and builders' merchants in the south. His chain of shops featured in all the main towns of Sussex and its green lorries were a familiar sight on the roads. While Mr Horn received 27s 6d a week, inclusive of the accommodation in the station house and of fuel, the salaries of porter signalmen varied from 20s to 12s 6d according to seniority, while a booking clerk received a weekly payment of 10s. In addition, railway staff received their uniforms. The stationmaster and the clerks had uniforms of cloth, the porter signalmen of corduroy. As clerk it was Louis Ford's job to despatch telegrams, and Lord Sheffield used to send very long ones which he had the task of tapping out on the telegraph instruments. He recalled the Earl's telegrams were often over a hundred words, and were real 'teasers', as his Lordship's writing was atrocious, particularly as he appeared to be at

loggerheads with various people and vented his spleen over the wires at great length, notably a running feud over manorial rights with Sir Spencer Maryon Wilson JP of Fletching Mill.

Each stationmaster in turn was well remembered. When George Harmer left on 6 February 1890, James Rawlins came over from Ardingly to take the reins, followed by another one of the Holdens, John, having been relieving clerk at the traffic superintendent's office. Eighteen months later Charles Horn took over, handing over to Stephen Sellwood on 12 March 1898. On 28 September 1904 George Fossey moved across from Ardingly, to hand over to Walter Hollamby on 14 June 1906. At the end of 1908 he was reduced to Beddington Lane over a reported incident concerning staff tokens. George Reddish (8 February 1909 to 15 June 1915) was well remembered and respected. The next appointee was Charles W. Skinner who, as a result of staff shortages arising from the war, proposed his 17-year-old daughter Amy as booking clerk. The approved appointment took effect on 20 May 1919. She recalls what living conditions were like at the close of the Brighton era.

Imagine a guided tour of the station around 1920, starting at the south end of the up platform, where stood the 22-lever South box. First came the milk trolley shed, the terminal of the hand-operated line which ran up from the dairy. The gate was still there until recent years, while further evidence remains in the grooved stone surface which facilitated the washing down of this section of the platform, the rest to the rear of the platform edge coping stones being strewn with small beach gravel. The fruit trees of the stationmaster's extra garden space next to the up platform buildings and facing Turner's yard were to disappear by the mid-1930s. Then came the gents' and ladies', no ordinary outbuildings these but the best the railway company could lavish on the station, for people had often to wait a considerable time for their return train after some great event at the Park. Washing and lavatory fittings were on a very elaborate scale, with huge brass taps and oak panelling. The ventilation shafts and glass roof lent a pleasing effect,

especially when freshly painted in light stone. The platform awning extended down to the footbridge, symmetrical in length on both platforms. Before reaching the steps of the footbridge came in turn the general waiting room (today's museum), while on either side of the central door outside were platform seats. Near the platform end stood and still stands the original 1881 water crane.

Crossing the footbridge (removed in 1949) to the down platform at the north end, and almost on the line of the Greenwich Meridian, stood the small 10-lever North box, later classified as a shunting cabin and taken out of use in 1934. Coming to the station house complex, first came the porter's room, then the coal store, screened by the descending steps of the footbridge. There was a seat under the stationmaster's house window, then a diminutive weighbridge and the office window, before reaching the main exit where the clerk collected the tickets. Over the door there still remained into the 1920s the legend 'Charles Horn, Station Clerk'. Through the door was the booking hall and general waiting room, with the ticket office on the north side, and to the right of the grand open fireplace on the south side the access to the ladies' waiting room and lavatory. There was a platform seat outside under the window. Finally came the gents' and the lamp room. Here the awning and building ceased and the platform continued to the water crane with enamel advertising plaques, the vogue of the day, much to the fore on this lengthy stretch of fencing, in front of which lay a bed of rose bushes bordered by whitewashed stones. Indeed at one time the railway employed a gardener to tend the displays at this high profile station.

No account can pass without mentioning that most prominent feature, the water tower containing the pump house on two floors. Regular drivers went out of their way to get Sheffield Park Ouse water, knowing that it was best for steaming compared to the chalky stuff further south. The water tank was often teeming with fish, chiefly eels pumped up from the stream and good catches were made by

A general view of Sheffield Park station c1920, providing a look inside the empty milk trolley shed on the up platform which encloses the terminus of the narrow gauge line from the dairy. Both canopy roof ends seem to have fallen on hard times. Inset is the stamp with Sheffield Park station postmark. *Bluebell Archives*

enthusiastic railwaymen. Until World War 2 kingfishers were a prominent part of the river scene there.

But returning to the station houses, whatever the merits of the style, they were for the time very adequately constructed, their fine, stout pitchpine doors the pride of the company. Sheffield Park by common opinion was the best of the three on the single line section. However, it had no drinking water, and in the early days this had to be brought up in churns from Barcombe, the only station house to have running water. Later an arrangement was made with the Mid Sussex Dairy Co for a supply of drinking water for the station house. The former supplied a large watercan which a porter on the late turn at 9 o'clock each morning fetched from a spring near the milk trolley line for, though a tap had by 1920 been installed in the kitchen, it was not to be used for personal consumption.

Amy Skinner, later Mrs Barford, describes the day's round at the station:

'We were aroused by the birds who were joined at 6.45am by the noise of the Mid Sussex Dairy milk trolley. Seventeen-gallon churns were being unloaded and taken across the line for the 7.4 am down train, together with one churn of cream which went daily to Brighton and another destined for Eastbourne. There would also be some milk for the up side to London. At 7 o'clock Messrs Turner & Sons Sawmill commenced work and their hooter could be heard for miles around. Their foreman would be crossing the line to the booking office to collect his mail.'

Two trains (7.2am up and 7.9am down) crossed at this 'rush hour'. The up train had the locked cash box in the guard's brake van. Each stationmaster had to place the small leather bag containing cash received the previous day into the box. These were then collected at London Bridge and taken to the treasurer's department. The other leather bag, which still had a brass plate showing 'Fletching', contained letters and passenger, parcels and goods accounts. These went loose in the

van to be collected by messengers and taken into the audit department. Off the up train came numerous parcels for all the surrounding area. Mr Bannister, the grocer at Nutley, was one of the carriers who each day came to the station to collect parcels and goods items for the local gentry like Lord Castle Stewart (Harold Macmillan's father), the Earl of Donoughmore, Sir Stephenson Kent and the like. Mr Stevenson and later Mr Bentley were the carriers for Fletching. A sealed mailbag came on this train from the postmaster at Lewes. The delivery took about 2½ hours and ran up as far as Lane End and Warren Wood farms, Chailey. The stationmaster was postmaster as well, selling postal orders and stamps, for parcels were sent by post as well as rail. Messrs Turner & Sons had their insurance stamps from him each month. The letter box outside the station was emptied twice daily and the contents put into a mailbag, sealed with wax, and sent on the 1.54pm and 6.8pm trains daily to Lewes. It was on the latter train and late stage of the day that the local newspapers came for Danehill and Fletching, bringing the *Sussex Daily News*, while the 5.8pm from Brighton delivered the *Evening Argus*.

The first of the carriers and carts, their packages sorted out to their satisfaction, had not long left before the lighter tread of carriage wheels began to clatter up the station road bringing passengers up for the 8.35am, a train patronised by those who wished to have a day's shopping in London, returning on the 4.10pm from London Bridge. Gradually the crowd disappeared their several ways and in the station house it was time for breakfast, cooked on two paraffin stoves. The dining room, which faced the platform, had a very nice open fire, and off this room was a larder whose cold marble slabs provided an adequate refrigeration. The milkman would come with his cart about 8.30am, bringing with it meat from Mr Glover, the butcher at Fletching. A baker from Scaynes Hill called thrice-weekly and the grocer from Fletching but once. In the kitchen was a big copper and a small oven which was alight each day. Consequently the stationmaster's family had a hot meal at midday, and also baked their own bread. The room which

This instruction was car[...]
concerned the 'double[...]
another dealt with spare[...]
and double bolster truck[...]
but kept on hand and [...]
instructions are receive[...]
sufficient accommodati[...]
forwarded to the sub-dis[...]

All this certainly ma[...]
Timber went by measur[...]
a Mr Turnbull was spe[...]
Kirkby, who worked i[...]
(London Central Divis[...]
from 1948-52, had th[...]
specialist timber loadi[...]
three or four men and [...]
Les Swallow. He lived[...]
support his family he [...]
the overtime money.[...]
because it was relati[...]
'checkers' were sent[...]
company, it was the a[...]
had to check all measu[...]
hence the charges. Un[...]
employed to draw eve[...]
centred by the Ouse t[...]
wartime expansion an[...]
its present site led to[...]
South box right to the[...]
which continues to t[...]
method of timber tran[...]

The first sign of th[...]
the mill particularly[...]
transport, and unfort[...]
trade stayed on the r[...]
1930s over a dispute[...]
end of the platforms i[...]
footpaths which had[...]
came was always a th[...]
to the timber yard, or[...]
north end of the stati[...]
from this was Frank [...]

Above: This little prin[...]
Turners timberyard in[...]
looking towards the v[...]
Park in the far distance[...]

Right: The dairy at S[...]
World War 1, with (le[...]
Fred Bray, Tom Dubl[...]
unidentified young a[...]
narrow gauge trolley[...]
a transfer shed halfw[...]
Bluebell Archives

Charles W. Skinner was appointed as stationmaster in June 1915, and is seen standing at the entrance porch of the station, its leaded stained glass windows here seen to good effect. The signboard above is a reminder that the station also served as a post office, and the letter box lodged in the booking hall wall can be discerned to the left of Mr Skinner. Note also the oil lamp above with its delicately patterned bracket. *Amy Barford/Bluebell Archives*

faced the station approach also had a very large fire on which oak logs were usually burnt. Oil lamps provided the only lighting. On Sundays Amy accompanied her mother to St Agnes' Church, a small 'tin' building at the end of the timber yard. The curate, Mr Mactravers, came in on his cycle from Chailey. On one occasion there was a congregation of only four people; on another Mrs Skinner and two cousins returned home because the curate decided not to hold a service with so small a number.

As for the station staff, there existed a good spirit of camaraderie, a railway fraternity that loved their days at Sheffield Park and later kept in contact with each other through visits or correspondence. The responsibility for the smooth working of the team lay with the stationmaster supported by two of the ubiquitous porter signalmen, or 'signal porters' as they were known among the staff. Despite the extra responsibility of crossing the trains, the starting wage was only 16s a week. There was no Sunday extra pay, none in fact till the 1911 strike, after which only drivers, guards and senior grades received such pay. Out of pocket railway staff did overtime on strike day fill-in turns. Staff moved around in small circles as, for example, Senior Clerk Reginald Pullinger, who had started at Barcombe in August 1902 as a learner clerk for 2s 6d a week, moved a year later on 4 July 1903 to Ardingly as full clerk at 10s and added another shilling when he moved to Sheffield Park on 1 July 1904.

A separate part of the station community was the p/way team. At the turn of the century this section was worked by Tom Hull (Ganger), George Tester (Assistant Ganger) and Platelayers Billy Gray and Harry Duplock. The teams generally remained very stable; George Tester had links going back to the beginning of the line, having worked for Firbank, helping in the strenuous work of digging the cuttings.

William Coney, member of a wide-ranging Brighton railway family, spent 45 years on the footplate until retirement in 1918. His son recalls: 'Each Christmas time Dad would have a large tree ready for us to collect at London Road station, Brighton, carried on his tender, and it came from Sheffield Park. Then again for many years Sheffield Park was the place for Sunday School outings and, if *Samuel Laing*, Dad's engine, was on the train (I can remember it at least once) I, at any rate, was the proudest boy of the lot!'

During the early part of World War 1, in the volunteer period, railway staff were sometimes considered vital to the war effort of the country but, with the late call of conscripts, gaps were left in the ranks. Booking Clerk Sidney Wall, who had arrived on 15 September 1914, joined up on the first day of July 1916 and as battalion runner in carrying messages

On the stairs of the former South box: in the rear are Signal Porters William Moorey and George Prevett; left on the bottom step are Miss Dolly Murrell (Clerk) and Miss Daisy Tester (Platform Porter). Taken in 1917 when the railway was short-staffed through so many of its men serving in the war. *Amy Barford/Bluebell Archives*

'Generalissimo'
between the dep
C. A. Perkins, ta
Sheffield Park (
Swallow, Rober

under very heavy f
received a DCM. To
in at many stations o
old Miss Dorothy (D
and Daisy Tester a le
influenza epidemic ir
daughter Amy to re
attending school. A t
on 6 February 1920,
held until July 1927,
10 months and th
accountant's departr

By 1920 the men
staff had been made,
shifts accordingly re
passenger service
challenge from the
roads, and it was a
fought a rearguard
public-spirited man.
to be fought. When
12s a week, his exp
work so that those
such hardship. For
Clerks' Association
Pension Fund del
LBSCR's pension f
make grants to me
receipt of prewar
management comm
at Woking. All thi
securing for clerks
greater opportunit
education. But righ
main, as did Willia
tide of traffic. One
King [George VI]
3,500 passengers t
see the illuminatio
1927, presented b

'C2X' 0-6-0 No 32539, entering the station with the 12.28pm East Grinstead-Lewes on 16 April 1955 with a Maunsell three-set in the carmine and cream livery of the early BR period. *Colin Saunders*

15.
Horsted Keynes

Arcadia

Soon after the opening in 1882 a visitor expressed astonishment at finding a station of such considerable size in so rural a district:

'The station at Horsted Keynes Junction is remarkably handsome and abundantly roomy; it has a long and wide central covered platform as well as up and down side platforms, and large yard space with sidings for goods, mineral and cattle traffic. This rural station greatly shames by contrast the ramshackle, unsightly property of the South Eastern Co at London Bridge. The link connecting the new line with the main line near Haywards Heath strikes off to the west at this station. A very pretty six-arch viaduct, built on a curve, is seen on the link line at a short distance from the station.'

The first stationmaster, William Yeomanson, arrived there on 14 July 1882, 2½ weeks before the actual opening on 1 August. Then 38, he received a weekly wage of £1 18s 4d less a rent reduction for living accommodation in the station house, where he resided with his wife and four young children. His early arrival enabled him to get the station set out and into shape for the commencement of train services, receiving the necessary station furniture, signs and equipment, registers, posters and tickets, together with an assignment of coal, and of course familiarising the newly-allocated staff with their duties. In this he had the assistance of a head porter, 27-year-old James Scutt, who certainly proved his worth, becoming two years later a station inspector at Haywards Heath. Soon after, Yeomanson also moved on to greater things at West Brighton (Hove) at the beginning of 1885, and the team he had led began to disintegrate and disgrace itself. Charles Mann, a signal porter, was dismissed for an assault on a girl; another, Charles Alder, resigned after just one month; while both a signalman, George Griffen from Three Bridges, and a booking clerk, John Sprinks of Oxted, were 'removed to Horsted Keynes because of incompetence'. One wonders whether Horsted Keynes was viewed as a penitentiary for miscreant staff, for there were to be several more cases.

Another early glimpse of the area comes from Lieut G. Harvey who wrote in *The Amateur Photographer* for September 1892:

'36½ miles from London Bridge lies a place of singular beauty and of exceeding interest to the men of art — a veritable Arcadia, as yet quite unknown and unfrequented by the artist or photographer. As a matter of fact the natives eyed my camera with evident suspicion, doubtless taking it for an infernal machine, and myself for a dynamiter. There are some of the most lovely spots imaginable in this neighbourhood. The village is two miles from the station, down some pretty lanes (be sure to enquire the way from the stationmaster).'

A Mrs Coon who lived at Leighton Cottage recalled in 1956 her memories of the locality at the turn of the century — the bonfire on the Downs for the Diamond Jubilee of 'Old Queen Victoria', the torchlight procession after the relief of Mafeking and Ladysmith, the memorial service after the Queen's death, the May Fair on the village green, the local gypsies carefully watched by the village policeman, Mr Turner, the stoolball and cricket matches and the quoit rink, the stock and village pound, the padding of the sheep's feet as the flocks were walked through the village, or the beagles barking up at the kennels. In the centre the two public houses, the Crown and the Green Man, faced each other across the green, while St Giles was half a mile down Church Lane, which was lit by oil lamps for the benefit and encouragement of evening churchgoers. There was a Bible class, a temperance class known as the 'Blue Ribbon Army' and for those not totally convinced, a 'moderate drinkers' class.

Sunday School and choir outings were red letter days; on May Day there was a maypole in the rectory garden, while biennial 'treats' were held at 'Treemans', owned by Captain Wyatt and hosted by Mrs Benson, widow of the Archbishop of Canterbury, who resided at Ludwell. At the latter place was one of the three village springs which never went dry. She recalls the instance in 1900 of a prospective resident come to look at 'Treemans' but who got no further than alighting from the train before saying that a place with three big platforms was not her idea of the country, and promptly re-entered the train. But later that same family did come, complete with a mound of luggage which included three parrot-stands which always stood in the hall!

On the west side of the station three carriage sidings were originally provided, used to berth special trains serving gala occasions at Sheffield Park, but the best of the cricketing days and visits by the Territorial volunteers were over by the turn of

Left: Taken just prior to the opening of the line at the start of August 1882, the line to Ardingly (left foreground) having yet to be connected. The Yeomanson family are on the left, Lucy (holding Ethel) at the edge of the picture, Ernest, William and Florence. On the opposite platform James Scutt heads a line of workmen putting the finishing touches to Horsted Keynes station.
H. M. Madgwick collection

William Yeomanson, first Stationmaster at Horsted Keynes (1882-5), from a portrait taken in 1875 at the age of 30. He kept a loyal and stable staff and lived on his job with his wife and four young children in the station house, for which he had to pay a rent of 4s out of his weekly salary of £1 18s 4d. *Joan Pearson/Bluebell Archives*

the century. In 1905 the LBSCR locomotive department found a use for the sidings, selecting them to store engines awaiting repairs or disposal, while Brighton Works was in the throes of extension and reorganisation and giving priority to the building of new engines. The three long sidings were at times host to upwards of 30 locomotives and 'the dump' became a mecca for the enthusiasts and photographers of those days. Through recorded and photographic evidence the following locomotives are known to have been residents:

Class	Nos
B4	45
C1	423-6/9/30/1
D	7, 17/8, 23/4, 237/95/6, 357
D2	309-13
E1	98, 110/4-6/32/56/9
E3	158/67/70, 453/6/7
E4	474/81-3/92/5, 519/62
E5	573
G	326/35/6/8/41/3/7/8/50

On to 26 May 1911 and the arrival upon the scene of a man who saw extensive though interrupted service on the line, for on that day George Prevett started as Porter for 12 hours a day at 16s a week. By doing some relief turns elsewhere, he was able to earn a shilling a day extra. That August he moved to Sheffield Park, was appointed Signalman on 5 May 1913, was there again in 1925, at Newick & Chailey in 1930, for a third time at Sheffield Park in 1938 and finally, in 1940, back where he started at Horsted Keynes. He gives us a picture of the station just before World War 1. He remembers the little North box, which controlled the crossover at that end of the station. The lines in order of nearness to the box on the east side were down Lewes, up Lewes, down Haywards Heath and up Haywards Heath, an arrangement which lasted until just prior to the war. The station was relatively busy with some 14 passenger trains a day, but it was the goods traffic that helped the line to pay its way.

A rare glimpse of the three sidings on the west side of the station at the turn of the century, empty, implying their use for stabling the 'specials' and additional workings in connection with the great festive occasions held at Sheffield Park. *John Minnis collection*

Following the decline of the gala events at Sheffield Park, these three sidings were selected to store locomotives awaiting repair or breaking up during the rebuilding and enlarging of Brighton Works between 1905 and 1909. This photograph, taken from the top of the water tower, affords a view across to the station with its complete set of canopies, and the tall topiary bushes on each platform. In the foreground is Stroudley's posthumous prototype 'E3' class 0-6-2T No 158 *West Brighton* and behind it one of his 'C' class 0-6-0 goods engines.
M. P. Bennett/Bluebell Archives

A head-on view of the 'dump' taken from the steps of the South box. A count of 29 chimneys gives some indication of the number of stored locomotives. On the left is 'D2' 0-4-2 *Splugen*, which arrived entire as No 309, but in June 1907 was renumbered on site as 609 in the duplicate list and at the same time lost its boiler and tender. *Bluebell Archives*

But hopes of a great interchange and the expectation that the line would carry much of the relief traffic to and from the coast (hence the two Lewes and two Haywards Heath sets of rails separately allocated for joining or terminating trains) never materialised. A plan of proposed alterations, stamped 13 August 1913, rationalising track and signalling arrangements came into force on 26 June 1914. Until 1914, the junction at Horsted Keynes was at the north end of the station, controlled by the North signalbox on the down side, and Haywards Heath line services used what were then Platforms 1 and 2 on the island platform. The island platform at this time possessed waiting rooms, canopy and finely trimmed bushes. The LBSCR plans included the removal from the block system of the North box (eight levers were moved to the South box) which became relegated to a shunting frame, together with some healthy exercise for the permanent way staff in moving the junction from the north end of the station to the south. A major change to the appearance and operation of Horsted Keynes came about as a consequence, as the island platform was divested of its structures and greenery in order to provide the South box signalman with a clear view of the north end of the station. Platform 1, formerly the up Haywards

Heath line, became a siding, with the old Platform 2 being used only for terminating up services from Haywards Heath. Through trains on the Ardingly line used the east platforms, previously the sole preserve of the Lewes line services. Platform numbers were all reduced by one from this time.

By the end of World War 1 the station had greatly changed in appearance, illustrated by the following description given by a railway enthusiast in 1914:
'At Horsted Keynes one is in a district remarkable for the beautiful scenery visible from the carriage windows. Here is a four-road, five-platformed station, one island used exclusively by Lewes trains, while both can be used by trains towards Haywards Heath. The down Lewes line has platform faces on both sides. The station as a whole is an exceptionally neat and artistic one.'

This odd situation led a wit to ask in the pages of the *Southern Railway Magazine*, 'What junction in this division has two up platform roads into which up trains from one route cannot run without a shunt, such trains having to run into one of the two down platforms? Answer: Horsted Keynes. Trains from Sheffield Park have to run to one of two down platforms.'

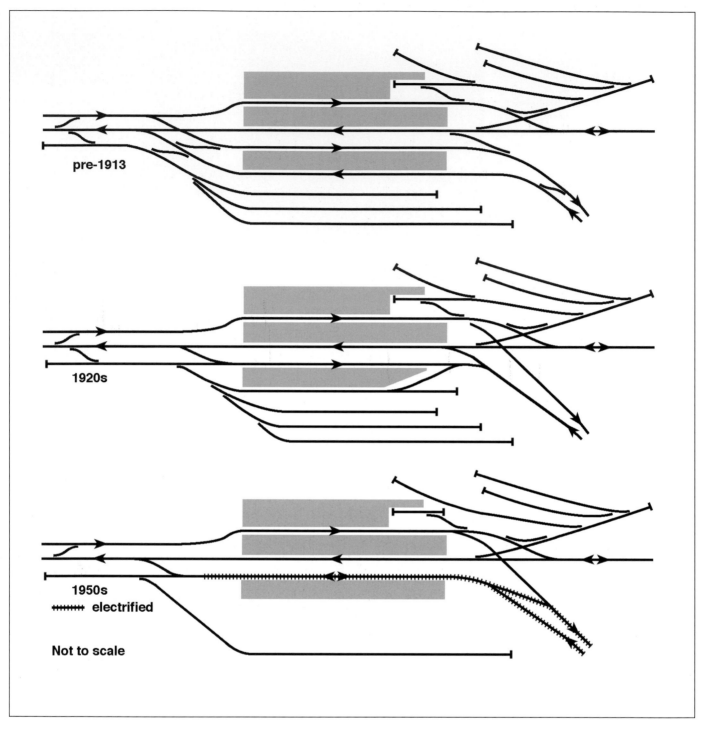

pre-1913

1920s

1950s
++++++ electrified

Not to scale

The Station Staff

The station team in those early days had mustered double figures: the stationmaster; two signalmen and two signal porters, one of the latter being head porter; two porters; one clerk and a couple or more learner clerks. Bertrams ran the refreshment room on the middle platform. Sunday nights were always a lively get-together. Beer sold better than tea, since all water had to be fetched from a pump. Not only was the station well run, but the flower beds and borders were reckoned to be second to none.

George Prevett's earliest remembered stationmaster was John Bromley, who came to Horsted under a cloud, having consented at Stoats Nest in April 1907 to allow the Clarendon Film Co to produce a train wrecking scene, resulting in a real fatality. Surprisingly he was not discharged but reduced in

grade and very conveniently a post was found for him at remotely situated Horsted Keynes, achieving this by allowing Bromley and Alfred Chalker, who had been in charge of Horsted Keynes since 1901, to swap stations. One gets the impression that the railway company wanted to forget the embarrassing incident as quickly as possible and banished the culprit deep into the heart of Sussex. Bromley was suspended from duty for several months, not arriving at Horsted Keynes until August 1907. His track record there was described as 'safe and popular'. Kathleen Turner, who lived at Horsted Keynes and began to use the station in 1919, remembers how on wintry mornings she would be let into the booking office to thaw out by the fire. He took the station through the war years, retired prematurely due to ill health at the end of April 1922 and went to live in Lewes. Until Ben Bowley took over on 1 December, station responsibilities were undertaken by the LBSCR's efficient system of relieving stationmasters.

Left: The changing layouts at Horsted Keynes (pre-1913, 1920s and 1950s).

Right: A close-up group photograph of the station staff, taken in 1892 outside the station's porch. The Stationmaster is Arthur W. Moore (1891-3), with his two children sitting at his feet. The only other member of staff positively identified is Porter Frank Geer standing on the right with his hand on his waistcoat pocket. He retired as Crossing Gatekeeper at Adams Well near Tunbridge Wells. He was the great uncle of Geoff Mantell, who passed on this photograph to the Bluebell Archives. *Bluebell Archives*

Stationmaster John Bromley found himself banished in 1907 to a 'rural retreat'. By 1912, when this photograph was taken, he had become much liked and respected by the local community. He stands here on the right with his station staff among whom are Frederick West (head porter), Ernest Bartlett (porter) and Frederick Simmons and William Moon (signalmen), together with the station dog. By the gate in the right background is his daughter Ethel, who was to become one of the first girls to be taken on by the railway as station clerks. *Bluebell Archives*

During World War 1, as with many other stations, the gentle sex lent a helping hand. Conveniently at hand was John Bromley's daughter Ethel, who on 27 August 1915 at the young age of 14 took on the duties of booking clerk at 10s a week. She was succeeded on 18 October 1920 by Emily Veness from Haywards Heath who resigned in December the following year, probably to have a child.

The porter-signalmen had to be jack of all trades, helping in the yard, chaining down round timber, double-sheeting goods trucks, or renewing the lamps of the distant signals — which involved a three-quarter-mile walk up all three ways twice a week, for the long-burning lamps of today (renewable once weekly) had not come on the scene. Indeed, there were several cases of lamps going out in 1911. There was the additional complication of the staff tokens. There were 18 at the South box but, there being one more train down than up, a linesman had to come up every so often and bring an even number of tokens with him. Of unusual locomotive workings, Mr Prevett remembers the trial trips of the Marsh tanks, *Abergavenny* and *Bessborough*, which came up on the 3.18pm ex-Brighton,

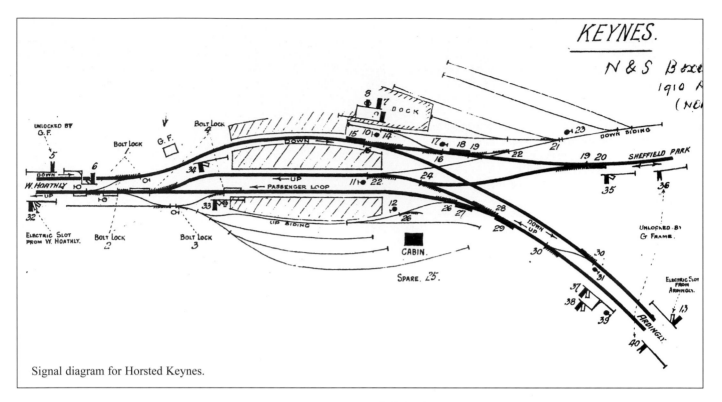

Signal diagram for Horsted Keynes.

Horsted Keynes Station. A846

An unusual view of the double-sided platform road at Horsted Keynes, showing the station house and, beyond, the loading dock and wagons in the goods yard, a pre-World War 1 scene.
James Young collection

arriving 3.45pm at Horsted Keynes, and away at 4pm after a quick run-round. On one occasion during this operation the former broke its coupling. After World War 1, many excursion trains originating from southeast London were, on bank holidays, routed to Brighton over the line and were frequently the preserve of SECR tender engines.

Another veteran of Horsted Keynes first arrived there as a signalman in June 1916 with 13 years of previous railway service to his credit. William Moon stayed at the South box right through to his retirement in 1950. He just remembers the late wartime economies, the west platform canopy and buildings which went first, followed on the same side by the up main and all but one siding behind the signalbox, while on the east side an extra short goods dock was taken out, involving a slight realignment. The station staff was at first scarcely reduced. Under Mr Bromley were two clerks and his daughter, who also lent a hand; two signalmen, head

porter, porter and learner porter, with someone usually out relieving.

Another character at the station was Harry Johnson, employed at a local nursery to take produce to the station for transport to Covent Garden. Harry had been a London cabby in his earlier days. When his pony trap was not required for nursery work, he would oblige and drive anyone to the station or even to East Grinstead for a day's shopping. Kathleen Turner recalls it was a great adventure to be taken to the station by this means. Harry would say, 'Nobby — Train's in!' and away Nobby would go at perilous speed, the grown-ups heaving a sigh of relief on reaching the station safely, the children dejected to think the excitement was over.

In his early days Bill Moon assisted with signal lamps and goods when required, but these demands grew less frequent as the decline of the interwar period set in. Kathleen Turner recalls how the station was a hive of activity in the mornings as the local farmers drove their milk floats down to get their milk on the London train. 'There were quite 20 floats tied up with others waiting for a space to become vacant while their owners unloaded the full churns and reloaded with empty ones.' But milk traffic soon dropped off. Horseboxes for Haywards Heath were required less as motor traffic took over on the roads. Bill Moon remembers the arrival by rail of the first tarmac mixer, pointer to the coming threat of road competition. More coal began to arrive, mainly from Kent, extremely dusty stuff which was put under the water crane and well hosed before shifting. The local coal merchant boasted the name of Reuben Baker. Arthur Friend held the field as corn merchant. A few old box trucks mounted on bricks to act as goods sheds remained as a sign of more prosperous times when they had been much in demand for the storing of goods. The lock-up goods shed was of normal size but had an extension with an additional railside door. At one period the local service of goods trains was run on different lines for a short while. The Lewes goods came up via Sheffield Park, on to Haywards Heath and back the same way. Another goods train came down from East Grinstead to Horsted Keynes, and then turned back. This experiment did not last long; the revised goods from Lewes to Kingscote usually detached a truck or two at Horsted Keynes to ease its load on the graded line further north, and on its return ran these over to Haywards Heath.

The signal staff had their moments too. The cutting between Horsted Keynes and West Hoathly was a favourite for minor landslips. On one occasion a 'push-pull' ran into a slip on the down road, while a goods train was stuck for four hours at the farther end. On another occasion, in Southern days, a Lewisham-Brighton excursion, which had topped 70mph south of East Grinstead, ran 550yd past the station signals. Once an engine crew heading north failed to surrender the staff token. Quick work on the telephone led to a good race between a clerk setting up the line from Horsted Keynes and a porter down from West Hoathly

Water was always a problem, there being but a 20-minute supply for local needs — engine drivers were asked not to take water from the crane except in an emergency — and this was accentuated when the Holy Well was tapped for water by the Mid Sussex Water Board to supply the rapidly growing built-up district around Haywards Heath. A deep bore had to be made at the pump house; when the results were poor this had to be rebored once again, and only in the early 1950s was new electrical pumping equipment installed.

Mention must be made of Horsted Keynes and its station vicinities being made the dumping ground for stored or withdrawn stock. During World War 1 the west sidings were filled with several ammunition trains, and, among other things, frequently with 'Lousy Lou', the Newhaven dock-workers' train of old six-wheeled coaches, a forerunner of the 'Lancing Belle'. A mobile coastal battery also put in frequent appearances but never stayed long. After that war, as soon as the rolling stock building programme got under way, a wonderful variety of old stock, trucks, small goods guard's brakes and the like, began to arrive, several of which ended up on bricks in the goods yard. Then all but one long siding was removed and this housed the engineer's service coaches during the mid-1930s when the line to Haywards Heath was electrified.

When the station was built, six railway staff cottages were constructed up on the western bank overlooking Leamland Cutting and serviced by the adjacent Leamland Bridge and what was called the 'long path'. Most staff preferred the 'short path' off the platform edge at the north end of the station and across 'the Platt', the area of bank leading up to the cottages.

Allan Parsons recalls the residents there in 1920. The cottages were then (although not now) numbered from the north end as follows: No 1, Fred Parsons (Ganger); No 2, Alf Parsons (Platelayer), Allan's father but no relation to Fred; No 3, The Tuletts (widow and daughter of George Tulett); No 4, Ernest West (Porter Signalman); No 5, Bill Moon (Signalman); No 6, Frederick Simmons (Signalman). Stationmaster Bromley lodged with Allan's family at No 2. They moved from there in 1921. 'We had a LBSCR truck shunted into the siding below and carried our furniture down the bank!'

A resident of the village, Bert King, relates that when he first left school around 1926, he had a job as errand boy for the village shop. The errand he dreaded most of all was the trek out to the railway cottages. Not only was it uphill for most of the way so that at times he had to dismount and push, but he would have to wait for trains to depart before he could manhandle his bike over the lines and climb the embankment to the cottages.

The Bowley Era

Mr Bromley's successor in December 1922 was Ben Bowley, who was to be Horsted Keynes's longest serving stationmaster, staying on into World War 2 because younger men were being called up, and retiring in 1941. He arrived with his wife and two sons; from Donald, the younger one, comes most of the information that follows.

The Bowleys soon fitted into village life and Ben knew all his regular passengers by their first names. Two brothers ran the local taxi service and the Green Man public house, the taxi being in the garage next door. Mains water did not arrive at the station until the late 1920s; until then water had to be pumped up from a well under the kitchen. The railway cottages were even worse off, serviced by a pump outside in one of the gardens. The residents would walk through each other's gardens to collect water. Lighting in the station house was by oil lamps. Even when the Bowleys left in 1941 they were still using oil but there was talk of the electric coming down from the village. As children, Donald and Cecil would play all over the station. Hide and seek was popular as none of the station rooms were locked. The porters' room was a good place to hide. This was where the station oil lamps were kept and cleaned, oil being stored in a wooden sleeper-built shed in the goods yard. One day, after a heavy shunting turn, this shed went up in flames. Apparently, great fun was had putting it out. After this incident a standard concrete SR lamp room was put on the dock.

The station was a bitterly cold place in winter. There was heating downstairs but the big bedrooms were difficult and expensive to keep warm. Donald would awake in the morning to find ice on the inside of the windows. Using the station coal for the house was against the rules; the coal room next to the porters' room was for the waiting rooms, signalbox and a supply for the locos if they ran short. Donald went to school in Haywards Heath and would take the electric train from Platform 1, where his father would hold it for a few minutes if he was late in getting up. The electric trains would often slip at Copyhold Junction in the winter and on one occasion one was stuck for 1½ hours due to ice on the line. Eventually a steam engine came to pull it out — a good excuse to be late for school that day!

The station never won any awards for best kept gardens but the few staff always kept them neat and tidy. Ben Bowley had an allotment at the back of the far platform but it was hard work, the weeds soon took over and, as he wasn't a keen

Ben Harry Bowley in LBSCR uniform at the early end of his career as Stationmaster. *Simon Baker collection*

followed by Mr Prevett when Mr Simmons retired. The Platform 1 canopy was taken down in 1914 along with the North signalbox but not all the canopy buildings were dismantled. Donald remembers a section of the waiting room and the ladies' toilet being there after 1935. Only the wooden top of the signalbox went, the lower brick base being kept for a gangers' store. He remembers helping the workmen to knock that down years later.

From 1934 Mr Bowley also had in his charge Ardingly and West Hoathly stations. He would usually check the books at the stations once a week on a Friday, when he would also take the wage slips with him. He went up on one train and returned on the next, with perhaps time to have a drink in the Bluebell Inn at West Hoathly or the Avins Bridge at Ardingly. For the rest of the week the 'governor' was always to be found at noon in the buffet at Horsted, enjoying a bite and a lunchtime drink. The buffet was run by Bertrams, who had a catering contract with the SR for many years. Miss Jenner, who lived in the railway cottages, worked in the buffet. The shelves were stacked out with bottles of beer, with spirits on the top shelves, much as it is today. Locals would just wander onto the station, have their pint and a snack and go again. Beer would arrive by train with the cellarman. The train would stop with the goods van directly outside the cellar doors and the fresh barrels were lowered down by rope. Sunday lunchtimes were always very busy, with the locals and farmers gathering and discussing the week's work and putting the world and station to rights over a few beers. In fact the station gained a reputation for selling more beer than the pubs in the village, much to the annoyance of the landlords. Mrs Tulett was a regular, a ganger's widow with one daughter who lived in the railway cottages and would come down to the buffet early every evening and sit at her regular seat in the corner to drink a glass of stout. The buffet remained open up until the 1955 closure. It did not reopen as the deafening quietness of the station during the obviously temporary reopening made it financially unviable.

Regular Ramblers' excursions started on 15 May 1932 from Victoria via East Grinstead. These cost 3s and attracted up to 600 people. They always finished at Horsted Keynes where the buffet would open up specially to do brisk business. The

gardener, he soon gave it up. He did, however, plant the honeysuckle that grows to this day around the south running-in board on the middle platform. The staff had their work cut out keeping the station running smoothly along with a busy goods yard with only a stationmaster and two porters, which was reduced to one senior porter as the war approached. There were also two regular signalmen, Mr Moon and Mr Simmons,

Snowscape at Horsted Keynes, with 'E5' 0-6-2T No 2592 making a crisp start with a local bound for East Grinstead. The length of electrified rail protruding just ahead of the locomotive indicates a post-July 1935 date. At this period the fortunes of the class were already on the wane, relegated to secondary duties. Withdrawals commenced in 1936 and only the outbreak of war saved this class from an early demise, old *Eastergate* here succumbing as late as 1953. *Courtesy Brighton Library*

In 1934 a Somerset farmer, Mr John Copp, moved his establishment to Sussex. His entire farm stock and implements came from Crewkerne by special train, which was photographed being unloaded beside the cattle dock at Horsted Keynes. The goods lock-up (now moved to Kingscote), the only covered accommodation, is seen near the top of the picture. Note also part of the ashphalt plant in the top left corner.
Bluebell Archives

last excursion before the war ran on 27 August 1939 at an increased price of 3s 2d.

Reuben Baker, a member of the Horsted Keynes Council and guardian of the public good, was also the local coal merchant who had his office built of railway sleepers in the goods yard. When electricity came to the village he could be contacted by telephone on Danehill 25. He was remembered as saying, 'I will not rest until Horsted Keynes has 12 electric street lamps.' Well, he must still be at unrest! Goods engines came every day to shunt wagons in and out. There were various goods — coal, cattle trucks with the baby animals wrapped in sacks with just their heads sticking out, and milk that went out in churns. One of the porters was famous for being able to roll two upright churns along with his hands.

A station survey in 1935 just prior to electrification noted, 'As far as rail traffic is concerned, the goods business is in agriculture, and a large quantity of granite and beach is dealt with in connection with Messrs Chittenden & Simmons Ashphalt plant which is situated in the goods yard.' Mr Bowley's main concern was the fumes that descended over the station from it.

Local farmers relied on the railway for transportation of feed, machinery and livestock and even a complete move of a farm. Such an occasion took place on Monday, 26 March 1934, when the first section of 25 trucks attached to a specially chartered train brought in the entire stock of a farm from Crewkerne in Somerset. Over 300 head of livestock made the journey, together with various agricultural machinery and implements. Mr John Copp, the enterprising farmer, was taking over a new business near Lindfield. Photographs in the *Sussex Daily News* indicate 'I' tank haulage and show the cattle dock at the south end of Platform 4 and some small sheds being unloaded from flat trucks.

The survey went on to report, 'During the fruit season a considerable quantity of fruit is dealt with for the Mid-Sussex Canning & Preserving Co, a business which is rapidly extending. Large orchards have been planted and present a grand sight when the trees are out in bloom. The surrounding land is owned by the well-known family of Stephenson Clarke & Co.' Donald Bowley recalls this traffic:

'During the fruit season large quantities of fruit arrived from local nurseries for the St Martins Preserving Co (later the Mid-Sussex Canning & Preserving Co) at Cinder Hill. This was the largest jam and canning factory in Sussex. Extensive orchards had been laid out and in the summer over 150 people, mostly girls from Brighton, would come up on the train to work there. The porters used to have great fun in teasing these factory girls while they waited for the trains back to Brighton.'

Electrification

On 8 July 1935 the station went through another upheaval as the third rail was extended from Haywards Heath. Mention has already been made of the significant change to the station track layout in 1914, when the effective junction of the Lewes and Haywards Heath lines was moved to the south end of the station. Now the 1935 electrification scheme went only as far as Horsted Keynes, and only Platform 1 was equipped to handle the terminating electric services. In order for electric trains to return on the right road, a new crossover was provided immediately south of the signalbox, and at the same time the facility to enter Platform 2 from the Ardingly branch was removed. A down starter was provided at the south end of Platform 1, and the junction now barely existed, being preserved at the south end by the single thread of a crossover from Platform 3 to the down Haywards Heath line.

The Southern Railway must have had it in mind to continue with the electrification north of Horsted Keynes in the 1930s, but instead then turned its attention and resources to the Portsmouth lines, despite the lobbying by residents of Oxted, East Grinstead and elsewhere. Only the outbreak of war in 1939 prevented plans for electrification going further north. Though electric services for Seaford, Eastbourne and Hastings had commenced on Sunday, 7 July, with the Ardingly branch being closed on Sundays, electric services did not start there till next day. The *Southern Railway Magazine* reported: 'At Horsted Keynes the block instruments and signalling have been modernised, the crossover road on the Ardingly line lengthened to make it suitable for the departure of down trains from the loop (renamed up main platform). The connection from the up Ardingly line to the up main platform has been abolished, and illumination converted to electricity.'

Above: The driver of 2BIL electric unit No 2039 has just handed the electric train staff for the section from Ardingly to the Horsted Keynes signalman, as he slows to enter Platform 1, which was originally the down Haywards Heath line. With electrification the layout was again revised to make it into a reversible track for terminating electric services. The date is 20 May 1961, when the section to Ardingly was operated as a single line. The goods yard was still in use at this stage, being closed the following year. *J. H. W. Kent*

Left: Many photographs were taken of track alterations to the goods yard at Horsted Keynes following the revision of the layout at the south end of the station for electric services in 1935. The district engineer's workforce ease the freshly assembled pointwork into the correct alignment. *D. Bowley/ Simon Baker collection*

The War Years

Goods traffic had been declining but a brief revival took place during World War 2. A sawmill was set up to cut pit props, while up at the village a jam factory was opened at 'The Blue Smock'. Truckloads of oranges arrived to join the apples from the local nurseries and a truck per day of jam was attached to a London train. All sorts of railway or war stock was berthed in the west siding that remained. Ships' propellers were stored here, to be sent back as replacements when required, as were ammunition trains, empty army tank flats in 1940, later with parts for tanks built at Brighton Works awaiting the invasion, although these were never required and were cut up on site with acetylene cutters after

the war. Both Pullman cars, secreted away from Preston Park Depot in bomb-prone Brighton, and sets of electric stock, mainly 2-NOL, 2-BIL & 2-HAL units, occupied the much-in-demand siding over this period. Sid Nash noted the following during his wartime journeys through Horsted Keynes:

16 Aug 1941
Electric Trailer units 1107/8 ('E4' No 2499 doing the morning shunting).
3 Apr 1943
1st Class Pullman Cars: *Juno, Padua, Sunbeam, Cynthia, Cadiz, Niobe* and *Sylvia*, also an SR dining car.
21 Mar 1944
Pullman Cars: *Sylvia, Cadiz, Sunbeam* and *Padua*.

Right: Horsted Keynes in the middle of the war — a rare picture taken from the top of the water tower, showing the station with blank nameboards to fox German parachutists, and wartime white stripes on the canopy supports to assist passengers on the unlit station. This photograph was most probably taken on a date close to the following one, for the leading electric unit next to the propellers is the same.
D. Bowley/ Simon Baker collection

Below: Signalman George Prevett poses by a consignment of ships' propellers, brought up from Newhaven in 1940 to escape the bombing of that port. Peeping out at the side of the signalbox is 2HAL unit No 2664, heading a line of stored electric stock.
Bluebell Archives

16 June 1945
Pullman Cars: *Calais, Padua, Sunbeam, Cadiz, Milan* (all painted red)

During the postwar period various sets of old rolling stock, bolster wagons, carriage frames, and towards the end condemned goods wagons for Polegate, were stored in the siding. The carriage underframes were reputedly for new electric stock, having been built at Ashford and en route to Eastleigh, using Horsted Keynes as a useful staging point.

During the war the signalbox had to be staffed day and night as the line was an important alternative secondary route between London and the coast. There was one porter who left to join the army. He rose to the rank of major and subsequently joined Lewes District Council after the war. Early in the war

evacuees from London were brought to Haywards Heath and East Grinstead by train and taken by bus to the surrounding villages. One busload was unloaded at the village green.

The war brought its problems too. A bomb hit the embankment near the waterworks, causing the line to be closed for a fortnight, and a bus service was run between Horsted Keynes and Sheffield Park. An air raid shelter was provided for the Bowleys. This was dug in the bank of the hill that is now the road to the car parking field. It was made out of station enamel signs and sleepers, topped with earth. The staff and public had to make do with the subway as a shelter and a platform seat was taken down there. The staff also used to take cover in the ticket office under the big, long, oak table that is still there today. On one occasion when Ben Bowley was going to check the books at Ardingly, the engine crew

The arrival of the Bluebell Railway, which had been granted permission to run into Horsted Keynes, under a rental agreement which included the cost of a pilotman for the final 300yd over BR tracks, meant that once more the station became an interchange junction. The scene on 12 October 1963, just a fortnight prior to the cessation of electric services, shows a train for Seaford strengthened to six coaches headed by 2HAL unit No 2624. Quite a number of passengers have disembarked and are seen crowding the subway stairs, intent on making their connection with the service to Sheffield Park standing in Platform 3/4, in charge of 'P' 0-6-0T No 27. *R. C. Riley*

occasions. Lingfield race specials from Brighton also used the route. One such day was as follows, on Friday/Saturday 4/5 July 1958 trains to Lingfield ran:

4/7/58	12.53 ex-Brighton, 1.17pm HK
4/7/58	5.25 ex-Lingfield, 5.46pm HK
5/7/58	12.11 ex-Brighton, 12.43pm HK
5/7/58	4.58 ex-Lingfield, 5.20 HK

'After the up line to East Grinstead was used as a siding (as from 9.00am on Monday 14 July 1958), the Lingfield race specials ran over the down line from East Grinstead under single line working, with a pilotman. A light engine was booked from East Grinstead to Horsted Keynes to open. Single line working was closed with the passing of the last down race special. The pilotman was usually Tom Apps from East Grinstead. On Friday 22 August 1958, the working was as follows:

LIGHT ENGINE 11.55 ex-EG arrive 12.27 at HK, depart 12.32 to EG to open single line working
12.53 ex-Brighton (race special) 1.26pm until 1.32 to EG

LIGHT ENGINE 1.55 ex-EG arrive 2.19 at HK, until 2.28 to HH to close single line working
5.25pm ex-Lingfield, 5.47 HK under normal working.

'When I first arrived at Horsted Keynes the box was fitted with Standard Three position instruments between Haywards Heath, Ardingly and Horsted Keynes, also between Horsted Keynes and East Grinstead South box. Ardingly box was normally closed except for shunting or Ardingly College luggage. There was a nasty incident at Ardingly station when the porter on duty went to close the door of a train as it moved out. His hand slipped, the window dropped, trapping him by the wrist. His wrist was very badly cut. The quick action of Alec Durrant (HK leading porter) saved his wrist and possibly his life; Alec was assisting at Ardingly with the College luggage. When the down line was made into a siding on 19 January 1959 to berth Kent Coast stock, single line working with electric train staff was introduced and the box at Ardingly required to be open all the time. I had to spend a few days at East Grinstead to learn how to use the staff instrument. They were memorable days, although I did not appreciate it at the time. It must have been January 1959;

Left: This aerial view of Horsted Keynes was taken in 1964, just prior to the lifting of the track from Ardingly, and the salient features are clearly defined in sunny conditions. At the bottom left are New Lane Bridge and Sheriff Mill Viaduct; at the top right Leamland Bridge and the staff cottages. The station layout and associated buildings can all be picked out. Though the Bluebell Railway had at this point been given permission to run into the station, all the lines seen here were in the ownership of BR, which had ceased all services, hence the total absence of any rolling stock. *R. G. Spalding/Meridian Airmaps*

A view of the station seen from the angle between the lines from Ardingly (left) and Sheffield Park taken in the late 1950s. There are wagon flats in the long siding behind the signalbox, while on the far right, part of the goods yard, somewhat grass-grown, can be seen still displaying a moderate amount of traffic. The shed is the original goods lock-up authorised at the end of 1890.
Lens of Sutton

there was a very cold spell with a lot of snow. All the train services at East Grinstead were steam-hauled and I remember all the coal braziers were burning continuously to stop the water cranes from freezing. Engines took water quite frequently at East Grinstead.

'After the condemned steam stock was cleared from the down line to Ardingly, the new Kent Coast electric stock was berthed on the down line (CEPs & BEPs), at one time seven 12-car trains were berthed. The new stock had to go out for mileage runs. A train crew would take the first train at the Ardingly end, then the other trains would all be moved towards Ardingly. When the first returned, it was berthed at the Horsted Keynes end, so they all had running trips in turn. To get in clear of the crossover to the down line (No 30), the 12-car trains had to pull up nearly to the railway cottages. It was the nearest electric trains ever got to East Grinstead from Horsted Keynes. I had a train on one occasion pull up nearly to Leamland Bridge; it was just on the 'juice'.

'In preparation for the arrival of the new trains, several test runs with longer than normal electric trains were run to and from Horsted Keynes to see if the traction current could cope, as there were not any sub-stations on the Horsted Keynes branch. The last sub-station was at Copyhold Junction, from where the traction current was said to be 'thrown' to Horsted Keynes. The tests consisted of trains starting simultaneously from prearranged positions to see if the circuit breakers held. For example, one train would be held on the down advance starting signal (No 13) to Ardingly and one held on Horsted home signal (No 38), then 'pull off' together so both trains were drawing current.

'When the Bluebell Railway first started, trains were only allowed to run to Bluebell Halt, situated just south of the over-road bridge on the single line to Sheffield Park, where a substantial fence was erected across the track. One summer evening, it must have been 1959, during a gap in the British Railways service, Fred Miles and I heard a train coming up from Sheffield Park, and went down to have a look. Shortly after the train arrived at Bluebell Halt, doors opened and out stepped a number of religious gentlemen with reversed collars. Fred Miles was dumbfounded. "My God," he said, "A Holy Special".

'In the early 1960s the Bluebell trains started running into Horsted Keynes with an engine at both ends, entering Platform 3 with a British Railways conductor. There were not any run-round facilities available to the Bluebell at this time. The electric trains were still running into Platform 1, where a sign was placed under the station nameboard reading, "ALIGHT HERE FOR THE BLUEBELL LINE". We did have problems with visitors on the track, particularly on the electrified lines. One day I caught a couple chatting away, standing astride the down line to Ardingly conductor rail with the current on; they thought it was off. In 1961 Horsted Keynes returned to junction status, connecting with the Bluebell Railway's services to Sheffield Park, but goods services, which needed to cross the latter's path to exit from the yard, were quickly withdrawn in March 1962. During the last few months of the electric train service the line to Ardingly was worked under the "one engine in steam" regulations, with one staff from Ardingly. Horsted box was unmanned and the signal arms removed.'

16.
West Hoathly

Description

The environs of this station witnessed both the beginning and the end of the northern section of the line. It was here that Firbank's men first set up their base close by the site of the tunnel that needed to be driven through the high Wealden ridge of sandstone and clay, and here that the demolition contractor set up his base for dismantling the panels of lifted rails in 1964. The tunnel lay below the small hamlet of Sharpthorne which gave it its local and popular name, but both station and tunnel received the official name of West Hoathley which lies a good mile further along the ridge to the west. In more modern times West Hoathly became the standard spelling.

The station was similar to the other double track stations on the line and lay just north of the tunnel. It was reached by a winding lane (today's Station Road) which meandered down to the west side of the line, where was sited the forecourt to the main station building, opposite which stood the Bluebell Inn. In common with Sheffield Park and Newick & Chailey it had a covered footbridge. There was also access from Hamsey Road on the east side via an ancient right of way. The signalbox at the north end of the down platform surveyed the goods yard opposite as well as the brickyard siding, which came off immediately north of the box.

The Brickyard

The earliest detailed recollections come from ganger Wilson, who started at Lewes with a re-laying gang on the South Coast line dealing with large slips and renewals, before being directed away for a period to help in the construction of the Lancing Carriage Shops. In 1922 he came to West Hoathly to replace the retiring Jimmy Merchant, whose associations with the line dated from earliest days, and settled in as ganger on the section West Hoathly-Kingscote (both stations inclusive). Four years later during the railway strike he worked for a spell in the brickyard. This too had connections with Firbank, for the navvies had a brickyard of their own on the west side of the station and it was here that the distinctive red brick so apparent on the line's viaducts, bridge parapets, station buildings, tunnel portals and linings was manufactured. The former navvies' brickyard was taken over by Alan Stenning who turned it into a workshop for making wooden barrows and concentrated all the brickmaking on the east site known as Coombe Brick Field. By 1899 Mr W. Hudson had taken over and from 1913 the firm was known as Hudsons Ltd, in 1976 becoming Ibstock Brick Hudsons.

Clifford G. Green of the Science Department of Brighton Technical College has been studying and excavating Sussex brickfields including the one at West Hoathly. He writes:

This sepia postcard view, giving excellent definition of the station and surroundings, taken from high up on the east side of the cutting near the tunnel mouth, shows cottages and the Station Inn in Station Road on the west side, and in the station itself a 'Terrier' and balloon coach pausing in the up platform. The smoke in the distance is close to the brickyard, with wagons discernible in the ramped siding alongside. *Bluebell Archives*

This view from the western side of the cutting near the tunnel shows the white sheds of the expanded brickworks. Standard Class 4 2-6-4T No 80105 leaves with the 12.3pm Victoria-Brighton on 30 April 1955, hauling Maunsell three-set 956 on a running-in turn following completion at Brighton Works, prior to being allocated to the London, Tilbury and Southend line.
R. C. Riley

A view of the station from platform level shows the imposing covered footbridge and staircases, the one on the up platform displaying a large enamel panel advertising Pears Soap. The woodwork appears well painted, the large coping stones at the platform edge give way to an area of fine gravel up to the line of whitewashed stones marking the limits of the hedgerows. By the up starting signal stands the daily goods engine, a 'C2' 0-6-0, which is shunting the yard, having left its train standing on the down line.
Bluebell Archives

West Hoathly Tunnel beneath the Sharpthorne ridge was a notoriously wet one, being built beneath a spring. Huge icicles would form during severe winters, endangering both crews and passengers who might have put their heads out in the dark to check whether they had arrived at West Hoathly. Before the first daily train, teams of gangers with sledgehammers would clear the threatening ice.
Bluebell Archives

'From early times up to today the disposal of waste in large towns and cities has been a major problem. In the mid-Victorian period brickmakers purchased materials from the London boroughs, which were then transported, mainly by rail, to the fields sited in the Home Counties and others nearby. The rubbish was screened, the ashes being used for brickmaking and the remainder dumped into disused pits or onto waste land. Towards the end of the 19th century there was a recession in the brick industry which made it uneconomical to purchase rubbish from London, so the boroughs, in order to dispose of this vast amount of unwanted material, gave it free of charge to the brickmakers — the brickfield at West Hoathly used London rubbish in this way, and in fact the station sidings were a collecting point for a number of brickmakers in the area and six wagons of rubbish were turned round daily, quite apart from loads of new bricks. An inspection report reads: "The firm who now operate the dump at Crayford also have a house refuse depot on the Southern Railway at West Hoathly, to which refuse from several districts, including certain London boroughs, is taken and stored. The refuse is later screened by hand into ashes and breeze, and a quantity of these separated materials is used in an adjoining brickworks, the remainder being distributed to small stock brickmakers in parts of Sussex. When this depot was inspected, there was a huge dump of crude refuse alongside the railway, and the main line and sidings were bestrewn with refuse."'

Clifford Green in his excavations at West Hoathly located a large dump of old ashes which came from London, and suspects that sites exist along the track, where extensive indiscriminate dumping of rubbish in pits and depressions in the land have taken place. The brickyard activity is still carried on today, only the loads go by lorry and no longer by goods truck from the lengthy siding whose traces, including a loading platform, can with some difficulty be made out today. This siding, worked from the signalbox off the down line, could hold a locomotive and 20 wagons. It was eventually closed in 1954 when the firm decided to switch to road transport.

The Goods Yard

Across the way were two coalyards belonging to Jack Moon and Frank Leppard respectively, which were still used for storage for some years after the line closed. Talking of coal, it is noted that in 1908 seven tons was contracted to be supplied by Hall & Co, delivered to West Hoathly for steamrollers of the East Grinstead Urban District Council. Farm produce traffic occupied the majority of space in the sidings but straight onto the station platforms went the milk from the local farms, aboard the 9am special whose arrival would be preceded by 14 or 15 milk floats carrying two or three churns apiece, a convoy which would trundle down the hill at breakfast time. The present-day course of the station approach road may seem steep but it was nothing compared to the roughness and inclination of the original course.

The event that marked a lessening of activity in the goods yard was the granting of road-hauling licences to lorries by the Government. Freight charges went up with such competition and big firms soon acquired their own fleet of lorries. Later the goods traffic was whittled down to twice weekly, and the box opened only at specific times as required, until World War 2 saw a brief revival. Canadian troops were billeted at Courtlands, near where the up distant signal stood at the other side of the tunnel, while the scenic woods at Gravetye became an ammunition dump, involving trains at night every week

The permanent way gang that covered Sharpthorne Tunnel was responsible for the length from West Hoathly right down to Sheffield Park. With the northern portal in the background, Jack Tulett on the left is photographed with the rest of the four-man team in the mid-1930s.
D. Bowley/Simon Baker collection

over a period. Other wartime recollections, particularly of the platelayers, concern various bombs that fell on the line. One landed halfway to Kingscote one night at 10pm in Birch Cutting near Mill Place where, although just one rail was crippled, both roads were stopped. Another was a delayed action bomb south of the tunnel; on each occasion the gangers with their trolleys worked hard to straighten things out for traffic to recommence.

The Ice Tunnel

No account of West Hoathly would be complete without mention of the adjacent and notoriously wet Sharpthorne Tunnel. The reasons for constant water seepage have been explained in the account of its construction. Its icing up was almost an annual event. Mrs Coon of Horsted Keynes recalls, 'Our railwaymen had some very hard winters when they worked day and night day to move with special poles the fantastic ice formations in the tunnel.' In February 1954 the *East Grinstead Courier* sent its correspondent to the tunnel for a first-hand account, headlined 'The Coldest Job of All':

'Where was the coldest place in Sussex last week — or in a large area of Southern England for that matter? Without any question at all, my vote goes to the tunnel immediately south of West Hoathly railway station. And unless I had experienced the truly arctic conditions there, I most certainly would not have believed any tales that the gangs of railway maintenance men told me.

'I heard stories of men fetching icicles out of the tunnel which were too heavy to lift, and it was in a dubious frame of mind that I went to investigate. Those stories were only too true. I spent my coldest couple of hours of the latest freeze-up in that tunnel. With gangers for guides I trod gingerly down the tunnel on a rocky floor of thick ice. The power lamps the guides carried lit up a scene that was a veritable fairyland.

Standard Class 4 No 80031 emerges from the north portal of Sharpthorne Tunnel with the 1.30pm Lewes-East Grinstead, comprising the solitary LBSC coach S3847S, on 21 March 1957. *Colin Hogg*

This is the only known staff photograph received into the Archives without any details as to staff and date. It shows West Hoathly with its full complement of staff. The stationmaster and his two daughters stand on the right. The number of milk churns visible is an indication of the importance of this traffic. The fully grown platform hedges and small bushes in the cutting leading up to the tunnel mouth suggest an Edwardian date. *Bluebell Archives*

From the roof of this 20ft high tunnel hung icicles 7ft and 8ft long, each of which weighed up to two and three cwts. The curved walls were one mass of ice formations, making all manner of fantastic shapes. That was not all. For the ganger guided me to their *pièce de résistance* — the wide airshaft at the centre of the tunnel. From this hung the biggest icicles I have ever seen. Not only did the ice hang perilously from the lip of the airshaft, but it was caked right up the centre. I did not stay beneath that airshaft any longer than I could help! The tunnel is some 200yd from the West Hoathly station and takes the line beneath the village of Sharpthorne. In addition to being a railway tunnel it is a wind tunnel, and it is the icy wind which immediately freezes any liquid, from water to oil.

'It is 731yd long, and from the bricked, domed roof there are hundreds of drainage points, for the hill above holds many springs which add to what would be normal seepage of water. There is a constant drip — and some of the drips are like rivulets in ordinary weather. Two gangs of men, one by day and one by night, have been constantly engaged in knocking down the icicles with special long poles and clearing them

away, together with the accumulation of ice on the tracks themselves. Last Friday night Ganger Charles Cottington, who lives at nearby Kingscote, was in charge of 15 men whose job it was to try and rid the tunnel of well over 100 tons of ice. During the day Ganger Leeves of West Hoathly had a similar number of men engaged on the same duty, but his job was made harder by the fact that he had to clear a passage for the rail traffic. Three times a day Ganger Leeves and his men had to traverse the length of the tunnel and take out the most dangerous icicles — for as soon as one was removed, the accumulated drips froze up again and there was another one!

'"It was worse than this in 1947," said one railwayman. "Then we had a ballast train in the tunnel of 49 trucks to remove the ice — and every one of them was full up." Said railwayman E. Robson of West Hoathly. "Each time there has been ice in the tunnel, I have been on duty for the last 30 years. This is not our worst freeze-up, but it has been pretty bad." The gangers and their men must have viewed the thaw with real relief. As for me, I shall keep out of the tunnel in future when the temperature drops. It's nothing but an ice-house!'

A nostalgic view of the erstwhile rural lane that formed the main street through Sharpthorne village, seen at the point where, from above the tunnel, a direct footpath led steeply down to West Hoathly station.
Bluebell Archives

Station Residents

The early stationmasters are unfortunately faceless characters who only feature in terse entries in the railway company's staff registers. Thomas Stone, the first, has recorded in 1890 that he paid his £4 annual rent for tenancy of the station house; Sidney Gladwin, who arrived in September 1893, was dismissed for inattention as from 7 April 1899, to be reappointed a humble clerk at Croydon Goods on 24 September 1899 and ordered to pay back £1 7s 6d. Henry Hewitt arrived on 17 April 1899, promoted from excess luggage inspector at Brighton, followed on 10 August 1904 by Charles Collins and on 10 May 1909 by Henry Holdaway. The earliest Stationmaster Ganger Wilson could remember was Charles Rook who arrived on 4 April 1914, whose 14-year-old daughter Myra worked from 23 September 1916 as a clerk in the booking office alongside Mabel Campbell, who had started that January and left on 10 October 1916 for Grange Road. Mr Rook bowed out in 1926, when West Hoathly came under the charge of Horsted Keynes.

Ganger Wilson retired on 1 April 1942, but his daughter Gladys wrote wistfully in 1991: 'My father worked on that part of the line from West Hoathly to Sheffield Park for 44 years and my late husband Fred Carter for 21 years until the line was shut.' To boot, her Uncle Will worked on the Seaford line, Uncle Jim on the Crowborough one and Uncle Pat was a guard on the 'Brighton Belle'. 'My parents and family lived in a railway house on top of the tunnel from 1922 till 1966. As children we would wait to hear the train's whistle just before entering the tunnel and then rush out of home and beat it to the station, lucky it was all downhill. Many a time I have walked through the tunnel with friends in our courting days. Sadly Sharpthorne has little outstanding beauty now. That was lost years ago, when all those houses were built between Vinols Cross and the brickworks.'

Ben Bowley's successor at Horsted Keynes in 1941 was Mr E. Corbyn, a devoted railwayman, whose wife assisted in the booking office during the war, and who regularly visited West Hoathly to see all was in order.

The Final Drama

Passenger traffic had always been moderate, though special trains were well patronised. The occasional flutter was produced by a Lingfield race special or a Ramblers' excursion, which often went on to berth its stock at Horsted Keynes. In Southern days head office would send every month or six weeks a special clerk as representative to check up on all the trade books, and this continued into the British Railways regime. But about 1.30pm one day a special train arrived, conveying Mr Bridger and members of the Ministry of Transport. Revenue enquiries began and an economy committee came round to see the books. Rumours of closure followed and before long there appeared the inevitable notices. Soon there was no work left for the two popular porter signalmen, Eddie Stevens and Henry Dry. The latter had come as a signalman to Kingscote in October 1925, transferred to a station south in December 1931 and served right through to the 1955 closure, but he was kept on, being sent to see the stationmaster at East Grinstead who gave him Brambletye Crossing on the single track to Forest Row, on which to fill in his three months until his retirement became due. The signalbox remained in use until the first closure, connected direct to East Grinstead to the north, Kingscote being opened only for shunting movements.

Another person who was not going to take the closure lying down was Mr Jack Leppard, Agent to the railway at West Hoathly since 1921, delivering goods and parcels besides operating as a Coal Merchant in his own right. He had not complained unduly when he had to change to collecting his deliveries from the railhead at East Grinstead in his lorry on Tuesdays, Thursdays and Saturdays, but with the coal now also travelling that way the additional cartage costs were considerable. At the time of the first closure the Coal Merchants' Federation extracted a preliminary enquiry at Charing Cross but British Railways dug its toes in. One interesting consequence of the first closing was that J. W. Boothroyd, who lived in the station house at West Hoathly and had also controlled Horsted Keynes and Ardingly, now had to travel by bus to and from his stations.

During the reopening period West Hoathly was reduced to an unstaffed halt and Mr Boothroyd had no part in its working, the guard issuing tickets on the train. Privilege tickets had to be exchanged at East Grinstead. It was after all a question of cutting as much of the losses as possible during this period of involuntary operation.

The penultimate drama in the history of West Hoathly was played out at the Lewes Court of Inquiry. The station's champions spoke out fearlessly. Mr Leppard, local Councillor and Railway Agent, posed as a local economist, stating plainly he was interested in the most economic way to run England. He pleaded congestion of roads that had been built for horse and cart, with no adequate bus service to counter the loss of the trains. In the interests of local

Smoke drifts from the tunnel through which 'C2X' No 32440 and its solitary coach are arriving at West Hoathly with the 11.30am working from Lewes on 13 March 1958. The signals were left permanently off during the period of 'one engine in steam' service. *R. C. Riley*

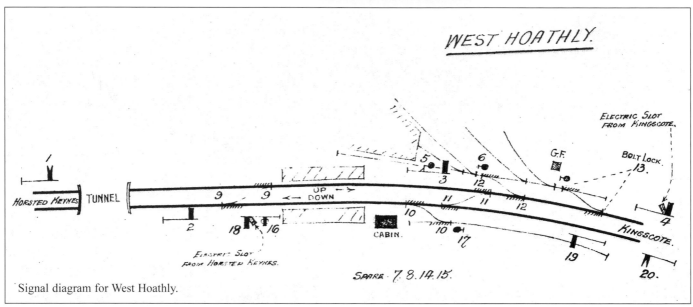

Signal diagram for West Hoathly.

needs railways were worth subsidising. Henry Dry, with more time now he had retired, carefully prepared his case for at least giving trial to a modified service. Prams could not go on buses, and even the Southdown's services were not paying! With more excursions in the summer months and a sensible service that had connections, what might not be achieved?

But the railway authorities took little notice of the arguments of these two men, well versed in the railway service; they had done the same between the wars despite recommendations from most of the local stationmasters. It only remained to ring down the curtain on the station though it took nine years to erase West Hoathly station from the map. The goods sidings were lifted in October 1960, the through lines went in 1964, together with the footbridge and down platform buildings, and September 1967 witnessed the demolition of the station house, lived in till the last, leaving behind a seeming air of finality.

The station house front recorded on 23 May 1964, shortly before the whole complex of buildings was razed to the ground. The building is already in a woebegone state, with broken window panes, beneath the 1882 commemorative stone. Behind the van the letter box can be seen in the wall, the window with its stained glass upper frame is open to vandals, tyres are stacked in the porch and the lower part of the next window is boarded up. *R. C. Riley*

17.
Kingscote

The Ward Era

Together with Rowfant this station held the all-time low record of the smallest traffic receipts on the Brighton system. It provided a classic example of a station built to serve the local gentry, who had sponsored the line and whose mansions lay dispersed across the adjoining countryside. The only buildings near the station in 1882 were the station cottages built for the railway staff.

Whenever local folk or former railwaymen are drawn into conversation about Kingscote, mention is made sooner or later of Thomas J. Ward, first Stationmaster through until his death on 28 April 1904, a most colourful character in the locality which, having no centre of population, tended to close in on the station. Hence Mr Ward held a position equivalent to a squire in other parts, and ran his domain in as independent a fashion as he chose. He was recommended for his appointment by the London & North Western Railway and had been Stationmaster at Rotherhithe for two years before arriving at Kingscote.

Many are the stories centred round his person, probably much embossed with legend, making it difficult to single out the true Mr Ward. He was certainly an officious personality, supervising the efficient running of the station which he constantly sought to present as the smartest on the Brighton system. It is on record that he won several station awards, particularly for the masses of roses which clustered the platform fences, but other flora also found their place in the display, including a special set of potted plants which resided on the oddly placed bench below the station house window for all to see as they stepped down to the subway. He was a religious man and used to hold open-air meetings on the station front if fine (if wet, on the down side platform). His wife sold lemonade and similar drinks from the station house to make up for the lack of a refreshment room. Sometimes during lengthy intervals between trains he went out with his clerk shooting rabbits; if anyone wanted him, his wife was to ring the old station handbell, which was used to warn folk that the train was due in five minutes.

A Victorian resident recalled such distant days:

'Kingscote, of which my first recollection is in 1888, was built in what may be fairly described at that time as a remote situation. It was still remote when I was there in 1901-2, and approached from the west by a road deep in sand, through woods thick with primroses (hence the designation of the section north of Horsted Keynes as the Primrose line) and only a farm and a market garden nearby. The station had, however, an almost national fame at that time, as its stationmaster,

Stationmaster Thomas Ward on the right with his three members of staff c1903: a signal porter, booking clerk and porter, enough to look after this station. Kingscote provided the classic example of a station built to serve the local gentry who had sponsored the line and whose mansions lay dispersed across the adjoining countryside but lay remote from any community, the nearest complex of dwellings being over two miles away at Turner's Hill.
Lens of Sutton

Stationmaster Thomas Ward (left) was in charge of Kingscote from the opening day, 1 August 1882, through till his death in harness on 28 April 1904. During this time more than 30 members of staff passed through his hands, so it is impossible to identify the young clerk or the signal porter on the track. But in the centre stands another veteran, side-whiskered William Cotterell, who arrived under a cloud, having been a relieving Signalman at Lewes. Behind him a pile of felled tree trunks await entry to the white-roofed sawmill shed. Note the well-trained rambling roses spreading their tendrils in orderly fashion along the awning valances. *H. M. Madgwick collection/Bluebell Archives*

Letter requesting report to London Bridge HQ of an accident to Kingscote's original loading gauge, which took place on 17 April 1885.
David Green collection/Bluebell Archives

Thomas Ward, a gentleman with a black bushy Victorian beard, devoted his time to gardening; as well as flower beds, there were dozens of baskets hung from the platform roof. The place was written up and illustrated in the newspapers of the time, and perhaps as a pioneer, long before the days of officially sponsored railway gardens, Thomas Ward and his Kingscote flowers deserve to be remembered.'

The Kingscote of that period is wonderfully captured in the above photograph. The year is 1895 and the unknown photographer must have waited to let a heavy shower pass over. On the left is the formidable Mr Ward with his beard still in youthful trim; his young clerk proudly displaying a chained watch; a veteran porter in full beard, sporting a half-buttoned-up waistcoat that became his seniority; and, on the southbound line, the tall porter-signalman. The veteran Porter was William Cotterell, who had come to Kingscote in 1892, reduced from Signalman to Porter because of signalling irregularities, and stayed there until 1912, leaving to become gatekeeper at Cooksbridge. He was remembered as 'a nice old chap'. He helped Thomas Ward's successors, Harold Hollingdale and William Goring, to maintain the station as a showpiece for flowers. The station house and main buildings were concentrated on the up platform. Off the picture at the south end the first buildings were the coal and porter's rooms, still so designated in recent times. Then followed the station house, coming into the edge of the picture; next the ticket office window with seat below, then steps leading down to the subway; the booking office door with a wall telephone close at hand; the ladies' waiting room; the gents'; culminating in a lamp room at the north end.

The left edge of the picture is framed with bushy plants growing high up the walls of the station house. Behind Mr Ward's right shoulder a well-trained rambling rose rises to spread its tendrils in orderly fashion along the awnings, under which large station oil lamps lurk in the shadows. More roses hedge the northern end of both platforms and lend some shade to the well-stocked flower beds at their feet. Behind the porter stands the lofty Brighton starting signal, a feature of nearly all the stations on this line, and further back a large pile of felled tree trunks await entry to the white-roofed timber shed. A tall, thin chimney behind the loading gauge (removed to the

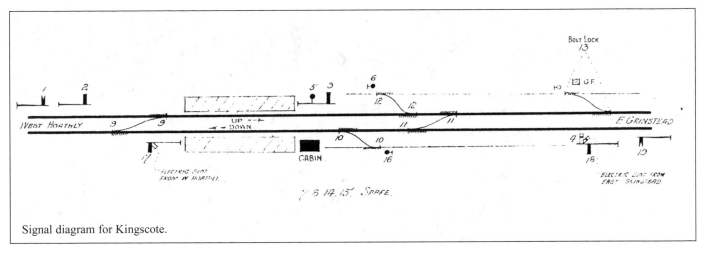

Signal diagram for Kingscote.

westernmost siding following an accident on 17 April 1885) belongs to a smaller shed. Part of the goods yard is lost to view as it curves away behind the signalbox.

There was just one signalbox, placed at the north end of the down platform. On the tall up starting signal was placed a shunting disc applying to anything shunting on the up line. There were two sets of points leading from the up siding to the up main and one set of points leading from the down siding to the down main, each of which was provided with a shunting disc. The points beside the cabin, which lead to the single down siding, can be seen clearly in the photograph. The points at the north end of the up siding, leading to and from the up main, were worked from a ground frame controlled by the signalbox.

The down platform had buildings too in the station's more prosperous days, including a waiting room and a store, their relative positions indicated by the chimney pots projecting from the roof of the down platform. Unfortunately, the Southern Railway's 'razor gang', which trimmed the Lewes & East Grinstead line between the wars, removed these and reckoned that the station could do without its down siding, a set of buffers and a few levers in the signalbox, reducing these to 19, seven of which were spare. The box in its latter days was switched in only when the Lewes goods arrived and terminated.

As at Horsted Keynes, Wolfe Barry chose to construct a subway to connect the platforms, though the station staff naturally used the boards to cross the line. Station seats, porter's trolleys and numerous advertisements complete the details of this fascinating photograph. An Edwardian railway enthusiast wrote, 'Although much praise might unreservedly be awarded to many stations, we think Kingscote, near Horsted Keynes, with its luxuriant growth of trailing creepers and geraniums, takes pride of place.'

Ganger George Coomber arrived in Kingscote in June 1906. He started as a platelayer at 18s a week, on the stretch down to West Hoathly, on such tasks as clearing the tunnel there of ice, 'a dangerous business,' draining the station platform area of water seeping down from the tunnel and dealing with slips on the embanked section between Kingscote and the Sanatorium Bridge, and, hardest of all, trolleying granite the first Sunday in the month. He became sub-ganger at East Grinstead in 1920 at 20s a week, taking charge of the line when the ganger was away. He was camping with the Territorials when World War 1 broke out but was invalided out in August 1917, soon returning to his former work. In 1926 he took over as ganger between East Grinstead and Dormans and, from 1937 till May 1953, was back on the line between East Grinstead and Kingscote.

The Mead Management

Memories of Mr Ward go back into the mists of time, but another much-loved Kingscote Stationmaster was William Mead, whose influence on the station is well documented through the memories of his son Leonard and from Eric Browning, who holds W. G. Mead's correspondence. He started work in 1884 as a signal lad in the tall signalbox at Clapham Junction which overlooked the road, and, following earlier stationmasterships at Wivelsfield and Hever, was appointed to Kingscote on 24 August 1916. In December 1916 the opening of Kingscote on a Sunday was obviously in question. In defence it was stated that the passengers using the station numbered 20 in winter and more in summer. Additionally there would be four churns of milk. The savings on alternate weekends when Mr Mead was not in attendance, since the signalbox was already closed on Sundays, was 9s. The Kingscote position was still a stationmaster third class at 35s per week. There were small increases subsequently and in 1919 the post was made up to second class with a salary of £200 per annum.

The period was one of many changes: men returning from the war, the introduction of the eight-hour day, the strike of 1919 and the Grouping of the railways, with William Mead's correspondence showing the station was under the auspices of the Southern Railway in 1924. Even at such a quiet station he still had his problems. The chocolate company would not refill the machine, and the railway company was reluctant to carry out essential repairs to the station residence. There were obviously long gaps between trains, which enabled various entrepreneurial sidelines to be developed. These mostly appeared to be unofficial and included the supply of plants, timber, apples, potatoes and tea to various locals and railway staff up and down the line. One of the more official sidelines was to act as agent for the Railway Passengers' Assurance Company. In connection with a policy for a Mr Holman of Turner's Hill, he wrote that 1s 11d, 'was poor remuneration for a compulsory five mile walk'. Presumably this was commission.

There were two other incidents of note. The first concerned a passenger who arrived at Kingscote at 3.15pm, under the illusion that he was at Dormans. Because there was no train back, he decided to walk to East Grinstead, some two to three miles. To William Mead's astonishment, he arrived back at Kingscote at 9.10pm. At this stage a local resident close to the station was recruited to drive the gentleman home.

William Mead, the last resident Stationmaster at Kingscote (1915-26), who fought hard to keep his job, defending the Sunday train services which were under question. His 1919 salary of £200pa led him to develop various sidelines, which included the supply of plants, timber, apples, potatoes and tea to various locals and railway staff up and down the line. His son Leonard, while still at school, helped out on deliveries by bicycle, put his hand to the well house pump and took the odd turn in the signalbox.
Leonard Mead/Bluebell Archives

The second incident involves what can only be described as unsolicited goods. Boxes of fish were sent from Hull to the station to be sold. In a letter of 30 May 1923 he wrote, 'I must point out that I did not order this fish: this is a country station with a very small staff. . . my wife actually took the trouble to take it to the neighbouring town of East Grinstead and asked a fishmonger to take it. He declined and advised sending it back.' This did not end the problem since in November a letter was sent to Hull saying, 'Oh yes, we received the box of fish and being hot weather, and not being able to dispose of it, it went bad.' Obviously a claim was made for the cost of the fish but in a letter to the fish department at Hull, reference was made to previous correspondence requesting no further deliveries and ended, 'I disclaim any liability. Please therefore decline the claim.' This seemed to end the matter.

In 1922 a learner, Charlie Browning, was rescued from West Hoathly and taken under William Mead's wing.

Browning lived at Birch Farm, his father being a gardener and his mother a cook on the estate. As a learner he started at 5s a week, but he ultimately became clerk at the station, which after William Mead's departure for Emsworth in 1925, left Browning as clerk-in-charge when control of the station was assigned to East Grinstead. In 1932 Browning married William Mead's daughter Kathleen. He ended up as assistant chief clerk at the Brighton booking office, with responsibility for continental traffic. But it is Mead's son Leonard's recollections which provide a fascinating cameo of the station during those years.

One of the most rural stations on the Brighton's system, it took its name from a small country house nearby. The nearest dwelling to the station was a farm cottage up the hill. The few passengers that brought their custom had for the most part walked over from Turner's Hill. As a result, the station community who lived in the station house and the two semi-detached staff cottages were very much left to their own devices.

The first train was around 7am and the last down some 12hr later, with a final up London train at 8pm. There was a much reduced Sunday service but the station staff had nevertheless to cover a seven-day week, living on the job so to speak, but could put the generous gaps between the trains to good use. There were a variety of specials in those pre-Grouping days: to pantomime and theatre in London and Brighton and football specials to the latter, which continued into BR times. Invariably these would come back with much joviality and singing, especially on Saturday nights up the lane to Turner's Hill. Len noted that the majority of the passenger workings through East Grinstead Low Level changed engines there, so the same crew would be quickly back through Kingscote on the next train. On the other hand, goods trains for many years during the Southern period terminated at Kingscote from either direction, apparently, according to Len, because the services at East Grinstead were too busy to allow for lengthy shunting there. As well as the yard on the up side at Kingscote, there was a long siding behind the signalbox in which to accommodate a medium-sized goods train.

One who never seems to have had a day off except for the annual holiday was Stationmaster Mead. Under him he had two porter signalmen. Alfred Hillman was proud of his Military Medal gained on the Western Front, covering a retreat with his machine gun. Alf's parents lived at Cuckfield, so he lodged with the Meads in the station house. He was a decent chap, giving the Meads a helping hand with the removal when the time came for them to leave Kingscote. The other Signalman was a Mr Parker. He and the line's Ganger 'Pedlar' Miles lived in the railway cottages. Pedlar was a rare character, very short in stature and in stride, and could not make the distance from sleeper to sleeper on his walks of inspection. He had to do his 'length' each morning before the first train, so he took to walking on the rails with a stick to balance him along. Some of the staff played for the Kingscote Lions, the local football team whose level playing field was a mile north near Hazelden.

When the Meads moved to Kingscote the LBSCR gave Leonard a free pass to complete his schooling at Edenbridge, an awkward railway journey, and young Len would think nothing of walking the five miles cross-country to Lingfield to catch a direct train home from there. As a young lad in search of the odd shilling, he would deliver perishable parcels on his bicycle. Later he took turns in the signalbox and partook of many a cab ride.

The pump house in the field behind the signalbox was frequently visited by Len for half-hour stints pumping the

Above left: Signalman Alfred Hillman stands at the top of the steps into Kingscote signalbox. He commenced his first appointment on the railway here on 7 February 1916 and stayed till the end of 1931. The platform side of the signalbox is enhanced by flowering shrubs, while a glimpse beyond shows the long timber store of Longley's yard. *Leonard Mead/Bluebell Archives*

Above right: An overview of the station taken in 1921, showing the well-kept flower beds and bushes tended by the staff between trains, which won Kingscote many station garden and best-kept station awards over the years. In the distance the timberyard is in full swing. Behind the down platform the ground fell away sharply, leaving the station perched on a plateau, hence the wooden buttress supports at the back of the station canopies. Water had to be pumped up to the station daily from the well house seen on the extreme right of the picture. *Leonard Mead/Bluebell Archives*

Right: Pedlar Miles, the local ganger, was a colourful character who walked his length every morning before the first train. Here he stands outside the door of the porter's room at the south end of the up platform. *Leonard Mead/Bluebell Archives*

water up to the station house, which had no running water. The field behind the down platform was railway property and Mr Mead let the ground out to a market gardener or for grazing out, £1 per animal per year. Len writes, 'Attached to the station house was enough ground to support about three apple trees, a greengage and a cherry tree, with a stream at the bottom of the area. I built it up and made a watercress bed. We had a large vegetable garden. To the right of the area: wired off, we had 20 chickens, four guinea fowl, a goose and gander for breeding, and we reared turkey chicks for Christmas. We also brought up a two-day old lamb (a ram) to full size, also a day-old pig.'

As the waiting room on the down platform was shunned by the public for the greater comforts of the main buildings opposite, this was stored full of apples, together with any spare corners of the station house and sold off at a shilling a gallon. All fallen apples were gathered into a large pile and when the cider press came round, they were collected by a farmer friend and in due course the Meads had nine gallons of cider indoors. With such an abundant yield, home-made cider was very much the order of the day. Geese and turkeys were kept, the occasional pig and one year they had a young ram which used to butt passengers as they approached the station. To add to that reception there was a jackdaw in a cage which shouted at them 'Hop it' and 'Go away' in quick succession! Thanks to Mr Ward, Kingscote had become renowned for its flower gardens and decorative setting. Hollowed tree stumps from the woodyard were placed at points on the platform with flowers planted in the core. There were clumps and clusters of flowers the length of both

When timber was king on the Lewes-East Grinstead line. The woodyard and sawmill at Kingscote, seen here in 1919, point to the more prosperous days of the line. The timberyard siding includes a loading gauge, beyond which the double track curves to the right up the 1 in 75 to East Grinstead. *Leonard Mead/Bluebell Archives*

The team at Longley's timber siding at the turn of the century. The dumb-buffered bolster wagon is noteworthy. The man standing on the left is Mr Gasson, Longley's foreman at the saw-mill. Next but one on his left is Obadiah Corke, while Frank Leppard is standing in the forefront with his elbow on the coupling hook. *May Ward/Bluebell Archives*

platforms. No wonder Kingscote won so many station garden competitions!

Finally there was the timber yard and sawmill, with Harry Gasson as Foreman. The trees came both by road and train, but all the main contracts went out by rail. The machinery included both hand and mechanical saws. There was a shed which contained a pit saw, worked by a man at each end cutting vertically, one man standing in the pit. In addition to the large timber, the smaller wood was particularly useful for making spokes for wheels. On Saturday mornings Len would earn a bit of extra pocket money by reporting to the mill to wheel away barrow-loads of sawdust. At the end of each day there would be numerous small pieces of wood over, and the good spirit of co-operation between the timberfolk and the railwaymen resulted in Stationmaster Mead being able to put sackloads of 'logs' onto trains for his various fellow railwaymen up and down the line.

The photograph showing Longley's Timber Siding in the early years of the 20th century comes from May Ward (no relation of Thomas Ward, although her father was Tom Ward, the Foreman of Longley's Farm), who lived at Selsfield

Common and commuted from Kingscote to East Grinstead (second class) from about 1908 to 1914.

World War 1 was about two years old when the Meads left Hever station to occupy the station house at Kingscote. Despite the distance inland, the windows on the station rattled day and night from the gunfire in France, and it was not long before German soldiers in uniform appeared on Kingscote station — but of course they were German prisoners of war and had coloured patches sewn into their uniforms to denote the fact. They had a British guard with them and went to work on the land. They were stationed at East Grinstead with others.

Some moments of high drama included the occasions when a group of men carrying rare young trees and bushes appeared at the station to catch the train down to West Hoathly. This frequent recurrence aroused Len's suspicions and the East Grinstead Police were tipped off. 'The West Hoathly policeman, dressed in navy clothes, straps under his knees, carrying his lunch in a red kerchief and a can of tea, walked through the woods and spoke to the men who were breaking bits off the trees to take to London. He then went on to

Kingscote Station, where other Police were waiting to catch them.' The trap was duly set and it was learned afterwards that these men had been pinching shrubs from the Gravetye Estate to sell elsewhere for profit. No direct reward came Len's way, but for many years after a sack of potatoes was given by the owners of Gravetye for the station community at Kingscote.

Then there was the station dog which would often travel with its guardian by train to West Hoathly, where the Railway Inn (recently the Bluebell Inn) was the most convenient hostelry within easy reach. On several occasions the dog's owner was called away on business and the dog, concluding that he must have gone for his regular drink, boarded the train and emerged at West Hoathly! A reassuring phone call and directive to send him back on the next up train to Kingscote was the order of the day. Another priceless incident was the case of the horsebox that was attached to its train one station early. It was the practice to manhandle the odd van out of the sidings by prising it under the wheels with bars to create leverage. The staff at West Hoathly got a horsebox moving out by the down line crossover, for attachment to the awaited train scheduled to run into the down platform. But they could not hold it and once it was out and onto the 1 in 122 down grade, it ran all the way to Kingscote where, slowed by the 1 in 75 up grade, it was retrieved by the staff. The scheduled train being already in the down platform, the horsebox was quickly attached and so caught its scheduled train after all!

Such was the life of a station community in those distant days when folk seemed to derive a lot more fun of their own devising. But it was the sunset of an era of comparative railway prosperity and when bus companies started up, serving places like Turner's Hill, the passengers disappeared from Kingscote's platforms.

The Prewar Period

Another railwayman who was close to the centre of life at Kingscote station was George Dry, who came in 1925 as a signalman shunter from Earlsfield after many years at the goods shed at Nine Elms Depot. The Southern, with an outlook already for economising, had lumped Kingscote in with the stationmastership of East Grinstead since January 1926, under Mr Edward Ernest Buck, a man of jolly disposition whose dog, Chum, used to go in trains during the course of his master's travels. Mr Buck retired at the end of 1930. Permanently at Kingscote was the Clerk, Mr Browning, and the two Porter Signalmen, Mr Dry's colleague being Mr Parker. The porters in the course of their various duties tended the oil lamps — there was no gas or electricity — cleaned the signals, assisted in the yard and pumped water for the station house.

Passenger traffic, though nothing to crow about, served the needs of the rural population, among whom were such notables as Mr Radcliffe of Fonthill, Col Rice of Kingscote House and the Longleys of Tickeridge. Of the ordinary trains the 8am down to Lewes paid best, taking Brighton season ticket holders who connected at Horsted with a train to Haywards Heath. Excursion traffic was a great draw, a situation the authorities never capitalised on, for the cheap day tickets to Hastings, Eastbourne and Brighton, and certain sports and Sunday excursions — on any train — always sold well. The most popular was the 1s 11d return to Brighton, which soon filled up the 9.36am. In 1939 these still sold at half a crown (12½p), and it was often impossible to fit another person in the train. These conditions were never repeated after World War 2. But the station only had a brisk look about it when a breakdown occurred on the Brighton main line and use was made of this secondary line. Then trains would be standing at the sticks, and the station staff could not get them through fast enough. On occasions this section of the line was used for running round stock when East Grinstead Low Level became overcrowded and the locomotives were required to take water at Horsted Keynes.

Another resident, who lived just 500yd from the station from 1933-7, was J. T. Rooth. He recalls it as a very busy place goodswise, as it was dominated by the large sawmill. There was considerable shunting and goods movements proceeding most days. For road transport to and from the yard J.B. West of Burgess Hill used a steam traction engine and trailer. From East Grinstead to Kingscote the line was quite steeply graded and the down trains, particularly the early morning 'D1'-operated motor train, rushed down the track from Imberhorne Cutting but always managed to stop!

Porter William Parker was in charge at this stage and it was he who made the classic statement as to the best train to catch to London. 'Take the 9.14am, stopping at East Grinstead, Dormansland, Lingfield and Oxted and then to "furrin parts".' (One hour 50 minutes for the 38 miles). He recalls that the station was always clean, oil-lit and the staff most helpful. The local goods was in the charge of Billinton 'C2s' and their Marsh 'C2X' rebuilds, passenger services with Marsh motor-fitted Stroudley 'D1s', Billinton 'D3s', Marsh 'I3s' and the occasional Stirling 'F1' 4-4-0, the latter with its large wheels being very sedate. Frank Leppard (see photograph of the sawmill team) was still working there in 1934 and Mr Rooth used to give him a lift home in his Model T Ford after work finished at 5pm.

In October 1936 the visiting correspondent of the *Southern Railway Magazine* reported, 'Kingscote is a very beautiful spot which would make a most enjoyable afternoon's visit. It has a pleasing appearance with flower beds on each of the two platforms, which are connected by a subway. The local scenery is almost entirely a mass of beautiful woodland with Gravetye Manor noted for its gardens which the owner, Mr W. Robinson, opens to the public at certain periods during the summer. From a railway point of view the chief traffic consists of agricultural produce and timber, the extensive timber yard of Messrs H. Longley & Sons (Lewes) adjoining the station. There is also appreciable business with the transport of alpine plants from Messrs W. T. Ingwerson Ltd of Sharpthorne, about 1½ miles distant.'

When Signalman Dry first arrived, the goods traffic was in a very healthy state, for the station was the transfer point of the two daily goods trains, one from Lewes and the other from East Grinstead, and the yard presented a busy appearance when both were shunting. Later the duality was stopped as the goods from the north was not warranted. Central to Kingscote freight traffic, as at Sheffield Park, was the sawmill, belonging to Frank Longley, though indeed later both mills were owned by Turners. The timber traffic was two way, raw wood coming in and being despatched partly prepared. There was a fair amount of agricultural traffic; milk was sent out while village commodities were received. In came coal, manure and bricks, five or six wagons a day. Occasionally there would be a special trainload of racehorses going to Ireland via Holyhead and returning by the same route. Lord Glendyne and Lord Dewar were the chief patrons of this horsebox traffic. An unusual line of goods was that of plants for Mr Ingwerson's Alpine Garden and Rockery, and for Mr Robinson at Gravetye whose nurture of rare plants employed the best part of the dozen or so people who lived at Kingscote.

The War Years

During World War 2 a train of tanks stood in the sidings opposite the signalbox. A document dated 3 September 1940, exactly a year after the outbreak of the war, in its introductory paragraph of regulations regarding the movement of trainloads of tanks, stipulated that trains transporting military tanks must not exceed a speed of 30mph, display a headcode of three white lights and carry a heavy brake van at each end. There was a special code of signal beats for easy recognition while in transit.

Eight special tank trains were berthed at various inland stations astride the Surrey-Sussex border: East Grinstead, Godstone, Horley, Kingscote, Lingfield (2) and Salfords (2). Five of these totalled 15 vehicles weighing about 700 tons in the following formation: Goods brake van, third class non-corridor coach, ramp wagon, nine tank wagons, ramp wagon, third class non-corridor coach, goods brake van. Those at Salfords and East Grinstead had only three tank wagons and one third class coach for the crews and the eight vehicles weighed 300 tons.

Destinations all lay to the west — the Meon Valley, the Mid-Hants and Basingstoke-Andover lines, and it was to the first or last mentioned that the Kingscote train was routed. The timings as required were as follows. Movement ordered by the military at midnight. Train in position for loading at 2am and departure from Kingscote at 5am. Arrival times were Alton 9.15am, Farringdon 9.25am, Tisted 9.30am, Privett 9.40am: Basingstoke 9.45-10am, Oakley 10.15am and Overton 10.25am. By inference these movements with their alternatives were invasion precautions. Not knowing exactly where Hitler would strike but most likely at Kent and Sussex, the tanks were at points south of London, but should the enemy thrust have been further west in Hampshire, plans had been devised to move the tanks swiftly overnight. The document closed with a strident footnote — 'Treat as a secret document.' In 1944 sidings like Kingscote's were again filled with tanks on wagons, this time awaiting D-Day.

The Final Days

Kingscote's last Stationmaster was Mr Clark (1945-53), who also managed East Grinstead and Grange Road. His sphere of authority went even further when the stationmaster at Horsted Keynes or Lingfield was off duty. The war had changed the pattern of travel and something drastic and attractive was required to lure people back onto the trains. Mr Clark fought hard for the restoration of the excursion services. He particularly made a case on behalf of the football traffic, for Brighton & Hove Albion had a good following in the area. The ordinary 1.30pm train was too late if there was an early kick-off, an hour later. Nor would the authorities give way to Mr Clark's application for cheap day tickets on the 12.5pm via Three Bridges. Failure to secure these facilities lost a considerable traffic potential. 'If they'd wanted to, they could have made it pay, but they'd made up their minds,' he maintained. 'A respectable service was of little value if the fares weren't right.' Soon, with the postwar fare increases, passenger traffic dwindled to 20 a day, and even the Girl Guides, who camped annually near West Hoathly, transferred to buses at East Grinstead. Soon, officious eyes were down taking statistics month after month before the threatened closure.

On the freight side there was very little postwar traffic: still some timber and a little agricultural goods; the sidings contained only a few trucks and trains only called at Kingscote if required. All small loads were taken off at East Grinstead and only full truckloads were sent through. There were some differences about the railway rates paid on the mileage of the sidings to the local councils. This may have been one of the reasons for the separate lifting of the yards at Kingscote and West Hoathly a couple of years after the closure.

After the war the signalbox was only brought into use for shunting, West Hoathly to East Grinstead forming one section, since cutting out cabins such as these reduced the turns of duty and the number of signalmen. Kingscote now had only a staff of one — a leading porter — who covered the duties of signalman, porter and booking clerk in one.

Marsh 'I3' 4-4-2T No 32086 enters Kingscote with the 3.35pm Oxted-Lewes service on 11 September 1950. The locomotive lasted another 13 months but this renowned historic class was extinct by May 1952.
R. C. Riley

Kingscote photographed from the north on 27 May 1955, the penultimate day of BR services. The view, from close to Milepost 15, shows the signalbox, station buildings and sidings serving the pen-less goods dock, all still retaining a neat appearance. *Denis*

Derek Coe lived at Kingscote from January 1947 until moving to East Grinstead in mid-1948, and his father had to commute through the terrible winter of early 1947. No local buses operated either early or late enough to benefit a London-bound commuter. To be in his office before 9 o'clock he would have to be out of the door a little after 5.30am and walk the two miles to East Grinstead to catch the 6.33am. The first up train from Kingscote was the 7.29am, by which he could reach London Bridge at 8.47am and his office 15 minutes late for work. Those taking the 7.29am would find it formed of a three-coach, ex-SECR, non-corridor set and two or three Maunsell coaches, unlikely altogether to be carrying more than a dozen people on leaving Kingscote. Getting home in the evening was always a chancy affair. There were several alternatives, the 5.40pm from London Bridge, regularly hauled by a Newhaven 'H1' or 'H2' Atlantic. The last option was the 8.20pm ex-Victoria with several changes, including a walk between Whyteleafe and Upper Warlingham, giving an arrival at Kingscote at 9.33pm. One bitterly cold day the engine on the latter train expired at Dormans, stranding the passengers awhile, and arrival time that night was near to 1am.

By this time William Charles Parker was the station's leading porter and only member of staff. In 1949 he got his photograph in the paper under the title 'A Hermit of North Sussex', in which he was shown pruning the celebrated station roses. 'One of the quieter stations in the Division is Kingscote, where W. C. Parker is the porter-cum-signalman-cum-booking clerk. He has occupied this position for 34 years and apart from his railway duties he takes pride in keeping the station flower beds and rose bushes in good order. No doubt that Kingscote owes its spick and span appearance entirely to his efforts. The 63-year-old widower started at Barnham Junction in 1910, going to Kingscote on 14 January 1915. He lives in the station house with his eldest son and says he is looking forward to retirement in 1951.' He had to prove a jack of all

trades, gathering into one the duties of a station staff that had originally numbered four. He undertook all the duties, ticket issue and collection, station accountancy, parcels receipts and despatch, goods recording, tending and lighting lamps, maintaining the waiting room fires, general cleaning and garden maintenance, and seeing to the trains. There was a public telephone at the station but positioned on the wall at a height out of Mr Parker's short reach, so a wooden box was permanently in place for his use. His duties also included opening the signalbox to facilitate the goods train which came up the line in the late morning, shunted the yard and returned to Lewes at 1.20pm. This limited opening of the box resulted in the running signals at other times being invariably in the off positions. Another marked feature of the station was a number of cans stacked under the awning. These were the daily water supply for the station house, coming down on the first train, implying that the pump house had by then fallen into disuse.

By Nationalisation the station was described as 'almost devoid of both passengers and freight traffic, and its continued existence for so many years is surprising, for it serves just a few houses in almost exclusively rural surroundings'. Soon the statisticians had their evidence and the orders for closure went through, despite Kingscote having won the best-kept station award only a few years previously. And for Kingscote there was only one closure, for, like Barcombe, it was not included among the four stations to be served in Miss Bessemer's reimplementation of the original Parliamentary Act. The remaining members of staff offered to work at Sheffield Park but the offer was in vain.

So for nearly 10 years Kingscote lived on, desolate though not quite bereft, its sidings a refuge for condemned wagon stock during 1960 until they were lifted on 21 October that year, Kingscote in the morning and West Hoathly in the afternoon. The final journeys of stored condemned wagons to Polegate took place behind Standard 2-6-4Ts and then silence

fell upon the scene, unbroken except for the ganger's trolley on routine duties. The last passenger train to call had been the first Bluebell special on 12 July 1959, which was greeted by almost the entire local population.

A visit in September 1961 revealed that some of Mr Ward's old station roses were still there; hanging wild of course, but actually in blossom. The sleepers were in position over a great part of the sidings, though mostly rotten; one length of rail remained; also the pieces of two smashed ganger's trolleys; while around the place lay the dismantled signals and points levers, among them the original weights inscribed 'Saxby and Farmers, Patentees, London, W' and embossed with the royal coat of arms. Milepost 15 stood out undisturbed opposite the gradient post, signifying the change from level to 1 in 75 north out of the station.

The demolition contractor arrived on the scene in 1964 but a private purchaser had bought the station area up to between the two platforms and, apart from removing basic mechanical railway equipment and the dilapidated signalbox, the station house and platform canopies were untouched, even to the large green and white glazed Southern Railway style running-in board at the south end of the up platform.

In the winter of 1976/7 the then owner of the station, Mr Morgan, wished to build a private swimming pool immediately behind the down platform and invited the Bluebell Railway to dismantle and take away the old down side canopy free of charge. He was offered an honorary life membership of the society for his wife and himself. With this act of controlled vandalism the fortunes of this station reached their nadir.

18.
Ardingly

'The Most Lovely of all Places'

The branch or link line through Ardingly opened on 3 September 1883 with just three trains running each way daily between Horsted Keynes and Haywards Heath which, at least on the opening day, 'were very well patronised'. Double track throughout, the branch curved away from Horsted Keynes and over the 117yd Sheriff Mill Viaduct, climbing all the way to the 218yd Lywood Tunnel, then to fall on a straight course for a mile at 1 in 75 to enter Ardingly station at 2m 22ch. After a further 1m 8ch of rising gradients the line reached Copyhold Junction just south of the famous Ouse Valley Viaduct. When the branch was first opened there was

no signalbox at this point and the branch trains ran on independent tracks beside the main line as far as Haywards Heath North box and, if terminating there, usually ran into the north-facing bay platform on the down side. In 1912 a box was installed just north of Copyhold Bridge and in 1932 Haywards Heath was rebuilt with up and down loop platforms and colour light signalling, commissioned on 12 June. The signalbox at Copyhold closed when the new Haywards Heath box was opened. The way of working was not changed from the old up/down/up/down principle at the new junction but it did allow the East Grinstead line to be used as a relief for the Brighton main line for two useful miles.

Ardingly station house followed the contemporary Firbank pattern, the design of which was described as one of the best ever built for the Brighton railway company and received a good deal of praise at the time of opening from the local

A well-organised photograph of the railway community at Ardingly, taken during the stationmastership of the portly George Fossey, seen standing by the signalbox. Apart from railway staff and possibly some prospective passengers, a nice touch has been added by the permanent way quartet posed on the track. *Lens of Sutton*

Though far from the clearest of prints, this photograph merits inclusion on two counts. It is the only early picture that has captured converging trains racing to Copyhold Junction, one of the pair of Marsh 4-6-2Ts, No 325 *Abergavenny*, on a Brighton-bound express while one of the Billinton 'B4' 4-4-0s displaced from such work brings a rather more mundane service from East Grinstead round the curve from Ardingly. The photograph also provides one of the few glimpses of Copyhold Junction signalbox, installed in 1912. The date is narrowed by the fact that in 1919 No 325 was fitted with oval-shaped buffers.
Lens of Sutton

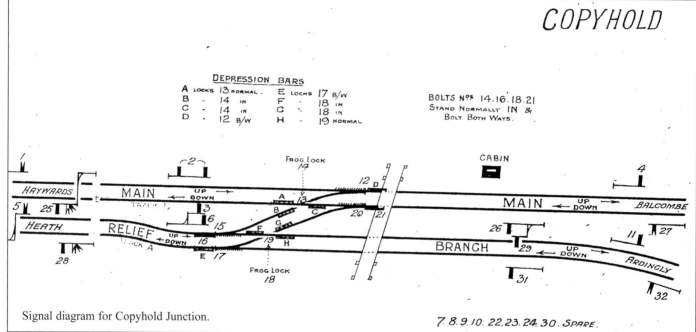

Signal diagram for Copyhold Junction.

A delightful posed postcard view of Ardingly station house, which stood some hundred yards away from the platforms below. Later it was tile-hung but after the line closed was splendidly restored to something akin to its earlier condition, with the floral patterns once more on view. *Lens of Sutton*

The scene north from Copyhold Bridge in 1910 shows 'Gladstone' 0-4-2 No 193 (formerly *Fremantle*) running tender-first, bringing a local off the Ardingly branch for Haywards Heath. *M. P. Bennett collection/ Bluebell Archives*

A pre-electrification motor train working from Horsted Keynes runs into Haywards Heath on 19 July 1930. The locomotive, 'D' tank No B623, featured a quarter century earlier in the Horsted Keynes locomotive store as No 23 *Mayfield* and lived to fight another day until 1934, when it was scrapped. *H. C. Casserley*

papers. It stood up at road level away from the platforms, necessitating an enclosed, corridor-like extension from the station entrance to the footbridge. The station house, unlike the others on the LEGR, was never tile-hung, retaining all the original flower patterns which survive today picked out in black on a white ground. It remains one of the best preserved examples of a Brighton station house in existence.

The facilities below were fairly basic with platform awnings and on the down platform an alcove-like waiting room, lacking doors to keep out the winter draughts and cold. The platform signal cabin stood at the west end, surveying the small yard behind. As elsewhere on the contract, there was local agitation that the goods accommodation was not ready until some three months after the line was opened. Its chief business was agricultural. Considerable inward traffic came in the shape of round timber, which went out in consignments of prepared boards after the timber had passed through a local sawmill. It was also noted for a special traffic in geese.

Ardingly had a station staff of four: stationmaster, signal porter, porter and assistant clerk. Its first Stationmaster was James Rawlins, who moved across to Sheffield Park on 5 February 1890. Next came Walter Odd, then on 4 October

1895 George B. Fossey, who on 28 September 1904 also moved on to Sheffield Park, succeeded by Thomas Muggeridge, William Peters, Frederick Hassall and on 9 February 1916, Frederick James Bone, displaced from Barcombe Mills, who stayed right through until June 1924, when he was posted just about as far as the SR could move him, to Halwill Junction in North Devon. The last stationmaster was W. Newman, who held the fort until the end of 1926 when the station came under the control of Ben Bowley at Horsted Keynes.

Ardingly was not without its black sheep among the staff. Porter Albert Burton was dismissed on 27 October 1896 for 'sending indecent letters to a young girl'; John Jeffery, who had come off the sick list from Grange Road on 30 October 1899, did not last long, being dismissed next 8 January for 'pilfering a parcel of tobacco'. There were many resignations and also retirements through ill health. One such was Miss Edith Sheppard, a wartime appointee on 21 May 1917, replaced by Edith Briggs on 15 July 1919, who left on 23 October 1920, 'Services dispensed with'.

A. L. Maycock adds a pre-World War 1 flavour of Ardingly: 'The local train eventually got away and jogged along

'Ardingly for Ardingly College' is the message on the station nameboard, denoting the station's most important source of traffic. An interesting feature is the tall up starting signal, whose upper board could be seen by approaching train crews and whose arm is repeated below at platform level to assist the enginemen when their locomotive was standing at the platform end. The date is 3 March 1934. *H. C. Casserley*

placidly, swinging from the main line at Copyhold and so down to Ardingly, where there was a porter who called out the name of the station in so splendid and melodious a baritone that you felt Ardingly must be the most lovely of all places and the goal of all journeys.'

The link line provided a useful alternative to the main line, not only in emergency situations but for munitions trains from Newhaven routed via Ardingly in both world wars, and till the end it was used for Lingfield race specials originating from the south coast. Ardingly became a popular destination for Ramblers' specials during its last 30 years, as betokened by the announcement in March 1930 that 'a camping coach will be stationed at Ardingly,' and a pleasant location it surely must have been. But local passenger traffic never materialised, and it never became the popular and well-housed district the forecasters had expected. Indeed LBSCR platform tickets with their red blob and inscribed 'Ardingly to Platform 1d' were still being sold in 1948.

Ardingly College

The station's only busy moments came with the College specials which served the public school at the beginning and end of term. In 1930 it was reported: 'The College sends away about 450 packages of luggage at each vacation to say nothing of the human freight which follows. The *Southern Railway Magazine* for May 1928 highlighted the schools specials: 'This traffic to and from schools at holiday time is very heavy for the Central Division. At the commencement of every holiday about 10,150 scholars from 256 schools have to be conveyed from 45 different locations, and brought back again when they reopen, not forgetting the several tons of baggage'. In an accompanying league table Ardingly was noted for its one school and 250 pupils. Old Ardinians certainly remember the hustle and bustle of these occasions. Early one term the

headmaster arrived during Sunday prep to deal with three boys caught smoking on the train at the end of the previous term. Another inmate writes: 'Almost every morning those of us of the railway enthusiast brigade would wait to see the steam trains above the trees bordering the line between Ardingly and Copyhold Junction.' Indeed years later another confessed (or boasted) that pupils of the war years or possibly earlier chose to prove themselves to their peers by walking across the nearby, and then electrified, Ouse Valley Viaduct.

A great day for those enthusiasts was 17 October 1933 when the new 'Schools' class 4-4-0 No 917 *Ardingly* visited the station and parties of boys from the college were invited to inspect the locomotive, whose shape was hardly recognisable for the number of boys standing on the buffer beam and running plate. Soon after 1935 electric trains often took over the college specials. A new pupil recollected, 'My first introduction to Ardingly station was in September 1939. Our train from Victoria was one of the 28 minutes past the hour semi-fasts composed of three 4LAV units. We were all contained in the last unit which was detached at Haywards Heath and reversed to run to Ardingly, where we all detrained. It then ran empty to Horsted Keynes for reversal.'

Ben Bowley at Horsted Keynes, who also had Ardingly under his wing, recalled: 'At such times the station became a hive of activity, the platforms literally covered with trunks, suitcases and tuck boxes for the local college. The luggage came in advance with the students arriving in specially reserved coaches. The boys often ran riot, throwing cushions out of the window. The staff never looked forward to the term times. Indeed extras were called in from other parts.' Frank Hyde was a Relief Stationmaster and in 1952 stood in at the Lewes-East Grinstead line stations. He was called in to serve at Ardingly to help with the termly specials and recalled how the station 'burgeoned into life'. The college special drew in with its inevitable and essential PMV luggage van; without it the 150-plus pieces of luggage could

The Ardingly College Cadet Force stand marshalled on the down platform by the signalbox, awaiting their train which will take them part of the way towards their destination, Shorncliffe near Folkestone, for their annual summer camp in 1938.
Courtesy The Ardinian

The 3.16pm Horsted Keynes-Seaford leaves Lywood Tunnel on 9 March 1959, shortly after the introduction of single line working. A clear view through this neatly constructed bore, 218yd in length, can be seen as 2BIL No 2149 emerges into the sunshine.
S. C. Nash

not have been accommodated on the train. In these later years Ardingly box was normally closed except for shunting college luggage. Even near the end in 1955, when numbers fell as the motor car came into general use, a reservation was made for a party of 90 from the College, travelling second class.

Electrification

The profile of the branch was considerably raised when it was included in the Southern Railway's 1935 electrification scheme to Lewes, Seaford, Eastbourne and Hastings. Haywards Heath had burgeoned into a rapidly expanding dormitory town serving the needs of local business travellers and commuters and, to minimise shunt movements at that busy station, the line to Horsted Keynes was to serve as a way of moving on what might otherwise be terminating electric trains from Seaford, to avoid blocking a valuable platform face. But at the back of the company's mind was eventual electrification through to East Grinstead and South Croydon. The main scheme was implemented on Sunday, 7 July, electric services through Ardingly starting the following day, the

branch being closed on Sundays until 1945. Colour light signalling was introduced at the approaches to Copyhold Junction. As at Horsted Keynes, the lighting at Ardingly was converted to electricity and standard type block instruments provided. The new service comprised some 18 electric trains on an hourly service to and from Horsted Keynes daily, about half of which commenced or terminated at Haywards Heath, the rest running as far as Seaford. Route indicators for the electric trains, 2NOL sets up to Nationalisation and latterly 2BIL or 2HAL units up to the closure, were as follows:

Horsted Keynes or Haywards Heath to Eastbourne	49
Horsted Keynes or Haywards Heath to Seaford	37
Horsted Keynes or Haywards Heath to Lewes	46
Horsted Keynes to Haywards Heath	1

An irregularity in working was noted on 18 January 1938 when the 7.56pm electric train from Horsted Keynes passed Haywards Heath down local inner home signal (No CH57) at danger at 8.4pm. Despite conflicting evidence given by both the motorman and guard about the aspects displayed by that signal and Ardingly down advanced starting signal (which acts as a 'distant' for CH57), the joint enquiry concluded there

Above: A 2HAL on the 2.16pm Horsted Keynes-Seaford passes the 'green snake' of new Kent Coast CEP electric stock berthed on the down line north of Ardingly on 9 May 1959.
S. C. Nash

Left: Not many months later, on 27 September 1959, the electric units have been taken into service and replaced by redundant Kent Coast steam stock, mostly Maunsell coaches.
S. C. Nash

was no irregularity with the signalling and the responsibility rested with the motorman for misreading the signal.

There was the occasional 4LAV working on the Ardingly College specials and an unusual 4COR set was also photographed on the branch but it was only near the end that a sudden influx of new stock appeared on the line, not in service but in store. The down line beyond the crossover east of the station was made into a siding on 19 January 1959 to berth new electric stock awaiting introduction of the first stage of the Kent Coast electrification scheme. For the following six months a two-mile line of 4CEP and 4BEP units occupied the down line while single line working with electric train staff was introduced on the up line for the ordinary services, requiring the box at Ardingly to remain open all the time.

The new stock had to go out for mileage runs in turn on a rotating basis. Twelve-coach trains were a tight fit at Horsted Keynes to get clear of the crossover to the down line. Test runs were carried out with longer than normal trains to see if the traction current could cope, the nearest sub-station being at Copyhold Junction.

By September 1959 the electric units had moved into employment on the Kent Coast lines, to be replaced in turn by the steam stock made redundant by the scheme. In May 1960 several coaches were damaged in the Sheriff Mill incident previously described. This stock was gradually whittled away for breaking up during late 1960 and the first part of the following year, only for the 'siding' to be filled up again with steam coaching stock made redundant by Phase 2 of the Kent Coast electrification. Late in 1961 David Wigley recorded 74 coaches stored there, mainly Maunsell sets and loose coaches but also ex-SECR coaches from Birdcage sets etc, the last LBSCR motor set No 714 and the single coach S6237S used for the Lewes-East Grinstead service during its temporary reprieve. The coaches were gradually removed in batches to Newhaven for breaking up during the following 12 months.

A recorded but not unprecedented interruption to services occurred in the winter of 1961. On New Year's Day the temperature fell below zero, causing the snow to freeze as it fell, covering the conductor rail. That day the branch electric trains were propelled by 'E4' No 32474 of Three Bridges shed.

'K' No 32343 swings round the curve off the Ardingly branch to join the main line at Copyhold Junction, with a long load of condemned wagons bound for Lancing in March 1960.
Derek Cross

The Final Curtain

The curtain came down on the branch in 1963 and a record of the final months survives in the Train Register of Ardingly signalbox, which has been analysed by Mike Garwood:

'This particular book starts at the end of March 1963 and finishes in late October 1963. It reveals that the bulk of the signal work during the remaining life of the line was handled by a total strength of two signalmen, with reliefs for leave and sickness. Their working day from Monday to Saturday started at 5.45am when the box was opened by the first man. The change of shift took place between 1.30pm and 2.30pm in between trains. Normally, the box was closed at 9.35pm, the signalman booking off some 10 minutes later. On Sundays, manning was by one person, who opened the box at 9.55am and closed it at 8.35pm. The length of the working day on Sundays was somewhat compensated by the number of trains, a regular seven each way; perhaps this was the day when the station gardens were attended to!

'During the period under review, only one goods train worked over the branch. This arrived Mondays to Saturdays at about 6am at Ardingly from Haywards Heath and departed about 6.20am, having left its mineral wagons in the sidings before the start of the working day of the Tarmac Co. There is evidence that some of the wagons returned to the outside system during this period bound for Frome via Havant and Salisbury.

'Normal incoming passenger trains were booked as originating from either Seaford or Haywards Heath, with certain exceptions. These were the first train of the day at 7.10am from Eastbourne and two in the late afternoon. The 4.59pm train came from Lewes and the 5.42pm from Brighton, this latter probably being a commuter train as it started its journey at 5.13pm. All these trains ran on to the single line to Horsted Keynes and returned about 20 minutes after leaving Ardingly. Without exception, all Sunday trains originated from Seaford.

'This was the general pattern throughout the summer, but occasionally it was broken — for instance, on Easter Monday the signalman had a sleep-in, as he did not have to open the box until 10.3am, and once during this period a train was terminated at Ardingly. Unfortunately the reason has not been recorded. Entries in the signal register also show that on most days the box was visited by an inspector who signed the book accordingly. The clock in the box appeared to vary during this summer, for it either "stopped" or was "fast". Also noted are derailments as far afield as London Bridge. Notice of these were phoned through from Haywards Heath for eventual posting on the station notice board.

'Towards the end of September there occurred a break in routine. On Thursday, 26 September, the current for the single line from Ardingly to Horsted Keynes was disconnected and the staff for the section withdrawn at 9.30am by permanent way men who proceeded into the section, first having advised Haywards Heath. The trolley returned and the current was restored at 11.4am. During the intervening period, there must have been an inspection of the Lywood Tunnel, as the following Saturday night saw a special working. On this night, the duty signalman closed the box at 9.27pm and signed off duty at 9.35pm as usual. Twenty-five minutes later, the deserted station was occupied by a fresh signalman who proceeded to reopen the box and then sat waiting patiently until 11.12pm when he noted in the register, "Gantry train arrived". At 11.20pm the electric current was disconnected, the single line staff withdrawn, and the train proceeded into the section. The next entry shows that this train returned at 1.4am on the Sunday morning and left immediately for Haywards Heath, leaving a lonely signalman to close the box at 1.15am. From these entries it is possible to deduce that this was the final inspection of the tunnel before the closure of the line. Naturally, there is no record of the make-up of the train involved. (See photograph page 146.)

'The most interesting entries in the register are those relating to special workings. Sunday, 26 May saw a special train denoted as "Victoria Rambler" on the record, arriving at 10.56am and returning from Horsted Keynes at 11.18. There is no comparable entry for the afternoon, so it is presumed that the balanced working back to Victoria was from Haywards Heath later in the afternoon. On Saturday, 24 August a special working from Portsmouth & Southsea passed through at 11.29am and returned at 11.45am, presumably to Haywards Heath for stabling. This returned at 5.15pm to Horsted Keynes, having passed the normal service train on the double track between Copyhold Junction and Ardingly, and was finally booked back through Ardingly at 5.36pm.

'Entries relating to the Bluebell Railway occur during the summer and show that the unbalanced working on the single line section meant additional manpower being employed and

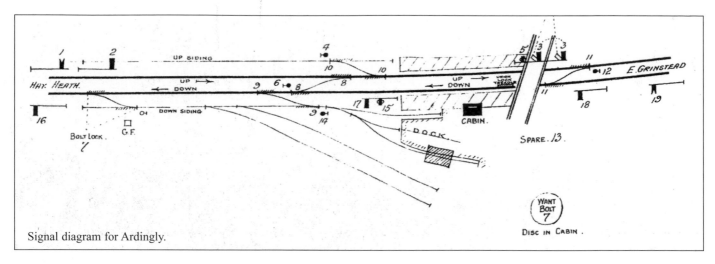

Signal diagram for Ardingly.

The last scheduled working between Ardingly and Horsted Keynes took place on 13 May 1964, when 'Terrier' No 32636, soon to recover its former name *Fenchurch*, propelled another recent Bluebell Railway acquisition, former LBSCR van No 270 of 1908, used for carrying milk and perishables like fruit, and especially strawberries in season, over the branch and onto its new home.
Courtesy Sussex Express

considerable road mileage used. On Saturday, 30 March, after the normal service train had departed for Haywards Heath at 9.26am, the single line staff was withdrawn from the box and taken by road to Horsted Keynes to enable *Birch Grove* to pass through at 10.10am to the main line and eventually to Victoria. This entry is simply described as "Light engine to Haywards Heath". The next day saw the running of the 'Spring Belle'. Once again a signalman was specially employed to take the staff by road to Horsted Keynes and returned at 11.47am with "2 engines Horsted Keynes to Haywards Heath". At 12.31pm the special arrived and left for Horsted Keynes, but this time the staff was not returned by road by the signalman until 1.20pm. At 4.20pm he withdrew the staff again and went to Horsted Keynes, returning at 5.6pm with the "Spring Belle". At 5.49pm the Bluebell locomotives returned from Haywards Heath, taking the staff with them to Horsted Keynes, whence

it was once again returned to its box by road at 6pm. As will be seen, all these operations necessitated the employment of at least one extra signalman as well as an inspector, but timings were so arranged that the train service was not disarranged. Similar arrangements were made on Sunday 15 September, for the "Scottish Belle". It is interesting to note that in March the signalman on duty unemotionally books his train as from "Sheffield Park" or "Horsted Keynes Spl" while his colleague later in the year refers to "Bluebell" trains.

'This train register stops on Thursday, 14 October 1963, the entry for which is actually on the hard back cover of the ordinary lined foolscap book. There were only three more days in the life of the branch and one rather wonders if it was thought worth while starting a new book for those three days. Anyway, the entries for the final day's running are not available, which is a pity as it would have been interesting to see if emotion had been allowed to creep into that day's entry!'

From 1959 the line was used to deliver rolling stock to the new Bluebell Railway and nearly all locomotives and rolling stock for the line took this route, the last recorded movement through Lywood Tunnel being on 13 May 1964, when 'Terrier' No 32636 propelling an LBSCR strawberry van passed through prior to the lifting of the line. With the closure of the line on 28 October 1963, the now truncated and newly designated 'Ardingly branch' was converted to a siding and reduced to single track, using the former down line. Access to the up main and up local lines at Copyhold Junction was severed, and the daily freight to Ardingly commenced travelling up the down local line from Haywards Heath to the junction. Workings soon reduced to 'As Required', serving the Amey Roadstone plant established on the goods yard and station site with its raucous grind of machinery spreading films of white dust around to render the station precincts a kind of lunar landscape, a far cry from the quiet, well-groomed station with its charming signalbox and homely platforms which provided a sanctuary of shade from the afternoon sun in the south.

The lifting of the section from just east of Ardingly station commenced on 15 July 1964 and by 21 September had reached Horsted Keynes. The last dramatic injury to the branch occurred in the summer of 1968 with the demolition of Sheriff Mill Viaduct. Although the southern face had suffered severe flaking of Firbank's deep red brickwork, it was only superficial. In reality the Mid Sussex District Council wished to straighten the bend of New Lane as it curved under the viaduct and BR was only too pleased to be shot of the considerable maintenance costs.

19.
Rationalisation

Retrenchment

By whatever name one calls the process of retrenchment, reorganisation or rationalisation, there was from the end of the Edwardian period an abridgement, a search for economies by making alterations, and a gradual diminution of the structure and staffing of the line, which gravitated towards its logical conclusion in 1955, culminating in the final solution. The line had been constructed on too lavish a scale for the relatively small local communities it was to cater for and brought with it no development commensurate with its facilities. It did not carry the equivalent of the traffic on the Mid-Sussex line south of Horsham, nor of the lines through Eridge and Uckfield which were double track throughout.

The first visible economies came just prior to and during World War 1 when the junction for the two diverging lines was moved to the south end of Horsted Keynes, the signalling arrangements rationalised and the North box reduced in status, quickly followed by the removal of most of the rooms and all the canopies of the western island platform, as has been previously noted.

Following the war the new Southern Railway took stock of this anomalous situation and saw an opportunity to cut down on the number of railway staff, especially the most expensive member, the stationmaster, having noted that in 1916

Horsted Keynes, showing the pre-1935 electrification layout, which existed from 1914, when the junction was moved from the north end to the south of the station. The single line to Sheffield Park continues straight to curve behind the loading gauge at the entrance to the goods yard, while the line of double track bends away towards Ardingly. *Lens of Sutton*

Barcombe had been lumped together with its twin station on the Uckfield line. At the end of 1926 Ardingly and West Hoathly were put under the control of the 'station agent' at Horsted Keynes, and Kingscote under East Grinstead, while in November 1931 a further regrouping was announced, whereby Barcombe Mills was taken together with Isfield under Uckfield, and Charles Perkins of Sheffield Park took Newick & Chailey and Barcombe under his wing.

Simplified it might seem but it also made for complications as A. J. Street, the literary clerk at West Hoathly, noted in a letter to the *Southern Railway Magazine* in February 1931, entitled 'Many links in a small chain':

'It may be of interest to your readers to know the unique position of the three stations controlled by Mr Bowley of Horsted Keynes, and I should imagine a similar position does not exist elsewhere. The three stations are Ardingly, Horsted Keynes and West Hoathly, and the following arrangements apply:

1. For distribution of freight rolling stock the stations come under Brighton, Lewes and Three Bridges respectively.
2. District Inspectors are at Brighton, St Leonards and Three Bridges respectively.
3. Permanent Way Inspectors are at Three Bridges for Ardingly and at East Grinstead for Horsted Keynes and West Hoathly.
4. Signal & Telegraph linesmen are at Brighton, East Grinstead and Three Bridges respectively.
5. Even for convalescent homes the three stations are allocated to two different district secretaries.
6. The same applies to the Southern Railway Orphanage.'

Not only were there economies with regard to station staff but also in the field of signalling. The stations on the single line section were, in relation to the traffic on the line, somewhat extravagantly appointed. Closure of boxes by taking out a run-round loop and timetabling the crossing of trains to suit could result in savings in staff and equipment, and were part of the Southern Railway's remit to counter the adverse trends of the recession of the 1930s and the loss of traffic to the roads. Barcombe's signalbox and part of the station canopies were demolished in 1932. Both boxes at Sheffield Park were demolished in 1934 and replaced with a platform ground-level frame with instruments housed in the booking office. The same took place at Newick & Chailey in 1938, where the up line was made into a loop siding and all the up platform buildings alongside were demolished. Sheffield Park yet again received further attention in 1949 when the footbridge was taken down, leaving passengers to and from trains having to cross the boards at the platform ends. Whether the original bridge was in poor condition or was sacrificed to some kind of economy is not certain, but its doubles at West Hoathly and Ardingly remained for the duration of the line. The demolition of the grand lavatories at the south end of Sheffield Park's up platform buildings appears to have escaped the records.

Electrification

The details of the branch from Haywards Heath to Horsted Keynes have already been touched upon in the respective station chapters. This was part of a grander strategy extending electrification to Seaford, Eastbourne and Hastings. On the one hand the Horsted Keynes stub was electrified to serve the needs of local business travellers at a time when Haywards Heath was rapidly expanding into a commuter dormitory town, and operationally to take the terminating services from Seaford out of the congested bottleneck there, but it was also an indication of future intentions presaging anticipated housing development along the Horsted Keynes-Sanderstead line when electrification was extended further north. The SR before the war was already talking in terms of electrifying through to East Grinstead, but Hitler intervened and it was pigeon-holed.

Had a decision been taken at this juncture the whole story of the line could have taken on a completely different aspect. Certainly comment at the time spoke of 'a great opportunity raised', with sound prospects of residential development, encouraging commuter villages to grow up near the stations. The scheme was heralded as the logical tidying up process of the second phase of Central Section electrification to follow that of the Mid-Sussex line, thus making available an alternative electrified route to the main line, but the major bottleneck it could not avoid was the double track portion through Haywards Heath Tunnel and southwards.

The line north from Horsted Keynes was again scheduled for electrification in the postwar plans of the SR but, after the company's impoverishment during the war years and the running down of plant, there were more urgent financial priorities on its agenda. Nationalisation in 1948, with its further enforced restrictions in capital expenditure, led the Southern Region to stall to the point of no return. The issue was raised again after Nationalisation but British Railways, particularly in view of the post war Green Belt legislation, decided to hedge its bets with a possible diesel option. However, this was also deferred until it was too late.

World War 2

Wartime incidents on the line have already been mentioned where they relate to the stations. In general terms the railways came under the control of the Government for more than five years. To be fair, what the railways were doing and faced up to between 1939 and 1945 was conveyed to the public, but only in general terms. For any breaks in the clouds of official secrecy one has to turn to the memories of railway staff and enthusiasts drafted into the services, who kept their eyes open to the interesting movements going on in many distant corners, to supply some of the richness of detail lacking from the few railway journals that carried on through the printing shortages of the war years, under a degree of censorship such as the elimination of all dates and place names, and the restrictions on photography. Wartime regulations, moreover, especially after the fall of France in 1940, made civilians who took notes or used a camera at stations or lineside objects of grave suspicion.

Turning to the line, one might have been led to conjure up a dramatic picture of troop and hospital trains, munitions specials and extra freights, main line diversions and cancelled trains, unusual locomotive workings, and untold damage creating havoc and chaos to the Central Section workings. In fact the services continued perfectly normally throughout the war period and, though there were plenty of things happening to remind folk that there was a war on, this fact would not have been easily gleaned by the lineside observer. True, the engines lost their green coats, and blinds and blue night lamps appeared in the compartments. People said that was really for the London area where things were more lively, but in fact the whole of the Southeast was in the front line.

A Civil Defence exercise took place just south of Sharpthorne Tunnel on 18 April 1943, involving two trains in charge of 'C2X' 0-6-0s, one involving a gas decontamination unit and the other, seen in this photograph, containing permanent way and other materials. The scene of much activity includes a participant using a chemical footwash. Staff dressed in protective clothing move all over the track, while above the tunnel mouth a crowd of interested spectators watch the proceedings.
Courtesy Railtrack Southern

It has been suggested that the exercise was a demonstration of emergency permanent way repairs practised under conditions of gas attack, hence the racks for gas masks attached to the command coach, in whose shade personnel take a welcome break during the exercise. Other photographs show a section of track taken up and men wearing gas masks shovelling material from a four-plank wagon.
Courtesy Railtrack Southern

The tank train at Kingscote and stored tanks at Horsted Keynes have already been noted, together with other wartime secretings at the latter's long west siding. Elsewhere on the line, as recorded by a set of official photographs, a Civil Defence exercise took place on 18 April 1943 in the cutting just south of West Hoathly Tunnel, seemingly a demonstration of emergency permanent way repairs under conditions of gas attack. Two unidentified 'C2X' 0-6-0s were in charge of a gas de-contamination train and one of permanent way materials on the up and down lines respectively. These proceedings were viewed openly by the locals who formed quite a crowd up above the tunnel's south portal. Looking through the dozen or so photographs held in Railtrack's archives, one can see gas masks hanging beside the running board of the support coach, a short section of the up track removed, contaminated material (sand/cement?) shovelled from an open goods wagon and decontamination procedures including liquid dips being used.

The only other way in which the war affected the line was through bombing, more often than not indirectly. The line itself was struck on several occasions, the most notable being near Mill Place between Kingscote and West Hoathly and on the embankment near Holywell Waterworks, causing the line to be closed for a fortnight and a bus service to be run between Horsted Keynes and Sheffield Park. During the night of 24 May 1943, in an attempt to cripple the rail centre of Brighton, an enemy bomb which had penetrated through three buildings exploded against Rastrick's great viaduct, 80ft high above the London Road, and brought down a pier and two arches. All Brighton trains from the Sheffield Park and Uckfield lines were terminated at Lewes which, during the month that followed while a temporary span was being installed, must have presented an interesting set of station workings. On 29 August at 7.15pm an up engineer's special was seen at Copyhold Junction coming off the Ardingly branch hauled by two 'C3s', Nos 2303 and 2307, unusual engines for these parts, and possibly connected with the repair to London Road Viaduct. The week ending 22 January 1944 saw an extra working, an emergency shuttle service between Lewes and Barcombe, for the line between Isfield and Barcombe Mills had been closed through bomb damage. The engine was 'D3' 0-4-4T No 2366 with a push-pull set. Later in the year there must have been similar trouble on the Oxted line, for the 10.50am Brighton to Victoria was diverted via Rowfant and Three Bridges, passing Redhill between 1.30 and 1.35pm. And then of course there were those 'tunnel chasing' incidents at Cinder Hill and Lywood, for Southeast England was not infrequently the scene of trains being shot up by lone raiders who found the return journey to the Channel somewhat dull. 'Train busting', as Hamilton Ellis mentions in his *British Railway History,* had a strong sporting appeal to the armed airman, and 'both sides delighted in it.'

Closure Plans

With the postwar recovery the family car began progressively to take traffic away from the railway, and British Railways, even in the pre-Beeching era, came to the conclusion that the line was a lossmaker and not worth including in its Modernisation Programme. It was no longer an economic proposition and in 1954, BR having decided not to proceed, the fate of the line was effectively sealed. In May 1954 British Railways (Southern Region) published a memorandum proposing 'Withdrawal of services between East Grinstead and Lewes'. It contained details of train services proposed for withdrawal, existing alternative facilities and appendices listing: (A) bus facilities in the area with proposed additional services, (B) train services and passenger carryings, (C) number of wagons dealt with at stations proposed for closure. A copy of this, together with other documentation regarding the closure, objections and enquiry, was donated in 1990 to the Bluebell Archives by B. W. Howe, who as former agent to the Sheffield Park Estate and occupier of the 307-acre Home Farm, had corresponded and contested the closure and attended the public meetings.

The unveiling of the memorandum was, of course, the culmination of work behind the scenes to gather overwhelming evidence to steam-roller through the closure. Waterloo's minions had from 1951 onwards been noted by station staff coming down to examine the books and cull information about traffic and costs. These had all been gathered in by November 1953, collated by the Branch Line Committee, whose report was made public at the enquiry the following year. These included a comparison of costs of working an hourly interval service by:

(a) two-car diesel electric set	£52,833
(b) Diesel-mechanical rail car (WR type)	£47,011
(c) three-car diesel-mechanical lightweight unit	£48,482

The figures included sections for the chief civil engineer, for repairs and renewals of bridges, fences, buildings and permanent way, for p/way staff, materials, clothing and weedkilling; for the signal engineer, for wages for labourers and linesmen; for train working regarding rolling stock repairs and renewals, wages of drivers and guards, for fuel and lubricants, for station expenses involving the operating department for staff listed as: two porters and two signalmen at East Grinstead, a stationmaster and two signalmen at Sheffield Park, two signalmen at Culver Junction and, at all the other stations listed for closure, two leading porters. There was also a further statement showing estimated costs of working original and new services by diesel mechanical railbuses (Western Region type). The former worked out at £40,072, the latter at £26,710.

Traffic Figures

The passenger traffic figures recorded in the memorandum are of interest, reflecting use of the line in the final years. It particularly footnoted the schoolchildren's journeys. The first up train, 6.44am from Lewes, carried an average of two dozen

The 2.59pm East Grinstead-Brighton leaves West Hoathly on 23 May 1955 behind Ivatt 2MT 2-6-2T No 41313, while Porter Henry Dry, heading for a premature retirement at the end of the week, recrosses the trackboards after attending to the train. Behind the signalbox at this late date, wagons still stand in use at the brickyard siding.
John Head

HAYWARDS HEATH — HORSTED KEYNES — E. GRINSTEAD
LEWES — BARCOMBE — HORSTED KEYNES — E. GRINSTEAD
THREE BRIDGES — GRANGE ROAD — E. GRINSTEAD

(*Italic Figures are A.M. times*) S.R. Table 7

WEEKDAYS

No. 1.																		SO		SO												
Brighton ....d	628	628	615	650	7 7	750	750	8 0	8 25	843	1023	1028	11 5	1128	12 8	1228		1228	1 8	1 28	1 20	1 58	228	3 8	2 58	3 28		346	428	428
Haywards Heath	651	7 6		713		737	812	815		8 48	911	1052	11 3		12 4	1226	1255		1 4	1 41	2 5		2 22	3 5	328	3 14	4 6		452	454
Ardingly		710			743		819				915		11 8		12 8				1 8	1 46	2 9			3 9	334		4 10			458
Lewes			637		726			820					1123							1 39									4 3	
Barcombe			647		735			831					1133							1 47									413	
Newick & C.			655		743			839					1140							1 54									421	
Sheffield Park			7 4		749			846					1146							2 3									426	
Horsted Keynes		714	716		747		823	855		919			1112	1156	1212				1 12	1 52	2 13	2 14		313	340		4 14		438	5 2
W. Hoathly			723					842	9 7						12 2					1 59	2 21				345					
Kingscote			729						914			STOP	12 8							2 5	2 27				350		STOP		5 9	
Three Bridges	7 8			732		832			9 6		1121				9 25				2 39					3 48					515	
Rowfant	714			738		838			9 12		1127				15	31			2 45					3 54					519	
Grange Road	718			742		843			9 16		1132				1 20	36			2 49					3 58	SX					
E. GRINSTEAD	724		734	748		848		920	9 23		1138	1210	1214		1 25	42	158		2 11	2T33	2 55		356	4	4 33				526	
Forest Row	733			820					9 42			1219			1 35	2 6			2 43		3 7				4 41				539	
Groombridge				840					10 1			1237			1 54	226			3 8		3 26				5 7				559	
Tun. Wells West				848					10 9			1244			2 2	233			3 17		3 32				5 18				6 6	

WEEKDAYS—continued | **SUNDAY**

No. 2.	SX	SO	SX	SO				SX																		
Brighton ....d	458	5 8	512	528	528	518	558	628	631	658		758	8 8	746	828	9 25		828	8 32	9 28	1128	1 28	328	528	650	7 8	728
Haywards Heath	522	536	512	552	6 6		625	653		722		822	835		9 6			852		10 5	12 6	2 6	4 5	6 5		731	8 5
Ardingly		540	540		610		629	658					839			910				10 9	1210	2 10	4 9	6 9			8 9
Lewes						537			658					818		9 43			8 52							7 8	
Barcombe						547			7 6					826		9 52			9 4							718	
Newick & C.						555			713					833		9 59			9 12							726	
Sheffield Park						6 4								838		10 5			9 19							732	
Horsted Keynes		544	544		614	615	633	7 2	STP			843	848	914	1013				9 29	1013	1214	2 14	413	613		743	813
W. Hoathly						623							855		1020				9 36							749	
Kingscote						629							9 1						9 42							755	
Three Bridges	6 3			6 8					738		850							920								747	
Rowfant	6 9			614					744		856							926								753	
Grange Road	614			619					749		9 1							931								758	
E. GRINSTEAD	623			624		635			7 3	754	811	9 7		9 7		1032	1035	937	9 48						8 1	8 4	
Forest Row	632			632					711		819	919		919			1042		10 4							814	
Groombridge									731		837	939		939			11 5		1024							837	
Tun. Wells West									738		844	946		946			1112		1031							845	

SO—Saturday only. SX or E—Saturday excepted. T—Arrives 2.36 p.m. on Saturday.

E. GRINSTEAD — HORSTED KEYNES — HAYWARDS HEATH
E. GRINSTEAD — HORSTED KEYNES — BARCOMBE — LEWES
E. GRINSTEAD — GRANGE ROAD — THREE BRIDGES

(*Italic Figures are A.M. times*) S.R. Table 7

WEEKDAYS

No. 1.					SX	SO															SO	SX	SX	SO				SX	SO
Tun. Wells West				7 6	736	736		8 50		10 6		1130						1 8	8	219									
Groombridge				712	742	742		8 56		1012		1136						1 15	1 15	226									
Forest Row	622			739	8 1	8 1		9 14		1032		1155						1 38	1 38	245									
E. GRINSTEAD	636	638		752	8 0	813	813	9 24	9 37	1040	1145	12 9		1 30				1 49	1 49	256	3 0			359			415	415
Grange Road	641				8 5			9 31			1150	1215						1 53	1 53	3 3								420	420
Rowfant	645			STP	8 9			9 34			1154	1219						1 57	1 57	3 6								423	423
Three Bridges	650				815			9 40			12 0	1224						2 3	2 3	312								429	429
Kingscote		643				818	818		9 42						1 35										3 5		4 5		
W. Hoathly		648				823	823	852	9 47						1 40										3 9		410		
Horsted Keynes		654	720	758		830	830	857	921	9 53	1116		1216	1 16	1 47	216	216			314				316	416	4 17		
Sheffield Park		7 7			8 0					10 2				2 1										322		429		
Newick & C.		713			8 5					10 8				2 0										328		434		
Barcombe		720			811					1014				2 15										334		442		
Lewes		734			821					1024				2 26										343		453		
Ardingly	729		724	8 2		834	834	9 3	925		1120		1220		1 20			220	220					320		4 21		
Haywards Heath			728	8 6		840	840	855	9 6	918	941	952	1014	1055	1151		1124		1228	1224	1259	1 24		224	224	327		324		4 25	455	5 1
Brighton ....a	752	8 4	752	840	840	855	9 6	918	941	952	1014	1055	1151		1250	1250	1 22	1 50	2 54	245	250	2 50	3 12	350	4 1		350	513	4 50	517	523

WEEKDAYS—continued | **SUNDAY**

No. 2.	SX	SO		SX	SO	SO	SX	SX	SO		SX									
Tun. Wells West		455	455					612			8 37		750				640			
Groombridge		5 2	5 2					619			8 43		756				647			
Forest Row		521	521					637			9 1		814				7 6			
E. GRINSTEAD		530	530	530				647	7 4	7 7	8 35	9 18	12 9	15	824	9 56		715		8 8
Grange Road		537	537						7 10			9 18			829			721		
Rowfant		540	540			STP			7 14			9 21			833			725		
Three Bridges		546	546						7 19			9 27			840			731		
Kingscote			537							712	8 39		9 20			10 3			815	
W. Hoathly			543							718	8 45		9 26			10 8			822	
Horsted Keynes	455	5 8		549	6 0	6 0	616	616	640	640	7 16	726	8 51	853	916	9 32	1015	1016	1216	216	416	616	816	829
Sheffield Park	5 3				6 4						738	9 1			1024			839	
Newick & C.	5 8			612							728	744	9 7			1031			846	
Barcombe	515			621							734	749	9 14			1038			854	
Lewes	528			635							744	758	9 23			1050			9 6	
Ardingly		512			6 46	620	620	644	644	7 20		858	920	9 38		1020	1220	220	420	620	820	
Haywards Heath		516	612	627	6 8	6	8	624	649	649	7 24	7T49		9 1	924	10 0	9 44	856		1024	1224	224	424	624	757	824	
Brighton ....a	556	541	629	650	656	629	641	650	655	717	722	8 57	51	8T13	818	10 2	941	951	1023	1023		920	1110	1051	1 21	321	521	721	821	921	925

SO—Saturday only. SX—Saturday excepted. T—10 mins. later on Saturday.

Southern Region Table 7 from the published timetable, illustrating the postwar timetable of services.

---

scholars from West Hoathly to East Grinstead, while the 8am from Sheffield Park brought 23 scholars, some from Newick & Chailey and Barcombe, down to Lewes. The 8.20am from Lewes carried 24 scholars from Barcombe to Newick & Chailey, the same number returning on the 2.59pm from East Grinstead (Newick 3.28pm). Seventeen returned from Lewes on the 4.3pm as far as Barcombe and Newick, while five Sheffield Park scholars arrived back at 6.3pm on the 5.35pm from Lewes. This latter was the busiest train on the line, loading up to 88 passengers in one day. The 'rush hour' period trains were the best patronised (on the 9.37am from East Grinstead 35 alighted at West Hoathly, while 14 joined at

221

No of Wagons:	Kingscote	West Hoathly	Sheffield Park	Newick & Chailey	Barcombe
Forwarded	4	11	53	50	30
Received	69	240	545	559	341
Highest No forwarded on any one day	1	1	12 (B)	4	4(E)
Highest No received on any one day	12 (A)	5	11 (C)	7 (D)	6 (F)

Notes
(A) Timber for store   (B) Timber (this includes eight wagons reconsigned from 11 received)
(C) Timber   (D) Coal
(E) Sugar beet   (F) Ashes for tennis courts

Barcombe), as were the lunchtime trains for shoppers to East Grinstead, Lewes and Brighton. The poorest figures were for the last two down trains from East Grinstead (8.38pm WSO and 9.17pm to Horsted Keynes and Haywards Heath), which mustered less than double figures. The Sunday custom was 54 and 43 on the 9.56am and 8.8pm from East Grinstead respectively, and from Lewes the 8.56am with 31 and the 7.9pm with 76.

There was also an appendix for the number of wagons dealt with in 1953 and this is best conveyed in tabulated form as shown in the table above.

Local Outcry

With the announcement of these proposals began the oft-repeated scenario of 'ushering' the closure of a line that was so typical of the period, and yet as a result of this particular one, British Railways, having received a sharp rap, learnt by painful process that it had to be rather more careful with its accounting procedures in the future. The usual objections to a railway closure had been lodged and there was a spate of protest meetings and remonstrative local groups and committees.

Bill Howe, a key player at Sheffield Park, received his personal letter on 4 July 1954 from Mr J. Bridger, the district traffic superintendent at Redhill. The threat of closure was electric. Already on 16 June, 200 people had come to a meeting in the Rainbow Ballroom at the Whitehall in East Grinstead, many being delegates from rural and parish councils affected and from town organisations. The press reported, 'The meeting heard that the closing of the line would save British Railways £59,000 a year (the line was costing £68,000 annually, with receipts realising only £9,000), and the unanimous retort to that was that British Railways were the authors of their own trouble.' A resolution was passed demanding the proposal be dropped forthwith and calling for the improvement of existing services, and that a deputation of five should attend a meeting of the Transport Users' Consultative Committee to put forward their protests.

Mr J. Bridger put the case for closure and said the line was making a big loss. A review had found the line's position 'rather bad'. The line did at one time pay, but since then the buses had come to the villages and the people's doorsteps. 'These buses have been a convenience to you, and you have left the railway, and that is why we find ourselves in this position today.' In a nutshell, if the local residents wanted the line to remain open they should have used it more, while the local council replied that it would have been better patronised if a more frequent and convenient service had been provided. But the damage had been done, and though BR was prepared to experiment with interval service push-pull trains and tickets issued by the guard, as later happened on the Three Bridges-Tunbridge Wells route, it was all too late.

The meeting's immediate response was to declaim the bus services as totally inadequate, and any rail closure would mean total isolation for many. The Ratepayers' Association representative described the closure proposal as a retrograde step. It was the duty of the BTC to provide the public with improved services, not to deny them services. Even then the argument of increasingly congested roads was being heard. The East Grinstead Urban Council decried the move, stating that under the County Development Plan the size of the town was about to be doubled. Every branch of society waded in to protest vigorously: the political parties, the coal merchants, market gardeners and shopkeepers, the clergy and even Kingscote Women's Institute. Delegates were appointed to make appropriate representations to the TUCC.

Bill Howe was not slow in making his personal case to the TUCC, posting it on 25 June, and including the following arguments and suggestions. He questioned using just the income receipts from the line's stations when the bulk of the traffic originated outside of the line, both passengers and goods, the latter consigned to stations on the line on which charges were paid at the forwarding station. The larger proportion of incoming traffic was not appearing in any accounts relating to the stations it was proposed to close. He challenged the still lavish staffing, quoting one of the platelayers who confided that 'his work was such a "potter" that he does not think he can put up with it much longer,' and suggested that more men were employed on track maintenance than was really necessary. He challenged the wagon figures as being reckoned as full wagon-loads, drawing attention to the 'road box' traffic, that is, goods consigned other than in full wagon-loads, and passenger service costs by stating that many of the services were return workings solely for the convenience of carriage working. With experience of the sugar beet traffic when Sheffield Park Estate loaded between 15 and 20 wagons each autumn, 'no farmer can contend with a seven-mile road journey to the station with farm transport'; just at a time when a new beet factory was being proposed in the south of Sussex. He also suggested singling the Horsted Keynes-East Grinstead section to save considerable expense on track maintenance. He concluded: 'Instead of sticking to a rigid system which admits of no change, let us have some initiative and the will to reduce expenses.' This was just the beginning of a thick file of correspondence to L. R. Bennett, secretary to the committee of five appointed at the East Grinstead meeting, to forward Bill's submissions; to J. Bridger at Redhill, and to J. W. Diplock, Manager of Turners sawmill.

On 20 August a detailed reply came from the TUCC for the Southeastern area dealing with the points mentioned, particularly the accounting and staffing. 'There must be a measure of supervision even at the smallest station, and the groups of stations under one stationmaster have been carried as far as is reasonably practical.' There would be new zonal

The tranquil scene at Sheffield Park in June 1954 gives no indication of the threat-of-closure bombshell which had exploded upon the community that same month. Ivatt 2-6-2T No 41307 takes water at the head of the 3.35pm Oxted-Brighton as does 'C2X' 0-6-0 No 32536 with the 4.3pm Lewes-Horsted Keynes. Both trains are formed of ex-SECR birdcage three-sets, while the station with the original LBSCR signal and water crane is pure 'Brighton'. *Peter Hay*

cartage arrangements from railheads and 'road box' traffic would cease. Lightly loaded passenger trains for balancing stock workings were a necessary function and, as to sugar beet, 'we should be prepared to offer cartage facilities if so desired,' but if the new beet factory was built, it was likely to transfer existing traffic to the road.

Closure

The TUCC met on 30 November at the Charing Cross Hotel, and Bill was invited to attend. He had to leave early to catch the last train to Sheffield Park after enduring three hours of quite irrelevant and unconstructive prattle by a number of complainants. On 6 December he was informed by the TUCC Secretary, C. W. G. Elliff, that the committee had decided to recommend that the railway proposals be approved. On 18 March 1955 the official closure letter arrived from Redhill stating: 'The necessity for withdrawing facilities in the manner indicated is much regretted.' The deputation was for pressing the Minister of Transport and Civil Aviation further to reconsider the closure but the battle was already lost, or so it seemed. Southdown Motor Services, in which the BTC had a large shareholding inherited from the Southern Railway, was ready to provide certain additional and extended services between Lewes and Sheffield Park on Service 20. Bill had resigned the line to its fate and even wrote on 28 May 1955, on the day the line closed, to enquire if he could purchase the four railway cottages at Sheffield Park station, 'as I am in need of additional housing for my workpeople here'. He received a letter back informing him of the undertaking that, 'the track shall remain *in situ* for a period of 12 months from the date of closure in case some subsequent development necessitates reconsideration of the abandonment of the line' — a wise proviso, with hindsight!

The line closed with the headline, 'Bluebell and Primrose Line officially dead.' It was at this period that the endearing name 'Bluebell' was inexorably linked to the line. Even back in 'Brighton' days it was known among enginemen and railway staff as the 'Bluebell and Primrose' line, and the section north of Horsted Keynes as purely the 'Primrose line', for the bluebells were more common along the single line section to the south. Driver Burgess of 'U1' No 31900 which hauled one of the last trips on the final day when interviewed said 'We used to get down and pick them.' Certainly the

phrase 'Bluebell' came into circulation when a member of the public (some suspect Madge Bessemer herself) related how, because of the lengthy station stops for taking on imaginary milk churns, 'there was time to leave the compartment and pick a bunch of bluebells'. Whatever the origin, it seems fairly certain that it was the *Sussex Express and County Herald* that latched on to this remark and coined the now famous name.

Closure, excepting for the electrified branch to Horsted Keynes, which left Ardingly as an anachronism, was scheduled for 13 June 1955 when the service of eight trains each way on weekdays and, as ever, the two on Sundays would be withdrawn, but an ASLEF strike brought the line to a premature close without ceremony on 28 May. The final trains to run on the Saturday were the 10.6pm from Lewes arriving at East Grinstead at 10.52pm, and the 8.38pm from East Grinstead to Lewes, arriving at 9.26pm. An attempt by Major Tufton Beamish, Conservative MP for Lewes, to get Mr Boyd Carpenter to reopen the enquiry had failed, he having claimed that the contrary views of the local authorities had received scant attention. But the Minister upheld the decision of the Central Committee. Local press comment was mixed and sentimental: 'The branch line that had served East Grinstead and Lewes faithfully for nearly 73 years "died" officially at 8.8pm on Sunday when the final train was to have pulled out of East Grinstead. But due to the walkout of the ASLEF footplatemen, the old line just petered out. No trains have run over the 17mile 13ch-long track since May 28, and so the celebrations planned for June 13 had to be cancelled', to the disappointment of Timothy Watson and Kate Longley, who had both travelled on the very first train. But other editorials were supportive of the closure. 'British Railways propose to close it at the beginning of the summer season. They are right to do so. Local sorrow at the loss of an old friend is quite understandable, but the verdict remains beyond dispute. The country cannot afford railways that are a dead loss.'

Mr H. J. Bellingham, Stationmaster at East Grinstead was interviewed about the arrangements that had been planned for the last train and he mentioned that a special railway enthusiasts' train was to have been run over the line on the Sunday, but this too had had to be cancelled because of the strike. 'It is an unfortunate ending to the old line and we were expecting a record business from that run.' He mentioned letter after letter arriving at his station, the majority asking for 'souvenir' tickets. East Grinstead-Kingscote return had been in great demand and had sold out, one man purchasing the

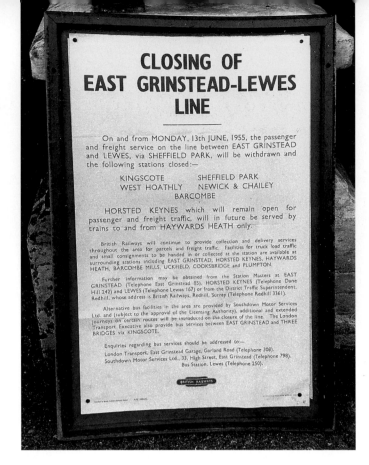

final eight. Letters came in from all parts of the country and most people wanted the tickets dated and clipped. Mr Bellingham hastened to mention that 'the track is not being pulled up because, it is understood, of a possibility that one day it may become electrified.' BR had, however, already contracted for the above-mentioned railtour sponsored by the RCTS for 12 June and, after negotiation, the 'Wealden Limited' behind 'H2' Atlantic No 32426 *St Alban's Head* rang down on 14 August 1955 what all assumed was the final curtain. The special was welcomed by quite a crowd and just before it majestically steamed through Barcombe, a black cat was seen walking along the track. The Holdens, through their historic connection with the station, were there to watch this 'last train' and Bernard, who as a young boy lived in the station house when his father was in charge, later wrote: 'I have often thought that the cat symbolised good luck, for today life is still strong further up the line.'

Photographers, some using cine film, were out in force, particularly at Horsted Keynes which was still accessible by rail. Everyone assumed 'rationalisation' had taken its logical and ultimate course. Nobody, least of all the Southern Region, expected it ever to be resumed.

The penultimate day of full service, 27 May 1955, with a footplatemen's strike looming, sees the usual 'K' replaced by 'N' No 31853 on the 3.28pm Haywards Heath-London Bridge near Mill Place, easing off on the downhill grade for the stop at Kingscote. *Denis Cullum*

The inhabitants of Barcombe say farewell to what was assumed then to be the last train along the line, the 'Wealden Limited' of the Railway Correspondence & Travel Society, behind Brighton Atlantic No 32426 *St Alban's Head*. This on-the-spot snap has captured well the bathos and sentiments of the occasion expressed by families with children, the finality of the last photograph and the general dumbfounded gaze of the 'mourners', one waving a white handkerchief. The suited figure by the trackside is Bernard Holden, who as a child was brought up in the station house where his father Charles was the Stationmaster. *R Holden*

20.
Respite

Madge Bessemer

Many groups had opposed the closure and none more so than the 'Fighting Committee' convened and chaired by the redoubtable Miss Rose Ellen Margaret Bessemer. Formidable, to say the least, and universally held in respect, if sometimes tinged with a modicum of awe, she was a person of public spiritedness and a 'natural' in taking a prominent part in local affairs.

The Rev Edwin Matthias, Rector of Chailey during his latter years, pinpointed her motivation when he wrote that she 'tried to emulate her father, Sir Henry Bessemer, with her straightforwardness and bull-terrier-like attitude of not letting things go once involved, like a dog with a bone.' A close neighbour described her as 'very concise and a born organiser. She had a wonderful brain. She was punctilious in her timing and expected it of others, and at times could be bossy in an imperious autocratic manner.' And yet, on the other hand, she was kind and generous, caring and concerned, an open character, and nearly always very friendly and charming. Frugal and monastic in lifestyle yet a hoarder by nature, there was in her a trace of a mean and stubborn streak that made her such a doughty protagonist. She was humorous, full of quips, and it is quite possible it was her comment about picking the spring flowers on the railway embankment at Newick & Chailey that led to the designation 'Bluebell Line'.

A member of Chailey Parish Council, she took her job very seriously and chaired the planning committee that vetted applications and advised the local planning authority of village views. This was organised on a far more formal and procedurally correct basis than the Parish Council meetings to which she reported. She did much quiet work for the village, teaching at the Chailey Heritage Craft Schools, as commandant of the local branch of the Red Cross Society, as Guide Captain in charge of the Girl Guide Rangers, together with involvement with the local sports association in providing the village with a sports ground and pavilion. She was normally somewhat retiring except when something struck her as important, when she would display surprising energy in impressing her views on others.

So, when the line that ran at the side of her Burchetts estate came under threat early in 1954, though not publicly announced by the BTC, her hackles were raised and she took up the cause. Jack Evans, Clerk at the time to the former Cuckfield Urban District Council, wrote a letter to the *Sussex Express* bitterly complaining over the proposed closure. She contacted him at once and quickly had Jack on the 'Fighting Committee', of which she took the chair and invited key local people onto it, including the Rev Bill Webb of Barcombe, Mr Sale, owner of the dairy at Sheffield Park, Frank Leppard, the coal merchant at West Hoathly, and others. She had monitored the East Grinstead protest meeting of 16 June, but nothing more was heard until notes referring to the impending closure were sent to the local and rural councils — with the exception

A rare portrait of Miss R. E. M. Bessemer (1898-1985), taken while attending a wedding at the Savoy Hotel. She was the queen that checkmated BR's attempt to snuff out the line in the first round of the closure stakes.
Courtesy Robina Kidd/Bluebell Archives

of Newick & Chailey, for reasons never explained. Consequently Miss Bessemer formed the Lewes & East Grinstead Railway and Transport Facilities Committee, who took their case to the South Eastern Transport Users' Consultative Committee in London and even marched up to the House of Commons to make their protest.

At this meeting on 30 November 1954 the public was admitted only at the discretion of the chairman, and the press was not invited. Having been admitted, representatives of the Lewes & East Grinstead Committee were not allowed to challenge the figures produced in evidence by the BTC or permitted to make any further challenge on legal points. Suggested economies and possible improvements were of no avail and the Consultative Committee recommended to the Central Consultative Committee that the line should close. The Lewes & East Grinstead Railway and Transport Facilities Committee stated that the public were not informed of their right of appeal, that at the Central Consultative Committee meeting representatives of the local body were not seen and as representatives of the BTC were there to state its case, the results were inevitably prejudiced, and the closure plans proceeded.

Madge Bessemer was still not satisfied that the local committee had done all that was possible. Her incredible determination was to prove a positive quality. Strong-minded, she had no uncertainty about any action she took or planned. Her almost single-handed research was to identify a flaw in the closure procedures followed by BTC, and she decided to see the original Acts of Parliament relating to the railway. The British Transport Commission was not forthcoming with copies, so she had photostat duplicate prints made from copies in the Record Office. Going over these with legal guidance, she discovered that under section 35 of the London, Brighton & South Coast Railway (Croydon, Oxted & East Grinstead Railways) Act of 1878, the LBSCR was under a legal obligation to provide four trains in each direction every day, Sundays included, for the carriage of passengers. This responsibility was taken over by the Southern Railway in 1923 and in 1948 by the BTC without being repealed, which amounted to the fact that the railway had been closed against an Act of Parliament, *an action which was therefore illegal.* To prove this point, Miss Bessemer's solicitors had a vast amount of correspondence with the Southern Region, British Transport Commission, the Ministry of Transport and Civil Aviation, and even the Minister himself. Meanwhile Maj Tufton V. H. Beamish, Conservative Member of Parliament for Lewes, asked the Minister questions on the closure and these combined factors forced the BTC to resume the service. Previously the Minister had refused to see a deputation from the local committee and said that the replacement facilities should be given a fair trial.

Madge Bessemer's discovery proved a sensation and a field day for the press, who milked it for all it was worth. 'Miss R. E. M. Bessemer, the lean sixtyish granddaughter of famed steelman Sir Henry Bessemer [incidentally, both father and grandfather were 'Sir Henry'], whose family home is within a stone's throw of the "Bluebell and Primrose" line as passengers call it, though she usually rode about in her own motor car, had an odd affection for the Bluebell and Primrose.: "We oughtn't to look at it as a wee strip of line, but as part of a whole principle."'

'Poring over documents on the line's past history, spinster Bessemer found just what she needed, an Act of Parliament passed when the railway was built, requiring the owners to run four trains daily. "They," said Miss Bessemer scornfully of the Transport Commission, with fire in her eyes, "have got to keep the law just like everyone else!"'

A visit on 16 April 1956 by Chris Campbell, one of the students who took the lead in saving the line, noted it covered in weeds a foot high and a 'For Sale' notice on the station house at Sheffield Park, while at Kingscote the porter living in the station house was of the opinion that the line would be reopened from Horsted Keynes to Lewes, not from East Grinstead. The stationmaster's wife at West Hoathly stated: 'We have not been told to start making the station usable. BTC may only run a goods train daily to comply with the Act.'

The newspaper headlines on 28 April trumpeted: 'So now the Bluebell Line will open again'; 'Reopening is a triumph for Miss Bessemer'; 'Bluebell Line gets reprieve'. Intriguing was the comment of the railway official who concluded: 'Those who fought for the line have won on a legal point. It is impossible to close a line without passing an Act, and that was not done. It will cost a great deal to reinstate the stations and the line can never be a paying proposition. I cannot say when it will be reopened as it will take time to get things running again.'

Another official said: 'I have heard that members of the stations' staff who were moved will be given an opportunity of returning to their old jobs.' Madge Bessemer meanwhile was magnanimous in victory, saying 'We shall admire the new Minister of Transport [Harold Watkinson] for upholding the rights of the public.' But a fortnight later, with support from the local councils, she was calling for a public enquiry into the legality of the closure.

However, after much local comment and rumour, a train traversed the line on 1 June. This was the weed-killing train hauled by No 32350 — a 'K' class 2-6-0, which included the line in its itinerary and brought a gleam of hope for the future, although no official announcement had been made regarding a resumption of service. This led to widespread rumour-mongering, with press headlines for 19 July proclaiming, 'Ghost train revives the rumours,' but railway officialdom was quick to play them down. 'We are bound by law to keep the weeds down, which seems to have been misconstrued as giving certain implications.' Another said: 'There is nothing we can say. Miss Bessemer's solicitors have brought out various points in connection with the legal position, which are now being considered.' But more than locomotive activity was reported on the line: 'There has been petty pilfering, and workmen have been seen on the line, but they have been moving equipment and not replacing it.' But that very week Sir Brian Robertson, Chairman of the BTC, informed Sir Tufton Beamish they would be prepared to reopen the line but the loss would have to be borne by other rail users.

The Reopening

The line reopened in a burst of publicity: 'Ghost line villagers cheer Bluebell train'; 'Bluebell Line comes to life again' and talked of victory celebrations in the Sussex villages served by the line. At stations all along the line villagers cheered, farm workers paused in the fields to wave their caps, housewives held their children high, and crowds gathered to view this wonder and wave flags. 'It was like an end of war celebration in Sussex today.'

'All aboard for a sentimental journey as Round 1 of the battle is won,' was the headline of the local reporter who, on Thursday, 7 August 1956, boarded the first train up from Lewes at 9.30am, headed by a 40-year-old goods engine, 'K' No 32342, crewed by Driver Arthur Norman of Newhaven and

Reopening day at East Grinstead Low Level, with 'C2X' No 32442 having run round its train before manoeuvring into the down platform for the return trip to Lewes with the 12.28pm. 'M7' 0-4-4T No 30052 stands in the High Level platform with a Three Bridges train. *T. Wright*

For the first months of the 'makeshift' service, former rail motor set No 504, comprising two veteran ex-LBSCR coaches, was used on the service, but negligible custom soon reduced this to a single coach. 'C2X' No 32438, with cab sheet drawn against the prevalent 'sou-westers' from the Channel, trundles the 2.28pm East Grinstead-Lewes near Sheffield Park on 14 August 1956. *John Head*

Fireman David Goather of Lewes, supervised on the footplate by Mr H. Copp, Locomotive Inspector of Brighton, with 63 passengers on board the two red LBSC coaches of Set 504. Passing Barcombe, where about 39 residents watched from the station yard, the first stop was at Newick & Chailey where Miss Bessemer and 16 other passengers boarded. As soon as she entered a compartment, she was besieged by newspaper reporters, cameramen and a BBC representative with a recording machine. During the journey she held a press Conference and distributed copies of the previous week's *Express & Herald's* leading article headed 'Boffins and the branch line' to the reporters. She asserted the Railway Executive had made no efforts to make the line pay and serve the needs of the public, and were still adopting the same attitude as they did before the line was closed. 'I want to protect the rights and interests of the public' she declared.

Railway officials turned out in force for the ride: W. C. Collins (District Traffic Superintendent), L. Fox (Chief Linesman, Lewes), H. Pettit (Signal Inspector, Brighton) and A. C. Streatfield (Public Relations Officer, Southern Region,

from Waterloo). Also on board was Frank Norman, 91-year-old retired master watchmaker who, leaning on his stick in the corridor, told how he remembered the line being opened 74 years before. There for the ride were a dozen lads from the Railway Enthusiasts' Club at Farnborough, Hants: 'We've been on plenty of trains making their last journey, but it's the only time we've been on one making the first journey', said 19-year-old Edwin Wilmshurst of Lancing. Ganger Charlie Cottington, who had been on the railway for 28 years, the last 12 at Kingscote said that, though the track had rusted over, 'It will come up nice and polished after a couple of weeks. The track is in good order.'

The reporters were obviously doing their mathematics. Five passengers left at Newick & Chailey and 18 embarked, seven more left at Sheffield Park and three at Horsted Keynes, nine getting on there. At West Hoathly 32 joined, to bring a total load of 107 into East Grinstead. Not a soul was seen at closed Kingscote. The only welcoming committee at journey's end was the station staff. Many of the passengers were railway enthusiasts armed with cameras, the majority of whom

Newick & Chailey station, deserted after the first closure. Note the 'CLOSED' board nailed across the entrance to the staircase exit, which was torn down with gusto the day the services recommenced on 7 August 1956. *Roy Hobbs*

reboarded the train for the return journey. Mr Bellingham, East Grinstead's Stationmaster, bombarded by the press, said no purpose could be served by discussing the matter at the moment. 'I have been told to run the trains and that is what we are doing. We must wait and see what happens in the future. It is the most economic service we can put on at the moment. I am not the leader of the opposition!'

On the return journey 105 passengers joined the train at East Grinstead, there were four passengers on and 31 off at West Hoathly, 16 on and four off at Horsted Keynes, four on at Sheffield Park and 11 on and 16 off at Newick & Chailey. A total of 83 alighted at Lewes. When Madge Bessemer alighted at Newick & Chailey, she made a point of shaking hands with Guard F. Bryant, who had been kept very busy because it was part of his duty to inspect and clip the tickets, issue handwritten ones for intermediate journeys and collect from alighting passengers. He recalled how people had hung from the carriage windows and pummelled each other for all they were worth. 'I've never seen anything like this,' said the amazed conductor. 'In the old days the passengers used to sit glumly, never speaking to each other.' As Madge Bessemer stepped down she called out, 'Good luck and fight on!' There were cheers as she left the station premises, where two young people were seen tearing down a board on which was painted 'Closed', and which had been nailed across the exit steps.

The Sulky Service

When the second train of the day started from Lewes at 11.30am, it carried a mere 15 passengers. A total of 383 passengers travelled on the eight trains of the day. After the first two, the numbers varied between 21 and 11. By the next day the traffic had already fallen to a fraction of that figure, the number travelling on the four morning trains being only eight.

On many days in the coming months there were to be many fewer than that. This was to come as no surprise and the following evening the Rector of Barcombe, the Rev Bill Webb, was interviewed in the TV programme *Highlight*, and spoke of the inadequacies and inconveniences of the reconstituted service, reintroduced with 'very bad grace' and a 'mere sop to the democratic process'.

He pointed out that the trains ran on a regular two-hourly headway but at such inconvenient times as to be largely useless to potential traffic. Taking his cue from Madge Bessemer, he stated that the present service was absolutely ridiculous and was so arranged as to be of no use whatever to the public, so that it could quite easily be shown to be unremunerative. The railway was acting very foolishly in not trying to make a success of the line and develop it so as to make it of real use to intending passengers. 'The service they are providing is quite stupid. If a family on this line want a day at Brighton, they will have to leave the seaside at 3pm to catch the last train from Lewes at 3.30pm.' No trains now called at either Kingscote or Barcombe, the latter station having formerly been a major source of revenue to the line. 'The villagers want to use this line but the railway authorities refuse to stop here, when the additional cost would be negligible. By not stopping at Barcombe, I think they are behaving like sulky children.' The intermediate stations open had been downgraded to unstaffed halts and the guard was required to issue tickets on the train. However, it was necessary to rebook at either East Grinstead or Lewes for travelling on further, or joining the line, and this could result in missing a connection, in the unlikely event that there was one. Why had the railway authorities waited until after the Bank Holiday, reopening the line the day after? And why passengers only, for, according to Stationmaster Bellingham's statement, 'We have received no instructions about parcels or goods traffic.'

WEEKDAYS / SUNDAYS

DOWN

Mileage M	Mileage C	DOWN	am	*Lewes arr. 11.17 am SO until 14th September inclusive*	PM	*Lewes arr. 1.14½ pm SO until 14th September inclusive*	PM	PM	*Until 26th October inclusive and again commences 27th January*	SX PM *From 28th October to 24th January inclusive*	SO PM *From 2nd November to 25th January inclusive*	am	PM	PM	PM	*Until 27th Oct. inclusive and again commences 2nd Feb.*	PM *From 3rd November to*
0	0	**EAST GRINSTEAD** dep	10 28		12 28		2 28	4 28		4 28	4 41	10 28	12 28	2 28	4 28		4 41
4	3	West Hoathly	10 36		12 36		2 36	4 36		4 36	4 49	10 36	12 36	2 36	4 36		4 49
6	28	Horsted Keynes ⓢ	10 40½		12 40½		2 40½	4 40½		4a41	4a54	10 40½	12 40½	2 40½	4 40½		4a54
10	66	Sheffield Park	10 50		12 50		2 50	4 50		4e53½	5e 6½	10 50	12 50	2 50	4 50		5e 6½
12	52	Newick and Chailey	10 55½		12 55½		2 55½	4 55½		5e 1½	5e14½	10 55½	12 55½	2 55½	4 55½		5e14½
17	16	Culver Jn. ⓢ	11 6½		1 6½		3 6½	5 6½		5 12½	5 25½	11 6½	1 6½	3 6½	5 6½		5 25½
20	35	**LEWES** arr	11 12½		1 12½		3 12½	5 12½		5 22	5 31½	11 12½	1 12½	3 12½	5 12½		5 31½

WEEKDAYS / SUNDAYS

UP

Mileage M	Mileage C	UP	am	am	*Starts 11.33 am and runs 3 mins. later throughout SO until 14th September inclusive*	PM	*Starts 1.33 pm and runs 3 mins. later throughout SO until 14th September inclusive*	PM	*Until 26th October inclusive and again commences 27th January*	PM *From 28th October to 25th January inclusive*	am	am	PM	PM	*Until 27th October inclusive and again commences 2nd February*	PM *From 3rd November to*
0	0	**LEWES** dep	9 30	11 30		1 30		3 30		3 30	9 30	11 30	1 30	3 30		3 30
3	19	Culver Jn. ⓢ	9 36	11 36		1 36		3 36		3 36	9 36	11 36	1 36	3 36		3 36
7	63	Newick and Chailey	9 47½	11 47½		1 47½		3b48½		3b48½	9 47½	11 47½	1 47½	3 47½		3b48½
9	49	Sheffield Park	9 53	11 53		1 53		3 53		3g57½	9 53	11 53	1 53	3 53		3g57½
14	7	Horsted Keynes ⓢ	10e 5	12e 5		2e 5		4e 5		4 7	10e 5	12e 5	2e 5	4e 5		4 7
16	32	West Hoathly	10 10½	12 10½		2 10½		4 10½		4b13½	10 10½	12 10½	2 10½	4 10½		4b13½
20	35	**EAST GRINSTEAD** arr	10 19	12 19		2 19		4 19		4 22	10 19	12 19	2 19	4 19		4 22

Timetable for the very basic reopened service for the period 7 August 1956-16 March 1958.

The curious use of tender engines was officially explained by the fact that the water columns at Sheffield Park and Horsted Keynes had been disconnected and therefore made it necessary to use an engine with sufficient water supply 'on tap' for the round trip, there not being time to go from Low Level to High Level at East Grinstead. It was ironical that most trains had a wait of about five minutes at Horsted Keynes, allowed for taking water that was not available even if required. The headlines said it all: 'A Cinderella Service'; 'A sulky service — just pique'; 'Sour Grapes'.

Many were the railway enthusiasts who, alerted by this resurrection wonder with all its attendant publicity, chose to travel the line, but few wrote up the experience at any length. One of the exceptions was Mike Esau, the well-known photographer. His account conveys something of the flavour of the line and, he admits, fired his youthful imagination, though of course he had no inkling of future events in this remote, mysterious part of the Sussex Weald. On Friday 28 December 1956, on a none too ideal day (for it rained or was dull for most of the time), Mike travelled to Brighton via Three Bridges and then behind steam to East Grinstead:

'There a short wait proclaimed the arrival of the train from Lewes, an amusing sight as it ambled in behind "E4" No 32502 with its one-coach load, a veteran LBSCR coach

'C2X' No 32440 passes through Imberhorne Cutting with the 12.28pm train from East Grinstead to Lewes on 21 March 1957, the service now down to a single coach. This was the site that East Grinstead District Council later selected for the town's rubbish tip. *Colin Hogg*

An interior view along the side corridor of the single coach used for the service in the last year or so of the line's life. Former LBSCR brake third No S3847S had no inside corridor doors to each 'compartment', over whose partitions one could look at one's immediate neighbours.
Martin Smith

and not very well filled at that, but a pleasing picture nevertheless. "C2X" No 32440 of Brighton shed, which had been inconspicuously shunting in the yard, now backed down onto the coach which the "E4" had propelled into the down platform, and prepared to leave. At East Grinstead seven passengers were in the train including myself, not a very inspiring number, although not surprising, considering the inconvenient service provided. We gathered speed down the bank and rushed through deserted Kingscote station at some 40mph, the old "C2X" swaying wildly. This station, together with Barcombe, was not provided for in the original LBSCR Act guaranteeing a service, rather ironical now as Barcombe has a large, developing housing estate near it, while Barcombe Mills station on the Uckfield line is nearly two miles away. The stops at West Hoathly and Horsted Keynes yielded nothing. The former station was unstaffed, but at Horsted the electric service from Haywards Heath warrants staff. It is odd to note that the whole station was completely repainted in 1955, just prior to the closure of the line.

'After a short stop at Horsted Keynes, we proceeded along the single track to Sheffield Park, where two passengers left. The up platform here is out of use and overgrown with weeds and grass but the old lamp standards are still in place, a nostalgic reminder of better days. All the signals have disappeared and the only ones are at East Grinstead, Horsted Keynes and Culver Junction. The fine LBSCR example on the down platform at Sheffield Park will be long remembered as part of that delightful country station. How well a day stands out in the spring of 1951, when an "I3" was glimpsed plodding out of the station on a misty afternoon, bound for Brighton. Continuing through undulating countryside, Newick & Chailey station was reached, perhaps the most rural on the line. Here we gained a passenger, even though the two villages which the station serves are a mile or so down the road. Then on we sped down to the levels around Lewes, rushing through the now closed Barcombe station with its nearby housing estate mentioned earlier, and thus to Culver Junction. The p/way slack over the wooden

The uninspiring end to Mike Esau's trip down the line on 28 December 1956. 'C2X' No 32440 stands at Lewes after arriving with the 10.28am from East Grinstead in pouring rain.
Mike Esau

The last visit of a Brighton Atlantic to the line took place on 24 February 1957. The last survivor, No 32424 *Beachy Head*, limps into Horsted Keynes with big-end trouble at the head of the Locomotive Club of Great Britain's 'Southern Counties Limited'. It had to be replaced by humble 'C2X' No 32437 on the next leg down the single line section to Lewes.
E. Wilmshurst

bridge is still in force as the junction is reached. In pouring rain No 32440 ran into Lewes with a total of six passengers, not an inspiring number, but nevertheless a train runs.'

Renewed Protest

But the threat of final closure remained and in 1957 the storm clouds gathered again and railtour societies once more pencilled in their specials to include a run over the line. To legalise the reclosing of the line, the Commission included in its British Transport Bill of March 1957 a clause to repeal the section of the original Act which imposed the statutory obligation to provide a service. This clause was opposed by all but two of the MPs in Sussex and petitioned against by Miss Bessemer. Once again the local telephone lines were abuzz as objectors to the closure talked of support. The BTC accountants had been busy behind the scene and had published a 'Marginal cost of working present restricted service' dated 12 May 1957, from which they deduced an annual net loss of £34,962, all to little purpose as this was discarded at the enquiry as of no relevance. On 2 August a letter was sent from the Central Transport Consultative Committee to all local bodies and registered objectors such as Bill Howe, giving formal notice of the Southern Region's intention to withdraw the service subject to the result of an enquiry to be held at the Town Hall, Lewes, between 9 and 11 October, together with a list of other addressees receiving the letter. On 21 August Bill was sent a further supplementary list and on 4 September a copy of the public notice that was to go out to the press. He had also received a letter from the Southern Region's Chief Commercial Manager, W. H. F. Mepsted, enclosing what was in fact a resubmission of the memorandum document presented back in 1954.

Meanwhile the next move of Miss Bessemer's local committee in the battle was to try and force a public enquiry into this illegal closure which was already being referred to locally as the 'Chailey Up' — being regarded as a parallel injustice to the recent Crichel Down affair. This enquiry would enable Members of Parliament to get the facts without bias and therefore allow them to decide for themselves the true course of the BTC's Bill to repeal the original Act.

On 29 August there had taken place a meeting of the local committee, at which Bill Howe felt rather put out, having received no invitation. He wrote to D. R. Walden-Jones, Clerk to the Chailey Rural District Council who would be preparing Counsel's brief, but received the reply that he was representing only local authorities and not other organisations or persons. Bill corresponded with S. R. Bostel of the Lewes-East Grinstead Railway & Transport Facilities Committee, who had solicited him regarding supporting their 'fighting fund', stating that 'Any balance left when this purpose has been achieved will be given to railway charities.'

On 24 September Bill sent Walden-Jones a memorandum setting out his grounds for objecting on much the same lines as his one of 1954, but additionally he charged the civil engineers of extravagant expenditure and wastefulness including the ruthless stripping of good signals, the lack of alternative bus facilities — just two at the end of the day for the convenience of children attending schools in Lewes — and he again stressed the strategic value of the line. He also enlisted the support of P.W.M. Lancaster of neighbouring Wapsbourne Farm, who sent in his reasons for retaining the line: 'Shopping and recreational facilities for my staff, and a good service for this farm, eg I bought a number of sleepers for a bridge. These could only be brought in as far as Haywards Heath. I bought a boar in Scotland which was sent by rail to Haywards Heath. From there I had to bring him on by hired lorry. Milk samples have to be taken to Haywards Heath.'

By July 1957 the press was once again hot on the closure trail. *The East Grinstead Courier* rallied the objectors, reminding them it was the last chance to state their case. 'The British Transport Commission is relying on a restatement of the 1954 case. It has not even taken the trouble to give up-to-date figures of traffic.' It was even accused of encouraging station staff to discourage use of the line by diverting passengers via Three Bridges. As to operating costs, the overall loss had been halved by using a basic service but the total takings had (not surprisingly) fallen to only £1,000 a year. 'BTC have stuck rigidly to the terms of the Act of Parliament, running just the requisite number of trains despite local protests,' eliciting the headline, 'Use of Bluebell Line is being discouraged.' An odd mention included electrification expected in 1962 or 1963 from London to East Grinstead to be extended down to Horsted Keynes and so reaching the coastal towns.

Above: While the British Transport Commission was in course of revoking the original Act of 1877, services continued. On 26 March 1957 Hither Green's 'C' 0-6-0 No 31724, which had come down to East Grinstead on the goods from Norwood, passes Milepost 16½ with the 10.28am East Grinstead-Lewes, having just crossed Imberhorne Viaduct as it heads towards Hill Place. *Colin Hogg*

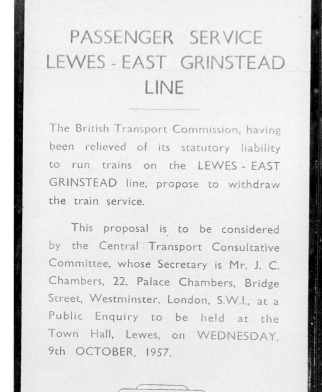

PASSENGER SERVICE LEWES - EAST GRINSTEAD LINE

The British Transport Commission, having been relieved of its statutory liability to run trains on the LEWES - EAST GRINSTEAD line, propose to withdraw the train service.

This proposal is to be considered by the Central Transport Consultative Committee, whose Secretary is Mr. J. C. Chambers, 22, Palace Chambers, Bridge Street, Westminster, London, S.W.I., at a Public Enquiry to be held at the Town Hall, Lewes, on WEDNESDAY, 9th OCTOBER, 1957.

SOUTHERN

Left: Notices were posted at all the stations open on the line, announcing the enquiry at Lewes, commencing on 9 October 1957, into the second proposed closure. This board was photographed at Newick & Chailey on 30 October. *John Beckett*

The Lewes Enquiry

So to what the local paper described as 'The last ditch fight to save from extinction the rail link between East Grinstead and the county town of Lewes'. The fate of the line was placed in the judicial balance of the Central Transport Consultative Committee as the public enquiry opened on Wednesday 9 October 1957. Lord Coleraine in his introduction stated that they were proceeding on the principle that the Transport Commission was there to serve the public. The public did not exist to serve the Transport Commission. 'We have not come here to hold an inquest upon previous proceedings in this case.' Mr Roland Adams QC, counsel for the BTC, was honest to admit 'The service we have provided since the line was reopened was intended to be not more than that which would enable us to comply with our statutory obligations at the least possible loss. It is my hope and my belief that you will consider irrelevant the costings etc of that service. The BTC had been running the line as cheaply as possible in fairness to their trust to the general body of railway users, having a duty not to see any more money sent down the drain than the whole national circumstances send down the drain anyhow. The real truth,' he said, 'is that the whole railway future as conceived in the 1920s has been revolutionised by the invention of the internal combustion engine and such branch lines do not pay.'

Much ground raked at the 1954 hearings was once more covered, but the battle was really joined over the vexed question of the reliability of costing formulae and sparks really flew on the second day over engine repair costs. Each of the three locomotives used on the 17-mile line cost the BTC £3,254 to keep in repair. This was almost twice the average for the whole railway system. Even the chairman was heard to comment: 'It seems quite extraordinary that such a large sum could be spent in repairs to these little engines pottering up and down this line.'

In the hot seat was David McKenna, the Southern Region's Assistant General Manager. He admitted that the actual cost of repairing engines had not been worked out, but calculated according to the engine's mileage, based on the average repair costs for all engines in the Region. In this he was taken to task by panel member R. G. M. Street who said 'it should not be beyond the Commission's ability to get a factual figure for the line rather than an average for the whole Region,' and talked

about 'coming against difficulties over our accounting apparatus'. Mr Percy Lamb, QC for the objectors, asked, 'Do you use the most modern and largest locomotives on the line?' and Mr McKenna replied, 'Not the largest, but modern ones.' Asked whether lightweight diesels had been considered before the proposal to close the line, he answered, 'We have not any lightweight diesel engines on the Southern Region.' He went on to say, 'The maximum we could ever see of the Bluebell line is a local line. We do not have the traffic potential to use this line in competition with the fast line.' Mr Lamb then told Mr McKenna, 'We have records of trains travelling at 60mph on the Bluebell line', leading to the most humorous moment of the enquiry when the latter, momentarily lost for words, replied, 'Well, they shouldn't!', to roars of laughter. A number of questions asked by individuals carried the proceedings to a third day, relating to Sunday services, attracting more passengers by reducing fares and the consideration of a cheaper push-pull service. It was significant that at this enquiry not one member of the public supported the proposal to close the line. All concerned parties left the Town Hall

'C2X' No 32437 passes Otye accommodation bridge with the 10.28am ex-East Grinstead on 30 September 1957, during the period of token service. *John Beckett*

'Little engines pottering up and down this line.' The driver of 'C2X' No 32536 has his eyes on the photographer as he approaches Freshfield with the 1.30pm Lewes-East Grinstead service. *J. J. Smith*

knowing they would have to wait several months before the result of the enquiry was made public.

Next month the *Railway Observer* passed comment:

'Somewhat unusually the hearing was in public and opponents of the closure were strongly represented. Although the basic fact that the line does not "pay" is probably beyond dispute, the railway did not help its case by producing a mass of figures purporting to be operating costs, some of which proved on detailed investigation to be quite fantastic. Notable in this respect was a figure which was claimed to represent the annual cost of repairing each of the "three tank engines which work the line". On being challenged this figure was admitted to be erroneous and was withdrawn, but the reference to three tank engines is itself somewhat puzzling, since on five days the number of engines working the line on the branch is four (two "C2X", one "E4", one BR 2-6-4T), none of which however spent more than a portion of its day on this line. On Saturdays and Sundays only two 2-6-4Ts are used.'

The Enquiry Report

The report of the Central Transport Consultative Committee, published in booklet form by HMSO for 2s in February 1958, is a mine of information, a snapshot of the line at this particular time. Would that such detailed surveys might have been recorded at earlier points in the history of the line, but it needed a case for closure to produce one!

After listing the members of the Committee, it proceeded to a description of the line to prove that 'Apart from the population of Lewes and East Grinstead, the inhabitants of the area served by this line do not amount to more than 7,000.' At Kingscote there were comparatively few houses near the station and West Hoathly was a village of 1,675 people. With regard to the double section of the line north of Horsted Keynes (pop. 1,148), 'It was the original intention of the Southern Railway and later that of the Southern Region to electrify the line at some future date. While this project has not entirely been abandoned, no definite work for carrying out such an electrification is at present contemplated.' Regarding the single track south, 'there is enough room for the track to be doubled without purchasing any further property or obtaining additional Parliamentary powers.' There were very few houses at Sheffield Park, Newick station was between the villages of Newick & Chailey , which together contained a fair rural population of about 3,000 people, and Barcombe, a village of 1,190 inhabitants, was the only station on the whole line near to the centre of a village. But only a mile away Barcombe Mills had an hourly service of steam trains, and it was the Southern Region's ultimate intention to electrify this route through Uckfield.

The following sections contained the general feeling of the committee, recording, 'their appreciation of the helpful manner in which Counsel made their representations'. The applicants, the Southern Region of British Railways, were represented by Mr Roland Adams QC and Mr H. Marnham. The Local Authorities concerned as objectors were represented by Mr Percy Lamb QC and Mr D. E. Peck. Ten members of the public appeared personally and 11 submitted evidence by letter. They had welcomed 'a spirit of consultation rather than litigation, and the cooperative and friendly manner which existed among all parties present'. The panel 'were left under no illusions about the depth of feeling which had been stirred by the decision to close the line, or about the very real measure of disturbance, inconvenience and

sometimes even hardship caused in a rural community by such a decision. We felt that unnecessary feeling had been created by the way in which the case for closing the Bluebell line had been presented in the past.'

Section 11 embraced the case for the objectors, which centred on the following main issues, which were countered in each of the following sections:

a) 'That the service could have been more economically operated than it was, and therefore that the losses were greater than they need have been.' The Committee's reply was that they did not feel that it was within their competence to sit in judgement upon the capacity of the BTC to operate a railway. A good deal of evidence, however, was put forward by objectors to show that the line had been managed uneconomically. A critical and interested public was quick to pick up any unusual event on the line, such as the occasional working of a Pacific heavy express engine (which sometimes happened for reasons of operational convenience), the undue time said to be spent at stations, and even the excess blowing-off of steam by engines — but the evidence amounted to no more than that. It may be that the number of permanent way staff on the line was higher than average, that heavier and larger engines were used than are usually seen on a branch line of this kind, or that porters were not always fully employed. All these things were alleged, but it was not seriously contended that any of them arose through operational incompetence. The committee felt that much of the evidence submitted to them was based upon a misunderstanding of the operational needs of a railway and upon lack of realisation that a branch line such as this had to be worked within the system as a whole. As to terminating at Lewes instead of running on to Brighton, Lewes had no depot, no locomotive staff and no facilities for cleaning, whereas the engines could be serviced at Brighton and had to go there in any case. As for introducing 'push-pull' trains, this was impracticable for operating reasons and many services went straight through to London.

(b) 'That if efforts had been made to modernise the service by the introduction of light diesel trains, it would have increased traffic receipts which, if it had not turned the loss into a profit, would have reduced it to manageable proportions.' It was countered by stating that despite adding £95,000 for the cost of vehicle and services, there would be no appreciably greater return, owing to the lack of traffic potential in the area.

(c) 'That the costs of an augmented service between East Grinstead and Three Bridges, introduced since the first closure, should have been set off against the savings shown by the closing of the Bluebell Line.' The reply was that the increase was not the result of closing the Bluebell line, but was mainly due to the growth of Crawley New Town.

(d) 'That the local bus services did not provide an adequate substitute for the railway passenger service, and that the 'zonal' service for freight was not as convenient as the railway goods service.' It was maintained that though the buses did not give services in the immediate vicinity of the stations equal to or as convenient as that provided by the trains, they formed an adequate network of country services. And again, there was no force in the argument that the zoning of goods traffic (that is, the system under which goods are

'Heavier and larger engines were used than are usually seen on a branch line of this kind.' Standard Class 4 2-6-4T No 80152 dwarfs its solitary lightweight coach as it storms through Hill Place Cutting with the 12.28pm train from East Grinstead to Lewes. *Mike Esau*

collected at a few railheads and transported to their destination by motor lorry) caused great inconvenience. In any case the zoning system was being applied generally throughout the country by the BTC.

(e) 'That the line was needed both as a relief to the main line from Lewes and Brighton to London via Haywards Heath, and as an emergency service in the event of the dislocation for any reason of that line.' The committee did not consider that the Lewes-East Grinstead line could be regarded as a relief line to London. It did not avoid congestion at Croydon near the point the line north of East Grinstead joined the main line. It would be impossible to run any fast trains over it unless it was both electrified and additional tracks laid for the passage of express services. This would certainly be an expensive and wasteful operation and the money would be better spent on improvements to the main line. As for being an alternative in an emergency, again it was not electrified and there were already alternative routes to London, one of which was already electrified (Mid-Sussex), and the other was likely to be electrified in the future (Uckfield).

(f) 'That the figures of savings were not based on facts but on costing formulae which were unsound, particularly in respect of the calculation of interest savings, renewals and locomotive repairs.' Here the committee were impressed by that part of the objectors' case which was based upon doubts as to the reliability of the costing formulae, eg locomotives which 'only spent part of a week, or even part of a day, on the line and the rest of the time at work on other parts of the system'. The report goes into considerable detail with regard to the 'costing exercise' listed in 10 separate appendices, many being repeats of the 1954 memorandum.

The report concluded: 'It is clear that a railway which loses at least £33,000 annually cannot be kept open in the public interest unless there is some major over-riding consideration of national policy which can only be satisfied by keeping the railway running. It seems to us to be clear, too, that the inconvenience and expense to individuals caused by the closing of the line is not in itself an over-riding consideration unless it is of exceptional proportions. No evidence was brought in the case before us to convince us that there was any over-riding circumstance of this nature. We must, therefore, recommend in the public interest that the train service between East Grinstead and Lewes be withdrawn.'

However, in conclusion the committee wished to make the following further recommendations regarding costing, asking that in future the BTC should furnish committees with detailed information covering the actual net outgoings which will cease to be incurred, the net income which may be expected to arise from the release or realisation of assets, and continuing or additional expenses, if any, following the cessation. 'We feel, therefore, that if a Railway Region cannot make out an adequate case for withdrawal of a service or the closure of a line on the direct factual savings arising therefrom, it should be prepared to continue to operate it until it can.' Their final word was to potential objectors to assist by stating how far their convenience and livelihood would be affected by such closure and, 'that they are of no assistance when their objections merely become prejudiced attacks upon the capacity and probity of the BTC, who are only trying in the national interest to save expense by rationalising their services.'

The Last Rites

Meanwhile the line continued to run with its token service. Newick & Chailey received a supply of new hurricane lamps, 'such is the only illumination on the station, the lamps being evenly spaced along the platform'. Bill Howe became resigned to the fact the line would close — there had been days at Sheffield Park when the takings were nil. It was no surprise when he heard that on 12 February 1958 the Minister of Transport had announced, in reply to the Hon Mrs Emmett (MP for East Grinstead), that the line would close from 17 March.

The media were quick to latch onto this as the story of the valiant fight by Madge Bessemer in the face of the big battalions hit the national headlines: 'The No 1 objector to closure of the Bluebell gives her views.' 'A battle lost with honour,' were the very words she used when interviewed and were carried by the local press on 18 February. She felt cheated in a way that an independent public inquiry had not

A delightful 1957 study, as in bright sunshine 'E4' No 32512 departs from Lewes station with the 3.30pm for East Grinstead, the guard having yet to close the door of his department. A vintage railway van stands parked in front of Bernard Thorpe & Partners' huge hoarding. *Peter Hay*

been called, and that the whole process had given grounds for serious misapprehension in the minds of the public. 'The commission may have achieved their object but they have done so in a manner which reflects little credit to themselves.' She concluded her long statement by thanking all her many supporters for their encouragement and assistance. Indeed, her

BRITISH RAILWAYS

CLOSING OF
EAST GRINSTEAD-LEWES LINE

On and from MONDAY, 17th MARCH, 1958, the passenger service on the line between EAST GRINSTEAD and LEWES, via SHEFFIELD PARK, will be withdrawn and the following stations closed :-

WEST HOATHLY
SHEFFIELD PARK
NEWICK & CHAILEY

HORSTED KEYNES will remain open for passenger and freight traffic, and be served by trains to and from HAYWARDS HEATH.

'Bus facilities in the area are provided by Southdown Motor Services Ltd.

(SOUTHERN)

Closure notice posted at local stations in February 1958. *E. Wilmshurst*

off-the-cuff statement that day was crystallised in a leaflet published by her Lewes East Grinstead Railway Transport and Facilities Committee: 'If the Bluebell line is closed, it will have been lost honourably after winning a moral victory which may benefit other branch lines.'

The biggest publicity event of her campaign came on 23 February when, according to the *Sussex Express and County Herald*, 'There were more people on Newick & Chailey railway station platform on Sunday afternoon than there have been for many years. They were not potential passengers on the famous Bluebell line, which is to be closed on 16 March, but had assembled because a BBC television team was there to make a film for inclusion in the feature *Tonight.*' It was a real hustle and bustle assembly with Mr Alan Whicker, TV commentator, interviewing local personalities including 'Miss R. E. M. Bessemer, the Rev W. P. Webb (Rector of Barcombe) who was Chairman of the Lewes & East Grinstead Railway and Transport Facilities Committee, and Mrs E. Pargitter, a school teacher at Danehill, who lived at Sheffield Park.' Also interviewed and filmed was Mr G. F. Manley, Chairman of the Society for the Reinvigoration of Unremunerative Branch Lines in the United Kingdom, with members who had travelled on the 12.28pm train from East Grinstead. Madge Bessemer had sought the aid of the SRUBLUK but found them 'sentimental and impracticable'. Keeping a watchful eye on the 50 or so audience was Mr J. W. Boothroyd, Stationmaster at Horsted Keynes, and Mr A. E. Kitcher from headquarters at Waterloo, together with other local officeholders. Miss Bessemer was the first to face the microphone and was questioned about the small number of people using the line — about 20 a day. She suggested that 'if properly handled, this line would carry a great many more, and goods as well'. The Rev W. P. Webb apologised to the stationmaster for not being in possession of a 2d platform ticket. 'We should have a job to find you one,' replied Mr Boothroyd. Mr Whicker hurled at him, 'You have lost this case, and the railway people are going to close this line.' Quickly the Rector replied, 'I suppose you may say we have lost, but that is only comparative. We hope that by our efforts we shall, at any rate, have succeeded in doing something — that it will lead to some kind of legislation that this kind of caper will not happen again.' As Philip Webb turned away, he said, 'That is the longest sermon I have preached for some time. A collection may now be taken!' By then another train was due, this time from Lewes, and as the

Mr G. F. Manley, Chairman of SRUBLUK, being interviewed by Alan Whicker for the BBC television programme *Tonight* on the down platform at Newick & Chailey. Miss Bessemer was among the crowd there on 23 February 1958 and was also interviewed. *Martin Smith*

Six Maunsell coaches were considered ample to cope with those making a last journey on the closing day of the line. Class 4 Tank No 80011 was in charge for the first two return journeys and is seen leaving East Grinstead with the 12.28pm for Lewes on 16 March 1958. *Geoffrey S. Robinson*

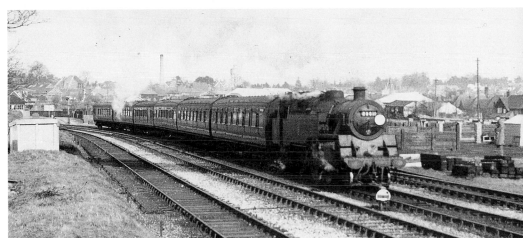

Class 4 Tank No 80154, the last new engine to emerge from Brighton Works, was chosen for the final pair of return journeys. It arrived on duty bearing a headboard support and is enterprisingly photographed approaching Sharpthorne Tunnel with the 2.28pm East Grinstead to Lewes. This ground-level view clearly shows the change of gradient into West Hoathly station. *John Beckett*

The Bluebell 'Victory' decorative headboard is adjusted by a member of the station staff at East Grinstead, prior to No 80154 shunting across to the down platform, where a crowd of almost a thousand wait to board the last train. *Mike Esau*

The animated scene as the throng of well-wishers await the somewhat belated departure of the 4.28pm to Lewes, the signal having been lowered some while back. The signalman at East Grinstead South Box waits patiently by, guarding against any illegal crossing of the tracks. *Gerald Daniels*

camera crew pulled their apparatus to a safer position, all six of the train passengers leaned out of the carriage window, wondering what on earth all the fuss was about.

The final day loomed up rapidly and whole sets of compartments were booked ahead by various groups in the county. There was even talk of including a buffet car in the formation. On the penultimate day 500 passengers were carried, anxious to see the line before it closed. Class 4 2-6-4T No 80011 worked the first two return journeys on the final day, with a rake of six Maunsell coaches, to be relieved for the final two round journeys by No 80154, the last locomotive built at Brighton Works, in 1957. Chris Gammell was aboard the 3.30pm from Lewes, where 'a large Sussex gentleman with a flowing beard and hobnail boots joined the train. The compartment in the Maunsell corridor coach was packed. A splendid, if doom-laden, discourse was delivered to the crowded compartment: "Someone's given me this 'ere leaflet about the Bluebell Railway — they don't stand a chance. Who's gowin' to travel to this place in the middle of nowhere?

I bet a fiver they pack up in a few months — wasting their time!" Well, today, we are still looking for this Sussex gentleman to claim our fivers!'

The 3.30pm up from Lewes arrived at East Grinstead at the time it should have departed. Further time was lost in adding three more coaches to the formation and fixing the fine colourful headboard in the shape of a large V with a handpainted bluebell in the middle, fringed with laurel leaves, heather and daffodils, betokening the moral victory won by the local people. Madge Bessemer had sat up late the previous night, cutting out more than 100 blue 'V' signs, and handed them out to be stuck on the train windows. The driver was 65-year-old Mr R. Roser of Brighton who was to retire on 27 March after 48 years' service, accompanied by Fireman Ernie Jackson. The train had two guards, Harry Stevens and Fred Bryant, both of Lewes, and also porter Bill Hobden to assist with checking the tickets on the train.

Some 870 people travelled on the final trip, though some estimates adding gatecrashers at intermediate stations gave a

The end, as passengers disembark at Lewes and throng round the engine and crew. The splendid headboard is being removed as the line is declared officially closed. *Lyndon Rowe*

figure of over 1,000. Stationmaster R. Neills of East Grinstead escorted two guests of honour who received complimentary tickets from the BTC, Miss Kate Longley (83) of Haywards Heath who rode on the first train and Charles Newnham (91) of Balcombe, who as a boy had worked on the construction of the line, receiving a wage of 9s a week of which he gave 8s 9d to his mother, and who said of the line: 'Like me, it has had a good life.' Also present was Mr Robert Coomber born 1875, a local builder, who was one of the schoolchildren taken to see the passing of the first train. Few noticed little Mark Faber, the Prime Minister's grandson, travelling incognito in the care of the wife of the local porter, arranged by Lady Dorothy Macmillan, but who could fail to notice Mr S. R. Bostel, secretary of Miss Bessemer's committee, a qualified miniature engine driver who made the journey wearing an engine driver's cap and overalls. He was president of the Sussex Miniature Locomotive Society, popularly known as 'The Shovel and Pump Club'.

The 'funeral' took place in anything but a funereal atmosphere. ITN and BBC newsreel crews covered the proceedings while photographers were at every vantage point along the line and the train frequently had to whistle to clear the tracks. The train left East Grinstead at 4.48pm, seen off by 1,000 people, and was to arrive at Lewes exactly an hour later, 36 minutes late. It departed exploding detonators every few yards and Driver Roser gave blast after blast on the whistle. At each of the six intermediate stations that Sunday crowds in jolly mood flocked to see the last train go through. Villagers crowded onto the weed-covered stations, singing, cheering, waving flags and letting off fireworks. There were more fog signals on the line, blasts from a hunting horn, but some spectators stood bareheaded with heads bowed. The speedometer in the cab registered 50mph on the down gradients, in between two interruptions in the hour's trip when the train had to stop through over-enthusiastic passengers pulling the communication cord. No one bothered to find the culprits. 'This is no day for nametaking,' said Guard Harry Stevens, grinning broadly. At Newick were Mrs West, aged 93, of Chailey and the 91-year old widow of Jared Brooks who had laid the first brick at the station and later was farm foreman to the Bessemer family. On arrival at Lewes passengers clambered out to rush and shake hands with the crew, one thrusting half a crown in

each's hand. Many enthusiasts took the opportunity to travel on the empty run as the stock was taken through to Brighton for stabling. The *Sussex Express and County Herald's* headline next day said it in a nutshell — 'Bluebell line closes in a blaze of glory'.

The contribution of an anonymous 'poet' provides a fitting close to this chapter:

'With Parliamentary precision
The Minister gave his decision
In terms concise and not too starchy.
It said that, round about mid-March, he,
Confronted by financial facts,
Would be compelled to wield the axe.
Sussex must face up to the blow,
The 'Bluebell line' at last must go,
For like so many charming folk,
It, too, was beautiful but broke.
Of course, the local population
Expressing righteous indignation
And rallying round from near and far
(As usual, by motorcar)
Characteristically enthused
About the line they seldom used.
Enthused, alas, but all in vain;
This was the death knell of the train
With no more puff-puffs on the go,
Nature resumes the status quo,
Ashes to ashes, dust to dust,
Naught can escape this mortal 'must',
Yet here's a thought that's comforting
There will be bluebells there next Spring!'

Ex-LMS 2-6-4T No 42070, based at Three Bridges, has arrived at East Grinstead Low Level and backs its train up the spur line to the High Level goods yard to face Londonwards with a departure from the High Level station. The year is 1958 following the closure of the line to Lewes. The up line had been placed out of use and the down line retained on a 'care and maintenance' basis. *Lens of Sutton*

The Avonside diesel *Kimberley* shunts at Barcombe as Pittrail commences the dismantling of the southern section of the line on 22 January 1960. *Klaus Marx*

The contractor's depot set up at Newick & Chailey, the area stacked with track panels which will be dismantled and removed by road. Meanwhile through all this, the local coal merchant carries on his business. Today the whole area has been redeveloped with housing. *Peter Hay*

21.
Resolution

Demolition South of Sheffield Park

The history of a line does not necessarily end with its closure. Things can and do happen, sometimes many years after the exploding fog detonators have sped the last train along its final journey, the crowds of sentimental enthusiasts and sorrowing local folk have dispersed and the station lamps have been dimmed by staff who will be moving elsewhere.

A few days after this a goods engine will chug down the line picking up any stray or derelict vans or trucks in any of the line's sidings, and that will truly constitute the last working before the demolition train arrives. This ritual was observed as far back as 7 July 1955, when the 8.34am (engine and brake van) left Lewes for West Hoathly, returning at 10.35am and clearing all empty wagons from West Hoathly, Newick and Barcombe (apparently there were none at Sheffield Park at that date!). Sometimes an enthusiasts' special travels the length of the line, usually on the day following the termination of public services. However, in this case, due to the 1955 rail strike, the RCTS 'Wealden Limited' in the end took place on 14 August 1955, the last date on which the track was to have been available. It was originally scheduled for 12 June, the day following the line's first closure (in fact the last public services ran on 28 May).

Within a year, on 7 August 1956, came a reopening, not in the usual run of fortunes of closed branch lines, and certainly unique in the way it was achieved. But the final closure was delayed only until the Act in question could be repealed in Parliament. On 23 April 1958, some five weeks after the final rites, the agents and representatives of most of the greater iron, steel and railway materials firms were taken over the line south of Horsted Keynes to formulate their tenders. This was neither the first, which took place in 1955, nor the last, for the new bids had to be re-tendered late in 1959 in view of the fact that the five mile section north of the bridge over the A275 at Sheffield Park was being negotiated with the Lewes-East Grinstead Railway Preservation Society. On 10 October 1958 Bill Howe received a letter, from BR's Estate and Rating Surveyor, inviting applications from those with property adjoining the line.

Next came the demolition of the southern part of the line to Culver Junction by Pittrail Ltd of Aldridge, Staffs. The contract was specified under three schedules and these provide a fascinating insight into how a line was lifted, what was taken away and what was left. They are reproduced below, having been transcribed at the time of the contract:

Schedule A
1. All permanent way from the tips of the points leading onto the main line at Culver Junction, up to and including the public road under-line bridge at 6m 11ch, except for items listed in Schedule B.
2. All sleeper-built platelayers' huts, including brick chimneys.
3. The steel/wrought-iron girders, troughing (gutters) handrailings and cross girders at the underline bridges at 1m 79ch, 2m 68ch, 5m 49ch and 6m 11ch. Steelwork to be taken down to the first joint above ground level of supporting columns where these exist.
4. The rail timbers and track only to be removed from the bridge at 1m 53ch.
5. Cattle pens at Barcombe and Newick & Chailey.
6. Platform roofing and supports at Barcombe and Newick & Chailey.
7. Notice boards not listed in Schedules B or C.
8. All gradient boards.
9. All gradient posts.
10. All telegraph poles, copper wire, signal posts, rodding, etc.
11. Dormant weighing machines No 2953/4 at Newick & Chailey.
12. Dormant weighing machine No 2525 at Barcombe station.

Schedule B
Details of items to be removed by purchaser and handed over to the district engineer at Horsted Keynes yard (loaded onto rail wagons) to his requirements.
1. All concrete track monuments.
2. All cast-iron notice plates worded, 'Stop, Look and Listen.'
3. All buffer stops complete, together with the fishplates, at Barcombe and Newick & Chailey.
4. Concrete load gauges at Barcombe and Newick & Chailey.
5. 'Beware of Train' board at Barcombe.
6. The concrete sectional 'Fogging' huts.

Schedule C
Details of items which are not included in the contract and must be left in position.
1. Station residences at Barcombe and Newick & Chailey.
2. Goods shed and brick-built platelayers' hut at Newick & Chailey.
3. All 'Trespass' and 'Right of Way' notices.
4. Bridge at 1m 53ch, excluding fixtures referred to in Schedule A item 4.
5. All underline brick arch bridges.
6. All boundary fencing and gates.
7. All mileposts.

This extremely rare photograph of an ex-SECR 'L' 4-4-0 on the line was taken on 14 November 1958. This Lingfield race special from Brighton via Ardingly climbs the grade from Kingscote past the long line of withdrawn goods wagons stored on the up line at this period. *John Beckett*

The last train to run was the contractor's diesel *Kimberley* with its rake of LNWR bogie trucks, a plate off one of which, inscribed 'Director of Stores Admiralty', found its way into the Bluebell Museum at the time. Several enthusiasts enjoyed rides aboard *Kimberley* during the spring but soon the rolling stock was trapped on the only remaining section of unlifted track at Newick & Chailey station. Huge, long lorries with trailers took away the materials throughout the summer. In August 1962 a bulldozer was noted scraping the ballast from the trackbed, and Newick & Chailey goods yard began a new lease of life as the local Urban District Council's rubbish dump. The station houses there and at Barcombe remained inhabited for several years by railway folk while the lineside railings and fences continued to be maintained by gangers from the East Grinstead and Lewes districts. Then came the establishment of a housing estate on the site of Newick & Chailey station, scotching any idea of the nascent Bluebell Railway expanding southwards. Still on the map, the earthworks and bridge abutments on this southern section will remain for many decades, for generations of antiquarians to walk along the overgrown and swampy trackbed and pick their way through the brambles which delight to flourish on derelict lines, as they attempt to reconstruct the past. Such is the fate of a rural branch line, certainly in degree more happy than those of urban areas, where the courses are soon virtually untraceable, so heavily are the areas redeveloped.

The line north of Horsted Keynes had a quite different and again virtually unparalleled story — a line in a state of suspense. Ever since closure, the fate of this section had been a subject of rumour, ill-informed comment, varying plans for its revival and indecision in high places. One week one heard of future electrification from South Croydon through East Grinstead to join up with the Ardingly branch at Horsted

Keynes in 1962, then probably in 1964, possibly at some time in the future. Then shortly afterwards one learned of plans for diesel services incorporated into the proposed conversion of the Tunbridge Wells area eliminating all steam services. Hopes were rising towards a reopening when news filtered in that the track was shortly to be taken up; enthusiasts rushed in to take last photographs of the stations with track in situ. 'No', said a local wiseacre, 'they're keeping the line for storing old goods wagons,' while elsewhere it was whispered that the line was to be left open for emergencies in the event of a blockage on the Brighton main line. Hopes rose again when a tracklaying unit visited East Grinstead; the condemned goods wagons would be going and the line would reopen this year, next year, sometime, never. The best one could make out of all this confusion was to examine the occasional reports of some of the better-reputed railway journals. Ever since the second closure, the line had been kept well in the public eye by the press, who were keen to report the fortunes of not only the Bluebell Railway Preservation Society but of the line through Horsted Keynes, which from early 1960 had become its only rail link with the national system.

A report at the time of closure stated that the northern section would remain open for use by occasional specials and emergency workings, and described this part of the line as, 'not dead but sleeping', since eventual electrification, it assumed, might well see a restoration of passenger traffic. The Lingfield race specials originating from Brighton were frequently reported. For instance on 19 and 20 March 1958, only a few days after the closure, they were running up through Ardingly. This was nothing new to this line but the locomotive circumstances were different. For example, the specials of 14 and 15 November 1958 were worked by 'L' class 4-4-0s Nos 31778 and 31777 on those respective days, a

Following the closure the down line from East Grinstead to Horsted Keynes remained open for limited use, including a number of Ramblers' specials. Earlier this train had been hauled from Greenford by the GWR record-breaking 4-4-0 No 3440 *City of Truro* as far as East Croydon, before 'K' No 32342 of reopening fame took over for the run to Ardingly, where its partial payload of enthusiasts, as opposed to ramblers, photograph the special at leisure. *Lens of Sutton*

'C2X' No 32535 in highly polished condition heads the new Bluebell Railway Preservation Society's pioneer railtour special across Imberhorne Viaduct on 12 July 1959. Another of the class stands in the Low Level yard at East Grinstead with the goods from Norwood. The special was on a circular route from Tunbridge Wells. *John Beckett*

class that had come over from the Eastern Section to Brighton to take over the duties of the Brighton Atlantics, the last of which had sadly been scrapped earlier in the summer. On their outward journey these race trains used the down line from Horsted Keynes to East Grinstead, the up line having been recently filled with stored wagons, and single line working using pilotmen was specially instituted for them.

Resuscitation

Meanwhile Madge Bessemer's magnificent rearguard action and 'never say die' attitude had not been in vain. It was the breathing space provided between 1955 and 1958 by her valiant intervention that procured the time and publicity which inspired a group of young students to call a well-attended meeting exactly a year after the second closure on 15 March 1959 in the Church Lads' Brigade Hall at Haywards Heath, to form a Lewes-East Grinstead Railway

Preservation Society. Chris Campbell, David Dallimore, Martin Eastland and Alan Sturt had caught the vision that what had been achieved on the narrow gauge Talyllyn and Festiniog Railways in North Wales in saving and reopening those lines could also be effected on a standard gauge line. They realised that something more than litigation was required if the Bluebell line was to be saved, and decided that private enterprise might succeed where public services had failed. They met with Madge Bessemer, but she wanted commuter services and the whole line back in operation, including her beloved Newick & Chailey. Having won the battle but lost the war, she eventually reconciled herself to the closure and got on with the many things that filled her busy life, leaving the enthusiasts to pursue their rather different interests. She died on 21 April 1985 at the ripe age of 87. The story of the Bluebell Railway is outside the remit of this volume, but it needs to be borne in mind that its birthpangs took place alongside the fading fortunes of the rest of the remaining sections of the former LEGR.

The final Ramblers' special to use the line, the 9.50am Victoria-Ardingly, passes West Hoathly on 27 September 1959 behind 'Battle of Britain' Pacific No 34068 *Kenley*. The leading coach was reserved for members of the Bluebell Railway Preservation Society on their way to Horsted Keynes and then on, by bus, to attend a rally day at Sheffield Park. *S. C. Nash*

That occasion was not the only public meeting that concerned the line, for earlier that week on 10 March one had been called by the local East Grinstead Urban Council. There Mr W. C. Collins, District Traffic Superintendent, not only soothed the complaints about the poor local services by promising that better rolling stock displaced from the Kent Coast services would be introduced on certain trains in the summer service, but further stated that 1964 would see the electrification of the London to East Grinstead line, prior to which diesel units would be introduced as an interim measure. Many read into this the revival of the section south to Horsted Keynes, for local people were much inconvenienced by the detour to Three Bridges involving a change of trains to reach destinations to the south.

For a while things continued to happen on the closed northern section. It was visited by a series of 'Bluebell' specials, the forerunner being a Ramblers' train on 11 May 1958 which had come through from Greenford behind *City of Truro* as far as East Croydon, and on to East Grinstead, Horsted Keynes and Ardingly headed by 'K' Mogul No 32342, the same engine incidentally which had hauled the first train up the Sheffield Park section at the first reopening on 7 August 1956. Fourteen months later followed the inaugural BRPS special behind 'C2X' No 32535, which made special stops for photography at Kingscote (which had last seen a passenger train call on 28 May 1955) and West Hoathly, before arriving at a very crowded Horsted Keynes. It continued via Ardingly and Lewes and paused at Culver Junction to enable participants to pay their respects. On 27 September another Ramblers' special behind unrebuilt Bulleid Pacific No 34068 *Kenley* travelled the section. It came down from Victoria with a BRPS Rally Day coach at the front and, after stopping for water at East Grinstead Low Level, carried on to Ardingly from where it returned in the evening.

Line in Limbo

The shadows of winter closed in, but they were not the only shadows. Foreboding increased as a speed restriction of 40mph was imposed between East Grinstead and Horsted Keynes, and a magazine reported: 'It is now believed that total abandonment of this section is now imminent.' During the summer it had not only been used by Lingfield race specials and Ramblers' excursions but also a number of times by the Sunday 4.45am London Bridge-Eastbourne. On 7 October ex-LMS tank No 42067 worked on a race special which remains on record as the last passenger train working over this section while in national ownership. The only other workings after that date were some ballast trains engaged in the recovery of material which had previously been deposited at the lineside in readiness for a programme of track renewals which had now been cancelled and the gradual clearance over the winter period to retrieve the several hundred condemned wagons stored on the up line north of Horsted and deliver them by the trainload for breaking up at Newhaven. Apparently simultaneously during this period, opportunity was taken to dispose of the sets of underframes that had been stabled in the siding by the signalbox at Horsted Keynes. One of these trips resulted in the accident on Sheriff Mill Viaduct when the rearmost frames broke away and ran down the gradient, crashing into the end of the line of redundant coaching stock still stored there at the time. The locomotive involved was 'K' No 32340, while there is a picture of No 32350 collecting further underframes in March 1960. Some of the damaged stock was still in the sidings on 17 May 1960, when the Bluebell Railway took delivery of its first locomotive, *Stepney*. The last workings of all by BR locomotives were in the autumn of 1960, when the sidings at Kingscote and West Hoathly were lifted. No 32353 was the engine involved at the latter on 21 October 1960. The outlook was ominous. The apparent intention to discontinue even occasional workings over this stretch was supported by the absence of the usual race specials from Brighton to Lingfield for the meeting on 13/14 November 1959. Passengers from the coast were invited to travel via Three Bridges and East Grinstead by ordinary trains with two changes en route. An observer commented in print that 'the local clientele are unlikely to take kindly to treatment of this sort after being 'spoilt' for so long; the traffic will presumably be lost to road transport in the future!'

At the end of the year all optimism vanished, judging by a report which filled many with gloom and concern. 'Hopes that the East Grinstead-Horsted Keynes line might be eventually revived as part of a through electrified route now appear to have become very slender, and the connecting Horsted Keynes-Haywards Heath line is itself reported to be under consideration for closure.' There was just cause for holding such opinions, since with the new winter timetable the Ardingly branch had lost its Sunday service, a fact always interpreted from recent experience as a sign of squeezing the

traffic out of a branch and producing substantial evidence for a closure in the none too distant future. One could sense among BRPS members a deep worry and misgiving as they visualised the possibility of their small 4½-mile stretch being totally severed from the main line system. Anxious questions were asked at the Society's Brighton Pavilion meeting in February 1960, which called forth the fighting reply that if the worst came to the worst they could manage without a rail link. Had not Pittrail brought down their demolition diesel, trucks and crane all by road? The point was further proven by the arrival soon after of the Dorking Limestone Quarry engines *Baxter* and *Townshend Hook* by the same method. However, and fortunately, this did not become the general rule yet, as during 1960 the tide of fortunes was to change once more. The

Above: Derek Cross took numerous photographs of the workings, mostly behind Class 4 2-6-4Ts, which cleared the up line north of Horsted Keynes of hundreds of stored goods wagons. Taking advantage of the low winter sunshine and cold morning air on 25 January 1960, he has captured a superb moment as No 80140 eases its load through West Hoathly, its yard still occupied by redundant wagons. *Derek Cross*

Right: In March 1960 'K' No 32350 brings a load of coach frames from Lancing for storage at Horsted Keynes. It is captured near Ardingly, whose down home signal is seen on the left. *Derek Cross*

21 October 1960 was the day the tracks in the goods yards at Kingscote and West Hoathly were lifted. The scene at the latter shows the last member of the 'K' class, No 32353, in charge of the P/way special. A heavy rail crane is seen at work on the up line by the goods yard. *S. C. Nash*

fate of the link sections to the outer world hung on the result of The Bluebell Railway Preservation Society's efforts to reopen the Sheffield Park section.

Truncation back to Ardingly

The Lewes & East Grinstead Railway's 1883 branch, running southwest from Horsted Keynes to join the Brighton main line at Copyhold Junction, also suffered vicissitudes, strangely, it may seem at first, in connection with the Kent Coast electrification schemes. At the beginning of 1959 it was proposed to use the down line between Horsted Keynes and Ardingly for berthing the new electric stock waiting to enter service, the approximately hourly train service between these points being catered for by single line working over the up line. Units assigned for storage were taken up as far as Horsted Keynes, run onto the down line and parked from the Ardingly end. An electrified track was essential to enable heaters to be kept in operation. The stored 4CEP units were taken out at frequent intervals for maintenance runs, so the branch was not exactly quiet. On the first day of March 1959 this long, green snake contained sets 7105/10/1/6-9/22/3/6-

31/3-7. The last day of the Ramsgate, Dover and Sheerness steam workings on the Chatham section was Sunday, 14 June, the great changeover being effected during the night of 14/15 June. The Ardingly branch must have been a stimulating sight that weekend, as the long electric snake split up into shorter sections and rolled away. Of the steam coaching stock displaced, a considerable portion was sent directly to Newhaven or transferred to other areas. Four of the Kent Coast steam sets totalling 41 vehicles were despatched to Horsted Keynes, where they were parked on the down line previously used for the new electric stock, to await transfer to Newhaven for breaking up. By the end of July an unbroken rake of withdrawn coaches was parked on the down line between Ardingly and Horsted Keynes, and in Horsted Keynes station and beyond. That ambitiously built junction seems always to have been chosen as a dumping ground for rolling stock right from its earliest Brighton days.

At this same time one interesting development took place regarding the future of the link line. Peter Hay, who was Rules Assistant to the Traffic Manager at Redhill, was asked to investigate a proposal by the Amey Roadstone Co to set up a base for a plant in one of the local goods yard sites. Peter was asked for his advice as to whether it should be at Ardingly or Horsted Keynes, and to report back within a week. He confirmed Ardingly as the more favourable location, the

The extraordinary scene taken on 9 May 1959 of the seemingly unending line of new Kent Coast electric stock awaiting entry to service in five weeks' time. The section is the straight from Ardingly, visible as far as the curve just short of Lywood Tunnel. *S. C. Nash*

The new electric units were replaced by steam stock rendered redundant as a result of the Kent Coast electrification. Nearest the camera, bearing the dreaded white circled cross of condemnation, is 'ironclad' BTK No 4047, seen with Maunsell stock on 7 August 1960, the day the Bluebell Railway opened for public services. *David Wigley*

A most unusual surprise was the use of Bulleid 'Q1' 0-6-0 No 33018 to remove a rake of condemned stored coaches near Ardingly station for breaking up, seen on 24 February 1963, towards the end of one of the most severe winters in recent memory. The photographer confesses, 'This was a disappointing day as the last thing I wanted to see on the job was a "Flying dustbin", then little realising its historic value.' *David Clark*

The Amey Roadstone plant was first set up on the site of the former goods yard at Ardingly. Later, following the demolition of the station platforms, it expanded to take in the whole area of the station site but kept the station house at road level for use as offices. The scene here in 1965 is already far removed from 'the most lovely of all places'. *Lens of Sutton*

The 'Blue Belle' return working from Sheffield Park passes Ardingly, carrying on board the ill-famed Dr Beeching, the BR closure specialist. He had been invited down that day to open a new halt on the Bluebell Railway at Holywell. It closed two years later, due to causing congestion on the country lanes. Perhaps that was no surprise as it was opened on April Fool's Day 1962. *Peter Hay*

continued full upkeep of Lywood Tunnel and Sheriff Mill Viaduct adding considerably to the costs if sited at Horsted Keynes — a decision the BRPS can be grateful for in view of its future developments.

At the time the closure beyond Ardingly was announced, some 50 condemned coaches remained on the former down line between Horsted Keynes and Lywood Tunnel, those between the tunnel and Ardingly having been removed a few at a time, mostly to Newhaven for breaking up. One load of 13 was noted on 11 October 1963 departing double-headed by 'N' 2-6-0s Nos 31831 and 31873.

It was at this time that the Bluebell became aware that the last surviving Brighton coach on the English mainland, typifying the LBSCR's conventional passenger stock, lay among the surviving stock at Lywood, and the Bluebell's General Manager Horace May promptly sought, but in vain, to put in a 'stopper' to reserve Set 714 for purchase. Alas, ex-

LBSCR coach No 6237 that had been used in solo for months on end on the 'sour grapes' service, had already been swept away to Newhaven, where little time was ever lost in putting arrivals there to the torch. By way of consolation, it is pleasing to note that four of the vehicles stabled there survive today.

Not only did the fledgling Bluebell Railway use the branch for the delivery of its locomotives and rolling stock ('Terrier' No 55 on 17 May 1960, the pair of 'P' Tanks Nos 323 and 27 on 27 June 1960 and 18 March 1961 respectively, Adams radial No 488 on 12 July 1961, 'Dukedog' 4-4-0 No 9017 on 15 February 1962, the North London Tank No 2650 on 28 March 1962, 'E4' No 473 on 16 October 1962 and another 'Terrier', No 32636 on 13 May 1964), but the Bluebell Railway's sole link with the national network saw a succession of 'Blue Belle' specials which brought several strangers past Ardingly. These are tabulated as follows:

Date	Title	Route	Locos Passing Ardingley
22.4.61	Bluebell Special No 2	Brighton-Horsham-Three Bridges-East Grinstead-Oxted-'Cuckoo' line - Lewes-Haywards Heath-Horsted Keynes (Bluebell connecting train to Sheffield Park) and back to Brighton via main line	'E4s' 32479 & 32564 (also made a return trip light-engine to Haywards Heath to take water)
1.4.62	The 'Blue Belle'	London Bridge-Sheffield Park and return (carrying the notorious Dr Beeching to the line!)	GNR 'J52' No 1247 (through to Sheffield Park)
21.10.62	The 'Victory Belle'	Victoria-Sheffield Park and return	'T9' No 120 to Haywards Heath Bluebell Nos 55 & 488
31.3.63	The 'Spring Belle'	Victoria-Sheffield Park and return	BR 'Cl4' No 80084 + 'E4' 473 to Haywards Heath Bluebell 473 and 488 top'n'tail to Sheffield Park
15.9.63	The 'Scottish Belle'	Victoria-Sheffield Park and return (120 & 123 light-engine visit to Horsted Keynes after turning at Brighton)	Caledonian Single 123 and 'T9' 120 to Haywards Heath Bluebell 473 and 488 to Horsted Keynes
27.10.63	The 'Brighton Blue Belle'	Brighton-Sheffield Park and return (last passenger train down Ardingly branch)	Bluebell 55 & 473

The Bluebell Railway's preserved 'E4' 0-6-2T No 473 *Birch Grove* takes a hire turn at the end of June 1964, as it heads a load of track panels lifted near Ardingly station. The eastern portal of Lywood Tunnel is seen on the extreme left and nearer to the train the fixed distant signal for Horsted Keynes. *Roy Hobbs*

On 17 October 1962 the daily papers carried a couple of small paragraphs reporting that formal notice had been given by BR to close the section between Horsted Keynes and Ardingly on 31 December. The headline — 'Bluebell Link Threatened' — soon had the press on the phone to the Bluebell's General Manager Horace May, who said that members were being asked if they wished to take over the closed section, their sole link with the national system and means of bringing in new rolling stock to their line. But the Southern Region stated it was unwilling to grant any further leases and it was now the Commission's policy to sell all unwanted lines. The asking price was somewhere between £25,000 and £30,000 and Sheriff Mill Viaduct would need to have £10,000 spent on it in the next three years.

Then on 16 November the *Evening News* was first to report, 'Bluebell Line Link reprieved', as two objections had been raised to the proposal and a TUCC enquiry was therefore necessary. A barely publicised enquiry took place in early spring, at which BR promised that if the section was shut down, they would continue cheap day excursions to Sheffield Park using a bus connection between Haywards Heath and the Bluebell Railway. The closure announcement for 27 October 1963, linked by the papers with 'Dr Beeching's Axe', came as no surprise. The last regular train, the 6.16pm Horsted Keynes-Seaford, was most unusually formed of 6PAN unit No 3033, BR having from previous experience learned that there was always a high turnout of mourners at their 'funerals'. Many dressed up in Victorian top hats and frock coats to pay their last respects, the majority, who were Bluebell members, choosing to travel in the 'Brighton Blue Belle' special that left Horsted Keynes at 6.40pm to the strident fanfare of locomotive whistles lasting at least half a minute. Setting out into the gathering twilight,

the two Bluebell engines, Nos 55 and 473, returning from Brighton about 9pm, were thought at the time to be the last working of all through Ardingly.

With the closure of the Haywards Heath link line from 28 October 1963, following the run of the 'Brighton Blue Belle' the previous day, the now-designated 'Ardingly Branch' was converted to a siding and reduced to single track, using the former down line. Access to the up main and up local lines at Copyhold Junction was severed, and the goods trains to Ardingly commenced travelling up the down local line from Haywards Heath to the junction.

Just prior to the disused tracks being lifted, the latest locomotive acquisition by the Bluebell Railway slipped through past Lywood on 13 May 1964. 'Terrier' No 32636 propelled the 1908 LBSCR van which it had collected from the yard at Haywards Heath, the very last traffic movement along the branch — and a 'Brighton' one at that. It was the twilight of the LEGR line leading to the darkness of night before the dawning of a new day. Lifting of the derelict track commenced on 15 July 1964 at the Ardingly end, and by 21 September the contractor had reached Horsted Keynes, completing the lifting of the former link to the Brighton main line. Any hopes of ever reopening that section was dowsed by the demolition of Sheriff Mill Viaduct in July/August 1968 in the interests of straightening out the country lane below. Not long after, Amey Roadstone rearranged the layout at Ardingly, demolishing the station and re-establishing a loop at the southern end of the former goods yard area. At the other end of the gap the Bluebell added a few lengths of rail to a point some 60yd short of the partly demolished northern abutments of the viaduct when turning the stub into a longer siding for the accommodation of some of its less sightly stock well out of view of passengers travelling the line. Time will tell in the

The scene on 29 June 1964 at West Hoathly station, the demolition contractor's base for dismantling the track panels, refuelling the locomotives, and office and mess accommodation for his small team. The contractor's defective Ruston & Hornsby diesel locomotive stands in the down platform, the Bluebell Railway's 'E4' *Birch Grove*, one of its hired replacements, stands in steam behind a freshly delivered load of track. The station footbridge that the Bluebell Railway had hoped to acquire has already fallen victim to the scrapmen. *Tom Martin*

new century whether talk of reopening the line to Ardingly is merely wishful thinking. But only too often wishful thinking has become a preservation reality!

Demolition North of Horsted

It seems quite extraordinary after reading accounts of how Firbank's navvies, several hundred of them, toiled away for the best part of four years on the construction of the Lewes & East Grinstead line and its branch to Haywards Heath, that a group of half a dozen men under one foreman should within the space of a few months clear away the disposable assets of half the original mileage and all double track section at that.

Ever since British Railways train services ceased between Lewes and East Grinstead, and the line north of Horsted Keynes lay in a state of suspense, it had been optimistically hoped that this section would survive as an emergency route alternative to the Brighton main line through Balcombe Tunnel and the ageing Ouse Viaduct. During 1959 the up line was given over to housing condemned wagons but in the winter of 1959/60 these were cleared and the goods sidings at Kingscote and West Hoathly removed, leaving only a crossover at the north end of the latter. It was the demise of the electric services that finally decided the Southern Region to tender the line between Ardingly and East Grinstead, excluding the immediate area of Horsted Keynes, reserved for the Bluebell Railway. The 'walk over' was arranged for 10.30am on 16 March 1964 — an ominous date, being exactly six years after the final closure — and the 'Tender for the recovery of redundant assets East Grinstead-Horsted Keynes-Ardingly' was to be in exactly a week later.

The original schedule for the tender included under its headings the clearing away and taking possession of permanent way materials excluding ballast but including rails, fishplates, baseplated and chaired sleepers, the loading of certain specified track and conductor rails into BR wagons, the demolition of bridges and structures including Sheriff Mill Viaduct just west of Horsted Keynes, and the removal of the materials. In the final event the last two groups were reduced

to cover a couple of bridges and the signalboxes at the two intermediate stations.

The final programme of work given to the successful contractor, the Demolition & Construction Co of Croydon, who had just previously completed the lifting of the Hawkhurst branch and the line to Newhaven West Quay, was contained under two schedules, both of which are of interest since they give an excellent picture of the duties and requirements devolving upon the men in charge of Dr Beeching's lethal work.

The first concerned the lifting of the track. Since the mileposts are numbered northwards, it will be more convenient to describe the specific directions commencing at Ardingly, that branch having a mileage reckoning of its own from Copyhold Junction, where it parts company with the main line. In order to leave a run-round loop for the locomotive serving the roadmaking plant at Ardingly, the contractor was instructed to commence at 1m 15ch, north of the station on the down line, while the up was allowed 3 ch more grace. The catch points on the up road were to be taken out and both tracks lifted as far as 3m 19ch on the south side of Horsted Keynes, just short of the crossover a few dozen yards from the signalbox. Throughout this stretch and beyond into Horsted, where the electrified section ends at 10m 68ch (reckoning from Culver Junction), the conductor rails, fishplates, insulators and brackets were to be removed and handed over to BR.

Lifting was to recommence at exactly Milepost 11 at Leamland overbridge, which carries a farm track and public footpath to the group of railway cottages which lie on the west bank of the cutting, and to proceed as far as 16m 55ch at the south end of Hill Place (Imberhorne) Viaduct, the northern part of which was still in use to accommodate trains reversing up the single line spur to the High Level station at East Grinstead. Other specific instructions concerned certain materials which were to be loaded up in wagons, the hire and use of which could be arranged with BR and handed over at East Grinstead Low Level yard: just under a mile of chaired sleepers on the down road immediately south of Kingscote, and to the north for half a mile from Milepost 15 a section of new 98lb flat-bottomed rails, fishplates, bolts, nuts and baseplated sleepers and spikes.

Dismantling has almost reached Horsted Keynes, as on 26 September 1964 the Bluebell Railway's No 473 *Birch Grove* passes through the station with rails and materials for delivery to West Hoathly. *S. C. Nash*

Schedule 1 concluded with a series of paragraphs enjoining the contractor to leave things tidy. No mileposts (many of the old wooden ones had been missing for some time) were to be taken, no damage was to be done to ditches, watercourses, drains or culverts, and the surfaces of public crossings or rights of way or lineside fencing interfered with by the removal of track was to be reinstated. At the close all debris was to be cleared away and the site left clean and tidy.

Schedule 2 concerned the demolition of specified bridges and structures. The brick underline bridge at Coombe, at 13m 24ch just north of West Hoathly, was to be demolished to 3ft above road level and the bank behind the abutment and wing walls trimmed to a 3:1 slope. Arrangements would have to be made with the SEEB for removal and reinstatement of electric power wires, with the GPO for the diversion of a telephone cable attached to the arch of the bridge, and with users of the road for temporary access and safety precautions, all in the day's work of a demolition contractor! Similar arrangements applied to the underline girder bridge at 1m 53ch near Ardingly. Only one other bridge was to receive the contractor's attention, that at 14m 71ch immediately south of Kingscote station, where only the brick parapet was to be taken down to rail level and concrete weathering capping to be laid on top of the exposed brickwork. A certain element of mystery surrounds the exclusion of all the other bridges from the contract; south of Sheffield Park few were missed out. One can only surmise that these structures must have been the particularly shaky culprits that gave the line engineer so much anxiety preceding the closure.

The signalbox at Kingscote was to be taken down, first the wooden superstructure, then the brick base to platform level, and the resulting void filled in with brick rubble. The same applied to the one at West Hoathly, where the station footbridge was also blacklisted. Though Mr Carey, the contracting firm's agent, remarked that the Bluebell Railway could have 'had it for nothing', this would probably not have been possible. Certainly the wooden parts were riddled with woodworm but the part of the structure on the up platform, the side framing and the timber-framed portal at the foot of the staircase were required to be left in position; the former to preserve the guttering to the store rooms, the latter as it supported the station awning. All other station buildings were to be left intact.

Such were the instructions. It was left entirely to the contractor to make his own plans and arrangements, and quite sensibly it was decided to commence at Ardingly and work northwards with temporary bases at West Hoathly and later at Kingscote. The advance party arrived on 9 July to set up their hutted quarters at West Hoathly and lifting commenced on 15 July.

The contractor's equipment consisted of two powerful cranes, a Grayston from Erith at West Hoathly and an NCK at the point of lifting. Though several wagons had been hired from BR, the contractor brought four trucks from Paddock Wood by rail, after lifting from Hawkhurst. Three were condemned four-wheel bolster trucks (dated Shildon 1957!), the odd one out a turquoise high-sided wagon with wooden frames, formerly belonging to the Metropolitan Water Board and labelled 'For internal use only from Sunbury'. The contractor also brought a four-wheel Ruston & Hornsby diesel, No 269 595 built in 1949. This failed on 15 July, getting out of control between West Hoathly and Horsted Keynes, the driver having tried to stop it by engaging reverse gear with disastrous results internally. This lay in the down Lewes platform at Horsted for several days but in early August was back at West Hoathly.

The same day it had met disaster was the first of working with a steam locomotive hired from the Bluebell Railway, producing both the adhesive and braking power necessary for the 1 in 75 grades which predominate on this northern section. The North London locomotive was on for the first three weeks, replaced by *Birch Grove* for a few days following 6 August, to enable No 2650 to have a proper boiler wash-out. The latter was on duty again until 30 August and No 473 filled in a few more days in late September. The crew did alternate weeks on this turn, booked away from Sheffield Park soon after 7am and usually returning coupled to the rear of the 5.25pm from Horsted Keynes. The Bluebell Railway also sent up to West Hoathly the spare 'Dukedog' tender to enable their locomotive to take water as required. The north end of the up platform there was stacked high with coal, for once lifting commenced north of Horsted the engine was isolated

The well-tarpaulined North London Tank stands by, apparently out of steam, as the demolition crew work through the wintry conditions on 23 January 1965. Track panels are dismantled by crane into rails and sleepers to be sent to their respective destinations from West Hoathly.
E. Wilmshurst

on its own. Only near the end of the contract had it to trek up to East Grinstead each time for replenishment.

The operation of lifting was carried out by just two men and the crane driver. The track was torn bodily out of the railbed, five or six lengths being loaded onto the bolster wagons, which were then taken up to the base, there being from two to four round trips a day. There they were off-loaded by crane in the station yard where the rest of the party proceeded to take the sections to pieces, rails, sleepers, chairs and bolts, etc going to their various piles. When sufficient to fill a wagon, these were loaded on to the trucks hired from BR and pushed early in the morning around 9am to East Grinstead, where arrangements were made for the Bluebell locomotive to cross the viaduct. The trip was not necessarily daily, running only as required.

The truckloads of materials were sent their various ways from the Low Level yard. The largest market for railway materials at the time was the National Coal Board, where serviceable chaired softwood sleepers were much in demand as well as relayable rail. Large quantities of both went to Keresley Colliery, Coventry; the stipulated 98lb rails with quantities of fishplates and fishbolts to Newstead Colliery, Walsall. The conductor rails departed on bogie bolsters to Meadow Hall Siding, ER Sheffield, while 10,000 plain sleepers went by lorry to Walsall, and a large tonnage of scrap metal, mainly railway chairs, were scheduled for Richard Thomas and Baldwin's blast furnaces at Ebbw Vale. Further smaller orders, often local, came in almost every day to keep the contractor at full stretch.

The work began very slowly at first, mainly due to labour problems and the removal of the electric third rail which proved a very tough proposition. By 6 August the lifting had only reached the first under-line bridge beyond Ardingly and by the end of the month had got as far as Lywood Tunnel, the jibs of the crane having been shortened to the required headroom. Horsted Keynes was reached late in September, and West Hoathly by Christmas. Soon after the contractor's arrival, Bluebell Railway General Manager Horace May put in a bid to secure the original station footbridge at West Hoathly and bring it to Sheffield Park for reassembly there to replace the missing footbridge removed in 1949, to avoid the public having to cross the platform ends there. To his dismay the reply came that the footbridge had already been demolished. What had happened was that the day the cranes arrived, both were delivered to West Hoathly whereas one was to have gone direct to Ardingly. While the culprit was being moved to the correct starting point, the men at West

Track-lifting on the up line has reached the south end of Imberhorne Viaduct at the end of February 1965, as panels are unloaded by crane to a position beside the track.
Ken Chown

March 1965, with the demolition contract completed. Forlorn and isolated, the North London Tank No 2650 stands under windswept tarpaulins on the goods shunting neck at East Grinstead. In the distance across Imberhorne Viaduct, the contractor's crane can be discerned. *J. J. Smith*

Hoathly were given the footbridge to occupy their attention as no rails were coming through until the NCK commenced lifting.

By the start of March 1965, the demolition contract had been completed, leaving the isolated North London Tank standing under minimum canvas wraps on the goods shunting neck at East Grinstead. From there it was transported back by road to Sheffield Park. The tracks across Imberhorne Viaduct were retained to stable the rush hour commuter stock overnight and during the weekends.

Restoration and Resurrection

The lifting of the lines and removal of equipment and the demolition of the odd bridge meant an added uphill task facing the Bluebell Railway Preservation Society, still with the millstone of a line purchase price for the Sheffield Park-Horsted Keynes section of £43,500, a formidable sum at that time, round its neck. In the end it had to opt for a single line of track north of Horsted when launching its Northern Extension scheme and, even before East Grinstead had been reached, the Bluebell Railway had with foresight purchased the trackbed of the Haywards Heath branch between the eastern end of the missing Sheriff Mill Viaduct right through to the approaches to the site of Ardingly station. The landmarks in the progress of the Bluebell Railway to date are summarised in the following table:

15 March 1959	Meeting called at Haywards Heath to form a Lewes and East Grinstead Railway Preservation Society.
12 July 1959	First Bluebell special traverses East Grinstead-Horsted Keynes and via Haywards Heath and Lewes pauses at Culver Junction.
24 December 1959	The Bluebell Railway Preservation Society offered a lease with option to purchase 4½ miles of track north from Sheffield Park but excluding Horsted Keynes for £34,000.
19 February 1960	Meeting at Royal Pavilion, Brighton, forms a limited company, The Bluebell Railway Ltd, closely allied to the Society.
17 May 1960	The Bluebell Railway takes delivery of its first stock, 'Terrier' *Stepney* and two coaches, all for £750.
7 August 1960	The Bluebell Railway opens for the first season of traffic following the grant of a Light Railway Order.
29 October 1961	Bluebell train services gain entry into Horsted Keynes for platform interchange with electric services to Haywards Heath.
27 October 1963	Bluebell Railway left in sole charge of Horsted Keynes station following withdrawal of services on the link line to Haywards Heath.
27 October 1968	Line purchase confirmed for £43,500 for the section Sheffield Park to Horsted Keynes inclusive.
Autumn 1972	A 'Northern Extension' first mooted as the possibility arises of acquiring some of the former trackbed.
30 November 1975	Purchase of former West Hoathly station site.
21 June 1983	Public enquiry at Oaklands, Haywards Heath, regarding permission for extending the railway north to East Grinstead.
January 1985	Acquisition of Kingscote station buildings and site.
April 1985	Secretary of State approves the application to extend northwards.

The scene at Ardingly as the first items of rolling stock make their way to the new Bluebell Railway on 17 May 1960. In charge is 'Terrier' No 55 (soon to be re-named *Stepney*) leading coach No 320, an LSWR lavatory third of 1900, and SR Maunsell brake composite No 6575 of 1929. *John L. Smith*

26 September 1987	Gala events celebrate electrification of the line from Sanderstead through Oxted to East Grinstead (Low Level).
13 March 1988	First track panel of the Northern Extension is laid by the Secretary of State for Transport, Mr Paul Channon.
13 April 1990	Approval is given by HM Inspecting Officer for the first phase to Horsted House Farm using a shuttle service.
17 April 1992	Further section of the extension is opened through Sharpthorne Tunnel up to the gap left by the missing bridge at New Coombe.
8 September 1992	BR hand over Hill Place (Imberhorne) Viaduct to the Bluebell Extension Company.
10 May 1993	Replacement bridge installed at New Coombe site.
23 April 1994	First public service train into Kingscote for 39 years.
1 October 1997	Trackbed from Horsted Keynes to 200yd short of the site of Ardingly station acquired as a long-term future project in the new millennium.

Today the wheel has almost come round full circle, as the Lewes to East Grinstead line has found the ultimate *resolution* of its destiny through the very *resolution* of those who, with a 'never say die' spirit, acted to include every shade of meaning of that word — of resolving the problem of its future, of its separation into component parts, of a progression from discord to concord, of undergoing an unexpected transformation, of a dogged and determined resolve and a formal statement of the intentions and views of a public democratic body, whether memorialists, 'fighting' committees or a preservation society. This 'never say die' spirit, exemplified in the determined promoters like Lord Sheffield and James Sclater, in persevering protagonists like Madge Bessemer and Bill Howe, and in enthused preservationists Capt Peter Manisty, who persuaded the powers-that-be at Waterloo to take the 'amateurs' seriously, and Peter Thomas, who was the driving force behind the extensions, has created a folklore saga unique in the annals of railway history — and may it long continue!

Index